Influence of Domestic Violence on Mental Health

Influence of Domestic Violence on Mental Health

Editors

Krim K. Lacey
Rohan D. Jeremiah

MDPI

Basel • Beijing • Wuhan • Barcelona • Belgrade • Novi Sad • Cluj • Manchester

Editors
Krim K. Lacey
Sociology and African and African American Studies
University of Michigan-Dearborn
Dearborn
United States

Rohan D. Jeremiah
Department of Human Development Nurse Science
University of Illinois-Chicago
Chicago
United States

Editorial Office
MDPI
St. Alban-Anlage 66
4052 Basel, Switzerland

This is a reprint of articles from the Special Issue published online in the open access journal *International Journal of Environmental Research and Public Health* (ISSN 1660-4601) (available at: www.mdpi.com/journal/ijerph/special_issues/Domestic_Violence_Health).

For citation purposes, cite each article independently as indicated on the article page online and as indicated below:

Lastname, A.A.; Lastname, B.B. Article Title. *Journal Name* **Year**, *Volume Number*, Page Range.

ISBN 978-3-7258-0676-8 (Hbk)
ISBN 978-3-7258-0675-1 (PDF)
doi.org/10.3390/books978-3-7258-0675-1

Cover image courtesy of Krim Lacey

Contents

About the Editors

Krim K. Lacey

Krim K. Lacey is an Associate Professor in the Department of Sociology and African and African American Studies at the University of Michigan-Dearborn. His primary research interest is intimate partner violence. Within the broader topic of intimate partner violence, Dr. Lacey's research has focused on understudied and marginalized populations and the intersection of race, ethnicity, culture, and environmental factors in shaping occurrences and experiences of interpersonal violence and related health outcomes. A focus of Dr. Lacey's more recent work has involved the investigation of risk factors and consequences of violence toward African American and Caribbean Black women. Along with his work on intimate partner violence, Dr. Lacey has explored the physical and mental well-being of Caribbeans living in the United States, England, Canada and within the Caribbean region to better understand the influence of social context, culture, and processes of migration on health outcomes.

Rohan D. Jeremiah

Rohan D. Jeremiah is a Global Public Health Scholar with cross-disciplinary training in Applied Medical Anthropology and Public Health. His research considers the interrelationship of substance use, violence, and HIV/AIDS and focuses on developing strategies to reduce trauma, disease risks, and mortality. Dr. Jeremiah integrates social science theories into public health and social service research by examining trauma through intersectionality to explain domestic and global health disparities affecting marginalized and vulnerable communities. Most notably, he led the most comprehensive research study about the United Nations-sponsored intimate partner violence (IPV) intervention (Partnership for Peace Program) in the Eastern Caribbean.

Preface

Years of research have enabled us to recognize the consequences of domestic violence and the impact it can have on individuals. Studies continue to highlight that this public health problem can be devastating to the health and well-being of victims of violence, particularly women and children, who are often the target of violent acts of aggression within the family and relationships. Research has pointed to the various mental health outcomes that are associated with domestic violence including mood, anxiety, and substance disorders, in addition to the increased risk of suicidality, just to name a few.

The recent COVID-19 pandemic has increased economic uncertainties, social isolation, and other stressors, which heightened some individuals' vulnerability to domestic violence and varied mental health conditions. The pandemic has highlighted the unique, complex, and unprecedented challenges that victims of domestic violence encounter in general, and particularly those under extreme circumstances. The rise in violence as a result of the pandemic has caused greater awareness of the growing need for and importance of access to resources and support systems for victims of violence. Importantly, it has encouraged ongoing dialogue about possible preventative and intervention measures to address this important public health concern.

This reprint helps to shed light on the mental health consequences of domestic violence, the impact of the COVID-19 pandemic, and the possible intervention and prevention measures to aid victims who are confronted with violence in their lives. In the initial chapters, this reprint highlights the association between mental disorders and domestic violence, and the associated influences across populations globally. This is followed by chapters that focus on the COVID-19 pandemic and its impact on the prevalence of violence, well-being, and service alternatives for victims of violence. In the later chapters, the reprint begins to address varying possibilities for intervention and preventative measures that could be employed to assist survivors of domestic violence.

This edited reprint would not be possible without the support and help of the Managing Editor and those who provided editorial comments. Importantly, I am eternally grateful to the authors of the chapters who dedicated their time and effort to raising awareness of this public health problem that continues to impact the health and well-being of individuals worldwide.

Krim K. Lacey and Rohan D. Jeremiah
Editors

International Journal of
Environmental Research and Public Health

MDPI

Article

Physical Intimate Partner Violence, Childhood Physical Abuse and Mental Health of U.S. Caribbean Women: The Interrelationship of Social, Contextual, and Migratory Influences

Krim K. Lacey [1,*], Regina Parnell [2], Sasha R. Drummond-Lewis [3], Maxine Wood [4] and Karen Powell Sears [5]

1 Department of Sociology and African and African American Studies, University of Michigan-Dearborn, Dearborn, MI 48128, USA
2 Department of Occupational Therapy, Wayne State University, Detroit, MI 48201, USA; ad9049@wayne.edu
3 Department of Behavioral Sciences, University of Michigan-Flint, Flint, MI 48502, USA; srdlewis@umich.edu
4 Department of Humanities, York University, Toronto, ON M3J 1P3, Canada; maxinew@yorku.ca
5 Department of Anthropology and Sociology, Denison University, Granville, OH 43023, USA; searsk@denison.edu
* Correspondence: krimlacey@gmail.com

Abstract: The literature has shown an increased risk for mental health conditions among victims of domestic violence. Few studies have examined the relationship between mental health disorders and domestic violence among Caribbean women, and how the association might be influenced by migratory and contextual factors. This study addresses the mental well-being of U.S. Caribbean Black women victims of domestic violence, and the relationships between acculturation, discrimination, and demographic influences. An analysis of data from the 2001–2003 National Survey of American Life (NSAL) re-interview, the first and most complete study on U.S. Caribbean Blacks, was conducted. Bivariate analysis revealed an association between acts of physical domestic violence and mental health conditions, with generally higher risk among women who reported both severe physical intimate partner violence and childhood physical abuse. Multivariate logistic regression indicates an association between specific mental disorders and acts of domestic violence. Acculturation, length of residence in the United States, age, education, poverty, and country of origin were also associated with mental health. The study highlights future directions for exploration including additional investigation of the influence of acculturation on the physical health of victims of domestic violence.

Keywords: childhood physical abuse; physical IPV; acculturation; discrimination; mental health

Citation: Lacey, K.K.; Parnell, R.; Drummond-Lewis, S.R.; Wood, M.; Powell Sears, K. Physical Intimate Partner Violence, Childhood Physical Abuse and Mental Health of U.S. Caribbean Women: The Interrelationship of Social, Contextual, and Migratory Influences. *Int. J. Environ. Res. Public Health* **2022**, *19*, 150. https://doi.org/10.3390/ijerph19010150

Academic Editor: Paul B. Tchounwou

Received: 31 October 2021
Accepted: 17 December 2021
Published: 23 December 2021

1. Introduction

The Black immigrant population has increased steadily since 1980 and is estimated to be about 9% of the Black population [1,2], with the majority being traditionally women [3]. Black women comprise 52% of the growing U.S. Black population and a high proportion of this group identifies as Sub-Saharan African or Caribbean [4]. As the number of immigrant Black women increases, the need to examine distinct cultural factors affecting their well-being becomes essential for addressing the needs of Black communities at large. Studies continue to find that Black and immigrant women are at greater risk for victimization [5,6], and the associated mental health risks are just as alarming [7]. One report estimates that half of the women in some Caribbean countries have reported violence by an intimate partner over the course of their lives [8]. Another study in the United States puts the physical intimate partner violence (IPV) rates for Black women at around 41 percent [9]. While we have made some progress in understanding more about the health consequences of victims of domestic violence, there is a paucity of research on factors that affect the well-being of U.S. Caribbean women.

In addition to intimate partner violence risks, the process of acculturation to host societies can be quite challenging and affect the well-being of immigrant women. Along with new experiences with social and structural conditions and stressors that can be consequential to mental health, some women face augmented exposure to violence (both family and intimate partner violence). The combination of the acculturation experiences and exposure to domestic abuse may place women at risk for poorer mental health outcomes. This research examines the influence of domestic violence (physical IPV and childhood physical abuse in particular) and migratory and contextual factors on the mental well-being of U.S. Caribbean Black women.

1.1. Background

Domestic violence across the life course in the form of adult physical intimate partner violence and childhood physical abuse is a serious and pervasive public health problem particularly within minority and immigrant communities [10,11]. Past research consistently links adult experiences with domestic violence to poor well-being [11–14]. Studies over the years have documented the association between adult intimate partner violence and a wide variety of mental health problems such as mood, anxiety, depression, and substance disorders [13,14]. Emerging yet scant research has also documented similar associations among U.S. Caribbean Black women [10]. In general, studies have also found an association between childhood abuse and mental health among adult women [15]. Documented mental disorders associated with physically victimized children include depressive disorder, suicide, PTSD, and personality disorder [16]. However, little is known about the influence of childhood abuse on the well-being of immigrant Caribbean women.

Domestic violence research shows that women of lower socioeconomic status, those living in urban areas, and those of minority status are more likely to be victimized [17]. While less studied, processes of acculturation have also been linked to domestic violence [18–20]. Varied studies suggest that low [21], intermediate [22,23], and even high levels of acculturation can increase the risk for intimate partner violence [24]. Given this, the likelihood for increased victimization during the acculturation process raises concerns about the potential health implications for immigrant women. A better understanding of the influence of acculturation on victimization and mental health risks becomes necessary considering the growing Black immigrant population in the United States.

Undoubtedly, migrating to a new country can be an exciting period that comes with endless possibilities to foster goal achievement and a better life [25,26]. However, for some immigrants, the process of migrating to a new country can bring a host of challenges including culture shock, family separation, and traumatic experiences with racial discrimination that might not have been experienced before migrating. These challenges can contribute to mental health problems including depression, anxiety, substance use, and poor physical conditions [27,28]. For some immigrants, poor health outcomes might be a consequence of a life of poverty in their new home as they seek to establish themselves. However, new immigrants to host countries may bring with them experiences and cultural attributes that serve as protective mechanisms and provide buffers against acculturative stress and subsequent poor health outcomes [29].

Generally, the literature suggests that the health of immigrants is initially more favorable than native-born residents early in the acculturation process and then appears to deteriorate with length of time in host countries [30,31]. The relationship between health and length of residence also holds for Caribbean immigrants to the U.S. [32–34]. Additionally, among immigrants to the United States gender differences exist in the health effects of acculturation with more physical symptoms, depression, smoking, and alcohol use for immigrant women than for immigrant men [28,35]. Although extant research has established the relationship between processes of acculturation and immigrant health, the interrelationship of physical domestic violence across the lifespan has rarely been examined.

1.2. Theoretical Frameworks

The Tridimensional Acculturation Model is useful when studying acculturative stress and well-being. The framework uses a multidimensional lens to explain the health of Caribbean Black immigrants who are seen as juggling three cultural worlds: Caribbean, African-American, and European-American [36,37]. Along with immersion within their own culture, Black immigrants are exposed to White mainstream culture as well to the culture of marginalized U.S. Black populations who face structural inequalities, including discrimination and poverty, which are known to create stress and increased risk for violence and poor health outcomes [38]. Each cultural world has a different set of challenges that require different responses, which can affect physical and emotional well-being.

Cumulative Stress Theory is also valuable when explaining the health outcomes from enduring stressors, whether due to acculturation or domestic violence. The theory posits that individuals exposed to continued adversity across their lifespan are more likely to experience diminished health and well-being than those who experience less chronic adversity [39]. The effects of stress over long periods are shown to have a cumulative negative impact on health especially among those experiencing racial discrimination and limited access to resources for coping in biased environments [40,41]. Negative health outcomes exist for all socio-economic levels but differ by gender, with Black women at an increased risk for poor health outcomes [42].

1.3. Research Aims

This study examined the association between mental health conditions (mood and anxiety disorders and suicide) and acts of domestic violence (i.e., severe physical IPV, childhood physical abuse) among U.S. Caribbean women. Another aim was to evaluate the combined effect of these forms of domestic violence (both forms of abuse) on the risk of particular mental health conditions. We further evaluated the interrelationship of specific acts of domestic violence, migratory factors, and contextual influences on mental health conditions. Based on extant literature, we expected to find an association between mental health disorders and specific acts of physical abuse. We also expected that the risk for mental disorders would increase with multiple victimizations. However, the nature of the interrelationships between life course domestic violence (childhood and adult), migratory factors, contextual influences, and mental health is presently unclear.

2. Materials and Methods

2.1. Participants and Sample

Data from the 2001–2003 National Survey of American Life (NSAL) re-interview were analyzed [43,44]. As part of the Collaborative Psychiatric Epidemiology Surveys (CPES), the NSAL is the most comprehensive study on the health of U.S. Blacks, and the first nationally representative study of Caribbean Blacks residing in the United States. Multi-stage probability sampling procedures were used to generate a sample of 6082 participants including 1623 Caribbean Blacks, a focus of this study. The Caribbean Black population was identified through two overlapping area probability sampling frames. A total of 266 Caribbean Blacks were interviewed in the NSAL core sample, while the remaining 1357 participants were selected from an area probability sample of housing units from high-density Caribbean areas. Eight primary areas were selected in five states: New York, New Jersey, Florida, Connecticut, Massachusetts, and the District of Columbia. Participants were included in the study if they were 18 years and older and were: (a) of West Indian or Caribbean descent, (b) from a Caribbean area country, or (c) had a parent or at least one grandparent who was born in a Caribbean area country [42]. Face-to-face interviews were primarily collected with a smaller proportion of interviews collected by phone. The analytic sample for the current study included 961 women of Caribbean descent with African ancestry.

2.2. Predictor Measures

Domestic violence. Two measures were used to address acts of domestic violence including severe physical intimate partner violence and childhood physical abuse. Severe physical intimate partner violence was assessed with the question, "Have you ever been badly beaten up by a spouse or romantic partner [34]. For childhood physical abuse, participants were asked, "As a child, were you badly beaten up by your parent or the people that raised you?" A composite of participants who reported severe physical intimate partner violence and childhood physical abuse was created and represented "both abuse" (severe physical IPV + childhood physical abuse). The measures had binary response options of "yes" and "no".

Acculturation. We considered two indicators of acculturation appropriately aligned with U.S. and Caribbean cultures. The items were measured on a Likert scale ranging from not at all, very little, moderately, very often, and almost always. U.S. acculturation consisted of a single item where participants were asked, "How often do you identify yourselves as only American?" Caribbean acculturation consisted of eight combined items. Participants were asked, how much they do each of the following: (1) "associate with Caribbean"; (2) "enjoy listening to Caribbean music"; (3) "have contact with Caribbeans"; (4) "have Caribbean friends as a child"; (5) "family cooks Caribbean food"; (6) "have Caribbean friends"; (7) "identify themselves as only Caribbean" and (8) "identify as Caribbean American". Altogether, the items had an internal consistency (α) of 0.89. The items were averaged for analysis.

Discrimination. Major discrimination was measured using a nine-item scale [45]. Participants were asked whether or not they had ever experienced the following events due to their race: (1) unfairly fired; (2) not been hired for a job; (3) unfairly denied a promotion; (4) unfairly stopped, searched, questioned, physically threatened or abused by police; (5) unfairly discouraged by a teacher or advising from continuing their education; (6) unfairly prevented from moving into a neighborhood because the landlord or realtor refused to sell or rent you a house or apartment (7); moved into neighborhoods where neighbors made life difficult for you and your family; (8) unfairly denied a bank loan; and (9) received service from someone such as a plumber or car mechanic that was worse than what others get. Response options of "yes" and "no" were provided. Major discrimination reflected the total count of the number of the categories of events due to race.

Control Variables. The control variables included are age (in years), poverty, education, country of origin, education, and length of residence. Poverty status is an income-to-poverty ratio measure consisting of the participants' household income divided by the 2001 U.S. Census poverty threshold for the number of adults and children living in that household. Ratios below 1.00 indicate that the participants' household income is below the official poverty threshold; a ratio of 1.00 or greater indicates income above the poverty level. For example, a ratio of 1.25 indicates that the income was 25 percent above the appropriate poverty threshold [46]. Education was separated into four categories: less than high school, high school graduate, some college, and college. Length of residence consists of Caribbean migrants living in the U.S. from 0 to 10 years; Caribbean migrants in the U.S. for 11 to 20 years; Caribbean migrants in the U.S. for more than 20 years; second generation consist of participants who were born in the United States to at least one Caribbean immigrant parent; and third-generation black participants who were born in the U.S. and had Caribbean born grandparents. Country of origin has four categories representing participants who had origins in English, Spanish, French, or Dutch speaking countries of the Caribbean.

2.3. Outcome Measures

The NSAL used a slightly modified version of a clinical assessment scale in accordance with the Diagnostic and Statistical Manual of Mental Disorders fourth edition (DSM-IV), World Health Organization Composite Interview (WHO-CIDI) to address lifetime mental disorders. In this study, we examined whether participants ever met the criteria for mood and anxiety disorders. Mood disorder was inclusive of major depressive disorder (MDD), major depressive episode (MDE), dysthymia, and bipolar disorder (any). Anxiety disorder consisted of panic, agoraphobia, generalized anxiety disorder (GAD), obsessive-compulsive disorder (OCD), and posttraumatic stress disorder (PTSD). We further evaluated suicide ideation and attempt. To address suicide ideation, participants were asked, "Have you ever seriously thought about committing suicide?" For suicide attempts, they were asked, "Have you ever attempted suicide?" The response option for both suicide measures was "yes" and "no".

2.4. Analytic Strategy

Univariate analysis and bivariate tests examining the association between specific acts of domestic violence (severe physical IPV, childhood physical abuse, both) and mental health disorders were conducted. This was followed by stepwise logistic regression analysis to assess mental disorders in association with acts of domestic violence, discrimination, acculturation, and socio-demographic factors. Block 1 examined acts of domestic violence and control variables. Block 2 added acculturation and discrimination. The last block (Block 3) examined all variables. We focus on the results from the last block of the analysis. Stata 15.1 was used to conduct the analysis. The sample was weighted and corrected for standard errors, clustering, stratification, and differential non-response. An alpha of 0.05 was set for significance.

3. Results

3.1. Sample Characteristics

Caribbean women averaged 41 years of age (m = 40.5) (see Table 1). Almost three-quarters (74.4%) of women lived above the federal poverty guidelines and less than a third (30.4%) of women had at least some college education. More than seven in 10 women (71.1%) had origins in English-speaking Caribbean countries. Many participants were foreign-born (67.7%) and had been living (24.0%) in the United States between 11 and 20 years. Almost two-thirds (65.2%) of Caribbean women reside in the Northeast region of the United States. Overall, the vast majority (85.1%) of women in the sample did not experience any physical domestic violence.

3.2. Bivariate Analysis Examining Domestic Violence and Mental Health Disorders

Table 2 illustrates the bivariate relationship between mental health and acts of domestic violence. An association was found between acts of domestic violence and anxiety disorder ($F = 18.20$; $p < 0.001$); a higher rate (40%) of anxiety was found among women who reported both childhood physical abuse and adult severe physical intimate partner violence than women who experienced only one act of domestic violence or those who did not report any at all. A similar association was found for domestic violence and suicide ideation. The prevalence (53.9%) of suicide ideation was substantially higher for women who reported both severe physical IPV and childhood physical abuse than those who experience one act or no domestic violence at all ($F = 10.86$, $p < 0.001$). This trend continued when examining the association between domestic violence and suicide attempt ($F = 16.7$; $p < 0.001$). About a quarter (26.9%) of women who attempted suicide also reported experiencing both severe physical IPV and childhood physical abuse. However, the results slightly differ for mood disorders, though a significant relationship was found ($F = 5.25$; $p < 0.01$). A higher percentage (36.9%) of women who met the criteria for mood disorder reported only severe IPV versus 22.3 percent who reported both severe physical IPV and childhood physical abuse. The lifetime prevalence of disorders was lowest among women who reported no childhood physical abuse nor IPV.

Table 1. Sample Characteristics (N = 961).

Characteristics	Std. Err	Percentage
Mean age (mean)	1.176	40.5
Poverty		
Below-at	0.0257	25.6
Above	0.0257	74.4
Education Status		
Less than HS	0.0197	19.4
HS Graduate	0.0247	29.5
Some College	0.0299	30.4
College	0.0143	20.8
Region		
Northeast	0.0540	65.2
Midwest	0.0222	3.9
South	0.0600	25.0
West	0.0280	5.9
Country of Origin (Language) [1]		
Spanish	0.0217	13.7
French	0.0250	14.3
English	0.0367	71.1
Dutch	0.0054	0.96
Length of Residence		
0–10 years	0.1518	15.2
11–20 years	0.2401	24.0
>20 years	0.2851	28.5
Second Generation	0.0297	21.7
Third Generation	0.0220	10.6
Immigrant Status		
US Born	0.0286	32.3
Foreign-Born	0.0286	67.7
Abuse		
No Abuse	0.0216	85.1
Childhood Abuse Only	0.0048	2.9
IPV Only	0.0178	9.3
Both IPV and Childhood Abuse	0.0105	2.7

[1] Note. **English-speaking countries:** Jamaica, Barbados, Guyana, Trinidad and Tobago, Anguilla, Antigua, Bahama, Bermuda, British Virgin Islands, Tortola, Cayman Islands, Dominica, Grenada/Grenadines, Montserrat, St Kitts-Nevis, St. Lucia, St. Vincent, Turks and Caicos, US Virgin Island, St. Croix, St. Thomas, West. Indies, and British W. Indies. **Spanish-speaking countries:** Puerto Rico, Dominican Republic, Cuba, Panama, Costa Rica, and Nicaragua. **French-speaking countries:** Haiti, French Guiana, Guadalupe, and Martinique. **Dutch-speaking countries**: Aruba, St. Eustatius, St. Maarten, Suriname, and Netherland Antilles.

Table 2. Bivariate Analysis of Domestic Violence and Mental Disorders and Behaviors Among Caribbean Black Women.

Domestic Violence	Anxiety Disorder		Mood Disorder		Suicide Ideation		Suicide Attempt	
	No	Yes	No	Yes	No	Yes	No	Yes
No Abuse	88.7	11.3	85.8	14.2	91.3	8.8	98.8	1.2
Child Abuse (Only)	79.4	20.6	75.4	24.6	88.6	11.5	93.8	6.2
IPV (Only)	63.3	36.7	63.1	36.9	79.1	20.9	90.8	9.3
Both Child Abuse and IPV	60.1	40.0	77.7	22.3	46.1	53.9	73.2	26.9
F-test		18.20		5.25		10.86		16.7
***p*-value**	***	0.0000	**	0.0086	***	0.0001	***	0.0000

** $p < 0.01$; *** $p < 0.001$.

3.3. Multivariate Analysis Examining Acts of Domestic Violence, Acculturation, Discrimination and Demographic Influences on Mental Health Disorders

Multivariate analysis shows that the odds (AOR = 4.51, $p < 0.01$) for mood disorder increased among participants from Spanish-speaking countries compared to English-speaking countries (see Table 3). The same was true for Caribbean women who experienced racial discrimination (AOR = 1.90, $p < 0.05$) and poverty (AOR = 2.66, $p < 0.05$). However, reduced odds (AOR = 0.211, $p < 0.05$) for mood disorders were found among Caribbean Black women who had resided in the United States between 11 and 20 years compared to those living in the country for fewer years. All things considered, acts of domestic violence were not associated with mood disorders.

Table 3. Multivariate Analysis Examining Domestic Violence, Acculturation, Discrimination and Demographic Factors on Lifetime Mood Disorder.

Variables	Block 1	Block 2	Block 3
Age	0.961 (0.936–0.984) **	0.972 (0.936–101)	0.970 (0.932–1.01)
Place of origin (language)			
English	1	1	1
Spanish	3.25 (1.62–6.50) **	3.90 (1.26–12.09) *	4.51 (1.49–13.67) **
French	0.801 (0.277–2.32)	1.56 (0.408–5.96)	1.71 (0.469–6.24)
Dutch	0.246 (0.014–4.33)	0.144 (0.003–5.63)	0.141 (0.004–4.73)
Length of residence			
0–10 years	1	1	1
11–20 years	1.12 (0.454–2.75)	0.207 (0.058–0.753) *	0.211 (0.061–0.753) *
>20 years	2.70 (1.09–6.68) *	1.46 (0.368–5.80)	1.17 (0.233–5.90)
Second Gen	1.88 (0.619–5.70)	0.759 (0.198–2.91)	0.766 (0.184–3.18)
Third Gen	8.57 (2.43–30.27) **	3.71 (0.509–27.03)	2.57 (0.331–19.99)
Education			
Less than HS	1	1	1
HS Graduate	1.08 (0.321–3.64)	1.24 (0.166–9.30)	0.745 (0.100–5.53)
Some College	2.65 (1.04–6.71) *	2.31 (0.485–11.04)	1.56 (0.307–7.89)
College	3.32 (0.836–13.21)	3.40 (0.326–35.37)	2.30 (0.192–27.53)
Poverty			
Above Poverty	1	1	1
Below	1.19 (0.687–2.07)	3.65 (1.69–7.88) **	2.66 (1.12–6.30) *
Discrimination		1.70 (1.12–2.58) *	1.90 (1.11–3.26) *
Caribbean Acculturation		0.958 (0.552–1.66)	0.953 (0.549–1.65)
U.S. Acculturation		0.911 (0.647–1.28)	0.891 (0.622–1.28)
IPV			
No	1		1
Yes	3.49 (1.41–8.65) **		2.12 (0.351–12.80)
Childhood Abuse			
No	1		1
Yes	2.37 (0.866–6.47) *		1.08 (0.126–9.22)
Both Abuse			
No	1		1
Yes	0.201 (0.047–0.849) *		0.053 (0.002–1.42)

$p < 0.10$; * $p < 0.05$; ** $p < 0.01$.

The opposite was found when examining the relationship with anxiety disorders; women who reported severe physical IPV had increased odds (AOR = 4.50, $p < 0.01$) for this condition (see Table 4). The odds (AOR = 4.79, $p < 0.001$) for anxiety disorders also significantly increased among Caribbean women who lived below poverty compared to those above the federal poverty level. Similarly, participants from Spanish-speaking Caribbean countries had increased odds (AOR = 2.99, $p < 0.05$) for anxiety disorders compared to those from English-speaking countries. In the analysis, however, the odds for this disorder reduced with age (AOR = 0.962, $p < 0.01$).

Table 4. Multivariate Analysis Examining Impact of Domestic Violence, Acculturation, Discrimination and Demographic Factors on Lifetime Anxiety Disorders.

Variables	Block 1	Block 2	Block 3
Age	0.967 (0.942–0.992) **	0.969 (0.945–0.993) **	0.962 (0.935–0.990) **
Place of origin (language)			
English	1	1	1
Spanish	1.69 (0.946–3.00)	3.04 (1.21–7.64) *	2.99 (1.11–8.10) *
French	0.807 (0.370–1.76)	0.467 (0.086–2.55)	0.525 (0.106–2.59)
Dutch	—	—	—
Length of residence			
0–10 years	1	1	1
11–20 years	0.720 (0.351–1.48)	0.758 (0.191–3.00)	0.710 (0.185–2.72)
>20 years	1.88 (0.767–4.63)	2.10 (0.495–8.97)	1.64 (0.398–6.74)
Second Gen	1.20 (0.525–2.73)	1.82 (0.466–7.11)	1.62 (0.490–5.37)
Third Gen	2.62 (0.950–7.24)	1.94 (0.371–10.10)	1.13 (0.219–5.82)
Education			
Less than HS	1	1	1
HS Graduate	1.21 (0.495–2.94)	3.17 (0.820–12.23)	2.78 (0.569–13.56)
Some College	1.54 (0.637–3.71)	1.56 (0.349–6.93)	1.60 (0.298–8.61)
College	1.17 (0.573–2.35)	1.96 (0.667–5.72)	2.30 (0.564–9.40)
Poverty			
Above Poverty	1	1	1
Below	2.42 (1.27–4.61) **	6.19 (2.42–15.82) ***	4.79 (1.96–11.70) ***
Discrimination		1.39 (0.960–2.01)	1.28 (0.869–1.89)
Caribbean Acculturation		1.02 (0.614–1.71)	0.977 (0.580–1.64)
U.S. Acculturation		0.985 (0.776–1.25)	0.969 (0.746–1.26)
IPV			
No	1		1
Yes	4.23 (2.43–7.35) ***		4.50 (1.44–14.06) **
Childhood Abuse			
No	1	1	1
Yes	2.75 (1.03–7.38) *		2.55 (0.400–16.20)
Both Abuse			
No	1	1	1
Yes	0.528 (0.139–2.01)		0.117 (0.012–1.13)

* $p < 0.05$; ** $p < 0.01$; *** $p < 0.001$.

The analysis examining suicide ideation showed both similarities and differences from previous models (see Table 5). The focus on suicide ideation as opposed to suicide attempts was due to sample size issues. Notably, the odds (AOR = 0.912, $p < 0.001$) for suicide ideation reduced with age. Acculturated Black women identifying with the Caribbean culture were also at reduced odds (AOR = 0.594, $p < 0.05$) for suicide ideation. Opposite to these findings, experiences with racial discrimination were associated with greater odds (AOR = 1.86, $p < 0.01$) for suicide ideation. No association between acts of domestic violence and suicide ideation was found in this model.

Table 5. Multivariate Analysis Examining Domestic Violence, Acculturation, Discrimination and Demographic Factors on Lifetime Suicide Ideation.

Variables	Block 1	Block 2	Block 3
Age	0.937 (0.909–0.966) ***	0.910 (0.875–0.947) ***	0.912 (0.877–.948) ***
Place of origin (language)			
English	1	1	1
Spanish	1.41 (0.483–4.10)	1.70 (0.386–7.54)	1.24 (0.247–6.24)
French	0.993 (0.266–3.71)	1.81 (0.312–10.51)	2.03 (0.406–10.20)
Dutch	—	—	—
Length of time/Gen			
0–10 years	1	1	1
11–20 years	1.31 (0.583–2.95)	0.923 (0.368–2.31)	0.713 (0.276–1.84)
>20 years	3.29 (1.13–9.55) *	4.29 (0.951–19.36)	4.20 (0.916–19.22)
Second Gen	2.87 (1.18–6.93) *	1.18 (0.310–4.48)	1.17 (0.207–6.68)
Third Gen	7.05 (1.70–29.22) **	1.05 (0.310–4.48)	1.20 (0.098–14.66)
Education			
Less than HS	1	1	1
HS Graduate	1.39 (0.538–3.59)	1.01 (0.174–5.81)	1.17 (0.163–8.33)
Some College	0.573 (0.228–1.44)	0.080 (0.011–0.589) *	0.133 (0.017–1.05)
College	1.48 (0.522–4.19)	1.00 (0.159–6.27)	1.72 (0.254–11.61)
Poverty			
Above Poverty	1	1	1
Below	0.532 (0.247–1.15)	0.602 (0.183–1.98)	0.534 (0.165–1.72)
Discrimination		2.38 (1.54–3.68) ***	1.86 (1.15–3.00) **
Caribbean Acculturation		0.571 (0.324–1.01)	0.594 (0.356–0.991) *
U.S. Acculturation		1.20 (0.788–1.84)	1.19 (0.760–1.86)
IPV			
No	1	1	1
Yes	2.23 (0.916–5.45)		3.84 (0.663–22.22)
Childhood Abuse			
No	1		1
Yes	1.41 (0.330–6.02)		3.07 (0.254–37.23)
Both Abuse			
No	1		1
Yes	4.22 (0.652–27.39)		0.982 (0.041–23.62)

* $p < 0.05$; ** $p < 0.01$; *** $p < 0.001$.

4. Discussion

This research provides further and supporting evidence of the potentially devastating health consequences that are associated with women's exposure to domestic violence [13,14,47,48]. Bivariate analysis revealed a direct association between specific acts (severe physical IPV and childhood physical abuse) of domestic violence and mental disorders as well as suicide (both ideation and attempt). The combination of various types of physical abuse increased the risk for poorer mental health outcomes among U.S. Caribbean women, lending support to the notion that women with multiple victimizations experience the highest level of distress [49]. This was especially evident for anxiety disorders and both suicide ideation and attempt.

The relationship between physical acts of domestic violence and mental disorders by and large was supported when adjusting for demographic factors (Block 1). However, when adjusting for other factors, only specific acts of domestic violence such as severe intimate partner violence were associated with anxiety disorders. Nonetheless, other factors contributed to mental disorders. For example, experiences with poverty and discrimination were associated with the increased risk for mood and anxiety disorders, suggesting that exposure to toxic or cumulative stressors can negatively affect the mental health of U.S. Caribbean women. Women with roots in the Spanish-speaking Caribbean region also had a greater likelihood for mood and anxiety disorders. While difficult to explain, it is known that Spanish-speaking individuals have faced a unique history of stressors including racial discrimination as they acculturate to the United States [50]. In light of this finding, additional investigation is warranted. Furthermore, Caribbean Black women who had lived in the United States for 11 to 20 years were less likely to meet the criteria for mood disorders, partly supporting the healthy immigrant effect hypothesis of the initial advantage health standing that some immigrant women might maintain after their arrival to host countries.

Our study further highlights the harmful effect that poor social and stressful conditions in host countries can have on Blacks and immigrant groups; certain stressors including racial discrimination may contribute to suicide ideation. Some immigrant women may be better protected from the negative health consequences than others. For example, our findings indicated that there was a lower likelihood for suicide ideation among acculturated Caribbean women who had stronger identification with the Caribbean culture, providing some support for the tridimensional framework. This finding suggests that acculturation may serve as a buffer or protective factor against certain mental health conditions. It should be noted that there are instilled cultural beliefs in the Caribbean countries and cultures that committing suicide is a sign of weakness which might explain this finding. Finally, the risk of developing suicidal thoughts was reduced with age and could be associated with greater resilience and effective coping mechanisms that come with maturity [51,52].

Limitations and Strength of Study

We recognize that this study is not without limitations and would like to highlight a few for consideration when interpreting the findings. Among the limitations of note is the age of the data. The data were collected during a time where social and political conditions may have differed from today. For example, we speculate that certain social movements (i.e., #MeToo) may influence victimized women's disclosure of violence and possible outcomes. Although the dataset is more than a decade old, to our knowledge the NSAL remains the most comprehensive representative sample on the U.S. Caribbean population that allows for addressing the research objectives. Additionally, the study focused only on physical violence. Other types of violence (i.e., psychological) were not included in the sample because of the manner in which the data were collected. It is also important to keep in mind that questions surrounding domestic violence (i.e., child abuse) are retrospective and are subject to recall bias which might affect the validity of the findings. Finally, as with cross-sectional samples, causal inferences cannot be drawn.

Regardless of the limitations discussed, this study contributes to the literature in many ways. To begin, it is one of few studies based on representative data that examines the interrelationship of domestic violence, migratory factors, and contextual influences on the mental health of Caribbeans residing within the United States. The study further examined mental disorders using a clinical assessment scale which is limited in domestic violence studies on the Caribbean population. Importantly, this study is one of few to examine the mental health of Caribbean women who reported childhood physical abuse. Finally, our study utilized valid measures of acculturation which have been limited in studies of this nature. Many studies are based on proxies (i.e., language), which may not provide a valid assessment of acculturation

5. Conclusions

Our research shows that domestic violence can adversely affect the health and well-being of Caribbean women, whether in the form of physical intimate partner violence or childhood physical abuse. This research further sheds light on the influence that migratory factors and poor social and structural conditions can have on women's well-being which adds to our understanding in finding effective prevention and intervention strategies.

Irrespective of the rather innovative approach in utilizing improved measures of acculturation, it is also vital that we examine other measures of acculturation in future studies. Furthermore, these measures should be considered in research that examines the physical health disposition of immigrant victims of violence. These studies are particularly necessary as research suggests an increase in victimization with different levels of acculturation. Independent of these important steps, our study has highlighted subsequent findings that warrant further exploration including the effects of multiple types of physical violence on the well-being of Caribbean women.

Author Contributions: K.K.L., R.P., S.R.D.-L., M.W. and K.P.S. contributed to the conceptualization and writing of the manuscript. K.K.L. contributed to the methodology and interpretation of data results. All authors have read and agreed to the published version of the manuscript.

Funding: This work was supported by the University of Michigan-Dearborn Office of Research and Sponsored Programs and funded by a scholar grant [P/G U)059355].

Institutional Review Board Statement: Data collection for the NSAL was approved by the University of Michigan's Institutional Review Board.

Informed Consent Statement: Secondary data were used for this study.

Data Availability Statement: The public use NSAL data is archived at the University of Michigan-ICPSR.

Conflicts of Interest: The authors declare no conflict of interest.

References

1. Anderson, M.; Lopez, G. Key Facts about Black Immigrants in the U.S. 2018. Available online: https://www.pewresearch.org/fact-tank/2018/01/24/key-facts-about-black-immigrants-in-the-u-s/ (accessed on 14 October 2021).
2. Anderson, N.B.; Bulatao, R.A.; Cohen, B. *National Research Council (US) Panel on Race, Ethnicity and Health in Later Life: Critical Perspectives on Racial and Ethnic Differences in Health in Late Life*; Immigrant Health: Selectivity and Acculturation; National Academies Press: Washington, DC, USA, 2004; Volume 7. Available online: https://www.ncbi.nlm.nih.gov/books/NBK25533/ (accessed on 14 October 2021).
3. Thomas, K.J.; Logan, I. African female immigration to the United States and its policy implications. *Can. J. Afr. Stud. Rev. Can. Études Afr.* **2012**, *46*, 87–107. [CrossRef] [PubMed]
4. U.S. Census Bureau. *Detailed Look at Sub-Saharan African and Caribbean Ancest*; U.S. Department of Commerce: Washington, DC, USA, 2019.
5. Sabri, B.; Bolyard, R.; McFadgion, A.L.; Stockman, J.K.; Lucea, M.B.; Callwood, G.B.; Coverston, C.R.; Campbell, J.C. Intimate partner violence, depression, PTSD, and use of mental health resources among ethnically diverse black women. *Soc. Work. Health Care* **2013**, *52*, 351–369. [CrossRef]
6. Frye, V.; Hosein, V.; Waltermaurer, E.; Blaney, S.; Wilt, S. Femicide in New York City: 1990 to 1999. *Homicide Stud.* **2005**, *9*, 204–228. [CrossRef]
7. Anderson, J.C.; Stockman, J.K.; Sabri, B.; Campbell, D.W.; Campbell, J.C. Injury outcomes in African American and African Caribbean women: The role of intimate partner violence. *J. Emerg. Nurs.* **2015**, *41*, 36–42. [CrossRef] [PubMed]
8. Le Franc, E.; Samms-Vaughan, M.; Hambleton, I.; Fox, K.; Brown, D. Interpersonal violence in three Caribbean countries: Barbados, Jamaica, and Trinidad. *Pan. Am. J. Public Health* **2008**, *24*, 409–421. [CrossRef]
9. Breiding, M.J.; Chen, J.; Black, M.C. *Intimate Partner Violence in the United States—2010*; National Center for Injury Prevention and Control: Atlanta, GA, USA; Centers for Disease Control and Prevention: Atlanta, GA, USA, 2014.
10. Lacey, K.K.; Mouzon, D.M. Severe physical intimate partner violence and the mental and physical health of U. *S. Black women. J. Women's Health* **2016**, *25*, 920. [CrossRef]
11. Stockman, J.K.; Hayashi, H.; Campbell, J.C. Intimate partner violence and its health impact on ethnic minority women. *J. Women's Health* **2015**, *24*, 62–79. [CrossRef]
12. Lacey, K.K.; Jeremiah, R.D.; West, C.M. Domestic Violence through a Caribbean lens: Historical context, theories, risks and consequences. *J. Aggress. Maltreat. Trauma* **2021**, *30*, 761–780. [CrossRef]
13. Lagdon, S.; Armour, C.; Stringer, M. Adult experience of mental health outcomes as a result of intimate partner violence victimisation: A systematic review. *Eur. J. Psychotraumatol.* **2014**, *5*, 24794. [CrossRef]
14. Dillon, G.; Hussain, R.; Loxton, D.; Rahman, S. Mental and physical health and intimate partner violence against women: A review of the literature. *Int. J. Fam. Med.* **2013**, *2013*, 313909. [CrossRef]
15. Horwitz, A.V.; Spatz, C.; McLaughlin, J.; White, R. The impact of children abuse and neglect on mental health: A prospective study. *J. Health Soc. Behav.* **2001**, *42*, 184–201. [CrossRef] [PubMed]

16. Springer, K.W.; Sheridan, J.; Kuo, D.; Carnes, M. The long-term health outcomes of childhood abuse: An overview and a call to action. *J. Gen. Intern. Med.* **2003**, *18*, 864–870. [CrossRef] [PubMed]
17. Gillum, T.L. Improving services to African American survivors of IPV: From the voices of recipients of culturally specific services. *Violence Women* **2009**, *15*, 57–80. [CrossRef]
18. Conwell, W.L. Domestic violence among the Black poor: Intersectionality and social justice. *Int. J. Adv. Couns.* **2010**, *32*, 31–45. [CrossRef]
19. Alvarez, C.; Lameiras-Fernandez, M.; Holliday, C.N.; Sabri, B.; Campbell, J. Latina and Caribbean immigrant women's experiences with intimate partner violence: A story of ambivalent sexism. *J. Interpers. Violence* **2021**, *36*, 3831–3854. [CrossRef]
20. Kasturirangan, A.; Krishnan, S.; Riger, S. The impact of culture and minority status on women's experience of domestic violence. *Trauma Violence Abus.* **2004**, *5*, 318–332. [CrossRef] [PubMed]
21. Kim, C.; Sung, H.E. The effects of acculturation on intimate partner violence among Chinese immigrants in New York City. *J. Fam. Violence* **2016**, *31*, 325–336. [CrossRef]
22. Bhuyan, R. The production of the "Battered Immigrant" in public policy and domestic violence advocacy. *J. Interpers. Violence* **2008**, *23*, 153–170. [CrossRef]
23. Caetano, R.; Schafer, J.; Clark, C.L.; Cunradi, C.B.; Raspberry, K. Intimate partner violence, acculturation, and alcohol consumption Among Hispanic Couples in the United States. *J. Interpers. Violence* **2000**, *15*, 30–45. [CrossRef]
24. Reyes, M.E.; Weiss, N.H.; Swan, S.C.; Sullivan, T.P. The role of acculturation in the relation between intimate partner violence and substance misuse among IPV-victimized Hispanic women in the community. *J. Interpers. Violence* **2020**, 1–25. [CrossRef]
25. Oberg, K. Cultural shock: Adjustment to new cultural environments. *Prac. Anthr.* **1960**, *7*, 177–182. [CrossRef]
26. Bradbury, L. *Five Stages of Acculturation*; Delta Discovery Inc.: Bethel, AK, USA, 2019; Available online: https://deltadiscovery.com/five-stages-of-acculturation-2/ (accessed on 17 October 2021).
27. Shekunov, J. Immigration and risk of psychiatric disorders: A review of existing literature. *Am. J. Psych. Res. J.* **2016**, *11*, 3–5. [CrossRef]
28. Livingston, I.L.; Neita, M.; Riviere, L.; Livingston, S.L. Gender, acculturative stress and Caribbean immigrants' health in the United States of America. *West Ind. Med. J.* **2007**, *56*, 213.
29. Cobb, C.L.; Branscombe, N.R.; Meca, A.; Schwartz, S.J.; Xie, D.; Zea, M.C.; Molina, L.E.; Martinez, C.R., Jr. Toward a positive psychology of immigrants. *Perspect. Psychol. Sci.* **2019**, *14*, 619–632. [CrossRef]
30. Consedine, N.S.; Chentsova-Dutton, Y.; Krivoshekova, Y.S. Emotional acculturation predicts better somatic health: Experiential and expressive acculturation among immigrant women from four ethnic groups. *J. Soc. Clin. Psych.* **2014**, *33*, 867–889. [CrossRef]
31. Lee, S.; O'Neill, A.H.; Ihara, E.S.; Chae, D.H. Change in self-reported health status among immigrants in the United States: Associations with measures of acculturation. *PLoS ONE* **2013**, *8*, e76494.
32. Williams, D.R.; Haile, R.; González, H.M.; Neighbors, H.; Baser, R.; Jackson, J.S. The mental health of Black Caribbean immigrants: Results from the National Survey of American Life. *Am. J. Public Health* **2007**, *97*, 52–59. [CrossRef] [PubMed]
33. Lee, S.; O'Neill, A.; Park, J.; Scully, L.; Shenassa, E. Health insurance moderates the association between immigrant length of stay and health status. *J. Immigr. Minor. Health* **2012**, *14*, 345–349. [CrossRef]
34. Lacey, K.K.; Sears, K.P.; Govia, I.; Forsythe-Brown, I.; Matusko, N.; Jackson, J.S. Substance use, mental disorders and physical health of Caribbeans at-home compared to those residing in the United States. *Int. J. Environ. Res. Public Health* **2015**, *12*, 710–734. [CrossRef]
35. Lopez-Gonzalez, L.; Aravena, V.C.; Hummer, R.A. Immigrant acculturation, gender and health behavior: A research note. *Soc. Forces* **2005**, *84*, 581–593. [CrossRef]
36. Ferguson, G.; Bornstein, M. Tridimensional (3D) acculturation: Culture and adaptation of Black Caribbean immigrants in the USA. In *Global Perspectives on Well-Being in Immigrant Families: Advances in Immigrant Family Research*; Dimitrova, R., Bender, M., van de Vijver, F., Eds.; Springer: New York, NY, USA, 2014; Volume 1. [CrossRef]
37. Ferguson, G.M.; Bornstein, M.H.; Pottinger, A.M. Tridimensional acculturation and adaptation among Jamaican adolescent-mother dyads in the United States. *Child Dev.* **2012**, *83*, 1486–1493. [CrossRef] [PubMed]
38. Christie-Mizell, C.A.; Leslie, E.T.A.; Hearne, B.N. Self-rated health, discrimination, and racial group identity: The Consequences of ethnicity and nativity among Black Americans. *J. Afr. Am. Stud.* **2017**, *21*, 643–664. [CrossRef]
39. Nederhof, E.; Schmidt, M.V. Mismatch or cumulative stress: Toward an integrated hypothesis of programming effects. *Physiol. Behav.* **2012**, *106*, 691–700. [CrossRef] [PubMed]
40. Simons, R.L.; Lei, M.-K.; Beach, S.R.H.; Barr, A.B.; Simons, L.G.; Gibbons, F.X.; Philibert, R.A. Discrimination, segregation, and chronic inflammation: Testing the weathering explanation for the poor health of Black Americans. *Dev. Psychol.* **2018**, *54*, 1993–2006. [CrossRef]
41. McClendon, J.; Chang, K.; Boudreaux, M.J.; Oltmanns, T.F.; Bogdan, R. Black-White racial health disparities in inflammation and physical health: Cumulative stress, social isolation, and health behaviors. *Psychoneuroendocrinology* **2021**, *131*, 105251. [CrossRef] [PubMed]
42. Stults-Kolehmainen, M.A.; Tuit, K.; Sinha, R. Lower cumulative stress is associated with better health for physically active adults in the community. *Stress* **2014**, *17*, 157–168. [CrossRef] [PubMed]

43. Jackson, J.S.; Torres, M.; Caldwell, C.H.; Neighbors, H.W.; Nesse, R.; Taylor, R.J.; Trierweiler, S.J.; Williams, D.R. The National Survey of American Life: A study of racial, ethnic and cultural influences on mental disorders and mental health. *Int. J. Methods Psychiatr. Res.* **2004**, *13*, 196–207. [CrossRef]
44. Neighbors, H.W.; Njai, R.; Jackson, J.S. Race, ethnicity, John Henryism and depression symptoms: The National Survey of American life reinterview. *Res. Hum. Dev.* **2007**, *4*, 71–87. [CrossRef]
45. Lacey, K.K.; Mouzon, D.M.; Parnell, R.N.; Laws, T. Severe intimate partner violence, sources of stress and the mental health of U.S. Black women. *J. Women's Health* **2021**, *112*, 482–492. [CrossRef]
46. Proctor, B.D.; Dalaker, J.; US Bureau of the Census. *Poverty in the United States 2001*; Current Population Reports 60–219; U.S. Government Printing Office: Washington, DC, USA, 2002.
47. Cimino, A.N.; Yi, G.; Patch, M.; Alter, Y.; Campbell, J.C.; Gundersen, K.K.; Tang, J.T.; Tsuyuki, K.; Stockman, J.K. The effect of intimate partner violence and probable traumatic brain injury on mental health outcomes for Black Women. *J. Aggress. Maltreat. Trauma* **2019**, *28*, 714–731. [CrossRef]
48. Messman-Moore, T.L.; Long, P.J.; Siegfried, N.J. The revictimization of child sexual abuse survivors: An examination of the adjustment of college women with child sexual abuse, adult sexual assault, and adult physical abuse. *Child Maltreat.* **2000**, *5*, 18–27. [CrossRef] [PubMed]
49. Kendall-Tackett, K. The health effects of childhood abuse: Four pathways by which abuse can influence health. *Child Abus. Negl.* **2002**, *26*, 715–729. [CrossRef]
50. Borrell, L. Self-reported hypertension and race among Hispanics in the National Health Interview Survey. *Ethn. Dis.* **2006**, *16*, 71–77. [PubMed]
51. Cavanaugh, C.E.; Messing, J.T.; Del-Colle, M.; O'Sullivan, C.; Campbell, J.C. Prevalence and correlates of suicidal behavior among adult female victims of intimate partner violence. *Suicide Life Threat. Behav.* **2011**, *41*, 372–383. [CrossRef] [PubMed]
52. Roberto, K.A.; McCann, B.R.; Brossoie, N. Intimate partner violence in late life: An analysis of National News Reports. *J. Elder Abus. Negl.* **2013**, *25*, 230–241. [CrossRef]

International Journal of
Environmental Research and Public Health

MDPI

Article

The Effect of Adverse Mental Health and Resilience on Perceived Stress by Sexual Violence History

Katherine M. Anderson [1,2,*], Kiyomi Tsuyuki [2], Alexandra Fernandez DeSoto [2] and Jamila K. Stockman [2]

[1] Department of Behavioral, Social, and Health Education Sciences, Rollins School of Public Health, Emory University, Atlanta, GA 30322, USA
[2] Department of Medicine, Division of Infectious Diseases and Global Public Health, University of California San Diego School of Medicine, San Diego, CA 92093, USA; ktsuyuki@health.ucsd.edu (K.T.); alf013@health.ucsd.edu (A.F.D.); jstockman@ucsd.edu (J.K.S.)
* Correspondence: k4anderson@health.ucsd.edu

Abstract: Sexual violence, including nonconsensual sexual initiation and rape, remains pervasive, with impacts including adverse mental health and dysregulated stress response. Resilience is a promising interventional target. To advance the science, we examined the potential for resilience as an interventional tool by estimating associations between resilience, adverse mental health, and perceived stress among women by sexual violence history and partner perpetration. We analyzed 2018–2020 baseline survey data from 65 women enrolled in a prospective case-control study of sexual violence and HIV susceptibility in San Diego, CA. Multiple linear regressions were performed to examine associations, stratified by sexual violence history. About half of women experienced nonconsensual sexual initiation and/or rape; half of rapes were partner-perpetrated. Post-traumatic stress disorder (PTSD) was significantly associated with perceived stress among survivors (in regressions with depression and resilience, nonconsensual initiation: $\beta = 6.514$, $p = 0.003$, $R^2 = 0.616$; rape: $\beta = 5.075$, $p = 0.030$, $R^2 = 0.611$). Resilience was associated with lower perceived stress for all women; the effect appeared stronger among survivors of sexual violence (nonconsensual initiation: $\beta = -0.599$, $p < 0.001$ vs. $\beta = -0.452$, $p = 0.019$; rape: $\beta = -0.624$, $p < 0.001$ vs. $\beta = -0.421$, $p = 0.027$). Partner perpetration of rape was not associated with perceived stress. Our findings support leveraging resilience and addressing PTSD to reduce perceived stress among women with lifetime experiences of sexual violence.

Keywords: sexual violence; depression; PTSD; resilience; stress

Citation: Anderson, K.M.; Tsuyuki, K.; Fernandez DeSoto, A.; Stockman, J.K. The Effect of Adverse Mental Health and Resilience on Perceived Stress by Sexual Violence History. *Int. J. Environ. Res. Public Health* **2022**, *19*, 4796. https://doi.org/10.3390/ijerph19084796

Academic Editors: Krim K. Lacey and Rohan D. Jeremiah

Received: 27 February 2022
Accepted: 12 April 2022
Published: 15 April 2022

1. Introduction

Sexual violence against women remains pervasive, and is associated with long-term negative health consequences [1]. In the United States (U.S.), approximately one in five women (21.3%) experience rape in their lifetime [2], and 8.8% experience rape by an intimate partner [3], with racial and ethnic minority women disproportionately affected [4–11]. Young women face the greatest burden of sexual violence, with 79% of women's first rape experiences occurring before the age of 25 and 40% before the age of 19 [3]. Further, nationally representative samples suggest that approximately 7% of U.S. women experience forced sexual initiation, with racial and ethnic minority women disproportionately impacted [12,13]. Of these, a large part is attributable to intimate partner violence (IPV) or domestic violence [12], wherein a former or current partner or spouse is the perpetrator [14]. While sexual violence estimates are already alarmingly high, national estimates often underrepresent the true burden, and two out of three survivors of sexual violence are expected to experience sexual violence revictimization at some point in their lifetime [15].

1.1. PTSD, Depression, and Stress among Survivors of Sexual Violence

Survivors of sexual violence may suffer long-lasting psychological morbidity, including post-traumatic stress disorder (PTSD) and depression [16–21]. Of traumatic experiences, rape is the most likely to be associated with PTSD, with almost one-third of survivors developing PTSD during their lifetime [22]. Additionally, one-third of sexual violence survivors experience major depression during their lifetime [23]. The relationships between depression, adverse mental health, and stress are well documented [18,24–26]: comorbidity of PTSD and perceived stress is higher among survivors of sexual violence than those who have not experienced sexual violence [27], and women who experience sexual IPV report more depressive symptoms, which in turn is associated with higher perceived stress, than survivors of non-sexual IPV. However, the impacts of trauma-related stress vary depending on the type of trauma experienced [28]. Survivors of sexual violence report significantly worse psychological and physical health outcomes compared to individuals without experiences of sexual violence, without experiences of trauma, and with experiences of non-sexual violence trauma [28]. Survivors of sexual violence have a heightened level of perceived stress [29], which is often measured by the lack of perception predictability or control of one's life, high extent of life changes, and lacking ability to cope with problems or difficulties [30]. Stress, in turn, has significant negative physiological implications. Chronic and acute stress impact immune responses and wound healing [31–37], increase allostatic load [38], and promote chronic inflammation [39,40]. Such impacts have been documented years following trauma [41], with implications for increased susceptibility to negative health outcomes [42,43].

1.2. The Role of Partner Perpetration

While all survivors of sexual violence may experience adverse mental health impacts, relationship to the perpetrator of violence may also impact outcomes [44]. Intimate partner sexual violence (IPSV), sexual violence perpetrated by a current or former spouse or romantic partner, including a dating partner [44], accounts for 45% of all sexual violence in the U.S. [3], with a significant proportion occurring in the context of domestic violence. Though sometimes used interchangeably with intimate partner violence [14], domestic violence may also refer to violence in other domestic relationships, such as partner–child or sibling relationships; however, sexual domestic violence significantly overlaps with IPSV. IPSV is often overlooked as a differentially impactful experience compared to non-partner sexual violence [44], despite evidence that IPSV is more strongly associated with depressive symptoms than non-partner sexual violence [45,46]. Women who experience IPSV also report significantly higher PTSD and anxiety scores compared to women with no sexual violence experiences [46].

1.3. Resilience among Survivors of Violence

Promisingly, resilience—the process of successfully adapting to adversity, trauma, or significant stressors [47]—may mitigate the relationship between psychological trauma, adverse mental health, and stress [18,48], but few studies have examined these associations [49,50]. Fewer still have examined this relationship among survivors of sexual violence, despite the high co-occurring prevalence of adverse mental health and trauma-related stress [18,51,52]. One study among Black women in Baltimore, Maryland, USA found that among survivors of sexual violence, resilience partially attenuated (mediated) the association between perceived stress and severe depression [18]. While women who experience domestic violence are reported to have lower resilience scores than the general population, women experiencing IPV in the domestic context had higher resilience than those experiencing paternal violence [53], indicating a solid foundation for resilience-based intervention work. Investigation of resilience, adverse mental health, and stress among sexual violence survivors, with consideration for type of sexual violence experienced and perpetrator of violence, is, therefore, critically needed.

To address this gap in research, we sought to model the associations between symptoms consistent with PTSD, depression, and resilience with perceived stress among survivors of nonconsensual sexual initiation and lifetime rape, with consideration for partner perpetration. Findings from this research may provide support for the development of trauma-responsive interventions to support survivors of sexual violence.

2. Materials and Methods

2.1. The THRIVE Study

The current analysis used baseline data from a sample of 65 participants aged 18 and older who enrolled from January 2018 to December 2020 into The THRIVE Study. Detailed methods for The THRIVE Study have been published elsewhere [42]. In brief, The THRIVE Study was a prospective case-control study designed to examine the impact of sexual violence on mental health and immune and stress response dysregulation, with implications for HIV susceptibility, among adolescent girls and adult women residing in San Diego, CA, USA. Participants were recruited through community organizations, a local rape crisis center, physical flyers, and social media advertisements. Eligibility criteria included being between the ages of 14 and 45, currently residing in San Diego County, CA, self-report being cis-gender female, and self-report having either experienced in the past month: (1) consensual vaginal sex with a male partner (controls) or (2) nonconsensual vaginal penetration perpetrated by a male (cases). Only women aged 18 and older expressed interest in the study. Eligible and interested participants provided written informed consent at a baseline study visit and attended two additional study visits over the course of three months, resulting in three study timepoints (Baseline, 1-Month Follow-Up, 3-Month Follow-Up). At each study visit, participants completed an interviewer-administered survey (30–60 min), pregnancy testing, blood draw for HIV testing, and a cervicovaginal exam performed by a female physician or nurse practitioner to collect (1) swabs for STI and bacterial infection testing, and (2) cervicovaginal lavage fluid for assessment of immune biomarkers local to the female reproductive tract. Following each visit, participants also self-collected nine saliva samples over the course of three consecutive days (three timed samples collected per day), which were then retrieved by study staff. Participants received $50 in compensation for each study visit and an additional $35 upon return of saliva samples; transportation assistance was provided in the form of complimentary rideshare services. All participants were also provided with a list of local resources for free or low-cost medical and social services as well as facilitated connection to services when requested. Robust protocols were employed to protect the safety and comfort of all participants, inclusive of integration of Trauma-Informed Care [54,55], screening for suicidality using the Suicide Behaviors Questionnaire (SBQ-R) [56], and screening for risk of homicide by an intimate partner using the Danger Assessment [57]. All procedures were approved by the University of California San Diego Institutional Review Board prior to enrollment of participants.

2.2. Measures

2.2.1. Mental Health Indices

The Perceived Stress Scale (PSS) [30] was used to measure perceived stress. The PSS consists of 10 items, each measuring the degree to which situations in one's life are appraised as unpredictable or uncontrollable. Example items included being upset because of something that happened unexpectedly and feeling unable to control the important things in one's life. Responses were coded on a 5-point Likert scale ranging from 0 (never) to 4 (very often). Scores were summed, with higher scores indicating higher levels of perceived stress (sample Cronbach's alpha = 0.974).

PTSD was measured using the Primary Care PTSD Screen (PC-PTSD-4) [58]. Participants were asked four questions about how a traumatic event over the course of their life affected them over the past week. Example items included having had nightmares about the traumatic event and being constantly on guard, watchful, or easily startled; response options were "yes" or "no". Scores were summed, and participants endorsing "yes" for three or more items were classified as having symptoms consistent with PTSD. Cronbach's alpha for the PC-PTSD-4 scale was good and acceptable (sample Cronbach's alpha = 0.721) [59]. Resilience was measured using the 10-item Connor–Davidson Resilience Scale (CD-RISC) [60]. Participants were asked questions that measured how well one is equipped to bounce back after stressful events, tragedy, or trauma in the past week. Responses were coded on a 5-point Likert scale ranging from 1 (not true at all) to 5 (true nearly all of the time). Scores were summed, with higher scores indicating higher levels of resilience (sample Cronbach's alpha = 0.888). Depression was measured using the 10-item Center for Epidemiological Studies Depression Scale (CES-D-10) [61]. The CES-D-10 is a self-report measure of depressive symptoms assessed in the past week using a 4-point Likert scale ranging from 0 (rarely or none of the time) to 3 (all of the time). Example items included being bothered by things that do not normally bother you, feeling depressed, and feeling that everything was an effort. Two positive affect statements were reverse coded. Scores were summed, with higher scores indicating higher levels of depressive symptoms (sample Cronbach's alpha = 0.923).

2.2.2. Sexual Violence History

Sexual initiation type was measured by asking "How would you describe your first [vaginal/anal/oral] sexual experience?" with the following response options: (1) wanted and not forced, (2) wanted but pressured, (3) unwanted and pressured, (4) unwanted and threatened with violence, (5) unwanted and physically forced, or (6) unwanted and forced to drink alcohol or take drugs. Nonconsensual sexual initiation included participants who endorsed any category between 2 and 6. Ever experiencing rape in their lifetime was assessed by asking participants the number of times a male or female partner or non-partner had used force or threats to make the participant have sex. Participants who endorsed > 1 times were classified as ever experiencing rape; those who endorsed 0 times were classified as never experiencing rape in their lifetime. Among those who ever experienced rape, an additional variable was created to capture whether or not they had experienced rape perpetrated by an intimate partner.

Of note, participants who endorsed a nonconsensual sexual initiation were not automatically classified as having experienced rape; rather, the measure for rape was based on self-defined experience of forced or threatened sexual activity. As such, neither variable is mutually inclusive of the other.

2.3. Statistical Analysis

Statistical analyses were performed in SPSS version 26 [62]. We assessed differences in symptoms consistent with PTSD, depression, and resilience on perceived stress stratified by sexual violence history. There were no missing data. We computed descriptive statistics for all variables, reporting means and standard deviations for normally distributed continuous variables, medians and interquartile range for non-normally distributed continuous variables, and frequencies and proportions for categorical variables. We conducted bivariate analyses using independent sample *t*-tests, chi-squared tests, Fischer's exact tests, and Pearson correlations. Multiple linear regressions were used to examine the influence of symptoms consistent with PTSD, depression, and resilience (independent variables) on perceived stress score (dependent variable), entering independent variables in six steps. Normality was graphically assessed using P-P plots, and scatter plots were used to assess homoscedasticity, together indicating linearity of the data. For each set of analyses, the first three models included one independent variable each (PTSD, depression, resilience). The fourth and fifth models in each set included resilience and either PTSD or depression, while the last model in each set included all three independent variables. Adjusted models were estimated that accounted for age, race, ethnicity, and employment status. We conducted two sets of regression analyses: (1) regressions wherein participants were stratified by consent status of sexual initiation and (2) regressions wherein participants were stratified by ever experiencing rape, with and without a covariate accounting for rape perpetrated by an intimate partner. Multicollinearity between predictors was assessed using variance inflection factor (VIF) values, in which a value greater than 5 indicates severe collinearity. We were unable to consider partner perpetration in association with nonconsensual sexual initiation due to insufficient cell sizes.

Theoretical covariates were included in each model, with the exception of education, due to a skewed distribution of responses (many participants were currently enrolled in college), and the sufficiency of income as a marker of socioeconomic status. Stratification was employed rather than interaction terms in an effort to assess comparative relationships between all variables within each stratified group, rather than to assess the joint effect of each independent variable and sexual violence on the outcome. Further, stratification was chosen based on interpretability for practice. Unadjusted coefficients are presented in regression tables. We assessed improvements in model fit at each step by the changes in adjusted R^2 values, the proportion of the variance in perceived stress score that the independent variables explain collectively. Significance was set at a level of $p < 0.05$.

3. Results

3.1. Demographic Characteristics

Table 1 presents the demographic profile of participants enrolled in The THRIVE Study. The median age of girls and women ($n = 65$) enrolled in The THRIVE Study was 22 years (IQR: 18–26). Approximately 25% of women identified as Black/African American, 19% were Asian/Pacific Islander, 34% were White, and 34% indicated "Other" race (Often, Hispanic/Latinx; racial identification not mutually exclusive). Forty-two participants ($n = 27$) identified an ethnicity of Hispanic/Latinx. In terms of mental health, 30% ($n = 19$) of women endorsed symptoms consistent with PTSD; mean depression score was 11.3 (SD: 7.6, possible range: 0–28), mean resilience score was 30.0 (SD: 6.2, possible range: 11–40), and mean perceived stress score was 16.2 (SD: 6.9, possible range: 1–32). Regarding sexual violence exposure, of 65 participants, 33 (51%) had ever experienced nonconsensual sexual initiation, 30 (46%) had ever experienced rape.

Table 1. Study Participant Characteristics, Mental Health, and Sexual Violence Exposure, San Diego, CA 2018 to 2020 ($n = 65$).

Variables	*n* (%)
Age in years, median (IQR)	22 (18, 26)
Race (Not Mutually Exclusive)	
Black/African American	16 (24.6)
White	22 (33.8)
Asian/Pacific Islander	12 (18.5)
Other	22 (33.8)
Ethnicity	
Hispanic/Latinx	27 (41.5)
Educational Attainment	
High School Diploma, GED, or Less	36 (55.4)
Some Trade, Vocational School, or College or more	28 (43.1)
Employment Status	
Unemployed	20 (30.8)
Employed Part-Time	29 (44.63)
Employed Full-Time	15 (23.1)
Mental Health	
Symptoms consistent with PTSD	19 (29.2)
Depression, mean (SD), possible range: 0–28	11.3 (7.6)
Resilience, mean (SD), possible range: 11–40	30.0 (6.2)
Perceived Stress, mean (SD), possible range: 1–32	16.2 (6.9)

Table 1. *Cont.*

Variables	*n* (%)
Sexual Violence Exposure	
Nonconsensual Sexual Initiation	33 (50.8)
Partner	31 (47.7)
Non-Partner	2 (3.1)
Ever Raped	30 (46.9)
Partner	17 (26.2)
Non-Partner	13 (20.0)

IQR, interquartile range; GED, general equivalency diploma; PTSD, post-traumatic stress disorder; SD, standard deviation.

Compared to those with a consensual sexual initiation, those who experienced nonconsensual sexual initiation were significantly more likely to screen positive for PTSD and had significantly higher depression scores and significantly lower resilience scores (Table 2).

Table 2. Bivariate Associations between Mental Health Outcomes, Resilience, and Perceived Stress by Sexual Initiation Consent Status, San Diego, CA 2018 to 2020 ($n = 65$).

	Nonconsensual Sexual Initiation ($n = 33$)	Consensual Sexual Initiation ($n = 32$)	*p*
PTSD, *n* (%)	14 (42.42%)	5 (15.6%)	0.017
Depression, Mean (SD)	13.82 (7.80)	8.65 (6.45)	0.002
Resilience, Mean (SD)	28.85 (6.81)	31.19 (5.36)	0.003
Perceived Stress, Mean (SD)	18.61 (6.68)	13.71 (6.24)	0.066

Compared to those who had never experienced rape, those who had experienced rape were significantly more likely to screen positive for PTSD, had significantly higher depression and perceived stress scores, and had significantly lower resilience scores (Table 3).

Table 3. Bivariate Associations between Mental Health Outcomes, Resilience, and Perceived Stress by Ever Experience of Rape, San Diego, CA 2018 to 2020 ($n = 65$).

	Ever Rape ($n = 30$)	Never Rape ($n = 35$)	*p*
PTSD, *n* (%)	16 (53.33%)	3 (8.57%)	<0.001
Depression, Mean (SD)	14.87 (7.04)	8.18 (6.67)	<0.001
Resilience, Mean (SD)	27.90 (6.71)	31.82 (5.17)	<0.001
Perceived Stress, Mean (SD)	19.47 (6.27)	13.38 (6.14)	0.005

Depression and perceived stress were significantly positively associated with screening positive for PTSD, while resilience was not associated with PTSD. Depression and resilience were moderately negatively correlated, while depression and perceived stress were weakly-to-moderately positively correlated, and resilience and perceived stress were strongly negatively correlated (Table 4).

Table 4. Bivariate Associations between Mental Health Outcomes, Resilience, and Perceived Stress, San Diego, CA 2018 to 2020 ($n = 65$).

	Positive PTSD Screen	Negative PTSD Screen	*p*
Depression, Mean (SD)	18.21 (6.15)	8.40 (6.09)	<0.001
Resilience, Mean (SD)	28.58 (6.48)	30.58 (6.07)	0.121
Perceived Stress, Mean (SD)	21.16 (6.01)	14.16 (6.16)	<0.001
	Pearson Correlation Coefficient, *r*		*p*
Depression × Resilience	−0.391		0.001
Depression × Perceived Stress	0.548		<0.001
Resilience × Perceived Stress	−0.687		<0.001

3.2. Survivors of Nonconsensual Sexual Initiation

In Table 5, regressions are presented by consent status of sexual initiation (nonconsensual (forced, pressured, or unwanted) or consensual (wanted and not pressured or forced)). VIF values (<5) indicated an absence of severe collinearity.

Table 5. Multiple Linear Regression Models of Independent Variables (PTSD, Depression, Resilience) on Perceived Stress Stratified by Consent Status of Sexual Initiation (n = 65).

	Nonconsensual Sexual Initiation (n = 33)						
	PTSD, β	p	**Depression, β**	p	**Resilience, β**	p	R^2
Model 1	**7.523**	**0.017**					−0.10
Model 2			**0.959**	**0.002**			0.161
Model 3					**−0.693**	**<0.001**	0.334
Model 4	**7.389**	**<0.001**			**−0.687**	**<0.001**	0.599
Model 5			**0.551**	**0.039**	**−0.532**	**0.002**	0.429
Model 6	**6.514**	**0.003**	0.306	0.175	**−0.599**	**<0.001**	0.616
	Consensual Sexual Initiation (n = 32)						
Model 7	**6.658**	**0.038**					0.183
Model 8			**0.927**	**<0.001**			0.504
Model 9					**−0.71**	**0.001**	0.427
Model 10	4.225	0.199			**−0.652**	**0.003**	0.446
Model 11			**0.696**	**0.003**	**−0.463**	**0.014**	0.612
Model 12	1.800	0.530	**0.657**	**0.007**	**−0.452**	**0.019**	0.601

All regressions are adjusted for age, race, ethnicity, employment status, and case/control status. **Bolded** effects are significance at a level of $p < 0.05$.

Among women with a history of nonconsensual sexual initiation, symptoms consistent with PTSD were significantly positively associated with perceived stress score across all models (β = 6.514 to 7.523), while depression was significantly positively associated with perceived stress when entered into the model alone (Model 2, β = 0.959, p = 0.002) and with resilience (Model 5, β = −0.532, p = 0.039). Across all models, resilience was significantly negatively associated with perceived stress score (β = −0.693 to −0.532). Upon the addition of both PTSD and resilience, depression was no longer significantly associated with perceived stress among women who had experienced nonconsensual sexual debut. Among these women, a model including only PTSD symptoms and resilience accounted for the most variance in perceived stress (R^2 = 0.559), with screening positive for PTSD associated with a 7.4 point higher perceived stress score (β = 7.389, possible range: 0–40, $p < 0.001$), while a 1 point higher reported resilience score (β = −0.687, possible range: 5–50, $p < 0.001$) was associated with a 0.7 point lower perceived stress score.

Among women who experienced consensual sexual initiation, symptoms consistent with depression (β = 0.657 to 0.927) and resilience (β = −0.452 to −0.71) were each significantly associated with perceived stress across all models, while PTSD symptomology was not associated with perceived stress in any models. The most variance in perceived stress was accounted for in the model including depression (β = 0.696, p = 0.003) and resilience (β = −0.452, p = 0.014) (Model 11, R^2 = 0.612). In this model, a 1 point higher depression and resilience score were each associated with a 0.7 point higher and a 0.5 point lower perceived stress score, respectively.

3.3. Survivors of Rape

In Table 6, multiple linear regressions models are estimated to understand the associations between mental health, resilience, and perceived stress score, stratified by whether women ever experienced rape in their lifetime. VIF values (<5) indicated an absence of severe collinearity.

Table 6. Multiple Linear Regression Models of Independent Variables (PTSD, Depression, Resilience, Partner Perpetration) on Perceived Stress Stratified by Ever Rape ($n = 65$).

	Ever Rape								
	PTSD, β	***p***	**Depression, β**	***p***	**Resilience, β**	***p***	**Partner Perpetration, β**	***p***	**R^2**
Model 1	4.817	0.125							−0.054
Model 2			**0.904**	**<0.001**					0.304
Model 3					**−0.659**	**<0.001**			0.434
Model 4	**5.939**	**0.004**			**−0.698**	**<0.001**			0.619
Model 5			**0.500**	**0.049**	**−0.483**	**0.006**			0.517
Model 6	**5.075**	**0.030**	0.193	0.450	**−0.624**	**<0.001**			0.611
Model 7	4.718	0.144					−0.777	0.770	−0.105
Model 8			**0.942**	**<0.001**			−2.356	0.270	0.314
Model 9					**−0.685**	**<0.001**	−2.476	0.178	0.456
Model 10	**5.715**	**0.005**			**−0.718**	**<0.001**	−2.016	0.202	0.633
Model 11			**0.530**	**0.032**	**−0.502**	**0.003**	−2.783	0.113	0.558
Model 12	**4.582**	**0.044**	0.247	0.327	**−0.626**	**<0.001**	−2.250	0.162	0.634
	Never Rape								
Model 13	7.063	0.054							0.418
Model 14			**0.694**	**0.009**					0.489
Model 15					**−0.563**	**0.008**			0.491
Model 16	5.679	0.087			**−0.507**	**0.013**			0.532
Model 17			**0.563**	**0.021**	**−0.459**	**0.019**			0.578
Model 18	4.770	0.119	**0.515**	**0.030**	**−0.421**	**0.027**			0.604

All regressions are adjusted for age, race, ethnicity, employment status, and case/control status. **Bolded** effects are significance at a level of $p < 0.05$.

Among women who had ever experienced rape, depression and resilience were significantly associated with perceived stress in all single-predictor models (Models 1–3), and PTSD, depression, and resilience were significantly associated with perceived stress in all dual-predictor (Models 4–5) models, with PTSD symptoms ($\beta = 5.939$, $p = 0.004$) and depression ($\beta = 0.500$, $p = 0.049$) positively associated and resilience negatively associated ($\beta = -0.532$ to -0.693) with perceived stress. These associations held when partner perpetration of rape was included as a covariate, in all single- (Models 7–9) and dual-predictor (Models 10–11) models. Upon inclusion of PTSD symptoms, depression, and resilience in a single regression, with or without the inclusion of partner perpetration as a covariate (Models 6 & 12), PTSD symptoms ($\beta = 4.582$ to 5.075) and resilience ($\beta = -0.624$ to -0.626) retained significance, while depression did not. Among survivors of rape, the model accounting for the most variance in perceived stress without accounting for partner perpetration was Model 4 ($R^2 = 0.619$), and, when accounting for partner perpetration, Models 10 ($R^2 = 0.633$) and 12 ($R^2 = 0.634$) accounted for similar amounts of variance in perceived stress. In each of these models (4, 10, and 12), screening positive for PTSD was associated with 4.6 to 5.9 points more perceived stress, while a 1 point higher resilience score was associated with a 0.6 to 0.7 point lower perceived stress score. Experience of partner-perpetrated rape was not significantly associated with perceived stress score in any regression.

Among women who never experienced rape, PTSD symptoms were not associated with perceived stress in any regression model, while depression ($\beta = 0.515$ to 0.694) and resilience ($\beta = -0.421$ to -0.563) were positively and negatively associated with resilience in single-, dual-, and three-predictor models, respectively. Model 18, including three predictors, accounted for the most variance in perceived stress among women who had never experienced rape ($R^2 = 0.604$). In Model 18, a 1 point higher depression score was associated with a 0.52 point higher perceived stress score, while a 1 point higher resilience score was associated with a 0.42 point lower perceived stress score.

4. Discussion

This study examined the associations of symptoms consistent with PTSD, depression, and resilience with perceived stress, stratified by experiences of nonconsensual sexual initiation and lifetime experience of rape among women. Results of this analysis indicate four key findings. First, symptoms consistent with PTSD played a significant role in perceived stress among all women who experienced sexual violence, irrespective of type of sexual violence experience, while depression was associated with perceived stress among their consensual sexual initiation counterparts and women who had not experienced rape. Second, resilience was consistently associated with less perceived stress among all women, accounting for symptoms consistent with PTSD and depression. Third, the attenuating association of resilience with perceived stress appeared stronger among women who experienced sexual violence than women who did not. Finally, counter to previous findings in the literature, perpetration of rape by an intimate partner was not significantly associated with perceived stress when accounting for PTSD and depression. We discuss these findings in the context of extant literature on stress, mental health, and resilience among women survivors of sexual violence.

Symptoms consistent with PTSD play a significant role in the perceived stress score of all survivors of sexual violence in our sample, wherein PTSD symptoms were significantly associated with greater perceived stress in adjusted models, irrespective of type of sexual violence. Among survivors, PTSD retained a significant association with perceived stress when accounting for depression, while depression did not remain significant. This finding is particularly significant, given that nearly one-third (30%) of our sample of women reported symptoms consistent with PTSD. By contrast, depression was significantly associated with perceived stress among women who did not experience the respective types of sexual violence, including when accounting for PTSD, indicating the importance of services tailored to survivors of sexual violence in relation to PTSD in particular. A range of traumatic events and childhood adversities, aside from sexual violence, can play an important role in PTSD among women, and our study revealed that symptoms consistent with PTSD significantly enhance perceptions of stress among women who experienced sexual violence. U.S. women are two to three times as likely to develop PTSD as men [63,64]; while sexual violence may contribute to this, it may also compound upon existing PTSD among women, further increasing stress and the negative sequalae of sexual violence. Moreover, mental health services are routinely underutilized, and survivors of sexual violence are likely to avoid care-seeking due to fear of re-traumatization [65]. Mental health conditions are likely to worsen if left untreated, often leading to additional adverse health outcomes and compensatory behaviors, including substance use and suicide [66,67].

Among our sample, resilience was significantly associated with lower perceived stress among all women, regardless of sexual violence exposure. However, the attenuating association of resilience with perceived stress appeared stronger in magnitude among women who experienced rape or nonconsensual sexual initiation than women who did not. These findings shine light on the importance of nurturing resilience among all women, especially survivors of sexual violence, which has also been shown to be protective against the development of PTSD in the aftermath of trauma [68]. We identify that resilience may be a critical tool for reducing perceived stress among women with experiences of sexual violence, who may be more vulnerable to the negative effects of perceived stress on mental health conditions compared to unabused women [69]. While screening positive for PTSD is significantly associated with a large increase in perceived stress, the breadth of possible scores in the measure of resilience, coupled with the statistically significant attenuation of perceived stress by resilience, indicate that augmented resilience can outpace the negative impacts of screening positive for PTSD. Despite the importance of resilience as a positive coping strategy, there are relatively few interventions that aim to promote resilience among women who have experienced sexual violence [70]; instead, interventions often address PTSD and trauma-related stress with strategies such as Cognitive Behavioral Therapy. Although most cognitive behavioral approaches focus their treatment on factors related to a traumatic memory, effective PTSD treatments have shown that trauma-focused treatment to promote resilience may be more effective than trauma-focused therapy [71]. Additionally, carefully tailored interventions that promote resilience can play a vital role in recovery following trauma [72]. Appropriate integration of resilience into interventions may be impactful against the robust negative effects of symptoms consistent with PTSD, depression, and sexual violence on stress in women.

Finally, the results of this analysis indicate no association between experiencing perpetration of rape by an intimate partner and perceived stress when accounting for PTSD, depression, and resilience. While previous research has identified associations between intimate partner perpetration of violence and PTSD, depression, anxiety, and other outcomes [44–46], our analyses cannot corroborate these findings nor suggest meaningful influence of partner-perpetrated sexual violence on perceived stress.

4.1. Strengths and Limitations

The present study was limited by several features that are common in sociobehavioral research, including self-reported measures of mental health, which can result in social desirability bias; cross-sectional data, which limit the ability to draw causal inferences; and recall bias, as it relates to recollection of sexual violence and first intercourse. These factors should be considered when evaluating the extent to which the findings can be generalized. While the sample was racially and ethnically diverse, its small size precluded the ability to examine racial and ethnic differences that likely exist. Future research should examine such differences, given high national prevalence estimates of sexual assault and PTSD among Black, Latinx, and Indigenous populations [73]. The age range of the sample was limited, precluding the ability to examine potential observed associations for children younger than 18 and women older than 45. Further, age of participants skewed younger, limiting the ability to generalize results to women 30–45. We were unable to determine whether symptoms consistent with PTSD and depression were directly attributed to sexual violence history or some other type of trauma over the life course. Likewise, we acknowledge that resilience is a dynamic process that we measured as a snapshot in time [74]. Moreover, we did not measure underlying variables that may have contributed to resilience, such as social connections with others and help-seeking behaviors. Future research should integrate qualitative research methods to elucidate these unmeasured factors to facilitate the development and implementation of interventions that promote resilience to mitigate the negative effects of adverse mental health. Finally, we acknowledge that the data are insufficient to assess the severity of experiences of sexual violence but rather assess whether participants conceptualize themselves as having experienced each type of sexual violence queried. This use of reported experiences kept the data and voices of women in the study as reflective of actual experiences as possible. Similarly, experiences of sexual violence other than those reflective of subgroup eligibility were not controlled for in analyses. Understanding the total mental health burden of women enrolled in the study associated with lifetime experiences of sexual violence allows for better responsiveness and anticipation of mental health outcomes based on the information likely to be provided to practitioners and public health interventionists. Similarly, there are significant associations between several of the independent variables, indicating the potential for multicollinearity [75]. However, VIF values indicated that no collinearity was severe (VIF > 5) [75].

Additional notable strengths are also worth discussion. On average, women enrolled in the study were younger, which decreased the likelihood of recall bias, as it pertains to assessment of lifetime history of rape and sexual assault. The sample was ethnically diverse, and over two-thirds of the sample were recruited through study advertisements on social media platforms, both of which increase the generalizability of study findings, as women who did not seek services or who are traditionally underrepresented in research were identified and enrolled.

4.2. Future Directions

Our study findings have several implications for future research and clinicians working with survivors of sexual violence. Through cross-sectional research, we found negative associations between resilience and perceived stress and positive associations between symptoms consistent with PTSD and perceived stress among survivors of nonconsensual sexual initiation and rape. Future analyses should investigate sustained and causal relationships between symptoms consistent with PTSD, resilience, and perceived stress among survivors of sexual violence and whether or not this relationship is consistent across sexual and gender identity. Additionally, qualitative research studies that elucidate the context of individual and collective resilience and coping strategies in the midst of experiencing PTSD symptoms is needed to inform interventions for survivors of sexual violence. Current trauma-focused interventions have been shown to both reduce PTSD symptoms and improve resilience [76]; however, to our knowledge, there is a lack of such interventions designed and tested among survivors of sexual violence. The high proportion of women experiencing sexual violence stresses the importance of promoting resilience while mitigating symptoms consistent with PTSD beyond in-person support to innovative methods such as therapist-assisted online support [77].

5. Conclusions

Overall, this study provides support for leveraging resilience and addressing symptoms consistent with PTSD to reduce perceived stress among women with lifetime experiences of sexual violence, as well as among women without such experiences. Among survivors of sexual violence, irrespective of type, PTSD and resilience were robustly associated with perceived stress. Resilience should be of considerable interest among violence researchers in search of identifying efficacious responses to traumatic stress and targets of PTSD prevention and treatment among sexual violence survivors.

Author Contributions: Conceptualization: J.K.S., K.T., K.M.A. and A.F.D.; data curation: K.M.A.; formal analysis: K.M.A.; funding acquisition: J.K.S. and K.T.; investigation: J.K.S., K.M.A. and A.F.D.; methodology: J.K.S., K.T. and K.M.A.; project administration: K.M.A.; resources: J.K.S.; software: K.M.A.; supervision: J.K.S.; validation: K.M.A.; visualization: K.M.A.; writing—original draft: J.K.S., K.T., K.M.A. and A.F.D.; writing—review and editing: J.K.S., K.T., K.M.A. and A.F.D. All authors have read and agreed to the published version of the manuscript.

Funding: The THRIVE Study is supported by the National Institute of Allergy and Infectious Disease (NIAID Grant #R01AI128803). J.K. Stockman is also supported by the National Institute of Mental Health (NIMH Grant #R34MH122014). K. Tsuyuki is supported by the National Institute of Alcohol Abuse and Alcoholism (NIAAA Grant #K01AA025009) and the National Institute on Minority Health and Health Disparities (NIMHD Grant #L60MD012089). We acknowledge the San Diego Center for AIDS Research (Grant #P30AI036214), the San Diego CFAR Disparities Core Community Advisory Board, the Center for Community Solutions for their contributions and support in the implementation of the THRIVE Study. The content of this article is solely the responsibility of the authors and does not necessarily represent the official views of the National Institutes of Health.

Institutional Review Board Statement: The study was conducted according to the guidelines of the Declaration of Helsinki and approved by the Institutional Review Board [Blinded for Review] (Project #181898).

Informed Consent Statement: Informed consent was obtained from all subjects involved in the study.

Data Availability Statement: Data are not available due to the sensitive nature of the study.

Acknowledgments: We extend our sincere appreciation to the participants for their contributions to the study and to Helen Zhu for her support manuscript development.

Conflicts of Interest: The authors declare no conflict of interest.

Abbreviations

CA	California, United States of America
CD-RISC	Connor–Davidson Resilience Scale
CES-D	Center for Epidemiological Studies Depression Scale
IPSV	Intimate Partner Sexual Violence
IPV	Intimate Partner Violence
PC-PTSD	Primary Care Post-Traumatic Stress Disorder Screen
PSS	Perceived Stress Scale
PTSD	Post-Traumatic Stress Disorder
SBQ-R	Suicide Behaviors Questionnaire-Revised
VIF	Variance Inflation Factor

References

1. Jina, R.; Thomas, L.S. Health consequences of sexual violence against women. *Best Pract. Res. Clin. Obstet. Gynaecol.* **2013**, *27*, 15–26. [CrossRef] [PubMed]
2. Smith, S.G.; Zhang, X.; Basile, K.C.; Merrick, M.T.; Wang, J.; Kresnow, M.-J.; Chen, J. The National Intimate Partner and Sexual Violence Survey: 2015 Data Brief–Updated Release. 2018. Available online: https://stacks.cdc.gov/view/cdc/60893 (accessed on 26 February 2022).
3. Breiding, M.J.; Smith, S.G.; Basile, K.C.; Walters, M.L.; Chen, J.; Merrick, M.T. Prevalence and characteristics of sexual violence, stalking, and intimate partner violence victimization–national intimate partner and sexual violence survey, United States, 2011. *Am. J. Pub. Health* **2014**, *63*, 1–18.
4. Draughon, J.E.; Lucea, M.B.; Campbell, J.C.; Paterno, M.T.; Bertrand, D.R.; Sharps, P.W.; Campbell, D.W.; Stockman, J.K. Impact of Intimate Partner Forced Sex on HIV Risk Factors in Physically Abused African American and African Caribbean Women. *J. Immigr. Minor. Health* **2014**, *17*, 1313–1321. [CrossRef] [PubMed]
5. Basile, K.C.; Smith, S.G.; Fowler, D.N.; Walters, M.L.; Hamburger, M.E. Sexual Violence Victimization and Associations with Health in a Community Sample of African American Women. *J. Aggress. Maltreatment Trauma* **2016**, *25*, 231–253. [CrossRef]
6. Stockman, J.K.; Lucea, M.B.; Bolyard, R.; Bertand, D.; Callwood, G.B.; Sharps, P.; Campbell, D.W.; Campbell, J.C. Intimate partner violence among African American and African Caribbean women: Prevalence, risk factors, and the influence of cultural attitudes. *Glob. Health Action* **2014**, *7*, 24772. [CrossRef]
7. Basile, K.C.; Smith, S.G.; Walters, M.L.; Fowler, D.N.; Hawk, K.; Hamburger, M.E. Sexual Violence Victimization and Associations with Health in a Community Sample of Hispanic Women. *J. Ethn Cult. Divers. Soc. Work* **2015**, *24*, 1–17. [CrossRef]
8. Cavanaugh, C.E.; Messing, J.T.; Amanor-Boadu, Y.; O'Sullivan, C.O.; Webster, D.; Campbell, J. Intimate partner sexual violence: A comparison of foreign- versus US-born physically abused Latinas. *J. Urban Health* **2014**, *91*, 122–135. [CrossRef]
9. Hazen, A.L.; Soriano, F.I. Experiences with Intimate Partner Violence among Latina Women. *Violence Women* **2007**, *13*, 562–582. [CrossRef]
10. Boykins, A.D.; Alvanzo, A.A.; Carson, S.; Forte, J.; Leisey, M.; Plichta, S.B. Minority Women Victims of Recent Sexual Violence: Disparities in Incident History. *J. Women's Health* **2010**, *19*, 453–461. [CrossRef]
11. Avegno, J.; Mills, T.J.; Mills, L.D. Sexual Assault Victims in the Emergency Department: Analysis by Demographic and Event Characteristics. *J. Emerg. Med.* **2009**, *37*, 328–334. [CrossRef]
12. Hawks, L.; Woolhandler, S.; Himmelstein, D.U.; Bor, D.H.; Gaffney, A.; McCormick, D. Association Between Forced Sexual Initiation and Health Outcomes Among US Women. *JAMA Intern. Med.* **2019**, *179*, 1551–1558. [CrossRef] [PubMed]
13. Tsuyuki, K.; Al-Alusi, N.A.; Campbell, J.C.; Murry, D.; Cimino, A.N.; Servin, A.E.; Stockman, J.K. Adverse childhood experiences (ACEs) are associated with forced and very early sexual initiation among Black women accessing publicly funded STD clinics in Baltimore, MD. *PLoS ONE* **2019**, *14*, e0216279. [CrossRef] [PubMed]
14. Centers for Disease Control and Prevention Prevent Domestic Violence. Available online: https://www.cdc.gov/injury/features/intimate-partner-violence/index.html (accessed on 26 February 2022).
15. Classen, C.C.; Palesh, O.G.; Aggarwal, R. Sexual Revictimization: A Review of the Empirical Literature. *Trauma Violence Abus.* **2005**, *6*, 103–129. [CrossRef] [PubMed]
16. Folayan, M.O.; Harrison, A.; Brown, B.; Odetoyinbo, M.; Stockman, J.K.; Ajuwon, A.J.; Cáceres, C.F. Associations between Forced Sexual Initiation, HIV Status, Sexual Risk Behavior, Life Stressors, and Coping Strategies among Adolescents in Nigeria. *PLoS ONE* **2016**, *11*, e0155210. [CrossRef] [PubMed]
17. McGuigan, W.M.; Middlemiss, W. Sexual abuse in childhood and interpersonal violence in adulthood: A cumulative impact on depressive symptoms in women. *J. Interpers. Violence* **2005**, *20*, 1271–1287. [CrossRef] [PubMed]
18. Catabay, C.J.; Stockman, J.K.; Campbell, J.C.; Tsuyuki, K. Perceived stress and mental health: The mediating roles of social support and resilience among black women exposed to sexual violence. *J. Affect. Disord.* **2019**, *259*, 143–149. [CrossRef] [PubMed]

19. Williams, M.J.; Grimley, D.M. Depressive symptoms and interpersonal victimization among African American women attending an urban STD clinic. *Women's Health Issues* **2008**, *18*, 375–380. [CrossRef]
20. Stockman, J.K.; Hayashi, H.; Campbell, J.C. Intimate Partner Violence and its Health Impact on Ethnic Minority Women. *J. Womens Health* **2015**, *24*, 62–79. [CrossRef]
21. Cole, J.; Logan, T.K.; Shannon, L. Intimate sexual victimization among women with protective orders: Types and associations of physical and mental health problems. *Violence Vict.* **2005**, *20*, 695–715. [CrossRef]
22. Nguyen, K.H.; Padilla, M.; Villaveces, A.; Patel, P.; Atuchukwu, V.; Onotu, D.; Apondi, R.; Aluzimbi, G.; Chipimo, P.; Kancheya, N.; et al. Coerced and forced sexual initiation and its association with negative health outcomes among youth: Results from the Nigeria, Uganda, and Zambia Violence Against Children Surveys. *Child Abus. Negl.* **2019**, *96*, 104074. [CrossRef]
23. Neilson, E.C.; Norris, J.; Bryan, A.E.B.; Stappenbeck, C.A. Sexual Assault Severity and Depressive Symptoms as Longitudinal Predictors of the Quality of Women's Sexual Experiences. *J. Sex Marital Ther.* **2016**, *43*, 463–478. [CrossRef] [PubMed]
24. Liu, Y.; Li, T.; Guo, L.; Zhang, R.; Feng, X.; Liu, K. The mediating role of sleep quality on the relationship between perceived stress and depression among the elderly in urban communities: A cross-sectional study. *Public Health* **2017**, *149*, 21–27. [CrossRef] [PubMed]
25. Anastasiades, M.H.; Kapoor, S.; Wootten, J.; Lamis, D.A. Perceived stress, depressive symptoms, and suicidal ideation in undergraduate women with varying levels of mindfulness. *Arch. Women's Ment. Health* **2017**, *20*, 129–138. [CrossRef] [PubMed]
26. Machado, C.L.; De Azevedo, R.C.; Facuri, C.O.; Vieira, M.-J.N.; Fernandes, A.-M.S. Posttraumatic stress disorder, depression, and hopelessness in women who are victims of sexual violence. *Int. J. Gynecol. Obstet.* **2011**, *113*, 58–62. [CrossRef] [PubMed]
27. Hu, E.; Koucky, E.M.; Brown, W.J.; Bruce, S.E.; Sheline, Y.I. The Role of Rumination in Elevating Perceived Stress in Post-traumatic Stress Disorder. *J. Interpers. Violence* **2013**, *29*, 1953–1962. [CrossRef] [PubMed]
28. Dworkin, E.R.; Menon, S.V.; Bystrynski, J.; Allen, N.E. Sexual assault victimization and psychopathology: A review and meta-analysis. *Clin. Psychol. Rev.* **2017**, *56*, 65–81. [CrossRef]
29. Garcia, E.R.; Stoever, J.K.; Wang, P.; Yim, I.S. Empowerment, Stress, and Depressive Symptoms Among Female Survivors of Intimate Partner Violence Attending Personal Empowerment Programs. *J. Interpers. Violence* **2019**, *36*, 9557–9579. [CrossRef]
30. Cohen, S.; Kamarck, T.; Mermelstein, R. A global measure of perceived stress. *J. Health Soc. Behav.* **1983**, *24*, 385–396. [CrossRef]
31. Campbell, J.C.; Baty, M.L.; Ghandour, R.M.; Stockman, J.K.; Francisco, L.; Wagman, J. The intersection of intimate partner violence against women and HIV/AIDS: A review. *Int. J. Inj. Control Saf. Promot.* **2008**, *15*, 221–231. [CrossRef]
32. Bauer, M.E.; Wieck, A.; Lopes, R.P.; Teixeira, A.L.; Grassi-Oliveira, R. Interplay between Neuroimmunoendocrine Systems during Post-Traumatic Stress Disorder: A Minireview. *Neuroimmunomodulation* **2010**, *17*, 192–195. [CrossRef]
33. Bauer, M.E. Chronic Stress and Immunosenescence: A Review. *Neuroimmunomodulation* **2008**, *15*, 241–250. [CrossRef] [PubMed]
34. Woods, S.J.; Wineman, N.M.; Page, G.G.; Hall, R.; Alexander, T.S.; Campbell, J.C. Predicting Immune Status in Women from PTSD and Childhood and Adult Violence. *Adv. Nurs. Sci.* **2005**, *28*, 306–319. [CrossRef] [PubMed]
35. Kalokhe, A.S.; Ibegbu, C.C.; Kaur, S.P.; Amara, R.R.; Kelley, M.E.; Del Rio, C.; Stephenson, R. Intimate partner violence is associated with increased cd4(+) t-cell activation among HIV-negative high-risk women. *Pathog. Immun.* **2016**, *1*, 193–213. [CrossRef] [PubMed]
36. Garcia-Linares, M.I.; Sanchez-Lorente, S.; Coe, C.L.; Martinez, M. Intimate Male Partner Violence Impairs Immune Control Over Herpes Simplex Virus Type 1 in Physically and Psychologically Abused Women. *Psychosom. Med.* **2004**, *66*, 965–972. [CrossRef] [PubMed]
37. Tsuyuki, K.; Cimino, A.N.; Holliday, C.N.; Campbell, J.C.; Al-Alusi, N.A.; Stockman, J.K. Physiological Changes from Violence-Induced Stress and Trauma Enhance HIV Susceptibility Among Women. *Curr. HIV/AIDS Rep.* **2019**, *16*, 57–65. [CrossRef] [PubMed]
38. Juster, R.-P.; McEwen, B.S.; Lupien, S.J. Allostatic load biomarkers of chronic stress and impact on health and cognition. *Neurosci. Biobehav. Rev.* **2010**, *35*, 2–16. [CrossRef] [PubMed]
39. Richman, A.D. Concurrent Social Disadvantages and Chronic Inflammation: The Intersection of Race and Ethnicity, Gender, and Socioeconomic Status. *J. Racial Ethn. Health Disparities* **2018**, *5*, 787–797. [CrossRef]
40. Goodman, E.; McEwen, B.S.; Dolan, L.M.; Schafer-Kalkhoff, T.; Adler, N.E. Social disadvantage and adolescent stress. *J. Adolesc. Health* **2005**, *37*, 484–492. [CrossRef]
41. Heim, C.; Shugart, M.; Craighead, W.E.; Nemeroff, C.B. Neurobiological and psychiatric consequences of child abuse and neglect. *Dev. Psychobiol.* **2010**, *52*, 671–690. [CrossRef]
42. Stockman, J.K.; Anderson, K.M.; Karris, M.Y.; Benson, C.A.; Tsuyuki, K.; Granger, D.A.; Weber, A.; Ghosh, M. The Role of Stress and Genital Immunity in Sexual Trauma and HIV Susceptibility among Adolescent Girls and Adult Women (The THRIVE Study): Protocol for a Longitudinal Case-Control Study. *JMIR Res. Protoc.* **2020**, *9*, e18190. [CrossRef]
43. Rivara, F.; Adhia, A.; Lyons, V.; Massey, A.; Mills, B.; Morgan, E.; Simckes, M.; Rowhani-Rahbar, A. The Effects of Violence on Health. *Health Aff.* **2019**, *38*, 1622–1629. [CrossRef] [PubMed]
44. Barker, L.C.; Stewart, D.E.; Vigod, S.N. Intimate Partner Sexual Violence: An Often-Overlooked Problem. *J. Women's Health* **2019**, *28*, 363–374. [CrossRef] [PubMed]

45. Decker, M.R.; Peitzmeier, S.; Olumide, A.; Acharya, R.; Ojengbede, O.; Covarrubias, L.; Gao, E.; Cheng, Y.; Delany-Moretlwe, S.; Brahmbhatt, H. Prevalence and Health Impact of Intimate Partner Violence and Non-partner Sexual Violence among Female Adolescents Aged 15–19 Years in Vulnerable Urban Environments: A Multi-Country Study. *J. Adolesc. Health* **2014**, *55*, S58–S67. [CrossRef] [PubMed]
46. Tarzia, L.; Thuraisingam, S.; Novy, K.; Valpied, J.; Quake, R.; Hegarty, K. Exploring the relationships between sexual violence, mental health and perpetrator identity: A cross-sectional Australian primary care study. *BMC Public Health* **2018**, *18*, 1410. [CrossRef] [PubMed]
47. Southwick, S.M.; Bonanno, G.A.; Masten, A.; Panter-Brick, C.; Yehuda, R. Resilience definitions, theory, and challenges: Interdisciplinary perspectives. *Eur. J. Psychotraumatol.* **2014**, *5*, 5. [CrossRef]
48. Leon, M.A.G.; Pérez-Mármol, J.M.; Gonzalez-Pérez, R.; García-Ríos, M.D.C.; Peralta-Ramírez, M.I. Relationship between resilience and stress: Perceived stress, stressful life events, HPA axis response during a stressful task and hair cortisol. *Physiol. Behav.* **2019**, *202*, 87–93. [CrossRef]
49. Machisa, M.T.; Christofides, N.; Jewkes, R. Social support factors associated with psychological resilience among women survivors of intimate partner violence in Gauteng, South Africa. *Glob. Health Action* **2018**, *11*, 1491114. [CrossRef]
50. Friedberg, A.; Malefakis, D. Resilience, Trauma, and Coping. *Psychodyn. Psychiatry* **2018**, *46*, 81–113. [CrossRef]
51. Mancus, G.C.; Cimino, A.N.; Hasan, M.Z.; Campbell, J.C.; Sharps, P.; Winch, P.J.; Tsuyuki, K.; Stockman, J.K. Greenness and the Potential Resilience to Sexual Violence: "Your Neighborhood Is Being Neglected Because People Don't Care. People with Power Don't Care". *J. Interpers. Violence* **2021**. [CrossRef]
52. Kuo, C.; LoVette, A.; Slingers, N.; Mathews, C. Predictors of Resilience Among Adolescent Girls and Young Women Who Have Experienced Intimate Partner Violence and Sexual Violence in South Africa. *J. Interpers. Violence* **2021**. [CrossRef]
53. Tsirigotis, K.; Łuczak, J. Resilience in Women who Experience Domestic Violence. *Psychiatr. Q.* **2017**, *89*, 201–211. [CrossRef]
54. Substance Abuse and Mental Health Services. *Administration SAMHSA's Concept of Trauma and Guidance for a Trauma-Informed Approach*; Substance Abuse and Mental Health Services: Rockville, MD, USA, 2014.
55. Center for Substance Abuse Treatment (US). *Trauma-Informed Care in Behavioral Health Services*; Substance Abuse and Mental Health Services Administration (US): Rockville, MD, USA, 2014.
56. Osman, A.; Bagge, C.L.; Gutierrez, P.M.; Konick, L.C.; Kopper, B.A.; Barrios, F.X. The Suicidal Behaviors Question-naire-Revised (SBQ-R): Validation with clinical and nonclinical samples. *Assessment* **2001**, *8*, 443–454. [CrossRef]
57. Campbell, J.C.; Webster, D.W.; Glass, N. The danger assessment: Validation of a lethality risk assessment instrument for in-timate partner femicide. *J. Interpers Violence* **2009**, *24*, 653–674. [CrossRef]
58. Prins, A.; Bovin, M.; Smolenski, D.J.; Marx, B.P.; Kimerling, R.; Jenkins-Guarnieri, M.A.; Kaloupek, D.; Schnurr, P.P.; Kaiser, A.P.; Leyva, Y.E.; et al. The Primary Care PTSD Screen for DSM-5 (PC-PTSD-5): Development and Evaluation within a Veteran Primary Care Sample. *J. Gen. Intern. Med.* **2016**, *31*, 1206–1211. [CrossRef]
59. Tavakol, M.; Dennick, R. Making sense of Cronbach's alpha. *Int. J. Med. Educ.* **2011**, *2*, 53–55. [CrossRef]
60. Connor, K.M.; Davidson, J.R.T. Development of a new resilience scale: The Connor-Davidson Resilience Scale (CD-RISC). *Depress. Anxiety* **2003**, *18*, 76–82. [CrossRef]
61. Radloff, L.S. The use of the Center for Epidemiologic Studies Depression Scale in adolescents and young adults. *J. Youth Adolesc.* **1991**, *20*, 149–166. [CrossRef]
62. IBM Corp. *IBM SPSS Statistics for Windows, Version 26.0*; IBM Corp: Armonk, NY, USA, 2018.
63. Olff, M. Sex and gender differences in post-traumatic stress disorder: An update. *Eur. J. Psychotraumatol.* **2017**, *8*, 1351204. [CrossRef]
64. Brody, D.J.; Pratt, L.A.; Hughes, J.P. Prevalence of Depression among Adults Aged 20 and Over: United States, 2013–2016. *NCHS Data Brief* **2018**, *303*, 1–8.
65. Reeves, E. A Synthesis of the Literature on Trauma-Informed Care. *Issues Ment. Health Nurs.* **2015**, *36*, 698–709. [CrossRef]
66. Chesney, E.; Goodwin, G.M.; Fazel, S. Risks of all-cause and suicide mortality in mental disorders: A meta-review. *World Psychiatry* **2014**, *13*, 153–160. [CrossRef]
67. Prasad, B. *Chronic Mental Illness and the Changing Scope of Intervention Strategies, Diagnosis, and Treatment in Advances in Psychology, Mental Health, and Behavioral Studies*; IGI Global: Hershey, PA, USA, 2016.
68. Thompson, N.J.; Fiorillo, D.; Rothbaum, B.O.; Ressler, K.J.; Michopoulos, V. Coping strategies as mediators in relation to re-silience and posttraumatic stress disorder. *J. Affect Disord.* **2018**, *225*, 153–159. [CrossRef]
69. Schneiderman, N.; Ironson, G.; Siegel, S.D. Stress and Health: Psychological, Behavioral, and Biological Determinants. *Annu. Rev. Clin. Psychol.* **2005**, *1*, 607–628. [CrossRef]
70. Herrman, H.; Stewart, D.E.; Diaz-Granados, N.; Berger, E.L.; Jackson, B.; Yuen, T. What is resilience? *Can. J. Psychiatry* **2011**, *56*, 258–265. [CrossRef]
71. Burton, M.S.; Cooper, A.A.; Feeny, N.C.; Zoellner, L.A. The Enhancement of Natural Resilience in Trauma Interventions. *J. Contemp. Psychother.* **2015**, *45*, 193–204. [CrossRef]
72. Feeny, N.C.; Zoellner, L.A. (Eds.) *Facilitating Resilience and Recovery Following Trauma*; The Guilford Press: New York, NY, USA, 2014.

73. Spoont, M.; McClendon, J. Racial and Ethnic Disparities in PTSD. *PTSD Res. Q.* **2020**, *31*.
74. Stainton, A.; Chisholm, K.; Kaiser, N.; Rosen, M.; Upthegrove, R.; Ruhrmann, S.; Wood, S.J. Resilience as a multimodal dynamic process. *Early Interv. Psychiatry* **2019**, *13*, 725–732. [CrossRef]
75. Kim, J.H. Multicollinearity and misleading statistical results. *Korean J. Anesthesiol.* **2019**, *72*, 558–569. [CrossRef]
76. Reyes, A.T.; Kearney, C.A.; Lee, H.; Isla, K.; Estrada, J. Interventions for Posttraumatic Stress with Resilience as Outcome: An Integrative Review. *Issues Ment. Health Nurs.* **2018**, *39*, 166–178. [CrossRef]
77. Ehlers, A.; Wild, J.; Warnock-Parkes, E.; Grey, N.; Murray, H.; Kerr, A.; Rozental, A.; Beierl, E.T.; Tsiachristas, A.; Perera, R.; et al. A randomised controlled trial of therapist-assisted online psychological therapies for posttraumatic stress disorder (STOP-PTSD): Trial protocol. *Trials* **2020**, *21*, 355. [CrossRef]

International Journal of
Environmental Research and Public Health

MDPI

Article

Intimate Partner Violence and the Role of Child Maltreatment and Neighborhood Violence: A Retrospective Study of African American and US Caribbean Black Women

Krim K. Lacey [1,*], Hira R. Shahid [2] and Rohan D. Jeremiah [3]

1 Department of Sociology and African and African American Studies, University of Michigan-Dearborn, Dearborn, MI 48128, USA
2 CASL, University of Michigan-Dearborn, Dearborn, MI 48128, USA; hrshahid04@gmail.com
3 Human Development and Nursing Sciences, College of Nursing, University of Illinois-Chicago, Chicago, IL 60612, USA; rjerem@uic.edu
* Correspondence: krimlacey@gmail.com

Abstract: *Background*: Research suggests that intimate partner violence (IPV) is associated with childhood maltreatment and violence exposure within the neighborhood context. This study examined the role of child maltreatment and violence exposure on intimate partner violence, with the moderating effects of mental disorders (IPV) among US Black women. *Methods*: Data from the National Survey of American Life (NSAL), the largest and most complete sample on the mental health of US Blacks, and the first representative sample of Caribbean Blacks residing in the United States was used to address the study objectives. Descriptive statistics, chi-square test of independence, *t*-test, and logistic regression procedures were used to analyze the data. *Results*: Bivariate results indicate an association between child abuse and intimate partner victimization among US Black women. Witnessing violence as a child as well as neighborhood violence exposure was also related to IPV but shown to differ between African American and Caribbean Black women. Multivariate findings confirmed the influence of mental disorders and social conditions on US Black women's risk for IPV. Moderating effects of child maltreatment and mental disorders in association with adult IPV were not found. *Conclusions*: The study addressed the short and long-term impact of child maltreatment and the contribution to the cycle of intimate violence among US Black women including African American and Caribbean Blacks. The study suggests the need for prevention and intervention efforts to improve structural conditions for at-risk populations and communities predisposed to violence and other negative outcomes. Possibilities for future research are also discussed.

Keywords: intimate partner violence; child maltreatment; violent exposure; mental health

check for updates

Citation: Lacey, K.K.; Shahid, H.R.; Jeremiah, R.D. Intimate Partner Violence and the Role of Child Maltreatment and Neighborhood Violence: A Retrospective Study of African American and US Caribbean Black Women. *Int. J. Environ. Res. Public Health* **2021**, *18*, 2245. https://doi.org/10.3390/ijerph18052245

Academic Editor: Ko-Ling Chan

Received: 1 January 2021
Accepted: 19 February 2021
Published: 24 February 2021

1. Introduction

Approximately half (41.7%) of US Black women, including Caribbean women, currently comprising of one of the fastest-growing ethnic groups, have reported physical intimate victimization in their lifetime [1–4]. Studies show that early childhood exposure to violence within families and the neighborhood context are precursors to intimate partner violence as an adult [5]. Statistics indicate the rate of child abuse among African Americans in the United States is second highest only to American Indian and Alaskan Native [6]. While there is general knowledge surrounding the association between adult intimate partner violence and child abuse, less is known about the role of neighborhood violence context exposure on intimate victimization among US Black women [7]. To inform intervention and preventative practices, research geared to understanding the interconnectedness of violence at the individual and community levels is necessary due to high and rising levels of child abuse and reported cases of violence within the Black population [8–11].

Child abuse is one of many childhood adversities that can be a precursor for violence in adulthood [12]. Studies suggest the link between child maltreatment and adult intimate partner violence may be influenced by childhood experience and mental disorders [5,13]. However, there is a void in the literature on how social behavior and mental conditions might moderate the relationship between child maltreatment and adult intimate partner violence among US Black women and other understudied populations (i.e., Latinx, Native American, Asian American, Immigrant and Refugees). This study utilized population-based data to explore IPV in association with child maltreatment and neighborhood violence among US Black women with a specific focus on African American and Caribbean Blacks.

1.1. Background

Research has long found a connection between a history of exposure to violence and intimate victimization [5,11,14–16]. Studies largely suggest that experiencing or witnessing acts of aggression can influence perpetration or victimization [11,14,17,18]. Social learning theory posits that acts of violence are learned through imitation; and such acts internalized may influence our approach to addressing disputes in interpersonal relationships [19,20]. The framework evaluates behaviors that are normalized and rewarded while examining operant methods that provide explanations on how experiences with child abuse or exposure to violence may be linked to adult victimization [21]. For example, children who are exposed and/or socialized in violent-prone environments may be more accepting of certain behaviors, and therefore, are more likely to resort to such practices during their relationships in later life. The intergenerational transmission hypothesis further contends that violent behavior is learned through modeling and imitation, and such behavior is particularly acquired in the early life course during childhood and through observation of parents and peer relationships [22,23]. Moreover, violence within the home or against children is rooted in the subconscious and intergenerational cycle of violence that perpetuates from one generation to the next [24,25].

1.2. Child Abuse and Intimate Partner Violence

Studies have demonstrated that there is a co-occurrence of child abuse and adult victimization [5,11,14,15,18,26]. Notably, harsh physical treatment and disciplinary measures in childhood have been found to increase the association of violence in adulthood [8,21]. For example, children growing up in violent homes are at risk of becoming victims of IPV [27]. Women in particular, who were raised in violent households, are at greater risk for suffering and becoming victims of intimate partner violence [26]. Although there is a general knowledge about the potential connection between child abuse and intimate partner violence, the understanding among ethnic groups where physical punishment is a method of disciplinary practice used by a parent or caretaker in rearing children, remains limited [28]. Nonetheless, there is some evidence that suggests childhood victimization increases the risk for physical, psychological, and sexual victimization and perpetration into adulthood among Caribbeans [29]. In recent years, more emphasis has been applied to understand the nuance of this problem from a more intersectional perspective [30,31]. However, more inquiries are needed to understand the association between child abuse and intimate partner violence among U.S. Black women, who are more vulnerable to victimization compared to other populations [1]. While considerable progress has been made to understand these issues among Black Americans, there are still considerable gaps that delineate the experiences of Caribbean Americans, a growing sub-population, that has its own experience with violence.

1.3. Childhood Exposure to Violence and Intimate Partner Violence

Along with direct acts of child abuse research further recognizes that children's exposure to violence increases the risk for adult perpetration and victimization, as well [5,13,18,32]. Particularly, children who bear witness to, or are exposed to family violence, were found to be at increased risk of battering later in life [5,13,32]. Research has established that early exposure to family violence results in males being 3 to 10 times more prone to partner violence than males without exposure to violence [26]. The connection between children's exposure to violence and adult intimate perpetration and victimization has also been noted by various international studies. For example, women in Jamaica who had witnessed parental or family violence were found more likely to be physically abused by an intimate partner [33]. Gage earlier found that compared to Haitian women who had not observed their father beating their mothers, those who had such experiences reported significantly higher rates of emotional and sexual violence [34]. In Grenada, Jeremiah et. al. explored how the failure to address adverse childhood experiences—such as witnessing abuse among their parents continued to affect adult women that were associated with domestic violence [35]. Despite these findings, we still lack an understanding of the role of cultural norms in the relationship between children's exposure to violence and the risk for adulthood victimization.

1.4. Neighborhood Violence Exposure and Intimate Partner Violence

While the literature is relatively new in providing an understanding of the effects of neighborhood violence on intimate partner violence, the association has been mixed [17,18,36]. Reed and colleagues (2009) established that neighborhood violence in addition to perception about intimate partner violence is associated with increased perpetration of IPV among urban African American men [10]. A systematic review further links neighborhood environment and disadvantage with physical and sexual IPV while noting the influence of socio-economic factors (i.e., poverty, unemployment, income, education) [17]. This was supported by an earlier study that linked neighborhood disadvantage to IPV [37]. Conversely, little variation was found in the likelihood of male IPV concerning neighborhood crime in other studies, even though there was an increased likelihood of IPV experiences among women whose partners were involved in male-to-male violence [38]. Raghavan and colleagues additionally found that living in a neighborhood with high levels of social disorder and substance use increased women's exposure to community violence and subsequent IPV in adulthood [7].

1.5. Mediating and Moderating Effects of Child Maltreatment and Intimate Partner Violence

Research suggests that the relationship between later intimate partner violence and child maltreatment including witnessing violence and child abuse, is not always linear and may be influenced by childhood adversities and mental conditions [39,40]. For some children or adolescents, the possibility of developing emotional and psychological problems in response to painful experiences with exposure to violence is not out of the ordinary during this critical stage of development. Studies have found experiences with maltreatment are accompanied by external and antisocial behaviors [5,18,40]. The association between child maltreatment and adult victimization may also be reflective of hostile behaviors often developed by abused children [18,40], particularly if the childhood trauma goes unacknowledged or untreated. Such hostile behavioral patterns, which may be a part of their coping strategy, are poor impulse control that may be present among perpetrators of violence [26].

There is evidence that child maltreatment might further be linked to the use and abuse of alcohol and other substances. Early substance abuse among children and adolescents is common, and often related to aggressive behavior that can continue into adult life [41,42]. Research additionally suggests personality disorders may have some influence on partner violence [40]. Ehresaft et al. found that personality disorder partially mediated the relationship between childhood family violence and adult partner violence [43]. Likewise, a prospective longitudinal study found that early behavior problems were associated with partner violence in adulthood [42]. Conduct disorder, in particular, was found to mediate the relationship between child abuse and partner violence [5,41]. Furthermore, conduct disordered behavior in early childhood and adolescence has been linked to IPV perpetration in later adulthood [44]. Irrespective of previous studies, potential moderators or mediators of intimate partner violence such as substance abuse, anti-social personality disorder, conduct disorder, and oppositional defiant disorder have yet to be fully explored in the relationship among US Black women using national data.

1.6. Goals and Summary of Hypothesis

Using a nationally representative sample, the present study sought to add to the body of knowledge by exploring the association between violence exposure and intimate partner violence among US Blacks with a focus on African American and Caribbean Black women. The specific aims of the study were to: (a) examine the relationship between child maltreatment (child abuse or witnessing violence as a child) and adult severe physical intimate partner violence (SPIPV); (b) address the relationship between exposure to neighborhood violence and intimate partner violence; (c) and to evaluate the moderating effects of substance abuse disorder, conduct disorder, anti-social personality disorder and oppositional defiant disorder in association with child abuse and later interpersonal violence. As with previous studies, we expected to find an association between severe intimate partner violence and both child maltreatment and exposure to neighborhood violence. We also expected that the relationship between child maltreatment and intimate partner violence would be moderated by mental disorders.

2. Materials and Methods

Data from the National Survey of American Life (NSAL), conducted over a three-year period between 2001–2003, were used to address the research aims. The NSAL to date is the most comprehensive study conducted on the mental and physical health of adult US Blacks, and the first nationally representative study of Caribbean Blacks residing in the United States (see Jackson et al. [45]). Multistage probability sampling methods were used to collect the data. Face-to-face interviewing was the primary method of data collection, with a smaller percentage (14%) collected by phone. In total, the sample consisted of 6082 participants: 3570 African American; 1621 Caribbean Black; and 890 non-Hispanic White respondents. African Americans were characterized as those with African ancestry but without Caribbean roots. Caribbean Blacks were those respondents of African descent who were either (a) of West Indian descent, (b) from a Caribbean-area country, or (c) had parents or grandparents who were born in a Caribbean area country [46]. Prior to the data collection process, informed consent was obtained from participants. Interviews on average were 2 h and 20 min in length. The response rate for the entire sample was 72.3 percent. Respondents received an honorarium of $50 for their participation in the study. For this study, approximately 3277 women of African descent were the focus of analysis. Data collection for the NSAL was approved by the University of Michigan's Institutional Review Board.

2.1. Predictor Measures

2.1.1. Control Variables

The control variables included age (in years), marital status, employment status, educational level, and poverty. Marital status was separated into married, partnered, separated or divorced, widowed, or never married. Employment status was divided into employed, unemployed, and not in the labor force. Educational level included less than high school, high school graduates, some college, and college-educated. Poverty status is an income-to-poverty ratio consisting of the participants' household income divided by the 2001 US Census poverty threshold for the number of adults and children living in that household. Ratios below 1.00 indicate that the income for the participants' household is below the official poverty threshold, while a ratio of 1.00 or greater indicates income above the poverty level. For example, a ratio of 1.25 indicates that income was 25 percent above the appropriate poverty threshold [47]. Two ethnic groups were examined: African Americans and Caribbean Blacks. Noted earlier, African Americans were persons who self-identified as Black but did not report Caribbean ancestry. By contrast, US Caribbean Blacks were persons who were descendants or had Caribbean roots [46]. US Blacks were inclusive of both ethnic groups.

2.1.2. Child Maltreatment

Child maltreatment is inclusive of two measures: child abuse and witnessing violence as a child. Child abuse was determined by the question, "As a child, were you ever badly beaten up by your parent or the people that raised you?" Response options were "yes" or "no." For witnessing violence, respondents were asked, "When you were a child, did you ever witness serious physical fights at home, like when your father beat up your mother (yes/no)?" These measured were combined for multivariate analysis.

2.1.3. Neighborhood Violence

Various markers of neighborhood violence exposure were used in the study. First, experiences with neighborhood crime were operationalized with the question, "How often are there problems with muggings, burglaries, assaults, or anything like that in your neighborhood?" Measured on Likert scale response options include: very often, fairly often, not too often, hardly ever, and never. The variable was recoded to reflect ever/often vs. never for bivariate analysis. Second, to address experiences with atrocities, respondents were asked, "Did you ever see atrocities or carnage such as mutilated bodies or mass killings (yes/no)?" Third, seen someone badly injured, was determined by the question, "Did you ever see someone being badly injured or killed, or unexpectedly see a dead body (yes/no)?"

2.1.4. Moderators

A modified version of the World Health Organization Composite International Diagnostic Interview (WHO CIDI) defined by the Statistical Manual of Mental Disorders, Fourth Edition (DSM IV) was used to obtain information on respondents that met criteria for substance abuse disorder, antisocial personality disorder, conduct disorder, and oppositional defiant disorder (yes/no) [48]. Substance abuse disorder refers to the presence of either alcohol or drugs, or both. In addition to alcohol, the substances included are cocaine, tranquilizers, stimulants, pain killers, other prescription drugs, such as heroin, opium, glue, LSD, peyote, or any other controlled substance. The criteria for substance abuse do not include drug-related consequences of tolerance, withdrawal, or a pattern of compulsive use, and instead include only the harmful consequences of repeated use. Antisocial personality disorder (APD) is a pervasive pattern of disregard for, and violation of, the rights of others that begins in childhood or early adolescence and continues into adulthood. The pattern has also been referred to as psychopathy, or sociopathy. Because deceit and manipulation are central features of APD, it may be especially helpful to integrate information acquired from collateral sources. For the diagnosis to be given, the individual must be at least 18 years of age and must have had a history of some symptoms of conduct disorder before age 15. Conduct disorder (CD) involves a repetitive and persistent pattern of behavior in which the basic rights of others or major age-appropriate societal norms or rules are violated. The specific characteristics of conduct disorder fall into one of four categories: aggression to people or animals, destruction of property, deceitfulness or theft, or serious violation of rules. The symptoms of CD include three or more of the following: deceitfulness, impulsivity, irritability or aggressiveness, reckless disregard for safety, irresponsibility, or lack of remorse. Oppositional defiant disorder (ODD) is a recurrent pattern of negativistic, defiant, disobedient, or hostile behavior toward authority figures that persists for at least 6 months, and is characterized by the frequent occurrence of at least four of the following: losing temper, arguing with adults, actively defying/refusing to comply with the rules of adults, deliberately doing things that will annoy other people, blaming others for his or her own mistakes or misbehavior, being touchy or easily annoyed, being angry and resentful, or being spiteful or vindictive. These behaviors occur more frequently than is typically observed in individuals of comparable age and must lead to significant impairment in functioning.

2.2. Outcome Measure

Intimate Partner Violence

IPV was operationalized with the question: "Have you ever been badly beaten up by a spouse or romantic partner?" Response options were "yes" and "no." We assessed this single measure's validity by comparing it to the National Comorbidity Study Replication (NCS-R) dichotomously defined Conflict Tactic Scale within the Collaborative Psychiatric Epidemiology Surveys (CPES) [49,50]. Two tests were conducted to assess the measure's validity. The probability of agreement (OR = 4.5, $p < 0.001$) [51–53], and area under the curve (AUC > 0.6) showed the item to have a fair association across estimates [54]. Five hundred and five (n = 505) Black women in the sample reported severe physical intimate partner violence.

2.3. Analytic Strategy

Descriptive statistics and bivariate (chi-square test, *t*-test) analytic procedures were employed to provide information on the sample distribution and SPIPV in associations with child maltreatment by a parent or caretaker, and neighborhood violent exposure within cohorts (e.g., US Black women, African American, Caribbean Black). Simultaneous multivariate logistic regression analysis was conducted to address the association between child maltreatment and adult intimate partner violence controlling for other factors. Within the analysis, moderating effects were assessed by including interaction terms for child maltreatment and mental disorders (e.g., child maltreatment X substance disorder). For these procedures, adjustments were made for complex sample design. Due to the underlying complex sample design, standard errors were corrected for weighting, clustering, and stratification. Adjustments were made for complex sample design and differential non-response. Stata 15.1 analytical software was used to produce statistical results. Significance was set at the 0.05 alpha level. Diagnostic test revealed an acceptable variance inflation factor (VIF), limiting collinearity concerns for the multivariate model.

2.4. Sample Characteristics

The average age of women within the sample was forty-three years (m = 42.5) old (see Table 1). A third (32%) of respondents never married. The socio-economic status of participants within the sample was different. Specifically, thirty-six percent of participants had a high school diploma. Almost two-thirds (63.7%) of respondents were employed. Meanwhile, nearly three-quarters (71.6%) of women lived at or above the federal poverty level. Finally, the majority of women in the sample were African American (93.8%).

Table 1. Sample Characteristics (N = 3277).

Variable	Total Sample (%)	Ever Report IPV	No IPV Report	F-Test Statistics
Age (mean)	42.5	42.7	42.0	0.46
Relationship Status				10.86 ***
Married	27.4	20.6	28.7	
Partnered	8.4	10.0	8.2	
Separated or Divorced	20.3	33.6	17.7	
Widowed	11.5	8.9	11.7	
Never Married	32.4	26.9	33.8	
Education				5.74 *
Less than High School	24.8	34.1	23.1	
High School Diploma	36.0	31.1	36.3	
Some College	24.8	24.0	25.2	
College	14.4	10.8	15.4	
Employment Status				6.82 *
Employed	63.7	58.8	65.0	
Unemployed	11.1	16.1	10.2	
Not in the Labor Force	25.2	25.1	24.7	
Poverty				14.95 **
At or Above	71.6	62.2	73.4	
Below	28.4	37.8	26.6	
Ethnicity				
African American	93.8	93.3	95.7	4.83 *
Caribbean Black	6.2	6.7	4.3	

Note. Statistics are weighted; * $p < 0.05$ ** $p < 0.01$ *** $p < 0.001$.

3. Results

3.1. Analysis Examining the Association of Adult IPV, Child Maltreatment and Neighborhood Violent Exposure Variables among US Black Women

Illustrated by Table 2 on US Black women in general, the rate at which they experienced child abuse was more than three times the percentage for victims of severe physical intimate partner violence (SPIPV) than non-victims (13.5% vs. 3.9%, $p < 0.001$). For women who witnessed violence in the household as a child, the percentage of SPIPV was almost two-fold that of non-victims (36.3% vs. 17.6%, $p < 0.001$). There were significantly higher percentages of SPIPV victims compared to non-victims (36.3% vs. 21.4%, $p < 0.001$) among respondents who had seen someone injured.

Table 2. Bivariate Analysis Examining Child Maltreatment, Violence Exposure on SPIPV and non-SPIPV US Black Women.

Variables	Total	Ever Report IPV	No IPV Report	Unadjusted OR	*p*-Value
Child Abuse					
No	94.4	86.5	96.1		
Yes	5.6	13.5	3.9	3.85 ***	0.000
Neighborhood Crime					
Never	24.0	20.4	24.1		
Very/often	76.0	79.6	75.9	1.24	1.000
Witnessing Violence					
No	79.1	63.7	82.4		
Yes	20.9	36.3	17.6	2.66 ***	0.000
Exposure to Atrocity					
No	98.2	98.0	98.2		
Yes	1.8	2.0	1.8	1.13	1.000
Seen Someone Injured					
No	75.9	63.7	78.6		
Yes	24.1	36.3	21.4	2.09 ***	0.000

Note. There were 505 US Black women in the sample who reported severe physical intimate partner violence. *** $p < 0.001$.

Among African American women, similar results were found as those previously noted (see Table 3). The proportion of severe physical intimate partner violence exceeded that of non-victims by three-fold (13.1% vs. 3.9%, $p < 0.001$) for those who were the victim of child abuse. For respondents that witnessed violence in the household, the rates were significantly higher (36.7% vs. 17.9%, $p < 0.001$) among those that experienced SPIPV than non-victims of IPV. The same was true for women who had seen someone injured; the percentage was significantly higher (36.0% vs. 20.9%, $p < 0.001$) for those who experienced severe intimate partner violence than non-victims.

The proportion of severe physical intimate partner victims significantly exceeded that of non-victims (22.2% vs. 3.3%, $p < 0.001$) for Caribbean Black women who reported child abuse (see Table 4). Among those women exposed to neighborhood violence, there was a higher percentage of SPIPV victims than non-victims (94.3% vs. 82.2%, $p < 0.05$). Although marginally significant, the percentage at which those who witnessed violence in the household were twice that for IPV victims than non-victims of SPIPV (27.8% vs. 12.9%, $p = 0.064$).

Table 3. Bivariate Analysis Examining Child Maltreatment, Violence Exposure on SPIPV and non-SPIPV African American Women.

Variables	Total	Ever Report IPV	No IPV Report	Unadjusted OR	*p*-Value
Child Abuse					
No	94.4	86.9	96.1		
Yes	5.6	13.1	3.9	3.67 ***	0.000
Neighborhood Crime					
Never	24.4	21.1	24.6		
Very/often	75.6	78.9	75.4	1.22	1.000
Witnessing Violence					
No	78.7	63.3	82.1		
Yes	21.3	36.7	17.9	2.65 ***	0.000
Exposure to Atrocity					
No	98.2	97.9	98.3		
Yes	1.8	2.1	1.7	1.23	1.000
Seen Someone Injured					
No	76.3	64.0	79.1		
Yes	23.7	36.0	20.9	2.12 ***	0.000

Note. There were 392 African American women in the sample that reported severe physical intimate partner violence. *** $p < 0.001$.

Table 4. Bivariate Analysis Examining Child Maltreatment, Violence Exposure on SPIPV and non-SPIPV US Caribbean Black Women.

Variables	Total	Ever Report IPV	No IPV Report	Unadjusted OR	*p*-Value
Child Abuse					
No	94.4	77.6	96.7		
Yes	5.6	22.2	3.3	8.43 **	0.001
Neighborhood Crime					
Never	17.1	5.7	17.8		
Very/often	82.9	94.3	82.2	3.57 *	0.033
Witnessing Violence					
No	85.3	72.2	87.1		
Yes	14.7	27.8	12.9	2.59	0.064
Exposure to Atrocity					
No	97.7	100.0	97.4		
Yes	2.3	0.0	2.6	1.00	1.000
Seen Someone Injured					
No	69.8	56.4	71.6		
Yes	30.2	43.6	28.4	1.95	1.000

Note. There were 113 Caribbean Black women in the sample that reported severe physical intimate partner violence. * $p < 0.05$ ** $p < 0.01$.

3.2. Multivariate Analysis Examining Associations and Moderating Factors of Intimate Partner Violence among US Black Women

Multivariate results show that the odds (AOR = 4.07, $p < 0.05$ CI 1.11, 14.92, $p < 0.05$) for severe physical intimate partner violence significantly increased among women who reported child maltreatment (see Table 5). In the absence of child maltreatment, however, there were other influences of severe physical intimate partner violence. First, the odds (AOR = 2.35, CI = 1.33, 4.16, $p < 0.01$) for SPIPV increased among women who met criteria for conduct disorder. Furthermore, anti-social personality disorder both increased the possibility (AOR = 4.87, CI = 2.28, 10.41, $p < 0.001$) and probability (AOR = 1.74, CI = 0.942, 3.22, $p = 0.076$; CI) of SPIPV. Moderating effects were not found between child maltreatment and severe intimate partner violence.

Table 5. Multivariate Analysis Predicting Adult Severe Physical Intimate Partner Violence.

Variable	Odds Ratio	SE	*p* Value	95% CI
Age	1.06	0.014	0.000 ***	1.03–1.08
Education Level				
Less Than HS	1			
High School Graduate	0.73	0.162	0.159	0.465–1.14
Some College	0.83	0.206	0.461	0.507–1.37
College	0.59	0.204	0.135	0.298–1.18
Marital Status				
Married	1			
Partnered	0.98	0.361	0.950	0.466–2.05
Separated-Divorced	2.51	0.878	0.010 **	1.25–5.06
Widowed	3.60	4.21	0.277	0.347–37.37
Never Married	1.07	0.276	0.789	0.640–1.80
Race/Ethnicity				
African American	1			
Caribbean Black	0.88	0.246	0.644	0.501–1.54
Poverty Level				
Above	1			
Below	1.77	0.396	0.014 *	1.23–2.77
Employment Status				
Employed	1			
Not employed	1.14	0.162	0.159	0.465–1.14
Not in Labor Force	1.24	0.310	0.385	0.298–1.18
Child Maltreatment				
No	1			
Yes	4.07	2.64	0.035 *	1.11–14.92
Crime Problem in Neighborhood	1.02	0.091	0.854	0.849–1.22
Atrocities				
No	1			
Yes	0.68	0.413	0.529	0.201–2.30
Injury				
No	1			
Yes	1.36	0.268	0.126	0.915–2.02
Anti-Social Disorder				
No	1			
Possible	4.87	1.85	0.000 **	2.28–10.41
Probable	1.74	0.535	0.076	0.942–3.22
Child Maltreatment X Anti-Social Disorder				
No	1			
Possible	0.37	0.295	0.218	0.077–1.81
Probable	1.01	0.655	0.987	0.276–3.70
Substance Abuse				
No	1			
Yes	1.63	0.521	0.130	0.861–3.09
Child Maltreatment X Substance Abuse				
No	1			
Yes	1.27	0.667	0.657	0.440–3.63
Oppositional Defiant Disorder (ODD)				
No	1			
Yes	0.93	0.316	0.834	0.472–1.84
Child Maltreatment X Oppositional Defiant Disorder				
No	1			
Yes	0.39	0.259	0.161	0.101–1.48
Conduct Disorder (CD)				
No	1			
Yes	2.35	0.669	0.004 **	1.33–4.16
Child Maltreatment X Conduct Disorder				
No	1			
Yes	0.526	0.246	0.175	0.207–1.34

Note. * $p < 0.05$ ** $p < 0.01$ *** $p < 0.001$.

The study results also indicate an association between socio-demographic factors and severe physical intimate partner violence. Notably, the odds (AOR = 1.06, CI = 1.03,

1.08, $p < 0.001$) for severe intimate partner violence increased with age. Compared with married respondents, those separated or divorced were at increased odds (AOR = 2.52, CI = 1.25–5.06, $p < 0.01$) for SPIPV. Finally, the odds (AOR = 1.77, CI = 1.13, 2.77 $p < 0.01$) for SPIPV increased among participants living at or below poverty almost by two-fold compared with those living above the poverty threshold. Collectively the independent variables in the model explained 14 percent of the variance in severe intimate partner violence.

4. Discussion

The results of the study provide theoretical support for social learning theory and the intergenerational transmission model. By and large, the study indicates that child abuse is linked to victimization in adulthood among US Black women, as with other populations [5,33,55]. This was evident in bivariate analysis across cohorts. While there was an association between exposure to violence and severe intimate partner violence, our study revealed that these experiences differ by ethnic groups. For Caribbean Black women, exposure to neighborhood violence was associated with adult victimization. Meanwhile for African Americans, witnessing violence and seeing someone injured was related to severe intimate partner violence. The findings and differences found between ethnic groups are difficult to explain. Quite possibly, this might be influenced by the cultural differences between Caribbean Blacks and African Americans in terms of how violence is defined and interpreted. However, the findings may point to the commonality of social, economic, and environmental conditions facing Blacks in the United States, including sources of stress, which might expose women to subsequent victimization. As evident in this study, racial and ethnic minorities including Caribbean blacks and African Americans face issues of poverty rate which might confine them to neighborhoods with higher criminal activities and violence, less economic resources and opportunities. There is also evidence that immigrant groups may more so face these challenges due to high rates of poverty after arrival and the absence of generational capital that has been accumulated by US Blacks [56].

Even though there was confirmation regarding the association between child maltreatment and severe intimate victimization in multivariate analysis, our study, in general, did not find any support concerning the moderating effects of mental health disorders. Nonetheless, we did find that independent of child maltreatment, the risk for adult intimate partner violence increased among US Black women who met criteria for conduct and anti-personality disorders. Although these results were either partially or fully supported by previous studies [40,57–59], the mechanism by which these factors influence intimate partner violence among US Black women is less clear.

The study results further showed that separated or divorced Black women were at an increased risk for intimate victimization. This could reflect the escalation of violence after the women leave or attempt to leave the relationship [60]. It should also be noted that some divorced or separated women may still be in abusive relationships, even though their relationship status had changed. Additionally, this research found that violence among women within this population increased with age. This finding contradicts other research trends that find that exposure to violence generally reduces with age [61]. Finally, women living in poverty were found to be at increased risk for intimate partner violence, which is consistent with previous research [5,62–66]. Known to many, poverty contributes to stress and increases the possibility of violent explosive encounters in relationships [67].

4.1. Limitations of the Study

We acknowledge that this study has a few limitations. First, cross-sectional data were used for this study, limiting causal inferences about the relationship between intimate partner violence and both child maltreatment and neighborhood violent exposure. As such, it is difficult to determine the temporal ordering of the relationship. Studies using longitudinal data are necessary for clarifying these relationships. Second, the study was retrospective and may be subject to recall bias, especially for those who have experienced victimization in early life. Therefore, memory lapses could cause participants to attribute certain conditions to other traumatic experiences. Third, the data used for this study is over a decade old and may not reflect current events, though the relationship is not likely to change over this period [68]. The data used for the study to our knowledge is the only available national data that allowed for the examination of the study goals, particularly in respect to ethnic groups within the US Black population. Furthermore, a single binary measure was used to address severe physical intimate partner violence. Even so, such a measure has been used in studies of this nature before [54,64]. Moreover, a comparison of the NSAL IPV indicator with the CTS found a fair agreement with the measure [54]. The measure used for this study also allowed for examining the relationship between child maltreatment, violence exposure, and adult victimization among black women. Additionally, only physical intimate partner violence was examined in this study. Other forms (e.g., psychological/emotional/verbal) of abuse were not evaluated due to data limitations. Finally, sample size issues prevented us from independently examining the moderating effects of child abuse and witnessing violence as a child on the mental disorders of women in this study.

4.2. Benefits of the Study

Despite the limitations, this study sheds light on the issue of child maltreatment as an important factor in the trajectory of victimized Black women, which has been lacking empirically using data at the national level. The study also addressed the contribution of other disorders on intimate partner violence. This research further provides insights into the significance of the potential role of structural and environmental conditions that are prominent in the lives of US Blacks which might influence victimization. Finally, this research highlights that while similar in some regards, there are differences that exist ethnically and culturally regarding the association of child maltreatment and neighborhood conditions in relation to Black women's experience with intimate partner violence.

5. Conclusions

The study has implications for prevention and intervention strategies for IPV. More notably, the findings reinforce both the short- and long-term outcomes of child abuse and witnessing violence as a child. Along with the immediate traumatic effects on the health and well-being of children, child maltreatment can contribute to a cycle of violence that has been known to influence intimate partner victimization or perpetration, placing US Black women at risk for poor outcomes. While some ethnic groups continue to endorse physical punishment, it is becoming more apparent that this method of discipline can contribute to a larger problem in later life. Therefore, other forms of non-violent disciplinary measures should be considered at the earliest stage of the life course. Along with child abuse, the study suggests possible exposure to violence resulting from poor social, economic, and environmental conditions circumstances may serve as a precursor for future violence. Hence, there is a need for preventative measures particularly in impoverished areas where individuals are likely to face these realities in their homes and neighborhoods. Likewise, primary, secondary and tertiary prevention of childhood exposure to violence (group and one on one counseling, addressing defiant behavior, engaging in restorative justice, etc.) can be used as a deterrence for adult IPV victimization and perpetration. Finally, additional studies are necessary to better understand the general and mediating effects of conduct and antisocial disorders and their association with intimate partner violence within minority populations.

Author Contributions: K.K.L., H.R.S. and R.D.J. contributed to the conceptualization and writing of the manuscript. K.K.L. contributed to the interpretation and analysis of the data. All authors have read and agreed to the published version of the manuscript.

Funding: This work was supported by the University of Michigan-Dearborn Office of Research and Sponsored Programs and funded by a scholar grant [P/G U059355].

Institutional Review Board Statement: Data collection for the NSAL was approved by the University of Michigan's Institutional Review Board.

Informed Consent Statement: Secondary data were used for this study.

Data Availability Statement: The public use NSAL data is archived at the University of Michigan-ICPSR.

Conflicts of Interest: The authors declare no conflict of interest.

References

1. Black, D.S.; Sussman, S.; Unger, J.B. A further look at the intergenerational transmission violence: Witnessing interparental violence in emerging adulthood. *J. Interpers. Violence* **2010**, *25*, 1022–1062. [CrossRef] [PubMed]
2. Breiding, M.J.; Smith, S.G.; Basile, K.C.; Walters, M.L.; Chen, J.; Merrick, M.T. *Prevalence and Characteristics of Sexual Violence, Stalking, and Intimate Partner Violence Victimization—National Intimate Partner and Sexual Violence Survey, United States, 2011*; Centers for Disease Control and Prevention: Atlanta, GA, USA, 2014.
3. Thomas, K.J.A. *A Demographic Profile of Black Caribbean Immigrants in the United States*; Migration Policy Institute: Washington, DC, USA, 2012; Available online: http://www.migrationpolicy.org/pubs/CBI-CaribbeanMigration.pdf (accessed on 10 October 2019).
4. Kent, M.M. Immigration and America's Black population. *Popul. Bull.* **2007**, *62*, 1–20. Available online: http://www.prb.org/pdf07/62.4immigration.pdf (accessed on 15 December 2010).
5. Heise, L.L. *What Works to Prevent Partner Violence: An Evidence Overview*; STRIVE, London School of Hygiene and Tropical Medicine: London, UK, 2011.
6. US Department of Health and Human Services. *Statista (2020)*; US Department of Health and Human Services, Administration for Children and Families: Washington, DC, USA, 2020.
7. Raghavan, C.; Mennerich, A.; Sexton, E.; James, S.E. Community violence and its direct, indirect, and mediating effects on intimate partner violence. *Violence Against Women* **2006**, *12*, 1132–1149. [CrossRef]
8. Lacey, K.K.; Jeremiah, R.D.; West, C.M. Domestic violence through a Caribbean lens: Historical context, theories, risks and consequences. *J. Aggress. Maltreatment Trauma* **2019**. [CrossRef]
9. Jackson, J.S.; Hamilton, T.G.; Ifatunji, M.A.; Lacey, K.K.; Lee, H.E.; Rafferty, J.A. Using Analytic Domains Within the Black Population to Understand Disparities in Population Health. Report to the Robert Wood Johnson Foundation. 2018. Available online: http://www.policylink.org/sites/default/files/ (accessed on 2 February 2019).
10. Reed, E.; Silverman, J.G.; Welles, S.L.; Santana, M.S.; Missmer, S.A.; Raj, A. Associations between perceptions and involvement in neighborhood violence and intimate partner violence perpetration among urban, African American Men. *J. Community Health* **2009**, *34*, 328–335. [CrossRef] [PubMed]
11. Sumner, S.A.; Mercy, J.A.; Dahlberg, L.L.; Hillis, S.D.; Klevens, J.; Houry, H. Violence in the United States: Status, challenges, and opportunities. *JAMA* **2015**, *314*, 478–488. [CrossRef]
12. Maguire-Jack, K.; Lanier, P.; Lombardi, B. Investigating racial differences in clusters of adverse childhood experiences. *Am. J. Orthopsychiatry* **2020**, *90*, 106. [CrossRef]
13. Millet, L.S.; Kohl, P.L.; Jonson-Reid, M.; Drake, B.; Petra, M. Child maltreatment victimization and subsequent perpetration of young adult intimate partner violence: An exploration of mediating factors. *Child Maltreatment* **2013**, *18*, 71–84. [CrossRef] [PubMed]
14. Hamby, S.; Finkelhor, D.; Turner, H.; Ormrod, R. The overlap of witnessing partner Violence with child maltreatment and other victimizations in a nationally representative survey of youth. *Child Abuse Negl.* **2010**, *34*, 734–741. [CrossRef] [PubMed]
15. Hamby, S.L.; Finkelhor, D.; Turner, H.; Ormrod, R. Children's Exposure to Intimate Partner Violence and Other Family Violence. *Natl. Surv. Child. Expo. Violence* **2011**, 1–12.
16. Stith, S.M.; Liu, T.L.; Davies, C.; Boykin, E.L.; Alder, M.C.; Harris, J.M.; Som, A.; McPherson, M.; Dees, J.E.M.E.G. Risk factors in child maltreatment: A meta-analytic review of the literature. *Aggress. Violent Behav.* **2009**, *14*, 13–29. [CrossRef]
17. Beyer, K.; Wallis, A.B.; Hamberger, K.L. Neighborhood environment and intimate partner violence: A systematic review. *Trauma Violence Abus.* **2015**, *16*, 16–47. [CrossRef] [PubMed]
18. Capaldi, D.M.; Knoble, N.B.; Shortt, J.W.; Kim, H.K. A systematic review of risk factors for intimate partner violence. *Partn. Abus.* **2012**, *3*, 231–280. [CrossRef]
19. Bandura, A. Social learning theory of aggression. *J. Commun.* **1977**, *28*, 12–29. [CrossRef]
20. Shorey, R.C.; Cornelius, T.L.; Bell, K.M. A critical review of theoretical Frameworks for dating violence: Comparing the dating and marital fields. *Aggress. Violent Behav.* **2008**, *13*, 185–194. [CrossRef]
21. Richards, T.N.; Tomsich Gover, A.R.; Jennings, W.G. The cycle of violence revisited: Distinguishing intimate partner violence offenders only, victims only, and victim-offenders. *Violence Vict.* **2016**, *31*, 573–590. [CrossRef] [PubMed]
22. Bell, K.M.; Naugle, A.E. Intimate partner violence theoretical consideration: Moving towards a contextual framework. *Clin. Psychol. Rev.* **2008**, *28*, 1096–1107. [CrossRef]
23. Black, M.; Basile, K.; Breiding, M.; Smith, S.; Walter, M.; Merrick, M.; Chen, J.; Stevens, M. *National Intimate Partner and Sexual Violence Survey 2010 Summary Report. United States, 2010*; Centers for Disease Control and Prevention: Atlanta, GA, USA, 2011.

24. Pollak, R.A. An intergeneration model of domestic violence. *J. Popul. Econ.* **2004**, *17*, 311–329. [CrossRef]
25. Powers, R.A.; Cochran, J.K.; Maskaly, J.; Sellers, C.S. Social learning theory, gender, and intimate partner violent victimization: A structural equations approach. *J. Interpers. Violence* **2017**, *35*, 3554–3580. [CrossRef]
26. Widom, C.S.; Czaja, S.; Dutton, M.A. Child abuse and neglect and intimate partner violence victimization and perpetration: A prospective investigation. *Child Abus. Negl.* **2013**, *38*, 650–663. [CrossRef]
27. Hamby, S.; Finkelhor, D.; Turner, H. Teen dating violence: Co-occurrence with other victimization in the National Survey of Children's Exposure to Violence (NatSCEV). *Psychol. Violence* **2012**, *2*, 111–124. [CrossRef]
28. Smith, D.E. Corporal punishment of children in the Jamaica context. *Int. J. Child Youth Fam. Stud.* **2016**, *7*, 27–44. [CrossRef]
29. van Wijk, N.P.L.; de Bruijn, J.G.M. Antecedents of the perpetration of domestic violence in Curacao. Risk factors for domestic violence in Curacao. *J. Fam. Violence* **2016**, *31*, 337–348. [CrossRef]
30. Kelly, U.A. Theories of intimate partner violence: From blaming the victim to acting against injustice intersectionality as an Analytic Framework. *Adv. Nurs. Sci.* **2011**, *34*, E29–E51. [CrossRef]
31. Barrios, V.R.; Khaw, L.B.L.; Bermea, A.; Hardesty, J.L. Future directions in intimate partner violence research: An intersectionality framework for analyzing women's processes of leaving abusive relationships. *J. Interpers. Violence* **2020**, 0886260519900939. [CrossRef]
32. Whitfield, C.L.; Anda, R.F.; Dube, S.R.; Felitti, V.J. Violent childhood experiences and the risk of intimate partner violence in adults: Assessment in a large health maintenance organization. *J. Interpers. Violence* **2003**, *18*, 166–185. [CrossRef]
33. Priestley, S. The prevalence and correlates of intimate partner violence in Jamaica. *Soc. Econ. Stud.* **2014**, *63*, 153–196.
34. Gage, A.J. Women's experience of intimate partner violence in Haiti. *Soc. Sci. Med.* **2005**, *61*, 343–364. [CrossRef]
35. Jeremiah, R.D.; Quinn, C.R.; Alexis, J.M. Exposing the culture of silence: Inhibiting factors in the prevention, treatment, and mitigation of sexual abuse in the Eastern Caribbean. *Child Abus. Negl.* **2017**, *66*, 53–63. [CrossRef] [PubMed]
36. Wilkinson, D.L.; Carr, P.J. Violent youths' responses to high levels of exposure to community violence: What violent events reveal about youth violence. *J. Community Psychol.* **2008**, *36*, 1026–1051. [CrossRef]
37. Benson, M.L.; Fox, G.L.; DeMaris, A.; Van Wyk, J. Neighborhood disadvantage, individual economic distress and violence against women in intimate relationships. *J. Quant. Criminol.* **2003**, *19*, 207–235. [CrossRef]
38. Kiss, L.; Schraiber, L.B.; Hossain, M.; Watts, C.; Zimmerman, C. The link between community-based violence and intimate partner violence: The effect of crime and male aggression on intimate partner violence against women. *Prev. Sci.* **2015**, *16*, 881–889. [CrossRef] [PubMed]
39. Holt, S.; Buckley, H.; Whelan, S. The impact of exposure to domestic violence on children and young people: A review of the literature. *Child Abus. Negl.* **2008**, *32*, 797–810. [CrossRef]
40. White, H.R.; Widom, C.P. Intimate partner violence among abused and neglected children in young adulthood: The mediating effects of early aggression, antisocial personality, hostility and alcohol problems. *Aggress. Behav.* **2003**, *29*, 332–345. [CrossRef]
41. Ehrensaft, M.K.; Cohen, P.; Brown, J.; Smailes, E.; Chen, H.; Johnson, J.G. Intergenerational transmission of partner violence: A 20-year prospective study. *J. Couns. Clin. Psychol.* **2003**, *71*, 741–753. [CrossRef]
42. Magdol, L.; Moffitt, T.E.; Caspi, A.; Silva, P.A. Developmental antecedents of partner abuse: A prospective—Longitudinal study. *J. Abnorm. Psychol.* **1998**, *107*, 375–389. [CrossRef]
43. Ehrensaft, M.K.; Cohen, P.; Johnson, J.G. Development of personality disorder symptoms and the risk for partner violence. *J. Abnorm. Psychol.* **2006**, *115*, 474–483. [CrossRef]
44. Boyle, D.J.; O'Leary, K.D.; Rosenbaum, A.; Hassett-Walker, C. Differentiating between generally and partner-only violent subgroups: Lifetime antisocial behavior, family of origin violence, and impulsivity. *J. Fam. Violence* **2008**, *23*, 47–55. [CrossRef]
45. Jackson, J.S.; Neighbors, H.W.; Nesse, R.M.; Trierweiler, S.J.; Torres, M. Methodological innovations in the National Survey of American Life. *Int. J. Methods Psychiatr. Res.* **2004**, *13*, 289–298. [CrossRef] [PubMed]
46. Williams, D.R.; Haile, R.; González, H.M.; Neighbors, H.; Baser, R.; Jackson, J.S. The Mental health of black Caribbean immigrants: Results from the National Survey of American Life. *Am. J. Public Health* **2007**, *97*, 52–59. [CrossRef] [PubMed]
47. Proctor, B.D.; Dalaker, J.; US Bureau of the Census. *Poverty in the United States 2001*; Current Population Reports P60–219; U.S. Government Printing Office: Washington, DC, USA, 2002.
48. American Psychological Association. *Diagnostic and Statistical Manual of Mental Disorders*, 4th ed.; American Psychological Association: Washington, DC, USA, 1994.
49. Kessler, R.C.; Molnar, B.E.; Feurer, I.D.; Appelbaum, M. Patterns and mental health predictors of domestic violence in the United States: Results from the National Comorbidity Study. *Int. J. Law Psychiatry* **2001**, *24*, 487–508. [CrossRef]
50. Straus, M.A. Measuring intrafamily conflict and violence: The conflict tactics (CT) scales. *J. Marriage Fam.* **1979**, *41*, 75–88. [CrossRef]
51. Agresti, A. *An Introduction to Categorical Data Analysis*, 2nd ed.; John Wiley: New York, NY, USA, 2007.
52. Hanley, J.A.; McNeil, B.J. The meaning and use of the area under a receiver operating characteristic (ROC) curve. *Radiology* **1982**, *143*, 29–36. [CrossRef] [PubMed]
53. Kessler, R.C.; Anguilar-Gaxiola, S.; Alonso, J.; Chatterji, S.; Lee, S.; Ormel, J.; Ustun, B.T.; Wang, P.S. The global burden of mental disorders: An update from the WHO World Mental Health (WMH) surveys. *Epidemiol. Psychiatr. Soc.* **2009**, *18*, 23–33. [CrossRef] [PubMed]

54. Lacey, K.K.; Powell Sears, K.; Matusko, N.; Jackson, J.S. Severe physical violence and black women's health and well-being. *Am. J. Public Health* **2015**, *105*, 719–724. [CrossRef]
55. Tsuyuki, K.; Al-Alusi, N.A.; Campbell, J.C.; Murry, D.; Cimino, A.N.; Servin, A.E.; Stockman, J.K. Adverse childhood experiences (ACEs) are associated with forced and very early sexual initiation among Black women accessing publicly funded STD clinics in Baltimore, MD. *PLoS ONE* **2019**, *14*, e0216279. [CrossRef] [PubMed]
56. Williams, D.R. Stress and the Mental Health of Populations of Color: Advancing Our Understanding of Race-related Stressors. *J. Health Soc. Behav.* **2018**, *59*, 466–485. [CrossRef]
57. Fergusson, D.M.; JBoden, J.M.; Horwood, J.M. Developmental antecedents of interpartner violence in a New Zealand birth cohort. *J. Fam. Violence* **2008**, *23*, 737–753. [CrossRef]
58. Kelley, M.L.; Braitman, A.L. Antisocial personality disorder and physical partner violence among single and dual substance-abusing couples. *J. Fam. Violence* **2016**, *31*, 423–431. [CrossRef]
59. Stalans, L.J.; Ritchie, J. Relationship of substance use/abuse with psychological and physical intimate partner violence: Variations across living situations. *J. Fam. Violence* **2008**, *23*, 9–24. [CrossRef]
60. Stockman, J.K.; Lucea, M.B.; Bolyard, R.; Bertand, D.; Callwood, G.B.; Sharps, P.W.; Campbell, D.W.; Campbell, J.C. Intimate partner violence among African American and African Caribbean women: Prevalence, risk factors, and the influence of cultural attitudes. *Glob. Health Action* **2014**, *7*, 24772. [CrossRef]
61. Wilke, D.J.; Vinton, L. The nature and impact of domestic violence across age cohorts. *Affilia* **2005**, *20*, 316–328. [CrossRef]
62. Mugoya, G.C.; Witte, T.; Bolland, A.; Tomek, S.; Hooper, L.M.; Bolland, J.; Dalmida, S.G. Depression and intimate partner violence among African American women living in impoverished inner-city neighborhoods. *J. Interpers. Violence* **2020**, *35*, 899–923. [CrossRef] [PubMed]
63. Wilson, P.; Thorpe, R.J., Jr.; Sharps, P.; Laughon, K. The relationship between housing instability and intimate partner violence: A retrospective study. *Public Health Nurs.* **2021**, *38*, 32–39. [CrossRef] [PubMed]
64. Flake, D.F.; Forste, R. Fighting families: Family characteristics associated with domestic violence in five Latin American countries. *J. Fam. Violence* **2006**, *21*, 19–29. [CrossRef]
65. Alexander, K.A.; Willie, T.C.; McDonald-Mosley, R.; Campbell, J.C.; Miller, E.; Decker, M.R. Associations between reproductive coercion, partner violence, and mental health symptoms among young Black women in Baltimore, Maryland. *J. Interpers. Violence* **2019**, 0886260519860900. [CrossRef]
66. Heise, L.; Kostsadam, A. Cross-national and multilevel correlates of partner violence: An analysis of data from population-based surveys. *Lancet Glob. Health* **2015**, *3*, e332–e340. [CrossRef]
67. Goodman, L.A.; Smyth, K.F.; Borges, A.M.; Singer, R. When crises collide: How intimate partner violence and poverty intersect to shape women's mental health and coping? *Trauma Violence Abus.* **2009**, *10*, 306–329. [CrossRef] [PubMed]
68. Stockman, J.K.; Hatashi, H.; Campbell, J.C. Intimate partner violence and its health impact on disproportionately affected populations, including minorities and impoverished groups. *J. Women Health* **2015**, *24*, 62–79. [CrossRef]

International Journal of
Environmental Research and Public Health

MDPI

Article

Interrelationships of Economic Stressors, Mental Health Problems, Substance Use, and Intimate Partner Violence among Hispanic Emergency Department Patients: The Role of Language-Based Acculturation

Carol B. Cunradi [1,*], Raul Caetano [1], William R. Ponicki [1] and Harrison J. Alter [2]

[1] Prevention Research Center, Pacific Institute for Research and Evaluation, 2150 Shattuck Avenue, Suite 601, Berkeley, CA 94704, USA; raul.caetano@utsouthwestern.edu (R.C.); bponicki@prev.org (W.R.P.)
[2] Andrew Levitt Center for Social Emergency Medicine, Oakland, CA 94602, USA; harrison_alter@levittcenter.org
* Correspondence: cunradi@prev.org

Abstract: We analyzed the interrelationships of economic stressors, mental health problems, substance use, and intimate partner violence (IPV) among a sample of Hispanic emergency department patients and probed if Spanish language preference, which may represent low acculturation and/or immigrant status, had a protective effect, in accordance with the Hispanic health paradox. Study participants (n = 520; 50% female; 71% Spanish speakers) provided cross-sectional survey data. Gender-stratified logistic regression models were estimated for mental health problems (PTSD, anxiety, depression), substance use (risky drinking, cannabis, illicit drug use), and IPV. Results showed that economic stressors were linked with mental health problems among men and women. Among men, PTSD was associated with greater odds of cannabis and illicit drug use. Men who used cannabis and illicit drugs were more likely to report IPV. Male Spanish speakers had lower odds of anxiety and cannabis use than English speakers. Female Spanish speakers had lower odds of substance use and IPV than English speakers. The protective effect of Spanish language preference on some mental health, substance use, and IPV outcomes was more pronounced among women. Future research should identify the mechanisms that underlie the protective effect of Spanish language preference and explore factors that contribute to the observed gender differences.

Keywords: Hispanic health paradox; language-based acculturation; emergency department; mental health; substance use; economic stressors

check for updates

Citation: Cunradi, C.B.; Caetano, R.; Ponicki, W.R.; Alter, H.J. Interrelationships of Economic Stressors, Mental Health Problems, Substance Use, and Intimate Partner Violence among Hispanic Emergency Department Patients: The Role of Language-Based Acculturation. *Int. J. Environ. Res. Public Health* **2021**, *18*, 12230. https://doi.org/10.3390/ijerph182212230

Academic Editors: Krim K. Lacey and Rohan D. Jeremiah

Received: 8 October 2021
Accepted: 19 November 2021
Published: 21 November 2021

1. Introduction

Hispanics constitute the largest ethnic minority group within the U.S., with 60.6 million individuals, representing 18.5% of the U.S. population [1]. The term Hispanic typically refers to individuals who have migrated to the U.S. from Central and South American countries and Spain, or their ancestors if they have lived in the U.S. for generations, and who identify as Hispanic and share a language, religion, and other cultural characteristics [2]. Mexicans account for the largest subgroup of Hispanics; other significant subpopulations include Cuban, Puerto Rican, Central American and Caribbean, and South American people [2]. Compared to non-Hispanic whites/Caucasians, Hispanics have poorer indicators of socioeconomic status (SES). For example, the poverty rate in 2019 for Hispanics was 15.7%, more than double the rate for non-Hispanic whites/Caucasians (7.3%) [3]. During the second quarter of 2020 (the outset of the COVID-19 pandemic), unemployment rates among Hispanics and non-Hispanic whites, respectively, were 16.7% and 12.0% [4]. Although unemployment rates have declined since the height of the pandemic, the disparities in rate persist [4]. In terms of education, Hispanics have the highest percentage among the major U.S. racial/ethnic groups of those age 25 or older who lack a high school diploma, a disparity that is greatest among Hispanics not born in the U.S. [5]. Finally, as of 2019 the percentage of those under 65 who remain uninsured is higher among Hispanics (19%) than any other racial/ethnic group, except Native Americans/Alaska Natives (21.8%); among non-Hispanic whites/Caucasians, 7.5% are uninsured [6]. Furthermore, among uninsured Hispanics, 33% are ineligible for ACA (Affordable Care Act) insurance coverage, due to their immigration status [6].

1.1. Hispanic Health Paradox

Despite these socioeconomic inequities, a substantial body of research has found that immigrant Hispanics have better health indicators [2,7–9] and a mortality advantage [10] compared to U.S.-born Hispanics and non-Hispanic whites/Caucasians. Often referred to as the Hispanic or immigrant health paradox [11,12], health advantages have been observed for physical health outcomes, such as perinatal outcomes (pre-term birth, low birth weight, and infant mortality) [7], coronary heart disease and stroke [13], and mental health outcomes [14], including substance use disorders [15]. Acculturation, generally described as 'the processes whereby immigrants change their behavior and attitudes toward those of the host society' [16], has been proposed as a sociocultural mechanism by which Hispanic immigrants lose their health advantage over U.S.-born Hispanics, as they navigate between prevailing American and traditional Latino cultures, and contend with adopting Euro-American behavioral practices, values, and cultural identities [17]. Levels of acculturation can be measured with multi-item scales, for example in [18–21]; another common approach is to use language as a proxy measure of acculturation [22]. Language is also correlated with other proxy measures, such as nativity, time in the U.S., and generational status [23].

1.2. Psychiatric Outcomes

Examples of the Hispanic health paradox can be seen for psychiatric outcomes. For instance, an analysis of data from the National Epidemiologic Survey on Alcohol and Related Conditions (NESARC) found that foreign-born Mexican Americans and foreign-born non-Hispanic whites had lower odds of DSM-IV substance use and mood and anxiety disorders compared with U.S.-born Hispanics and non-Hispanic whites [15]. Moreover, U.S.-born Mexican Americans had a lower risk of psychiatric morbidity compared to U.S.-born non-Hispanic whites [15]. Similarly, in a nationally representative sample from the National Comorbidity Survey Replication (NCS-R), Mexican immigrants had a lower lifetime risk of anxiety, mood, impulse control, and substance use disorders than U.S-born Hispanics and non-Hispanics [14]. Interestingly, the researchers found that those who immigrated to the U.S. at age 12 or younger had the same risk as non-immigrants for mood and impulse control disorders [14]. An analysis of a nationally representative sample of Hispanics from the National Latino and Asian American Study (NLAAS) found that the prevalence of psychiatric disorders varied among ethnic subgroups, with Puerto Ricans having the highest overall prevalence rate [24]. Other factors associated with elevated rates of psychiatric disorders were being U.S.-born, English-language-proficient, and third-generation Hispanic [24].

1.3. Intimate Partner Violence

In terms of intimate partner violence (IPV), a recent review found that Hispanic women who were U.S.-born reported greater prevalence rates of victimization, compared to those not born in the U.S. [25]. In an analysis of Hispanic men who participated in the NESARC study (Wave II), no differences in rates of past-year IPV perpetration were found between U.S.-born and immigrant men [26]. Among this sample, however, the U.S.-born men reported greater anxiety symptoms, alcohol dependence symptoms, and drug dependence symptoms than the immigrant men [26]. In a study among all married/partnered NESARC participants, Hispanics had higher IPV prevalence (victimization, perpetration, and bidirectional IPV) than whites, but lower prevalence than Blacks/African

Americans [27]. Acculturation-related factors, such as nativity and language preference, were not included in the analysis [27]. An analysis of a national sample of married or cohabiting Hispanic men and women who participated the National Household Survey on Drug Abuse found no significant differences in the proportion of men and women reporting IPV perpetration (6.1% vs. 6.5%) or IPV victimization (8.8% vs. 7.8%) [28]. The results of the study's gender-stratified multivariate analyses did not show an association between acculturation-related factors (survey language; nativity) and past-year IPV perpetration or victimization [28].

1.4. Study Goals and Significance

The purpose of this study is to analyze the interrelationships of economic stressors, mental health problems, substance use, and IPV among a sample of Hispanic ED patients, and to assess if Spanish language preference has a protective effect. Assessing these outcomes among Hispanics in an urban ED setting is significant for several reasons. For example, the emergency department (ED) increasingly serves as a safety net for underserved patients to receive medical care, especially those on Medicaid [29]. Compared to whites/Caucasians, Blacks and Hispanics are more likely to report receiving routine healthcare in an ED and are less likely to report having a primary care provider [30–32]. Urban ED patients comprise an at-risk, socially disadvantaged population, with elevated rates of unemployment, substance use, and mental health problems [33,34]. A recent ED-based study found that 37% of participants screened positively for social risks, defined as adverse social conditions associated with poor health, such as housing instability and food insecurity [35]. Additionally, compared to adults in the general household population, ED patients have an elevated prevalence of IPV. For example, rates of past-year IPV among male and female patients screened in ED-based studies range from 8.7% to 37% [36]. In contrast, the results of representative U.S. household population surveys indicate that between 4–7% of adults reported past-year IPV involvement [37]. Given the essential function of urban EDs in providing care to socially disadvantaged patients, including racial/ethnic minorities, the results of the current study can provide insights into how economic stressors may be associated with mental health problems, and thereafter substance use and IPV among Hispanic patients, as well as if those with a Spanish language preference have lower odds of these outcomes than those with an English language preference. The results can inform future research studies and interventions aimed at reducing health disparities among low SES Hispanic populations.

Our study hypotheses are as follows:

Hypothesis 1 (H1). *Economic stressors will be positively associated with mental health problems (PTSD, anxiety, depression).*

Hypothesis 2 (H2). *Mental health problems will be positively associated with substance use (risky drinking, cannabis, illicit drug use).*

Hypothesis 3 (H3). *Substance use will be positively associated with IPV perpetration and victimization.*

Hypothesis 4 (H4). *Spanish speaking study participants will have lower odds of mental health problems, substance use, and IPV perpetration and victimization than English speaking participants.*

2. Materials and Methods

2.1. Sample and Data Collection

Data for this cross-sectional study on drinking and IPV were obtained at the ED of an urban Level I trauma center in Northern California. As part of a county-wide integrated public health care system, the hospital's ED provides care for the poor and uninsured. Patients seeking non-emergency care at the ED were considered eligible for the study if they met the following eligibility criteria: 18–50 years old; English or Spanish speaker;

resident of the county in which the hospital is located; and married, cohabiting, or in a romantic (dating) relationship for the past 12 months. Exclusion criteria were patients who were intoxicated, experiencing acute psychosis or suicidal or homicidal ideation; cognitively/psychologically impaired and unable to provide informed consent; held in custody by law enforcement; or in need of immediate medical attention. The Alameda Health System Institutional Review Board approved the project's protocol for the protection of human subjects.

The research staff conducted survey interviews with 1037 participants (53% female) between February and December 2017. Data collection procedures have been described elsewhere [38]. The study participant recruitment sequence is illustrated in Figure S1. As a first step, trained research assistants (RAs) identified potentially eligible participants through the ED's electronic patient information system. They conducted face-to-face screening in the ED waiting room or in a treatment cubicle. If a patient screened eligible, the RA conducted the survey interview in the patient's room, without others present, using computer-assisted personal interview (CAPI) techniques. Before being interviewed, participants provided informed consent. Recruitment of the sample occurred during weekdays from 9 a.m. to 9 p.m. Patients could opt to be interviewed in English or Spanish. Participants who chose to be interviewed in Spanish were interviewed by bilingual, Spanish-speaking RAs. The Spanish version of the questionnaire had been validated through translation into Spanish and retranslation into English, followed by verification. Average survey interview completion time was 37 min (SD = 20.7). Participants received a USD 30 grocery store gift card as an incentive for completing the survey. The current analysis is limited to those participants who self-reported their race/ethnicity in the survey as Hispanic or Latino (n = 520).

2.2. Measurements

Gender. Self-reported gender was coded as male or female.

Age. This was used as a continuous variable.

Household food insufficiency. Participants rated their level of agreement with the statement, 'In the past 12 months, the food we bought ran out and we didn't have money to get more' (never; sometimes true; often true). We dichotomized and compared those who responded 'sometimes' or 'often' to those who responded 'never' [39]. Those in the latter category comprised the reference group.

Household financial strain. Participants were asked, 'How would you describe the money situation in your household right now?' Response options were: (1) comfortable with extra; (2) enough but no extra; (3) have to cut back; (4) cannot make ends meet. We dichotomized and compared those who chose responses 3–4 to those who chose responses 1–2 [39]. Those in the latter category comprised the reference group.

Fired/laid off from job. Participants were asked if in the past 12 months they had been fired or laid off from a job. We dichotomized and compared those who responded 'yes' to those who responded 'no'. Those in the latter category comprised the reference group.

Anxiety. This was measured with 7 items on a 4-point Likert-type scale, from the Hospital Anxiety and Depression scale [40]. A cutoff point equal to or greater than 8 identified those positive for anxiety. The reference group were those who scored less than 8. Cronbach's α was 0.81.

Depression. This was measured with 7 items on a 4-point Likert-type scale from the Hospital Anxiety and Depression Scale [40]. A cutoff point of 8 or more identified those positive for depression. The reference group were those who scored less than 8. Cronbach's α was 0.69 for depression.

Post-Traumatic Stress Disorder (PTSD). We measured PTSD with the 4-item Primary Care Screener for PTSD [41]. A score of 3 or more was considered positive. A dichotomous variable was created for those who scored positively; the reference group were those who did not have a positive score. Cronbach's α was 0.83.

At-risk drinking. We asked participants who drank alcohol in the past 4 weeks, 'What was the greatest number of drinks you had on any day in the past 4 weeks?'. A 'drink' was defined as a 12-ounce can of beer, a five-ounce glass of wine, or a one-ounce shot of liquor. We asked participants who did not use alcohol in the past 4 weeks the same question over the past year. Women/men were considered at-risk drinkers if they had had four/five or more drinks on any one day in the past 4 weeks (past 12 months for past year drinkers) [42]. For women, the reference group was those who had less than four drinks on any one day; for men, the reference group were those who had less than five drinks in one day.

Cannabis use. We asked participants, 'How many times during the past 12 months, or 365 days, did you use marijuana or hashish (weed, pot, hash) without a doctor's instruction?'. We created a dichotomous variable representing any past-year cannabis use. The reference group were those who did not report any past-year cannabis use. Recreational cannabis use was legalized in California for those 21+ years old in November 2016.

Illicit drug use. We asked participants, 'How many times during the past 12 months, or 365 days, did you use amphetamines, cocaine, heroin, and pain relievers not prescribed for you?'. We created a dichotomous variable representing any past-year illicit drug use. The reference group were those who did not report any past-year illicit drug use.

Intimate partner violence: We measured past-12-month physical IPV victimization and perpetration with the 12-item physical assault subscale of the CTS2, Revised Conflict Tactics Scale [43]. Participants were asked how many times in the past 12 months their spouse or partner did each type of aggressive behavior to them, and how many times they did each physically aggressive behavior to their spouse or partner. Separate dichotomous variables were created for any IPV perpetration and any IPV victimization. The reference groups were those who did not report any past 12-month IPV perpetration or IPV victimization, respectively. Cronbach's α for the scale in the dataset under analysis was 0.85.

2.3. Statistical Analysis

We conducted data analyses using IBM SPSS v. 25 (IBM, Armonk, NY, USA). We used Fisher's exact test to analyze gender differences in categorical participant characteristics. An independent-samples *t*-test was used to analyze gender differences in mean age. We then estimated a series of gender-stratified multivariate logistic regression models for three mental health outcomes (PTSD, anxiety, depression), three substance use outcomes (at-risk drinking, cannabis use, illicit drug use) and two IPV outcomes (IPV perpetration, IPV victimization). The models generated adjusted odds ratios (AORs) and 95% confidence intervals (CIs) that quantified the strength of the association between the independent (exposure) variable and the outcome (dependent variable) after accounting for the other variables in the model. We stratified the models by gender, due to previous results showing significant gender differences in drinking, drug use, and IPV [44,45], and prior studies showing a more robust association between acculturation and alcohol use outcomes among Hispanic women than men [17]. In accordance with H1, we analyzed the association between economic stressors (being fired/laid off from a job, food insufficiency, financial strain) and each mental health outcome. For H2, we analyzed the association between PTSD, anxiety, and depression and each substance use outcome. For H3, we analyzed the association between at-risk drinking, cannabis, and illicit drug use and each IPV outcome. To test H4, we included a language preference variable in each model. All models were adjusted for age. Missing data for the variables in the study were minimal (range 0–1.6%); these were removed through list-wise deletion from the analysis.

3. Results

3.1. Sample Characteristics

The sample characteristics are shown in Table 1. Most participants (>70%) chose to have their survey interview conducted in Spanish. Substantial proportions of the sample reported economic stressors. For example, more than one third of men reported having been fired or laid off from a job in the past year, as did over one quarter of women. Approximately half the sample reported food insufficiency. More than 40% of men and nearly half of women reported financial strain. A greater proportion of women than men screened positively for depression (19.5% vs. 12.1%; $p = 0.02$). In terms of substance use, there were significant gender differences in at-risk drinking (38.7% of men vs 14.1% of women; $p < 0.001$) and illicit drug use (12.6% of men vs 4.3% of women; $p = 0.001$). A similar proportion of men and women reported past-year IPV perpetration.

Table 1. Sample Characteristics.

Variable	Males (n = 256) % or Mean (SD)	Females (n = 262) % or Mean (SD)	p Value *
Age	35.89 (8.25)	34.88 (7.87)	0.16
Spanish survey	72.3	70.6	0.70
Economic stressors			
Fired/laid off from job	38.6	28.8	0.02
Food insufficiency	46.5	52.1	0.22
Financial strain	43.9	48.3	0.33
Mental health problems			
PTSD	15.6	22.1	0.07
Anxiety	25.0	31.4	0.12
Depression	12.1	19.5	0.02
Substance use			
At-risk drinking	38.7	14.1	<0.001
Cannabis use	12.3	8.6	0.19
Drug use	12.6	4.3	<0.001
Intimate partner violence			
IPV perpetration	9.9	9.6	1.00
IPV victimization	15.0	9.6	0.08

* Fisher's exact test or independent-samples t-test for gender differences in sample characteristics.

3.2. Multivariate Results

3.2.1. Economic Stressors and Mental Health Problems

Associations between economic stressors and mental health problems are shown in Table 2. Among men, the results of the adjusted models show that food insufficiency was associated with a more than four-fold increase in the likelihood of PTSD, anxiety, and depression. In addition, men who had been fired or laid off from their job were more than twice as likely to screen positively for anxiety. Male Spanish speakers had lower odds of anxiety compared to English speakers (AOR = 0.42; 95% CI 0.20, 0.90; $p < 0.05$). Among women, results of the adjusted models showed that food insufficiency was associated with a five-fold increase in the likelihood of PTSD. Financial strain was associated with more than double the odds of anxiety. None of the economic stressors were significantly associated with depression, nor were Spanish speakers less likely to have mental health problems than English speakers.

Table 2. Associations between economic stressors and mental health problems.

	PTSD		Anxiety		Depression	
	Men	Women	Men	Women	Men	Women
	AOR (95% CI)	AOR (95% CI)	AOR (95% CI)	AOR (95% CI)	AOR (95% CI)	AOR (95% CI)
Age	0.93 (0.89, 0.98)	1.01 (0.96, 1.05)	1.02 (0.98, 1.06)	1.02 (0.99, 1.06)	0.99 (0.94, 1.04)	1.02 (0.99, 1.07)
Spanish lang. survey	2.23 (0.87, 5.69)	0.94 (0.47, 1.86)	0.42 (0.20, 0.90) ^{a}	0.77 (0.41, 1.43)	0.56 (0.22, 1.44)	0.99 (0.48, 2.03)
Fired/laid off from job	1.68 (0.81, 3.49)	0.71 (0.35, 1.42)	2.17 (1.17, 4.04) ^{a}	1.42 (0.77, 2.61)	1.20 (0.54, 2.66)	1.00 (0.50, 2.02)
Food insufficiency	4.59 (2.03, 10.39) ^{c}	5.09 (2.32, 11.19) ^{c}	4.29 (2.21, 8.28) ^{c}	1.61 (0.85, 3.03)	4.33 (1.74, 10.76) ^{b}	1.94 (0.91, 4.13)
Financial strain	0.52 (0.23, 1.18)	0.96 (0.47, 1.95)	1.38 (0.70, 2.74)	2.67 (1.42, 4.99) ^{b}	1.44 (0.60, 3.45)	1.97 (0.94, 4.14)

^{a} $p \leq 0.05$; ^{b} $p \leq 0.01$; ^{c} $p \leq 0.001$.

3.2.2. Mental Health Problems and Substance Use

Associations between mental health problems and substance use outcomes are shown in Table 3. Among men, the results of the adjusted models showed that those who screened positively for PTSD had a more than three-fold increased likelihood of cannabis use, and were more than twice as likely to use illicit drugs. Male Spanish speakers had decreased odds of cannabis use compared to English speakers (AOR = 0.22; 95% CI 0.20, 0.90; $p < 0.01$). Men's mental health problems were not associated with increased odds of risky drinking. Among women, the results of the adjusted models showed that mental health problems were not associated with any of the substance use outcomes. Female Spanish speakers had lower odds of risky drinking (AOR = 0.31; 95% CI 0.15, 0.66; $p < 0.01$), cannabis use (AOR = 0.08; 95% CI 0.03, 0.25; $p < 0.001$), and illicit drug use (AOR = 0.21; 95% CI 0.06, 0.80; $p < 0.05$) compared to English speakers.

Table 3. Associations between mental health problems and substance use.

	Risky Drinking		Cannabis Use		Illicit Drug Use	
	Men	**Women**	**Men**	**Women**	**Men**	**Women**
	AOR (95% CI)	**AOR (95% CI)**	**AOR (95% CI)**	**AOR (95% CI)**	**AOR (95% CI)**	**AOR (95% CI)**
Age	1.01 (0.99, 1.05)	1.01 (0.97, 1.06)	0.93 (0.88, 0.99) [a]	0.98 (0.92, 1.05)	0.95 (0.91, 1.00)	1.01 (0.99, 1.07)
Spanish lang. survey	0.71 (0.39, 1.30)	0.31 (0.15, 0.66) [b]	0.22 (0.20, 0.90) [b]	0.08 (0.03, 0.25) [c]	0.60 (0.25, 1.42)	0.21 (0.06, 0.80) [a]
PTSD	1.10 (0.51, 2.36)	1.03 (0.43, 2.47)	3.31 (1.18, 9.33) [a]	1.11 (0.34, 3.61)	2.67 (1.03, 6.91) [a]	0.78 (0.15, 4.09)
Anxiety	1.30 (0.68, 2.46)	1.08 (0.44, 2.66)	1.24 (0.47, 3.29)	1.00 (0.30, 3.32)	1.42 (0.57, 3.53)	1.16 (0.24, 5.56)
Depression	1.21 (0.55, 2.64)	1.08 (0.39, 2.975)	0.65 (0.70, 2.74)	0.36 (0.06, 2.04)	0.96 (0.31, 2.96)	0.36 (0.04, 3.72)

[a] $p \leq 0.05$; [b] $p = <0.01$; [c] $p \leq 0.001$.

3.2.3. Substance Use and Intimate Partner Violence

Associations between substance use and IPV outcomes are shown in Table 4. Among men, the results of the adjusted models showed that cannabis use was associated with a four-fold increased risk of IPV perpetration, and illicit drug use was associated with a more than three-fold increased likelihood of this outcome. Men who used illicit drugs had four-fold elevated odds of IPV victimization. Among women, the results of the adjusted models showed that substance use was not associated with IPV perpetration or victimization. Women Spanish speakers had reduced odds of IPV perpetration compared to English speakers (AOR = 0.30; 95% CI 0.11, 0.82; $p < 0.05$); there was no protective effect for IPV victimization.

Table 4. Associations between substance use and intimate partner violence.

	IPV Perpetration		IPV Victimization	
	Men	**Women**	**Men**	**Women**
	AOR (95% CI)	**AOR (95% CI)**	**AOR (95% CI)**	**AOR (95% CI)**
Age	0.98 (0.92, 1.05)	0.96 (0.91, 1.03)	0.96 (0.91, 1.01)	0.96 (0.90, 1.02)
Spanish lang. survey	0.63 (0.22, 1.76)	0.30 (0.11, 0.82) [a]	0.48 (0.21, 1.11)	0.41 (0.16, 1.07)
Risky drinking	2.48 (0.97, 6.30)	2.30 (0.77, 6.85)	1.84 (0.85, 3.95)	2.25 (0.75, 6.74)
Cannabis use	4.02 (1.35, 11.95) [a]	2.52 (0.73, 8.76)	1.13 (0.40, 3.20)	1.44 (0.39, 5.37)
Illicit drug use	3.32 (1.22, 9.05) [a]	1.33 (0.26, 6.70)	4.30 (1.78, 10.39) [b]	1.85 (0.38, 9.06)

[a] $p \leq 0.05$; [b] $p \leq 0.01$; [c] $p \leq 0.001$.

4. Discussion

Among a socially disadvantaged sample of Hispanic men and women seeking medical care at an urban safety-net hospital ED, a substantial proportion reported economic stressors and screened positively for mental health problems. For example, regarding economic stressors, more than one quarter of the women and nearly 40% of the men reported having been fired or laid off from their job. Nearly half of respondents reported food insufficiency; over 40% of men and nearly 50% of women reported financial strain. In terms of mental health, anxiety was the most prevalent problem reported by men and women. While men had greater rates of risky drinking and illicit drug use than women, no gender differences were seen for self-reported IPV perpetration or victimization. Previous analyses of the data showed that Hispanic study participants had lower rates of past-year substance use and IPV compared to study participants who self-reported their race/ethnicity as white, Black/African American, or multiethnic/multiracial [38].

4.1. Impact of Economic Stressors on Mental Health

The H1 hypothesized associations between economic stressors and mental health problems were partially confirmed, with some gender differences. Specifically, food insufficiency was associated with PTSD, anxiety, and depression among men; among women, food insufficiency was only associated with PTSD. Being fired/laid off from a job was only associated with anxiety among men; financial strain was only associated with anxiety among women. The results suggest that Hispanic ED patients who experience economic stressors are significantly more likely to screen positively for mental health problems than those who are not exposed to these stressors. In contrast with past research [46], economic stressors were not associated with depression among women. One explanation is that the impact of economic stressors may be mitigated by other sample characteristics. For example, family separation is associated with depression among Mexican-origin women residing in the U.S. [46]; however, the current sample consists entirely of married or partnered participants. The women's married/partnered status may, therefore, help buffer the influence of economic stressors on depression.

4.2. Men's, Not Women's, Mental Health Problems Linked to Substance Use

The results showed that the H2 hypothesized associations between mental health problems and substance use were not confirmed among women. Among men, no associations were observed between mental health problems and odds for risky drinking. Men who screened positively for PTSD, however, had elevated odds of cannabis use and illicit drug use, compared to men who did not screen positively for PTSD. Men's anxiety and depression were not associated with elevated odds of cannabis or illicit drug use. Other factors besides mental health problems may be more salient correlates of substance use among socially disadvantaged Hispanics. For example, a longitudinal study among Hispanic young adults found that exposure to adverse childhood experiences was associated with binge drinking and cannabis use, even after accounting for culturally relevant variables [47]. Other potential correlates of substance use outcomes among Hispanic populations are impulsivity traits [48] and emotion dysregulation [49].

4.3. Men's, Not Women's, Cannabis and Drug Use Associated with IPV

The H3 hypothesized association between substance use and IPV was partially confirmed, but only among men. No association was observed between women's substance use and IPV perpetration or victimization. It may be that each partner's psychosocial traits, such as level of impulsivity, are more likely to contribute to the expression of aggressive dyadic behavior among Hispanic couples [50]. Among men, cannabis and illicit drug use were associated with IPV perpetration; illicit drug use was also associated with IPV victimization. The lack of an observed association between risky drinking and IPV perpetration or victimization is consistent with the findings reported by Caetano and colleagues [51]. In their longitudinal follow-up study, which accounted for acculturation and acculturation stress among Hispanic couples, binge drinking by either partner did not predict IPV perpetration or victimization [51].

4.4. Protective Effect of Spanish-Language Preference: Gender Differences

The H4 hypothesized protective effects of Spanish language preference on mental health problems, substance use, and IPV were partially confirmed, with notable gender differences. For example, in terms of mental health problems, Spanish language preference was associated with lower odds of anxiety among men; no protective effect was observed for women. On the other hand, Spanish language preference was associated with lower odds for risky drinking, cannabis use, and illicit drug use among women; for men, a protective effect was only seen for cannabis use. The gender differences in the association between Spanish language preference and risky drinking are consistent with those described in two previous reviews, both of which noted more robust findings for this association among women [17,52]. The consistent protective effect of Spanish language preference among women may be attributed to sharper differences in gender roles in Latino cultures compared to Anglo culture. In the former, the consequences of behavioral problems such as risky drinking and drug use are more severe for women than for men. Societal drinking norms are stricter for women than men. Spanish language preference may be a marker for women that adhere to these stricter gender-related norms. Finally, Spanish language preference was associated with lower odds of IPV perpetration among women, but not men. The protective effect of Spanish language preference may be due to Latino cultural factors centered around family life, or perhaps the positive side of machismo where men are 'protectors' of the family. It is also possible that the group with language preference for Spanish is a selected special group, with more people born abroad and therefore more immigrants who could be more resilient than others (i.e., self-selection). The acculturation process may also result in dyadic stress that increases the likelihood of IPV. For example, an analysis of a national sample of Hispanic couples found that compared to couples in which both partners were categorized as low acculturation, based on a multi-item scale, couples in which both partners were categorized as medium acculturation had the highest odds for female-to-male partner violence [50]. Similarly, in a longitudinal follow-up, lower acculturation among the men was associated with higher acculturation stress, which was directly related to greater likelihood of IPV. The same associations were observed among women; additionally, higher levels of acculturation among women were directly linked to IPV [51].

4.5. Study Strengths and Limitations

This study is characterized by various strengths. For example, the study is among the first to examine the interrelationships of economic stressors, mental health problems, substance use, and IPV among a sample of Hispanic ED patients, and to assess if Spanish language preference has a protective effect. The persistence of socioeconomic disparities among the U.S. Hispanic population underscores the importance of identifying how economic stressors are associated with mental health problems, and how mental health problems are related to substance use and IPV. Another study strength is the near-equal number of men and women study participants. This allowed for a gender-stratified analysis, to compare the prevalence and correlates of the study outcomes. Since IPV is most often bidirectional (i.e., men and women report both perpetration and victimization) [27,28,53–55], it is important to measure both behaviors independently. By measuring IPV perpetration and victimization among all study participants, this study helps to overcome a limitation of some previous IPV research among Hispanics, in which factors related to IPV perpetration were confined to male study participants [26,56,57], and factors related to IPV victimization were confined to female study participants [58–61].

There are several study limitations that should be considered. First, due to the cross-sectional study design, causality cannot be inferred. It is also important to note that many of the associations observed in this study could be bidirectional. For example, risky drinking may increase the odds of experiencing IPV, but experiencing IPV could lead to increased substance use [62]. Similarly, our models tested the association between economic stressors and mental health problems; we did not test the association between IPV exposure and mental health problems. Prior research has shown that IPV victimization is associated with elevated odds for PTSD, anxiety, and depression [63]. Second, because the sample was obtained from a single safety-net ED, the generalizability of the findings may be limited. Third, the survey did not assess acculturation stress, nativity, or immigrant status, nor were multi-item measures of acculturation collected. We therefore largely refrain from using the term acculturation, as suggested by Doucerain et al. [64], using instead language preference, to identify the measurement more clearly in the analysis. Fourth, the study lacks concurrent dyadic reports on IPV, since the participants' spouses and romantic partners were not interviewed. This may result in an underestimate of IPV [65]. Fifth, we note that due to the study's exclusion criteria, the sample did not include those with suicidal ideation. As those with suicidal behavior exhibit elevated rates of substance use disorders, impulsivity, and aggressive behavior [66], inclusion of this group would likely have produced significantly different results than the current study findings. Finally, recall bias may have affected participants' ability to recall past-year drinking, drug use, and other behaviors.

5. Conclusions

The results of this study suggest that socially disadvantaged Hispanics seeking non-acute care at urban EDs may be especially vulnerable to mental health problems. This has important implications for clinical providers in similar urban safety-net settings. For example, given the high levels of food insufficiency observed in this sample, ED staff should be aware that their patients may benefit from referrals to community resources, such as food banks, to bolster household nutrition. Similarly, ED staff may want to consider using brief screeners to assess for anxiety and other mental health problems among their patients. ED staff can provide brief counseling to those who screen positively and provide referrals to outpatient mental health services. A fundamental concern for ED staff should be ensuring that low English proficiency patients receive appropriate Spanish language assistance during their ED visit [67].

The study results indicate that Spanish language preference, which may represent low acculturation and/or immigrant status, was protective against men's anxiety and cannabis use, and against women's risky drinking, cannabis, and illicit drug use, and IPV perpetration. Future research should identify the mechanisms that underlie this protective effect and determine the factors that contribute to a greater protective effect among women. Obtaining dyadic reports using a longitudinal study design and using appropriate dyadic modeling techniques will enhance these goals.

Supplementary Materials: The following are available online at https://www.mdpi.com/article/10.3390/ijerph182212230/s1, Figure S1: Study sample recruitment.

Author Contributions: Conceptualization, C.B.C.; formal analysis, C.B.C.; writing—original draft preparation, C.B.C.; writing—review and editing, R.C., W.R.P., H.J.A.; funding acquisition, C.B.C. All authors have read and agreed to the published version of the manuscript.

Funding: This research was funded by the National Institute on Alcohol Abuse and Alcoholism of the National Institutes of Health, award number R01AA022990. The content is solely the responsibility of the authors and does not necessarily represent the official views of the National Institutes of Health.

Institutional Review Board Statement: The study was conducted according to the guidelines of the Declaration of Helsinki and approved by the Institutional Review Board of Alameda Health System (protocol code IRB16-02093A—Environmental Drinking Contexts & Intimate Partner Violence, 5 April 2016).

Informed Consent Statement: Informed consent was obtained from all subjects involved in the study.

Data Availability Statement: The data are not publicly available, due to Institutional Review Board restrictions.

Acknowledgments: The authors gratefully acknowledge the work of the research assistants Anna Balassone, Steffani Campbell, Leah Fraimow-Wong, Christian Hailozian, Reika Kagami, Lori Lujan, Jose Padilla-Hernandez, Simone Phillips, Karla Prodigue, Vanessa Rubio, Marissa Vasquez, Frances Vernon, Eve Zarate, and clinical research coordinator William R. Stewart, M.S.W.

Conflicts of Interest: The authors declare no conflict of interest. The funders had no role in the design of the study; in the collection, analyses, or interpretation of data; in the writing of the manuscript, or in the decision to publish the results.

References

1. U.S. Census Bureau. Hispanic Heritage Month. 2020. Available online: https://www.census.gov/newsroom/facts-for-features/2020/hispanic-heritage-month.html (accessed on 15 September 2021).
2. Alarcón, R.D.; Parekh, A.; Wainberg, M.L.; Duarte, C.S.; Araya, R.; Oquendo, M.A. Hispanic immigrants in the USA: Social and mental health perspectives. *Lancet Psychiatry* **2016**, *3*, 860–870. [CrossRef]
3. Creamer, J. Inequalities Persist Despite Decline in Poverty for All Major Race and Hispanic Origin Groups. Available online: https://www.census.gov/library/stories/2020/09/poverty-rates-for-blacks-and-hispanics-reached-historic-lows-in-2019.html (accessed on 15 September 2021).
4. U.S. Bureau of Labor Statistics. Labor Force Statistics from the Current Population Survey. Available online: https://www.bls.gov/web/empsit/cpsee_e16.htm (accessed on 15 September 2021).
5. U.S. Census Bureau. Without a High School Education. Available online: https://www.census.gov/dataviz/visualizations/035/ (accessed on 15 September 2021).
6. Artiga, S.; Orgera, K.; Damico, A. Changes in Health Coverage by Race and Ethnicity since the ACA, 2010–2018. Available online: https://www.kff.org/racial-equity-and-health-policy/issue-brief/changes-in-health-coverage-by-race-and-ethnicity-since-the-aca-2010-2018/ (accessed on 15 September 2021).
7. Montoya-Williams, D.; Williamson, V.G.; Cardel, M.; Fuentes-Afflick, E.; Maldonado-Molina, M.; Thompson, L. The Hispanic/Latinx Perinatal Paradox in the United States: A Scoping Review and Recommendations to Guide Future Research. *J. Immigr. Minor. Health* **2021**, *23*, 1078–1091. [CrossRef]
8. Franzini, L.; Ribble, J.C.; Keddie, A.M. Understanding the Hispanic paradox. *Ethn. Dis.* **2001**, *11*, 496–518. [PubMed]
9. Velasco-Mondragon, E.; Jimenez, A.; Palladino-Davis, A.G.; Davis, D.; Escamilla-Cejudo, J.A. Hispanic health in the USA: A scoping review of the literature. *Public Health Rev.* **2016**, *37*, 1–27. [CrossRef] [PubMed]
10. Ruiz, J.M.; Steffen, P.; Smith, T.B. Hispanic Mortality Paradox: A Systematic Review and Meta-Analysis of the Longitudinal Literature. *Am. J. Public Health* **2013**, *103*, e52–e60. [CrossRef] [PubMed]
11. Markides, K.S.; Coreil, J. The health of Hispanics in the southwestern United States: An epidemiologic paradox. *Public Health Rep.* **1986**, *101*, 253–265.
12. Feliciano, C.; Lanuza, Y.R. An Immigrant Paradox? Contextual Attainment and Intergenerational Educational Mobility. *Am. Sociol. Rev.* **2017**, *82*, 211–241. [CrossRef]
13. Fang, J.; Yuan, K.; Gindi, R.M.; Ward, B.W.; Ayala, C.; Loustalot, F. Association of Birthplace and Coronary Heart Disease and Stroke among US Adults: National Health Interview Survey, 2006 to 2014. *J. Am. Heart Assoc.* **2018**, *7*. [CrossRef]
14. Breslau, J.; Aguilar-Gaxiola, S.; Borges, G.; Kendler, K.S.; Su, M.; Kessler, R.C. Risk for Psychiatric Disorder Among Immigrants and Their US-Born Descendants: Evidence from the National Comorbidity Survey Replication. *J. Nerv. Ment. Dis.* **2007**, *195*, 189–195. [CrossRef] [PubMed]
15. Grant, B.F.; Stinson, F.S.; Hasin, D.S.; Dawson, D.A.; Chou, S.P.; Anderson, K. Immigration and Lifetime Prevalence of DSM-IV PsychiatricDisorders Among Mexican Americans and Non-Hispanic Whites in the United States: Results from the National Epidemiologic Survey on Alcohol and Related Conditions. *Arch. Gen. Psychiatry* **2004**, *61*, 1226–1233. [CrossRef]
16. Rogler, L.; Cortes, D.; Malgady, R. Acculturation and mental health status among Hispanics: Convergence and new directions for research. *Am. Psychol.* **1991**, *46*, 585–597. [CrossRef]
17. Lui, P.P.; Zamboanga, B.L. A Critical Review and Meta-Analysis of the Associations between Acculturation and Alcohol Use Outcomes among Hispanic Americans. *Alcohol. Clin. Exp. Res.* **2018**, *42*, 1841–1862. [CrossRef] [PubMed]
18. Cuellar, I.; Harris, L.; Jasso, R. An acculturation scale for Mexican American normal and clinical populations. *Hisp. J. Behav. Sci.* **1980**, *2*, 199–217.
19. Szapocznik, J.; Scopetta, M.; Aranalde, M.; Kurtines, W. Theory and measurement of acculturation. *Interam. J. Psychol.* **1987**, *12*, 113–130.
20. Burnam, M.A.; Hough, R.L.; Karno, M.; Escobar, J.I.; Telles, C.A. Acculturation and Lifetime Prevalence of Psychiatric Disorders among Mexican Americans in Los Angeles. *J. Health Soc. Behav.* **1987**, *28*, 89. [CrossRef]
21. Caetano, R. Acculturation and Drinking Patterns among U.S. Hispanics. *Br. J. Addict.* **1987**, *82*, 789–799. [CrossRef] [PubMed]
22. Lara, M.; Gamboa, C.; Kahramanian, M.I.; Morales, L.S.; Hayes Bautista, D.E. Acculturation and Latino Health in the United States: A Review of the Literature and its Sociopolitical Context. *Annu. Rev. Public Health* **2005**, *26*, 367–397. [CrossRef]

23. Hunt, L.M.; Schneider, S.; Comer, B. Should "acculturation" be a variable in health research? A critical review of research on US Hispanics. *Soc. Sci. Med.* **2004**, *59*, 973–986. [CrossRef]
24. Alegría, M.; Mulvaney-Day, N.; Torres, M.; Polo, A.; Cao, Z.; Canino, G. Prevalence of Psychiatric Disorders Across Latino Subgroups in the United States. *Am. J. Public Health* **2007**, *97*, 68–75. [CrossRef]
25. Gonzalez, F.R.; Benuto, L.T.; Casas, J.B. Prevalence of Interpersonal Violence among Latinas: A Systematic Review. *Trauma Violence Abus.* **2018**, *21*, 977–990. [CrossRef]
26. Maldonado, A.I.; Cunradi, C.B.; Nápoles, A.M. Racial/Ethnic Discrimination and Intimate Partner Violence Perpetration in Latino Men: The Mediating Effects of Mental Health. *Int. J. Environ. Res. Public Health* **2020**, *17*, 8148. [CrossRef]
27. Reingle, J.M.; Jennings, W.G.; Connell, N.M.; Businelle, M.S.; Chartier, K. On the Pervasiveness of Event-Specific Alcohol Use, General Substance Use, and Mental Health Problems as Risk Factors for Intimate Partner Violence. *J. Interpers. Violence* **2014**, *29*, 2951–2970. [CrossRef] [PubMed]
28. Cunradi, C.B. Intimate Partner Violence Among Hispanic Men and Women: The Role of Drinking, Neighborhood Disorder, and Acculturation-Related Factors. *Violence Vict.* **2009**, *24*, 83–97. [CrossRef] [PubMed]
29. Tang, N.; Stein, J.; Hsia, R.Y.; Maselli, J.H.; Gonzales, R. Trends and Characteristics of US Emergency Department Visits, 1997–2007. *JAMA* **2010**, *304*, 664–670. [CrossRef]
30. Doty, M.; Holmgren, A. Health care disconnect: Gaps in coverage and care for minority adults. *Commonw. Fund* **2006**, *2*, 1–12.
31. Hong, R.; Baumann, B.M.; Boudreaux, E. The emergency department for routine healthcare: Race/ethnicity, socioeconomic status, and perceptual factors. *J. Emerg. Med.* **2007**, *32*, 149–158. [CrossRef]
32. Parast, L.; Mathews, M.; Martino, S.; Lehrman, W.G.; Stark, D.; Elliott, M.N. Racial/Ethnic Differences in Emergency Department Utilization and Experience. *J. Gen. Intern. Med.* **2021**, *5*, 1–8. [CrossRef] [PubMed]
33. Beaudoin, F.L.; Baird, J.; Liu, T.; Merchant, R.C. Sex Differences in Substance Use among Adult Emergency Department Patients: Prevalence, Severity, and Need for Intervention. *Acad. Emerg. Med.* **2015**, *22*, 1307–1315. [CrossRef] [PubMed]
34. Bazargan-Hejazi, S.; Kim, E.; Lin, J.; Ahmadi, A.; Khamesi, M.T.; Teruya, S. Risk Factors Associated with Different Types of Intimate Partner Violence (IPV): An Emergency Department Study. *J. Emerg. Med.* **2014**, *47*, 710–720. [CrossRef] [PubMed]
35. Molina, M.F.; Li, C.N.; Manchanda, E.C.; White, B.; Faridi, M.K.; Espinola, J.A.; Ashworth, H.; Ciccolo, G.; Camargo, C.A., Jr.; Samuels-Kalow, M. Prevalence of Emergency Department Social Risk and Social Needs. *West. J. Emerg. Med.* **2020**, *21*, 152–161. [CrossRef]
36. Harland, K.K.; Peek-Asa, C.; Saftlas, A.F. Intimate Partner Violence and Controlling Behaviors Experienced by Emergency Department Patients: Differences by Sexual Orientation and Gender Identification. *J. Interpers. Violence* **2021**, *36*, NP6125–NP6143. [CrossRef]
37. Okuda, M.; Olfson, M.; Wang, S.; Rubio, J.M.; Xu, Y.; Blanco, C. Correlates of Intimate Partner Violence Perpetration: Results from a National Epidemiologic Survey. *J. Trauma. Stress* **2015**, *28*, 49–56. [CrossRef] [PubMed]
38. Caetano, R.; Cunradi, C.B.; Alter, H.J.; Mair, C.; Yau, R.K. Drinking and Intimate Partner Violence Severity Levels Among U.S. Ethnic Groups in an Urban Emergency Department. *Acad. Emerg. Med.* **2019**, *26*, 897–907. [CrossRef] [PubMed]
39. Okechukwu, C.A.; el Ayadi, A.M.; Tamers, S.L.; Sabbath, E.L.; Berkman, L. Household Food Insufficiency, Financial Strain, Work–Family Spillover, and Depressive Symptoms in the Working Class: The Work, Family, and Health Network Study. *Am. J. Public Health* **2012**, *102*, 126–133. [CrossRef] [PubMed]
40. Zigmond, A.; Snaith, R. The Hospital Anxiety and Depression Scale. *Acta Psychiatr. Scand.* **1983**, *67*, 361–370. [CrossRef]
41. Prins, A.; Ouimette, P.; Kimerling, R.; Camerond, R.P.; Hugelshofer, D.S.; Shaw-Hegwer, J.; Thrailkill, A.; Gusman, F.D.; Sheikh, J. The primary care PTSD screen (PC–PTSD): Development and operating characteristics. *Prim. Care Psychiatry* **2004**, *9*, 9–14. [CrossRef]
42. National Institute on Alcohol Abuse and Alcoholism. What's "At-Risk" or "Heavy Drinking"? Available online: https://www.rethinkingdrinking.niaaa.nih.gov/How-much-is-too-much/Is-your-drinking-pattern-risky/Whats-At-Risk-Or-Heavy-Drinking.aspx (accessed on 10 December 2018).
43. Straus, M.A.; Hamby, S.L.; Boney-McCoy, S.; Sugarman, D.B. The revised Conflict Tactics Scale (CTS2): Development and preliminary psychometric data. *J. Fam. Issues* **1996**, *17*, 283–316. [CrossRef]
44. Cunradi, C.B.; Caetano, R.; Alter, H.J.; Ponicki, W.R. Adverse childhood experiences are associated with at-risk drinking, cannabis and illicit drug use in females but not males: An Emergency Department study. *Am. J. Drug Alcohol Abus.* **2020**, *46*, 739–748. [CrossRef]
45. Cunradi, C.B.; Ponicki, W.R.; Alter, H.J.; Caetano, R.; Mair, C.; Lee, J. Drinking Context–Specific Dose-Response Models of Intimate Partner Violence Among an Urban Emergency Department Sample. *J. Stud. Alcohol Drugs* **2020**, *81*, 780–789. [CrossRef]
46. Shattell, M.M.; Smith, K.M.; Quinlan-Colwell, A.; Villalba, J.A. Factors Contributing to Depression in Latinas of Mexican Origin Residing in the United States: Implications for Nurses. *J. Am. Psychiatr. Nurses Assoc.* **2008**, *14*, 193–204. [CrossRef]
47. Grest, C.V.; Cederbaum, J.A.; Lee, J.O.; Unger, J.B. Adverse childhood experiences and the substance use behaviors of Latinx youth. *Drug Alcohol Depend.* **2021**, *227*, 108936. [CrossRef] [PubMed]
48. Stevens, A.K.; Blanchard, B.E.; Shi, M.; Littlefield, A.K. Testing measurement invariance of the UPPS-P Impulsive Behavior Scale in Hispanic/Latino and non-Hispanic/Latino college students. *Psychol. Assess.* **2018**, *30*, 280–285. [CrossRef] [PubMed]

49. Paulus, D.J.; Bakhshaie, J.; Lemaire, C.; Garza, M.; Ochoa-Perez, M.; Valdivieso, J.; Velasco, R.V.; Bogiaizian, D.; Kauffman, B.Y.; Robles, Z.; et al. Negative Affectivity and Problematic Alcohol Use among Latinos in Primary Care: The Role of Emotion Dysregulation. *J. Dual Diagn.* **2016**, *12*, 137–147. [CrossRef] [PubMed]
50. Caetano, R.; Schafer, J.; Clark, C.L.; Cunradi, C.B.; Raspberry, K. Intimate Partner Violence, Acculturation, and Alcohol Consumption Among Hispanic Couples in the United States. *J. Interpers. Violence* **2000**, *15*, 30–45. [CrossRef]
51. Caetano, R.; Ramisetty-Mikler, S.; Vaeth, P.A.C.; Harris, T.R. Acculturation Stress, Drinking, and Intimate Partner Violence Among Hispanic Couples in the U.S. *J. Interpers. Violence* **2007**, *22*, 1431–1447. [CrossRef]
52. Zemore, S.E. Acculturation and Alcohol among Latino Adults in the United States: A Comprehensive Review. *Alcohol. Clin. Exp. Res.* **2007**, *31*, 1968–1990. [CrossRef]
53. Caetano, R.; Ramisetty-Mikler, S.; Field, C.A. Unidirectional and bidirectional intimate partner violence among white, black, and Hispanic couples in the United States. *Violence Vict.* **2005**, *20*, 393–405. [CrossRef]
54. Cunradi, C.B. Drinking Level, Neighborhood Social Disorder, and Mutual Intimate Partner Violence. *Alcohol. Clin. Exp. Res.* **2007**, *31*, 1012–1019. [CrossRef]
55. Cunradi, C.; Dellor, E.; Alter, H.; Caetano, R.; Mair, C. Problem drinking and marijuana use as risks for unidirectional and bidirectional partner violence. *Partn. Abus.* **2020**, *11*, 57–75. [CrossRef]
56. Mancera, B.M.; Mungal, A.S.; de Santis, J.; Provencio-Vasquez, E. Reflections of Men of Mexican Origin: A Grounded Theory Study of Intimate Partner Violence Risk Factors. *Am. J. Men's Health* **2018**, *12*, 1784–1798. [CrossRef]
57. Gonzalez-Guarda, R.M.; Ortega, J.; Vasquez, E.P.; de Santis, J. La Mancha Negra: Substance Abuse, Violence, and Sexual Risks among Hispanic Males. *West. J. Nurs. Res.* **2009**, *32*, 128–148. [CrossRef] [PubMed]
58. Lown, E.A.; Vega, W.A. Prevalence and predictors of physical partner abuse among Mexican American women. *Am. J. Public Health* **2001**, *91*, 441–445. [CrossRef] [PubMed]
59. Garcia, L.; Hurwitz, E.L.; Kraus, J.F. Acculturation and Reported Intimate Partner Violence among Latinas in Los Angeles. *J. Interpers. Violence* **2005**, *20*, 569–590. [CrossRef] [PubMed]
60. Sabina, C.; Cuevas, C.A.; Schally, J.L. The effect of immigration and acculturation on victimization among a national sample of Latino women. *Cult. Divers. Ethn. Minor. Psychol.* **2013**, *19*, 13–26. [CrossRef]
61. Zadnik, E.; Sabina, C.; Cuevas, C.A. Violence against Latinas. *J. Interpers. Violence* **2014**, *31*, 1141–1153. [CrossRef]
62. Foran, H.M.; O'Leary, K.D. Alcohol and intimate partner violence: A meta-analytic review. *Clin. Psychol. Rev.* **2008**, *28*, 1222–1234. [CrossRef]
63. Free, B.L.; Lipinski, A.J.; Lewin, R.K.; Majeed, R.; Zakarian, R.J.; Beck, J.G. Using a Person-Centered Approach to Identify Patterns of Exposure to Intimate Partner Violence and Child Abuse in Women: Associations with Mental Health. *Child Maltreatment* **2021**, *26*, 376–386. [CrossRef] [PubMed]
64. Doucerain, M.M.; Segalowitz, N.; Ryder, A.G. Acculturation measurement: From simple proxies to sophisticated toolkit. In *The Oxford Handbook of Acculturation and Health*; Schwartz, S., Unger, J., Eds.; Oxford University Press: New York, NY, USA, 2017; pp. 97–117.
65. Cunradi, C.B.; Bersamin, M.; Ames, G. Agreement on Intimate Partner Violence among a Sample of Blue-Collar Couples. *J. Interpers. Violence* **2008**, *24*, 551–568. [CrossRef]
66. Costanza, A.; Rothen, S.; Achab, S.; Thorens, G.; Baertschi, M.; Weber, K.; Canuto, A.; Richard-Lepouriel, H.; Perroud, N.; Zullino, D. Impulsivity and Impulsivity-Related Endophenotypes in Suicidal Patients with Substance Use Disorders: An Exploratory Study. *Int. J. Ment. Health Addict.* **2020**, 1–16. [CrossRef]
67. Taira, B.R.; Orue, A. Language assistance for limited English proficiency patients in a public ED: Determining the unmet need. *BMC Health Serv. Res.* **2019**, *19*, 56. [CrossRef]

International Journal of
Environmental Research and Public Health

MDPI

Brief Report

Crisis Work Embedded in a Global Crisis: The Early Phase Impact of COVID-19 on Survivors of Intimate Partner Violence and Service Provisions

Vithya Murugan [1,*], Terri L. Weaver [2], Theresa Schafer [1] and Quin Rich [1]

1 School of Social Work, Saint Louis University, St. Louis, MO 63103, USA; tschafer301@gmail.com (T.S.); quin.rich@slu.edu (Q.R.)
2 Department of Psychology, Saint Louis University, St. Louis, MO 63103, USA; terri.weaver@health.slu.edu
* Correspondence: vithya.murugan@slu.edu

Abstract: COVID-19, as a global pandemic, was a public health inflection point for individuals affected by intimate partner violence (IPV) and those who provide IPV services. Public health guidelines that were intended to reduce risk of exposure to the virus impacted vulnerability factors for IPV survivors and associated systems of services. We aimed to (1) explore the effect of COVID-19 on survivors of IPV; (2) assess the effect of COVID-19 on IPV-related service provisions and service providers; and (3) explore challenges and opportunities in the wake of COVID-19 on broader IPV services and advocacy. Method: Twelve directors of IPV shelter, criminal justice, and other advocacy services within a diverse, Midwestern metropolitan area were recruited to participate in in-depth, semi-structured interviews in June–August 2020. Interviews were transcribed verbatim and analyzed using Dedoose. Data were coded and analyzed through thematic analysis. Results: Four major themes, contextualized by COVID-19 and racial injustice, emerged from the data analysis: (1) IPV-related trends; (2) impact on IPV survivors, services, and agency morale; (3) inter-agency collaborations; and (4) future opportunities for innovative service delivery. Gaps and opportunities for developing culturally congruent, trauma-informed services were identified. Conclusion: Findings suggest that responsive and accessible IPV resources and associated advocacy services can make the difference between life and death for survivors.

Keywords: COVID-19; intimate partner violence; service providers; resiliency

Citation: Murugan, V.; Weaver, T.L.; Schafer, T.; Rich, Q. Crisis Work Embedded in a Global Crisis: The Early Phase Impact of COVID-19 on Survivors of Intimate Partner Violence and Service Provisions. *Int. J. Environ. Res. Public Health* **2022**, *19*, 4728. https://doi.org/10.3390/ijerph19084728

Academic Editors: Ko-Ling Chan and Jagdish Khubchandani

Received: 23 February 2022
Accepted: 12 April 2022
Published: 14 April 2022

1. Introduction

Public health officials asserted in March 2020 that it is safest to be at home to reduce risk of exposure and to curb the spread of COVID-19 virus. However, professionals who work with survivors know the home can magnify risk of exposure to another public health hazard: intimate partner violence (IPV), including emotional, physical, psychological, and sexual violence. Individual and relational level stressors exacerbated by the pandemic, including anxiety and fear related to unemployment, sickness, and death, may increase the likelihood of conflict and the use of maladaptive coping mechanisms, such as alcohol and substance use [1]. These stressors are nested within structural contexts that include chronic and persistent poverty, which may exacerbate the frequency and severity of IPV [2,3]. Self-isolation forced those affected by IPV and their children to be confined, in proximity, with their abusive partners with no definite endpoint. Additionally, early public health recommendations, such as social distancing, limited individuals' options for access to IPV agencies and associated resources—at least in their conventional form. Research has confirmed that COVID-19 lockdowns have led to decreased service utilization by IPV survivors, increased severity of IPV, and experiences of isolation [4–10]. Concerted efforts by IPV service providers to effectively respond to the COVID-19 pandemic have been identified as crucial for positive survivor outcomes [11]. However, perspectives from IPV service providers on the early stage of the pandemic have received limited scholarly attention.

Previous quantitative research conducted in the same Midwestern city and over the same time as the present study identified survivor concerns with decreased safety, loss of access to support services, increased economic precarity, and forced contact with perpetrators as key concerns [12]. According to service providers, the isolation of the pandemic highlighted particularly acute elements of intimate partner violence, including substance use coercion, reproductive coercion, and control around heath care and service seeking [13]. While the pandemic has increased vicarious trauma and exacerbated pre-existing barriers for culturally specific agencies, service providers have responded creatively, such as utilizing technology to connect with survivors [14]. In line with findings from the present study, Black survivors have been particularly affected by pandemic barriers to accessing IPV services. Data from Chicago, a nearby city, indicated that IPV-related police reports from the majority of Black neighborhoods decreased at almost twice the rate of the general population due to stay-at-home orders [15].

The present study builds on the findings of previous studies by exploring service providers' perspectives on the specific factors that promote or inhibit survivor safety in greater depth. As articulated by Ragavan and colleagues [13], service providers can share information about how COVID-19 has affected survivors without causing safety concerns intrinsic to data collection with survivors during a global pandemic. As such, we aimed to (1) explore the effect of COVID-19 and associated public health guidelines on individuals affected by IPV; (2) assess the effect of COVID-19 on service provisions for individuals; and (3) explore challenges and opportunities in the wake of COVID-19 on IPV services and advocacy.

2. Materials and Methods

2.1. Participants

Participants were recruited through convenience sampling via the End Domestic Violence Network (EDVN) listserv consisting of over 20 member agencies in the Midwest metropolitan area. To participate in the study, participants needed to be 18 years or older and needed to have worked at an IPV agency in the Midwest metropolitan area as an executive director, program director, and/or advocate. Interested participants were asked to phone or email the researcher, who then provided them with additional information about the study. If the participant indicated that they were interested, an interview date and time was arranged. Interviews took place over Zoom and ranged in duration from 60 to 90 min. Participants were compensated with a USD 20 Amazon gift card. A total of 12 participants were interviewed by the first and/or second authors, both of whom are doctoral-level researchers trained in qualitative methods. The sample of 12 women was sufficient for the analysis because saturation was achieved such that no new data or theoretical insights continued to emerge [16]. The majority of participants were women (92%, n = 11). Their ages ranged from 25 to 70 years with a mean of 42.25 years. The participants' length of time with their respective agencies ranged from 1 to 20 years with a mean of 8.85 years at their current agency and 4.25 years in the current position.

2.2. Interview Guide

Semi-structured interviews are used as a method of data collection to gather information from participants who have "personal experiences, attitudes, perceptions, and beliefs related to the topic of interest" [17] (p. 2). The semi-structured interview guide contained approximately 15 questions and addressed the following topics: service providers' perceptions of how COVID-19 has affected survivors of IPV; how COVID-19 has affected services available to survivors; and what is needed to effectively support similar agencies in helping survivors. Planned and unplanned follow-up probes were utilized to deepen the PIs' understanding of the service providers' responses. Planned follow-up questions are questions that ask for more details about particular aspects of the core questions [17].

For example, one question on the interview guide asked how COVID-19 affected survivors of IPV. Planned follow-up questions included: How has it affected severity/frequency of abuse? How has it affected mental and physical heath? How has it affected caregiving of children? Work? How has it influenced the tactics used by batterers? Unplanned follow-up questions were also utilized to seek clarification on words and phrases to avoid assuming shared meaning. For example, the PIs would ask "Could you tell me what that means or looks like for you?" or "Could you give me an example?" to encourage elaboration.

2.3. Data Analysis

The interview data were transcribed and analyzed using Dedoose, a cross-platform software often used for qualitative and mixed-methods research. The research team employed a thematic analysis approach, defined as "a method for identifying, analyzing, and reporting patterns within data" [18] (p. 79). Due to its flexible approach, thematic analysis allows for rich, detailed, and complex descriptions of the data.

The first and second authors and a master's-level research assistant (third author) began by familiarizing themselves with the data by reading each transcript in its entirety. Each documented their thoughts about potential codes which they shared and discussed during a debriefing session. Next, a preliminary codebook, containing codes and their definitions, was developed based on questions from the interview guide and codes that were discussed during the debriefing session. One transcript was then selected for preliminary coding by the first, second, and third authors, ensuring that the initial codebook adequately captured patterns in perspectives across the interview. Coders then met to review and compare their coding, and discrepancies were discussed until a consensus was reached. This led to the first refinement of the codebook which included the addition of new codes, clarification of code definitions, and inclusion of exemplars. The three authors then recoded the initial transcript using the refined codebook.

As the discrepancies between coders were minimal and not code-specific (i.e., the length of excerpt coded), all remaining transcripts were double-coded by the authors. The full team met, as needed, to discuss and resolve any coding discrepancies until minimal discrepancies emerged. The team then met and discussed the consolidation of codes into broader themes. Quotes were extracted from codes for each theme and then re-evaluated to ensure they captured the meaning of themes [18]. Further, to ensure the accuracy and reliability of the qualitative data, member checking was conducted with the participants. Following the completion of analysis, the researchers sent a draft of the report to the study participants. The participants were asked if the findings reflected their experiences and if they wanted to change or add anything. Participants generally confirmed the findings as reported.

3. Results

Interviews revealed four, early-phase COVID-19 themes: (1) intimate partner violence (IPV)-related trends; (2) impact on IPV survivors, services, and agency morale; (3) interagency collaborations, and (4) moving forward—lessons learned and ongoing needs.

3.1. IPV-Related Trends

All participants discussed IPV-related trends since the emergence of COVID-19 and the subsequent implementation of stay-at-home orders. The most palpable trend was the precipitous decrease in hotline and emergency shelter calls. For example, an executive director reflected on the dwindling number of hotline calls that her agency received, "I [also] work our crisis line and our [call] numbers went down ... "

The executive director, who oversees emergency housing, shared:

> The biggest thing [COVID trend] that I can speak to right now is the decrease in calls [shelter] that we have seen since the pandemic started. When the pandemic was officially declared [a national emergency] in mid-March, we had six families in [the] shelter so we were not full and that is abnormal for us. We typically are

> always full. And if we have a space, we have like one space [available]. So, to have three [spaces available] . . .

The executive director shared that she partially attributed the decreased volume in calls to the rapidly evolving news cycle. At the outset of the pandemic, media outlets covered the effects of COVID-19 on domestic violence by interviewing service providers. Information that was presented at one time may have quickly changed or even become obsolete soon thereafter. The executive director stated: "There was a lot of misinformation out there. There was a lot of news articles reporting that shelters were not taking people. And we were [taking people]. So, we did our best to reach out [to the media] every time we'd see those stories . . . "

Despite the decrease in calls for supportive services, many participants noted an increase in the incidence and severity of abuse reported by the survivors with whom they did have contact. A service provider described her perception of the escalating violence severity:

> Now [during the stay-at-home orders] it seems that that abuse is consistent and escalating. I have several women [clients] right now who are in the middle of extremely abusive relationships. Um, I've had two women within the last couple of weeks that actually had to go to the hospital for their injuries.

In fact, some participants attributed these trends to survivors' diminished prioritization of their physical safety during COVID-19. More specifically, participants noted that the pandemic has forced survivors to prioritize other competing demands (e.g., employment, childcare), sometimes at the expense of their physical safety. While these demands are omnipresent in the lives of survivors outside of the COVID-19 context, participants reflected on how the pandemic has caused an inflection of diminished prioritization of safety due to role strain. For example, another service provider shared:

> It [survivors' personal safety] kind of has had to be deprioritized as they've [survivors] had to homeschool and had to figure out employment and childcare and all the things that all of us are dealing with in the midst of [the pandemic] . . . you know being in an abusive relationship and having to potentially live with the abuser. I would say that's one of the biggest trends we've noticed is just sort of the de-prioritization of safety measures that normally, we would very much be prioritizing under normal circumstances if those other, you know, [other] resources were in place

In addition to using stay-at-home orders to further isolate survivors, participants described how perpetrators have used economic abuse strategies to control survivors, including forcing them to work or not work, or to intercept their stimulus checks upon arrival. Another service provider discussed how perpetrators attempt to get money from survivors' stimulus checks:

> When the checks were going out, a number of women that were speaking to me [shared] that their significant other [was] trying to like control . . . like checking the mailbox and, and [asking] 'has your check come yet?' like constantly badgering . . . to make sure that they kind of got first dibs on the [survivors'] check.

Many participants underscored the importance of clarifying misconceptions that suggested that COVID-19 caused IPV. Instead, participants shared that the pandemic increased the incidence of IPV by exacerbating existing stressors:

> COVID did not cause domestic violence. COVID has amplified [IPV] that, and made those pressures even greater, that has led to increase incidence and an increased impact. So, so often people will ask, like, so is COVID causing more domestic violence? No, you need to know the root of domestic violence and that COVID is a layer on top of that, that influences the impact of incidents.

3.2. Impact on IPV Survivors, Services, and Agency Morale

3.2.1. Survivors

All participants explicitly discussed the adverse economic effects experienced by survivors that were either caused or exacerbated by the pandemic. Participants shared that largely due to COVID-19, many survivors and their families grappled with job loss or instability, housing insecurity or homelessness, and lack of childcare. For survivors of color, the economic implications of the pandemic have been especially pronounced, largely due to systemic inequality. For example, one participant shared: "Eighty percent of the people we serve are Black. And because they may not have other resources, because they, you know, they're also living below the poverty line and they didn't graduate high school and none of that's a coincidence." Additionally, participants shared that most of the jobs that have been available to Black survivors during the pandemic have been in essential roles, thus increasing their risk of exposure to COVID-19. Another participant shared:

> [Most] of my ladies are African Americans, and we're finding them jobs in these essential roles. That means they're going to be overrepresented in those essential worker positions where they're going to be exposed to COVID-19 at a higher rate, than those of us who could work from home ...

Participants reflected on how these economic challenges intensified already precarious relationships and placed survivors at an increased risk of experiencing IPV. For example, a participant explained:

> The biggest complaint [from survivors] is that a lot of people [survivors and their families] lost their employment. I think that financial stability does play a part in the stability of the home. And so, now, if you take a situation that may have [already] been volatile, and then now put on top of it financial stress, right, you know, the question, is that at a tipping point [for IPV]?

Many participants shared survivors were acutely aware of the risk that financial insecurity during the pandemic created for them whilst experiencing IPV. Another provider described how a survivor anticipated that her partner's unemployment and increased alcohol consumption would foster a dangerous dynamic within the home:

> She [the survivor] knew the triggers well enough to know he's [her partner] going to be home, he's going to be drinking, he's not going to be getting a paycheck until his unemployment starts, this [the violence] is going to get bad, it's [the violence] going to get worse.

Furthermore, some participants shared how economic hardships exacerbated by the pandemic coupled with the stay-at-home orders have halted survivors' plans of leaving abusive relationships. One participant shared how many survivors who considered moving in with family and/or friends were unable to do so because of social distancing guidelines:

> So [survivor's] family and friends, what I heard ... were not an option [to stay with] because of social distancing. As they [survivors] were kind of working towards independence, that [staying with family and friends] wasn't going to be an option because of social distancing.

Additionally, in some instances, participants shared that they returned to their abusive partners during COVID-19 out of financial necessity. Another participant shared:

> Folks [survivors] need a car, they need [financial] stability ... to be able to be independent, you know, it's like, the lack of financial stability, often we [service providers] see folks going back to an abusive partner because they're just not making it [financially]. And I worry about that a lot.

Participants also reflected on the challenges that survivors experienced in accessing support services during the pandemic. Although they shared that their respective agencies were able to quickly pivot certain services (e.g., counseling, protection order filing, safety planning) to virtual platforms, barriers to accessibility persisted for survivors. One barrier that survivors encountered was the lack of privacy in their households (due to stay-at-home orders) that often prevented them from being able to meaningfully participate in counseling and/or safety planning sessions.

Additionally, participants noted that many survivors do not have access to computers in any form and may have limited data on their smart phones, and thus, are unable to take advantage of virtual support services. In fact, some participants noted that this was an issue that was especially pronounced for clients located in a Midwest City. This service provider shared: "A lot of the clientele that I work within the city do not have access to desktop or laptop, laptop computers ... we're trying to figure that out a little bit." Although participants acknowledged that smartphones and tablets are virtually ubiquitous, they shared that certain services (i.e., court filing systems) are not mobile-friendly and, therefore, may not be accessible to all survivors. Additionally, in some cases of IPV, survivors were limited in their phone use to access services for fear of their abusive partner accessing and tracking their call logs.

Many participants openly reflected on systemic racism and ongoing police brutality against Black men and women. Specifically, participants shared how these insidious social issues serve as barriers to Black survivors calling the police for assistance, even in acute circumstances. This participant explained: "There are in the current climate, there are some victims that are rightfully 100% afraid to seek police assistance ... [Black] Victims don't often call the police because they're scared ... ".

3.2.2. Services

All participants discussed the adaptations that their respective agencies made to IPV services in response to the pandemic. When COVID-19 was declared a national emergency, participants shared that their respective agencies devised and implemented safety protocols to reduce the risk of exposure to the virus. These protocols included limiting the number of in-person staff members; procuring COVID-19 testing and protective personal equipment (PPE); and, where possible, pivoting service offerings to a virtual format.

After barring minor roadblocks that included limited access to stable WiFi and concerns about firewall security, participants shared that their respective agencies made relatively quick transitions to virtual service offerings. Yet, many participants shared that the quantity and quality of the services offered were largely affected. For example, many participants shared that the way their agencies approached outreach with survivors of IPV was affected by the pandemic. Participants shared that their agencies began to rely heavily on social media to reach out to survivors of IPV during the pandemic. A participant shared:

> There's been a continued focus on the use of our social media, to reiterate to folks that we're still providing services. They [the agency] started up a newsletter, oh, gosh, it was probably about two months ago. And what they [the agency] would do is highlight each of our services and explain what that looks like with COVID.

Participants shared that many services, such as intake, safety planning, and counseling, were significantly altered in their virtual transition. All participants shared that the lack of in-person, tactile interactions with their clients adversely affected the nature of services being offered, specifically related to rapport building with clients. Additionally, participants relayed that the lack of privacy in survivors' homes often inhibited their ability to provide quality services to their clients. Another provider described the complexity of offering virtual counseling services to clients, especially when they were cohabitating with their abusive partner:

> With phone appointments, sometimes that person [abusive partner] is there ... And so, it's kind of a situation where we [survivor and counselor] must text in advance to see if they're [abusive partner] there. And then, you know, sometimes we're [survivor and counselor] on the phone and then that person [abusive partner] comes home and then [the survivor says] 'Okay, we got to get

off the phone real quick.' Whereas, you know, in the past, like I said, you know, [survivor and counselor are] meeting like at a library or something like that, we just never had to worry about that kind of stuff, you know.

Participants also reflected on services that were difficult to translate to a virtual platform, including clinical therapeutic interventions used to treat trauma or play therapy with children. This participant shared the challenges of virtually administering eye movement desensitization and reprocessing (EMDR):

> Our counseling services, as they still are currently all either virtual through telehealth or they're on the phone. What's kind of tough about that is in talks with counselor friends that I have it's [counseling] very different and so there may be certain techniques such as EMDR [eye movement desensitization and reprocessing], which is a form of really beneficial [therapy] for trauma victims … you can do it [EMDR] virtually, in some cases, but it's like a really heavy form of therapy that we really don't want to do with somebody over the phone or over video calls. So I know that's been impacted.

The participant continued by describing the challenges associated with providing therapy to children and the adaptations that her agency made to accommodate children's needs. The participant shared:

> [The agency's] Our child therapists … I've talked to multiple of them, I've talked about how realizing that kids' attention spans virtually is very different [than in] their [face-to-face] life. So we've gone from hour [therapy] sessions to like 30 min because kids don't have that attention span to look at a screen and do therapy.

Participants shared that some services, especially those offered in group formats (e.g., group therapy, children's support groups), had been suspended due to social distancing guidelines. A participant expressed her fear for children exposed to IPV who may not be getting the communal, peer-based support that they were receiving before COVID-19:

> It's terrifying to think of children who aren't in shelter because we were so much more than just a roof over their head … We had community nights, we had art therapy, we had support dogs and we really had a great program. And just knowing that there's so many kiddos that are stuck and not being in school and not having sort of all those normal mechanisms, and that are stuck in homes.

The effect of COVID-19 on IPV service provisions was especially palpable for under-resourced agencies that predominantly worked with ethnic minority survivors and/or survivors living in a Midwest City. When it came to legal and court services continuing through the pandemic, the economic disparities between courts in certain geographic jurisdictions became acutely highlighted. Because the Midwest County has a specific court dedicated to domestic-violence-related issues, participants shared that the county courts were able to renegotiate court services and access virtually more easily and quickly, whereas city courts struggled to shift with the same ease. Specifically, with regards to filing orders of protection, the county adopted an online filing system early in the pandemic, while the city was slower to adopt these measures.

Participants shared that survivors' IPV-related needs are unique and often require services that are not typically housed within a traditional IPV agency (e.g., substance abuse treatment and acute mental health services). Unfortunately, participants noted that many agencies providing such services were forced to suspend services or close due to COVID-19, thus leaving gaps in service provisions for survivors. Another participant explained:

> With COVID, a lot of those [allied services] agencies are folding up. It's, it's you know, frustrating that, you know, they just closed up and there's no real safety net to kind of, to continue to provide some of these services [for survivors], particularly, like I said, some of the drug treatment ones, those are the ones that I'm, I'm pretty concerned about right now.

3.2.3. Agency Morale

Agency reflections on morale and the response to low morale highlighted the juxtaposition of the crisis worker embedded within a global crisis and the associated constraints on the work that reflects the mission and worker identity. Most participants mentioned the strain on personnel during this time, including increased role strain associated with having family and extended family, childcare and work coalesce at home, as well as the challenges to the mission and identity of domestic violence advocacy with COVID-related restrictions abruptly limiting available space or types of service activities. Reflecting upon her staff, one participant said: "We got a lot of pushback when we had to say, 'we have to limit the number of intakes,' or 'we can't do intakes for a few days.' Like they were really pissed because it was like, 'This is what we do. Women are still at-risk; women are still dying'".

Effectively coping with threats to morale included transparent communication (what was known and what was not known at the time regarding COVID-19 safety protocols or shifting policies), leaning on one another for support, flexibility, and allowing work-related accommodations. Thus, personal limit-setting and self-care were supported. One provider shared: "I think that, I think that we keep a positive attitude around here. We, like I said, are each other's support system. We have a great chemistry with each other. And so we feed off of each other". Another service provider reflected: "I think we just, you know, hear what the needs are and try to honor and help kind of navigate as best as we can".

Several of the agencies mentioned the importance of tangible supports, including external as well as internal funding that helped to secure employees' jobs, and at least one agency highlighted the importance of formalizing health-related organizational policies to protect their employees. The service provider from this agency stated: [We found] that if we had a public health leave policy, staff would still get paid in full. So we very quickly developed a policy and got it approved by the board.

Other tangible support included staff group activities that could be completed remotely and shared with the group—often with a focus on health and personal wellness, such as a yoga or walking challenge. Additional morale boosters mentioned by at least one group were tokens of appreciation, such as food or T-shirts.

3.3. Inter-Agency Collaborations

Almost all participants discussed agencies that they collaborated with during the pandemic. Yet, many participants noted that the IPV sphere, pandemic or not, seldom operates in isolation, and that inter-agency collaboration is crucial to optimally assisting survivors of IPV. For example, an IPV court advocate explained:

> I would say, pre-COVID and post-COVID and under any normal circumstances, the domestic violence [IPV] court does not operate in isolation. I mean, we exist partially because of our community partnerships and collaboration. We [IPV court] consider ourselves very much a part of the community wide efforts. People's experience with the court system is usually fleeting, you know, they may come to court once and then we never see them again, they may be there more continually. But the reality is we if we have that opportunity to connect with a victim, we need to make sure that we're connecting them to those long-standing community resources . . .

All participants represented agencies that were members of the EDVN. When COVID-19 was declared a national emergency, participants shared that an EDVN meeting commenced, which assessed the functionality and capacity of member agencies during the pandemic. A working list was disseminated across EDVN member agencies and updated as the pandemic unfolded.

Some participants shared that they collaborated with agencies outside of EDVN to meet survivors' needs during the pandemic. For example, one participant shared that her agency formalized a collaboration with the local counseling center to incorporate trauma-informed services

3.4. Moving Forward and Lessons Learned

Participants were asked to reflect upon the lessons learned as they navigate the process of providing domestic violence-related services during the pandemic and priorities for moving forward. Most of the participants highlighted the key role of technology and the importance of investing in technological upgrades for the agency, including boosting WiFi capacity and enhancing firewalls, purchasing new computers for staff, and supporting survivors in becoming more technologically savvy to engage in telehealth services. Several agencies mentioned that this focus on technology was a significant shift in budgetary emphasis; thus, agencies had to reframe their perceptions of this investment as integral to connecting survivors with existing services and keeping them safe while doing so. Several agencies also mentioned some of the funding limitations of existing grants with allowable expenses primarily for direct services. Other agencies mentioned emerging grants with a focus on building technological infrastructure. One service provider explained: "We have gone into the technology world kicking and screaming the whole way. And that is only for good reason. Like, you know, but so when something like this hit, we did have to like . . . we had to buy laptops for everybody".

At least one agency mentioned the importance of developing or adapting existing technology platforms to enhance access while also reducing risk to the safety of survivors as they communicate remotely. One service provider noted:

> . . . if somebody got a hold of her phone or, you know, are there certain platforms that you can do that will sort of like Snapchat that will instantly delete text or so we started researching it not in connection to this just something in the long term. Would that be part of our technology goal. I wish we would have had it, it would have made a big difference.

4. Discussion

Our study sought to explore the early-phase impact of COVID-19 on survivors of IPV and related service provisions. Taken together, the trends highlighted in this study demonstrate how COVID-19 amplified the risk for an exacerbation of IPV by inflated IPV-related relational dynamics, including economic abuse, isolation, and more severe assaults. Additionally, COVID-19 created additional barriers to accessing supportive services, including role strain, thus limiting opportunities for women to focus on their health and well-being and proximity to abusive partners precluding opportunities to reach out to services and to have private conversations. IPV is interwoven with macrosystems [19] and changes within those macrosystems, including pandemic-related environmental stressors, which have a profound impact on both exposure and IPV, particularly for those who are more disadvantaged. These findings also underscored the multiplicity of safety threats during this time, both within and outside the home, and the resulting challenges for safety planning and decisional processes about reducing risk of harm [20]. With the expanded landscape of COVID-19-related risk factors, respondents reported that survivors made fewer overall calls but ultimately reported serving survivors who experienced more severe violence. This increase in severity suggests that there may have been new benchmarks for turning points as survivors struggled to navigate fewer available resources, thus increasing responsibility and the uncertainty associated with the early phase of the virus. Holistically acknowledging the compounding intersection of diseases and the social, environmental, and economic barriers to freedom and healing already faced by IPV survivors is an essential first step in understanding the experience of survivors during the COVID-19 pandemic and could serve as a model for including the influence of macro-systems, including systemic racism, within individualized safety plans.

Specifically, our study revealed the added vulnerability of BIPOC survivors, exacerbated by the intersection of IPV, COVID-19, and ongoing systemic racism [13,19]. Findings also underscore the ways in which some conventional recommendations intended to enhance survivor safety, as advice to 'call the police if you are in imminent danger' may not be a viable option for BIPOC survivors or for those who witness IPV happening to BIPOC survivors due to concerns of enhanced risk [21]. These findings serve as a clarion call for IPV resources and services to evaluate the degree to which they are offering culturally congruent services for diverse populations and raise critical questions about whether this is a time for new paradigms for survivor-centered services. IPV services have hardly changed over the past forty years and the voices of minoritized individuals have been largely absent from the design of extant services [22–24].

Additionally, our study found that the effects of COVID-19 were especially palpable for under-resourced agencies that predominantly serve BIPOC survivors, underscoring the financial fragility of these systems and the need for increased investment of resources into the formal and informal agencies serving these women. While the overall prevalence of IPV has decreased with the infusion of resources (e.g., Violence Against Women Act (VAWA)), disparities for marked or increased risks of homicide, and the different impacts of preventive policies faced by Black women (compared with other racial groups)) [25]. These findings highlight the eminence of creating intervention strategies that address IPV, service provisions, and COVID-19 within the context of existing systemic and structural inequities to better serve survivors of marginalized identities [13].

Furthermore, our study documented the effects of COVID-19 on service providers and agency morale. The pandemic intensified role strain related to the personal (e.g., family, childcare, fear of illness) and professional demands for service providers. Macro-systems not only affect those who experience victimization, but also those who provide crisis services. Bolstering resilience efforts within the work setting is paramount in order to retain a healthy and engaged workforce [26]. Resilience building efforts must also acknowledge the intersectional identities of their advocates and consider the disproportionate effects that these macro-factors have on advocates who are also BIPOC. Despite these demands and challenges, providers' remarked that their commitment to the mission of IPV advocacy, survivors, and to one another were sources of meaning, strength, and resilience.

There are several limitations to this study that must be acknowledged. First, our interviews were conducted with IPV service providers. However, we recognize that their sentiments may or may not be congruent with the lived experiences of survivors themselves, especially survivors who did not seek IPV-related services. Additionally, the study sample was recruited from IPV agencies in a medium-sized Midwestern city. Since the sample represents a small subset of IPV service providers, findings cannot be generalized, although they are still exploratory and idea-generating for IPV service providers in other locations. Additionally, the data were collected from June to August 2020, i.e., during the early phase of the pandemic. Therefore, our study was unable to explore the exacerbation of, and additional challenges raised by, the ongoing pandemic. Notwithstanding the limitations, this study is integral to shedding light on the issue of service providers' thoughts on the impact of COVID-19 for IPV survivors and service provisions.

5. Conclusions

Our study highlights how COVID-19 sharpened a focus on the macro public health context of white privilege, racial inequity, and social and economic disparities. As eloquently stated by our participants, these themes share fertile ground with IPV vulnerability as they confer risk for exposure, more deleterious outcomes, and disparate access to resources for Black and Brown women [19]. Therefore, as next steps, our intent is to explore the ways in which these macro-contexts have shaped IPV services and whether there are gaps in culturally congruent services for Black and Brown women.

Author Contributions: Conceptualization, V.M. and T.L.W.; data collection, V.M. and T.L.W.; coding, V.M., T.L.W. and T.S.; analysis, V.M. and T.L.W., writing—original draft preparation, V.M., T.L.W. and T.S.; writing—review and editing, V.M., T.L.W., T.S. and Q.R. All authors have read and agreed to the published version of the manuscript.

Funding: This research was funded by Saint Louis University's Office of the Vice President for Research Spark Microgrant.

Institutional Review Board Statement: The study was conducted in accordance with the Declaration of Helsinki and approved by the Institutional Review Board of Saint Louis University (protocol #31272, approved 15 May 2020).

Informed Consent Statement: Informed consent was obtained from all subjects involved in the study.

Data Availability Statement: Not applicable.

Acknowledgments: We would like to thank the community of IPV service providers for their time, expertise, commitment, and creativity for maintaining continuity in domestic violence services during a global health crisis.

Conflicts of Interest: The authors declare no conflict of interest.

References

1. Rodriguez, L.M.; Litt, D.M.; Stewart, S.H. Drinking to cope with the pandemic: The unique associations of COVID-19-related perceived threat and psychological distress to drinking behaviors in American men and women. *Addict. Behav.* **2020**, *110*, 106532. [CrossRef] [PubMed]
2. Goodman, L.A.; Smyth, K.F.; Borges, A.M.; Singer, R. When crises collide: How intimate partner violence and poverty intersect to shape women's mental health and coping? *Trauma Violence Abus.* **2009**, *10*, 306–329. [CrossRef] [PubMed]
3. Klein, L.B.; Chesworth, B.R.; Howland-Myers, J.R.; Rizo, C.F.; Macy, R.J. Housing interventions for intimate partner violence survivors: A systematic review. *Trauma Violence Abus.* **2021**, *22*, 249–264. [CrossRef] [PubMed]
4. Bracewell, K.; Hargreaves, P.; Stanley, N. The consequences of the COVID-19 lockdown on stalking victimisation. *J. Fam. Violence* **2020**, 1–7. [CrossRef]
5. Campbell, A.M. An increasing risk of family violence during the Covid-19 pandemic: Strengthening community collaborations to save lives. *Forensic Sci. Int.* **2020**, *2*, 100089. [CrossRef]
6. Moreira, D.N.; Pinto da Costa, M. The impact of the Covid-19 pandemic in the precipitation of intimate partner violence. *Int. J. Law Psychiatry* **2020**, *71*, 101606. [CrossRef]
7. Ravi, K.E.; Rai, A.; Schrag, R.V. Survivors' experiences of intimate partner violence and shelter utilization during COVID-19. *J. Fam. Violence* **2021**, 1–12. [CrossRef]
8. Smyth, C.; Cullen, P.; Breckenridge, J.; Cortis, N.; Valentine, K. COVID-19 lockdowns, intimate partner violence and coercive control. *Aust. J. Soc. Issues* **2021**, *56*, 359–373. [CrossRef]
9. Wright, E.N.; Miyamoto, S.; Richardson, C. The impact of COVID-19 restrictions on victim advocacy agency utilization across Pennsylvania. *J. Fam. Violence* **2021**, 1–7. [CrossRef]
10. Davis, M.; Gilbar, O.; Padilla-Medina, D. Intimate Partner Violence Victimization and Perpetration among U.S. Adults during COVID-19: A Brief Report. Available online: https://www.medrxiv.org/content/10.1101/2020.06.08.20125914v1 (accessed on 20 February 2022).
11. Slakoff, D.C.; Aujla, W.; PenzeyMoog, E. The role of service providers, technology, and mass media when home isn't safe for intimate partner violence victims: Best practices and recommendations in the era of COVID-19 and beyond. *Arch. Sex. Behav.* **2020**, *49*, 2779–2788. [CrossRef]
12. Wood, L.; Baumler, E.; Schrag, R.V.; Guillot-Wright, S.; Hairston, D.; Temple, J.; Torres, E. "Don't know where to go for help": Safety and economic needs among violence survivors during the COVID-19 pandemic. *J. Fam. Violence* **2021**, 1–9. [CrossRef] [PubMed]
13. Ragavan, M.I.; Risser, L.; Duplessis, V.; DeGue, S.; Villaveces, A.; Hurley, T.P.; Chang, J.; Miller, E.; Randell, K.A. The impact of the COVID-19 pandemic on the needs and lived experiences of intimate partner violence survivors in the United States: Advocate perspectives. *Violence Women* **2021**, 1–21. [CrossRef] [PubMed]
14. Garcia, R.; Henderson, C.; Randell, K.; Villaveces, A.; Katz, A.; Abioye, F.; DeGue, S.; Premo, K.; Miller-Wallfish, S.; Chang, J.C.; et al. The impact of the COVID-19 pandemic on intimate partner violence advocates and agencies. *J. Fam. Violence* **2021**, 1–14. [CrossRef] [PubMed]
15. Baidoo, L.; Zakrison, T.L.; Feldmeth, G.; Lindau, S.T.; Tung, E.L. Domestic violence police reporting and resources during the 2020 COVID-19 stay-at-home order in Chicago, Illinois. *JAMA Netw. Open* **2021**, *4*, e2122260. [CrossRef] [PubMed]
16. Charmaz, K. *Constructing Grounded Theory: A Practical Guide through Qualitative Analysis*; SAGE Publications: Thousand Oaks, CA, USA, 2006.
17. DeJonckheere, M.; Vaughn, L.M. Semistructured interviewing in primary care research: A balance of relationship and rigour. *Fam. Med. Com. Health* **2019**, *7*, e000057. [CrossRef] [PubMed]
18. Braun, V.; Clarke, V. Using thematic analysis in psychology. *Qual. Res. Psychol.* **2006**, *3*, 77–101. [CrossRef]
19. Dworkin, E.R.; Weaver, T.L. The impact of sociocultural contexts on mental health following sexual violence: A conceptual model. *Psychol. Violence* **2021**, *11*, 476–487. [CrossRef]
20. Nnawulezi, N.A.; Sullivan, C.M. Oppression within safe spaces: Exploring racial microaggressions within domestic violence shelters. *J. Black Psychol.* **2014**, *40*, 563–591. [CrossRef]

21. Petrosky, E.; Blair, J.M.; Betz, C.J.; Fowler, K.A.; Jack, S.P.D.; Lyons, B.H. Racial and ethnic differences in homicides of adult women and the role of intimate partner violence—United States, 2003–2014. *Morb. Mortal. Wkly. Rep.* **2017**, *66*, 741–746. [CrossRef]
22. Waller, B.Y.; Harris, J.; Quinn, C.R. Caught in the crossroad: An intersectional examination of African American women intimate partner violence survivors' help seeking. *Trauma Violence Abus.* **2021**, 1–14. [CrossRef]
23. Reisenhofer, S.; Taft, A. Women's journey to safety—The transtheoretical model in clinical practice when working with women experiencing intimate partner violence: A scientific review and clinical guidance. *Patient Educ. Couns.* **2013**, *93*, 536–548. [CrossRef] [PubMed]
24. Monterrosa, A.E. How race and gender stereotypes influence help-seeking for intimate partner violence. *J. Interpers. Violence* **2021**, *36*, NP9153–NP9174. [CrossRef] [PubMed]
25. Wallin, M.A.; Holliday, C.N.; Zeoli, A.M. The association of federal and state-level firearm restriction policies with intimate partner homicide: A re-analysis by race of the victim. *J. Interpers. Violence* **2021**, 1–25. [CrossRef] [PubMed]
26. Seville, E. Building Resilience: How to have a positive impact at the organizational and individual employee level. *DLO* **2018**, *32*, 15–18. [CrossRef]

International Journal of
Environmental Research and Public Health

MDPI

Article

Effects of the Response to the COVID-19 Pandemic on Assault-Related Head Injury in Melbourne: A Retrospective Study

Juan F Domínguez D [1], Johnny Truong [1], Jake Burnett [1], Lata Satyen [2], Hamed Akhlaghi [1,3], Julian Stella [4], Nick Rushworth [5] and Karen Caeyenberghs [1,*]

1 Cognitive Neuroscience Unit, School of Psychology, Deakin University, Geelong, VIC 3220, Australia
2 School of Psychology, Deakin University, Burwood, VIC 3125, Australia
3 Department of Emergency Medicine, St. Vincent's Hospital, Melbourne, VIC 3065, Australia
4 Department of Emergency Medicine, Geelong Hospital, Geelong, VIC 3220, Australia
5 Brain Injury Australia, Sydney, NSW 2112, Australia
* Correspondence: k.caeyenberghs@deakin.edu.au; Tel.: +61-3-924-68301

Abstract: Assault is the leading preventable cause of death, traumatic brain injury (TBI), and associated mental health problems. The COVID-19 pandemic has had a profound impact on patterns of interpersonal violence across the world. In this retrospective cross-sectional study, we analysed medical records of 1232 assault victims (domestic violence: 111, random assault: 900, prison assault: 221) with head injuries who presented to the emergency department (ED) at St Vincent's Hospital in Melbourne, Australia, a city with one of the longest and most severe COVID-19 restrictions worldwide. We examined changes in prevalence in the assault group overall and in domestic violence, random assault, and prison assault victims, comparing data from 19.5 months before and after the first day of COVID-19 restrictions in Melbourne. Moreover, we investigated differences driven by demographic factors (**Who**: age group, sex, and nationality) and clinical variables (**Where**: assault location, and **When**: time of arrival to the ED and time from moment of injury until presentation at ED). Descriptive statistics and chi-square analyses were performed. We found the COVID-19 pandemic significantly affected the **Where** of assault-related TBI, with a shift in the location of assaults from the street to the home, and the increase at home being driven by random assaults on middle-aged adults. Overall, we observed that 86% of the random assault cases were males, whereas 74% of the domestic assault cases were females. Meanwhile, nearly half (44%) of the random assault victims reported alcohol consumption versus a fifth (20%) of domestic violence victims. These findings will have direct implications for developing screening tools and better preventive and ameliorative interventions to manage the sequelae of assault TBI, particularly in the context of future large-scale health crises or emergencies.

Keywords: head injury; COVID pandemic; traumatic brain injury; domestic violence; random assault; physical assault

check for updates

Citation: Domínguez D, J.F.; Truong, J.; Burnett, J.; Satyen, L.; Akhlaghi, H.; Stella, J.; Rushworth, N.; Caeyenberghs, K. Effects of the Response to the COVID-19 Pandemic on Assault-Related Head Injury in Melbourne: A Retrospective Study. *Int. J. Environ. Res. Public Health* **2023**, *20*, 63. https://doi.org/10.3390/ijerph20010063

Academic Editors: Krim K. Lacey and Rohan D. Jeremiah

Received: 15 September 2022
Revised: 13 December 2022
Accepted: 14 December 2022
Published: 21 December 2022

1. Introduction

Physical assault, by which we mean any intentional and unlawful physical force applied by a person to the body of another person [1], is a leading preventable cause of death, traumatic brain injury (TBI), and associated mental health problems, particularly amongst women and vulnerable populations. The COVID-19 pandemic and associated restrictions have had a profound impact on patterns of interpersonal violence across the world [2], be it domestic violence (DV), which in this paper includes family violence (FV), gender-based violence, violence against women and intimate partner violence (IPV), or violence from strangers or nonfamily acquaintances (which we refer here as random violence, (RV)). Therefore, there is an urgent need to understand the effect of the pandemic on assault-related TBI.

Two and a half years from the start of the pandemic, the picture that emerges of the effect of COVID-19 on DV is a complex one, particularly when focusing on physical assault. Regarding DV, owing to the potential confinement and increasing isolation of victims with violent partners brought about by the restrictive measures adopted to manage the pandemic, the United Nations (UN), barely two weeks after the World Health Organization declared COVID-19 a pandemic, issued a statement warning that this form of violence could escalate. The statement urged governments around the world to renew their efforts to minimise the increasing risks of violence [3]. In April 2020, Phumzile Mlambo-Ngcuke, Executive Director of UN Women, referred to violence against women as the 'shadow pandemic' [4], citing reports of increasing DV from helplines and shelters from various countries. Consistent with this, systematic reviews have reported an increase in DV in several jurisdictions across the world since the start of the pandemic [5–8].

There is still, however, substantial variability in the findings reported by these reviews. For example, Piquero and colleagues (2021) found an increase in DV in 29 out of 37 instances reported, with the remaining eight exhibiting a decrease [6]. Both Bazyar et al. (2021) and Lausi et al. (2021) reported an increase in IPV [5,7]. In the case of Lausi et al. (2021), however, the increase was observed when including both physical and nonphysical instances of violence (e.g., sexual, economic, psychological) [7]. Considering physical IPV on its own, while the severity was reported by victims to increase, the number of physical assaults decreased. Moreover, results from a more recent review were inconclusive regarding the prevalence of physical DV during COVID-19, with studies reporting both increases and decreases. This review paper also showed a change in severity of psychological/emotional and sexual DV during the COVID-19 pandemic [9].

A closer look at the literature suggests that when considering all reported cases of DV, there were only slightly more instances where DV increased versus decreased following the introduction of COVID-19 restrictions. Moreover, when focusing on cases of DV more likely involving physical assault (i.e., from worldwide studies using police crime data, rather than calls to hotlines), the number of reported instances where DV decreased or stayed the same outnumbered the instances where DV increased [10–31]. This finding, however, could be due to victim-survivors' reduced ability to report an incident of DV and access services during the pandemic [32]. This is consistent with previous findings showing that law enforcement is frequently the last resort for DV victims who often choose community-based services such as emergency hotlines before reaching out to law enforcement [33]. Moreover, the mixed findings in prevalence estimates for DV can also be attributed to the differences in data collection.

Regarding RV, COVID-19 restrictions led to no change or a reduction in reported incidents [10,11,13,15,16,19,24,25,29]. In studies that did not distinguish between DV and RV, most cases exhibited a decrease in assaults, followed by no change [14,28]. This pattern was the same including or excluding hotline or survey data.

The above findings show substantial heterogeneity in the effect the COVID-19 pandemic had on interpersonal violence, particularly DV. In addition to demographic and socioeconomic factors, there is considerable variability across jurisdictions in the timing, severity, and geographic coverage of policies that countries have implemented to manage the pandemic, including policies pertaining to containment and closure strategies, economic responses, health system programs, and vaccine roll-out [34,35]. Government responses to COVID-19 ranged, for example, from keeping society mostly open, as in the case of Sweden, to a 'zero community transmission' approach adopted in countries such as Australia, New Zealand or Vietnam, prior to achieving vaccination targets.

Australia is a particularly interesting case, as it offers the opportunity to evaluate the effect of one the longest and most stringent regimes of COVID-19 restrictions in the world (see Table 1), on interpersonal violence and more specifically, assault. Figure 1, for example, shows how mobility was largely restricted to the home, grocery stores, and pharmacies, and substantially reduced to workplaces, retail, and recreation venues, parks, and transit stations starting in March 2020, and mandatory COVID-19 isolation periods ended in Australia on 14 October.

Table 1. Dates and duration of COVID-19 restrictions and lockdowns in Melbourne, Australia.

Event		Dates	No. of Days
Restrictions	Start	16 March 2020	-
Lockdown	1	30 March to 12 May 2020	43
Lockdown	2	8 July to 27 October 2020	111
Lockdown	3	12 February to 17, 2021	5
Lockdown	4	27 May to 10 June 2021	14
Lockdown	5	15 July to 27 July 2021	12
Lockdown	6	5 August to 21 October 2021	77
Restrictions	End	19 November 2021	-
Total–lockdowns	**6** [1]	**-**	**262** [2]
Total–restrictions	**-**	**-**	**613** [3]

[1] Total No of lockdowns, [2] Total No of lockdown days, [3] Total No of restrictions days.

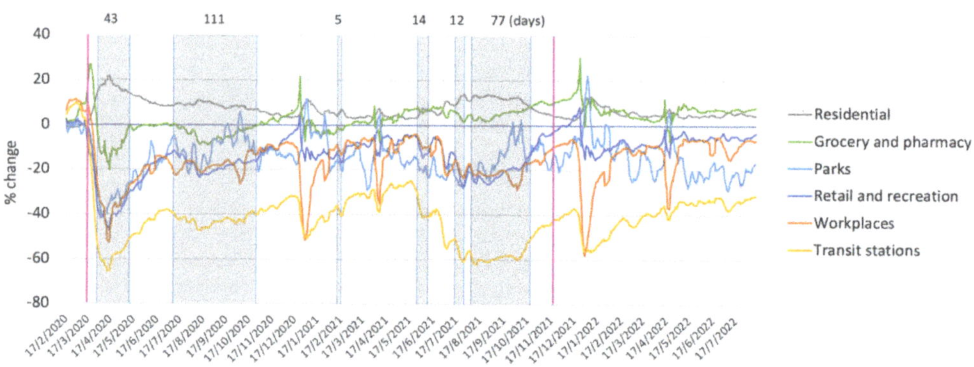

Figure 1. Changes in community movement in specific locations in Australia relative to the period before the COVID-19 pandemic. The 'Residential' category shows percent change in duration of time spent at home; the other categories measure a change in total visitors (compared to baseline days: the median value for the 5-week period from 3 January to 6 February 2020). First (16 March 2020) and last (19 November 2021) days of restrictions are indicated by magenta reference lines. Shaded areas represent Melbourne lockdowns. The duration of each lockdown (in days) is indicated above each lockdown period (Note: Mandatory COVID-19 isolation periods ended in Australia on 14 October 2022). Source: Google COVID-19 Community Mobility Trends–last updated 16 August 2022 (https://www.google.com/covid19/mobility/ accessed on 18 August 2022).

Initial evidence suggests that the pandemic restrictions in Australia have had an effect on interpersonal violence. Despite 2020 being referred to by the media as 'the worst year for domestic violence', and support services reportedly struggling to meet demand [36], the Australian case is, similarly to the rest of the world, more complex. In the state of Victoria, studies have variously reported an increase in violence against women (via survey of help professionals), family common assaults and FV incidents (police crime data), and assault-related injuries at home (emergency department (ED) records) in both male and female victims [13,31,37]. However, a decrease in Victoria was reported for serious domestic assaults related to FV [13] and in family-related assaults (overall, without distinguishing severity) [25]. Moslehi and colleagues found that the decrease in family-related assaults was almost half of the decrease in other assaults [25]. Moreover, their analysis revealed that this was only true for local government areas in Victoria below the median income, further illustrating the role of place-related variability in the effect of pandemic restrictions [25].

However, again, the decrease may not present a true picture of the extent of domestic violence experienced, due to under-reporting or differences in data sources.

National statistics show that situational stressors during the pandemic possibly exacerbated the main drivers of violence and increased the rates, complexity, and severity of violence [38], while other reports show, in contrast, a decrease in domestic assaults in New South Wales (police crime data), and no change in breaches of DV orders (official offence rates) in Queensland [13,25,29]. Many women also experienced violence for the first time during COVID-19 [38]. Those who had previously experienced violence reported increased rates of physical and sexual abuse and emotionally abusive, harassing, or controlling behaviours during COVID-19; several women also reported that they were unable to seek assistance from services during this period [38]. Regarding RV, all available Australian studies reported a decrease in assault overall, but also in common and serious assault [13,25,29].

As noted at the outset, there is an urgent need to investigate the effects of COVID-19 restrictions on physical assault, particularly when it is most serious and may result in traumatic brain injury. While TBI ranges in severity (80% of TBI patients are mild [39]), it can result in various long-term physical, cognitive and emotional sequelae [40–42]. Moreover, the pathophysiology of assault TBI is likely unique compared to other TBI causes due to the coupling of the physical and psychological trauma of intentional violence. However, studies investigating the impact of the COVID-19 crisis on assault-related TBI are sorely missing. Data from presentations to EDs can provide unique insight into this problem as they comprise information regarding location and type of injury.

Another gap in the literature is the effect of COVID-19 restrictions on physical assaults in places with the most severe and longest restrictions. Most of the studies focus on the months of March to June 2020. The city of Melbourne, Australia, offers an ideal case to assess the sustained effect of the COVID-19 pandemic restrictions on assault-related TBI: Melbourne was the place with the second longest lockdown in the world by the end of 2021 (263 days across six separate lockdowns [43]), in addition to other restrictions and stay at home orders spanning from 16 March 2020 to 21 October 2021.

This study investigated changes to the **Who, Where,** and **When** of assault-related TBI brought about by COVID-19 in Melbourne using ED presentation data from St Vincent's Hospital, an inner-city hospital in Melbourne. Regarding **Who**, the paper studied changes in prevalence and demographics in the assault-related TBI population, comparing data from 19.5 months before and 19.5 months after 16 March 2020 (the first day of restrictions in Melbourne). We examined changes in the assault TBI group overall, but also in subgroups of assault victims (DV victims and RV assault victims), and vulnerable populations (prison population and Aboriginal and Torres Strait Islanders). We also investigated differences driven by demographic factors including age group, sex, and nationality. The study also tracks changes in the assault location, **Where**, and the timing of victims presenting to ED, **When**. Finally, we report on the data without partitioning into pre-COVID and COVID periods, to provide an overall picture of interpersonal violence across the whole period.

2. Methods

2.1. Study Design

This study utilised a retrospective cross-sectional design of all patients with assault-related head injury (as an indicator of likely TBI) who were admitted to the Emergency Department (ED) of St Vincent's Hospital in Melbourne (SVHM). SVHM is a comprehensive adult health service for people aged 18 years and older who live in the inner urban east area of Melbourne. SVHM catchment includes vulnerable populations (such as Aboriginal and Torres Strait Islanders and prisoners), which are generally more disadvantaged and have higher health care needs than the wider Australian population. There is currently limited data available to understand the extent to which COVID-19 has impacted prisoners' health in particular. We therefore decided to include this vulnerable group in the present study. Of note, there were no changes in policy by the ED regarding accepting patients relative to their injury severity given the challenges associated with the pandemic and the health care system's response to the pandemic. The patients were identified from the electronic medical record system of SVHM (H.A.). Their data were extracted from this medical record system and nonidentifiable data collected in an independent database for further analyses. Ethics approval for the study was obtained from St Vincent's Hospital Human Research Ethics Committee (Project ID: 66135, LRR 167/20).

2.2. Study Population

Figure 2 depicts an overview of the inclusion/exclusion criteria to select patients for our study sample. Any patient admitted from the ED who met the following criteria was included in the present study: (i) aged 18 or older; (ii) ED discharge date between 30 July of 2018 and 30 October of 2021; and (iii) presenting with 'head injury' using the injury descriptor, or ED diagnosis using International Classification of Disease Tenth Revision (ICD-10) codes (namely S00–S09.2 and S09.7–S09.9). Patients were excluded if: (i) the head injury occurred outside Victoria (e.g., transferred to SVHM from other states); or (ii) the head injury was a result of police intervention or self-harm. Some patients had multiple ED presentations resulting from the same assault event. In this case, we only retained the first presentation and discarded subsequent presentations. In the case of subsequent admissions for new injuries of different assault events, we included these cases in our study population.

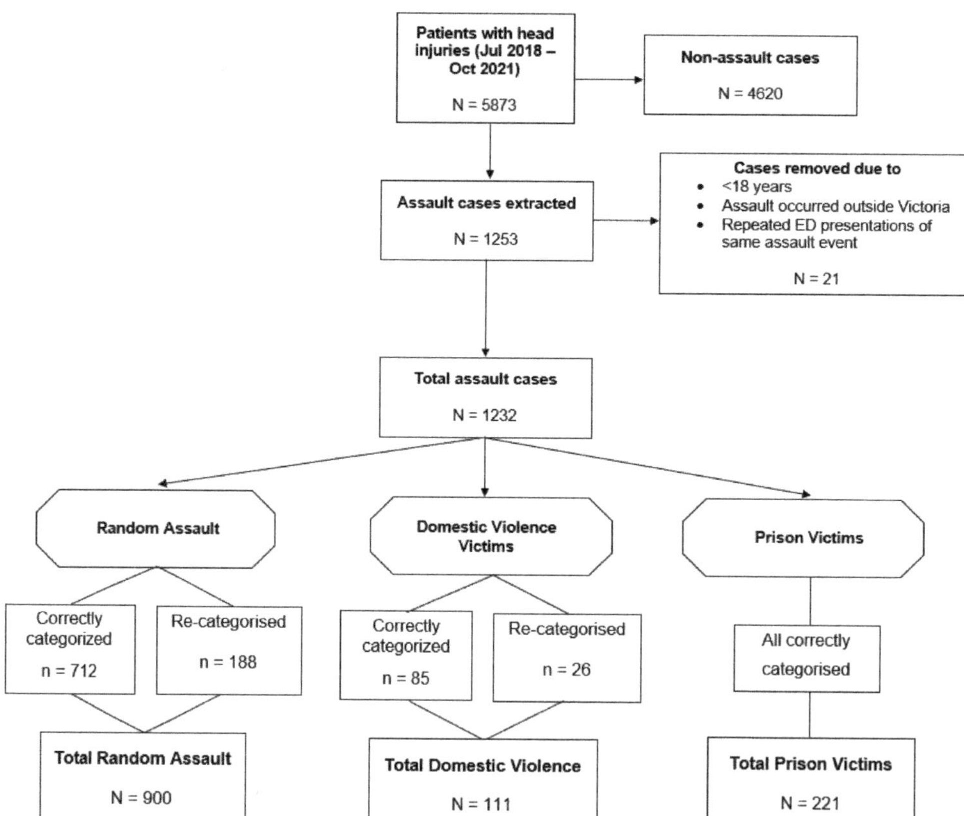

Figure 2. Flowchart of study sample selection along with inclusion and exclusion criteria.

In the present study, we categorised the assault patients with head injury into three subgroups: (i) RV assault (defined as assault by a stranger or an acquaintance that is not a family member or prison mate), (ii) DV assault (involving the assault by a partner, ex-partner, or family member), and (iii) prison population (PP) assault. We utilized three descriptors in the database to distinguish the three assault subgroups and avoid ambiguity. Specifically, we used (i) the human intent descriptor, which described whether the aggressor was an intimate partner; (ii) the description of the injury event, which provided a short description of the assault; and (iii) the presenting complaint comments, which encompassed accompanying narratives from patients written by the triage nurses. Importantly, several assault cases were incorrectly categorised as unintentional head injury (see Figure 2). These cases were included in the analysis if the corresponding ED presenting complaint comments provided unambiguous mention of assault (~1.5% of cases were therefore excluded for this reason). ED presenting complaint comments were thoroughly checked in every single case in the dataset. Data cleaning and quality control (including correction of miscategorised cases) was performed by J.T. under the close supervision of clinician H.A. and in consultation with K.C. and J.F.D.D.

As can be seen in Figure 2, 5873 patients were presented with a head injury (using the ICD-10 diagnosis codes) at the ED of SVHM during the 39-month data collection period. Of these head injury patients, 1232 were due to assault, with 900 RV assault cases, 111 DV assault cases (9%), and 221 cases (18%) occurring in PP. Within RV and DV assault subgroups, approximately 20% of included cases had incorrect human intent descriptors and needed to be corrected and recategorised.

To investigate changes to the **Who, Where,** and **When** of assault-related TBI brought about by COVID-19, we subsequently extracted demographic variables from the selected sample. Concerning the 'Who', we obtained the following demographic data: (i) sex; (ii) age group, which here we define as younger adults (18–39), middle-aged adults (40–59), and older adults (60+) (in close agreement with the literature [44–46]); (iii) nationality, categorised as Australian, Aboriginal, and Torres Strait Islander Peoples, non-Australian, or unknown; and (iv) alcohol consumption (self-reported). Regarding 'When' and 'Where', we collected time of arrival to the ED (grouped into four time windows, i.e., morning (6:00 a.m.–12:00 p.m.), afternoon (12:00 p.m.–6:00 p.m.), evening (6:00 p.m.–12:00 a.m.) and night (12:00 a.m.–6:00 a.m.), whether patients were admitted to the ED within 24 h of injury and the location where the head injury was sustained (home, road/street, place for recreation, workplace and other public areas, prison, unspecified).

2.3. Data Analysis

Descriptive statistics were calculated for all the demographic and injury-related variables. Specifically, frequency tables were computed for age group, sex, nationality, alcohol consumption, and time of injury. These frequencies were stratified by assault subgroups (i.e., RV, DV, and PP assault victims). Chi-squared analyses were conducted to examine changes in the frequency of assault cases before and during the COVID-19 pandemic. Differences in variables between these time periods and across assault subgroups were also explored with chi-square tests. Specifically, we categorised the data from 19.5 months before and 19.5 months after 16 March 2020. An additional chi-squared analysis was performed explicitly and specifically investigating if lockdowns (as different from all COVID-19 restrictions), differentially affected the proportion of assault across assault groups. Cases during the lockdowns were compared to cases during the equivalent periods before the pandemic, in 2019. We focused our analysis on lockdowns 1 and 6 as these represent lockdown periods at the beginning and end of COVID-19 restrictions and as they lasted for a substantial amount of time. Specifically, lockdowns 1 and 6 lasted 43 and 77 days respectively, as opposed to lockdowns 3, 4, and 5, which lasted between 5 and 14 days. We drew cases in 2019 from 30 March to 12 May (as the equivalent period for lockdown 1), and 5 August to 21 October (as the equivalent for lockdown 6). Statistical analyses were conducted using JASP Version 0.16.3 (JASP Team, 2022).

3. Results

3.1. Effect of the COVID-19 Pandemic

3.1.1. Who Were Victims of Assaults with Head Injuries in Melbourne during the COVID Pandemic?

A total of 689 cases of assault resulting in head injury were recorded in the pre-COVID period, compared to 543 cases during the COVID pandemic (see Figure 3 for an overview). This represents a 21.2% decrease in these cases. Overall, the COVID pandemic did not significantly affect proportions of cases by assault subgroup, sex, age, or nationality (for all variables, $p > 0.05$). When restricting analysis to lockdown periods 1 and 6, we also did not find any differences in proportions of cases by assault subgroup compared to the corresponding period in 2019, prior to the pandemic ($p > 0.10$). However, we observed a significantly lower number of middle-aged PP assault victims (aged between 40–59 years) during the COVID period compared to the pre-COVID period [χ^2 (1) = 9.10, $p < 0.01$; Figure 4] (there were not enough individuals aged 60 or older for this test). Frequencies of demographic variables by COVID period and stratified by assault subgroup are presented in Table 2.

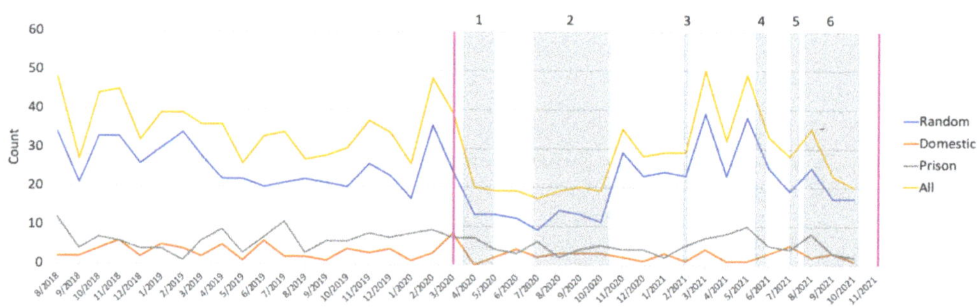

Figure 3. Time series showing the monthly number of assault cases for every assault group and in total. Onset and end of restrictions are indicated by magenta reference lines. Numbered shaded areas represent the Melbourne lockdowns.

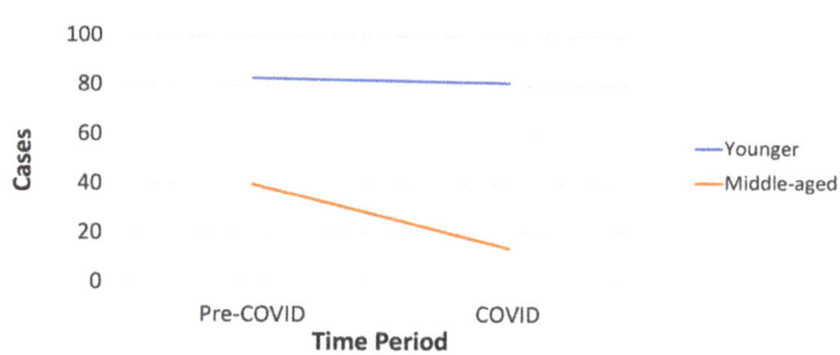

Figure 4. Change in assault-related TBI cases by age group for prison victims between pre-COVID and COVID periods.

3.1.2. Where Were Victims of Assaults with Head Injuries during the COVID Pandemic?

We found that the location of injury significantly differed between the pre-COVID and COVID periods [χ^2 (3) = 23.78, $p < 0.001$, Cramer's V = 0.17]. Examination of the adjusted residuals (FWE corrected) revealed that home (3.82, $p < 0.001$) and road/street/highway (−3.14, $p < 0.01$) contributed significantly to this result, with home exhibiting an increase in assault-related TBI victims during the COVID period, compared to the pre-COVID period, and the inverse occurring for assault cases occurring on the streets (Figure 5A). No pandemic effect was found between assault subgroups (random and domestic victims) at home or on the streets [χ^2 (1) = 0.22, $p > 0.05$]. This 2 × 2 × 2 cross tabulation analysis had one cell with an expected frequency less than 5. For these two locations, post hoc analyses of sex and age across assault subgroup and time period revealed only an effect on middle-aged adults at home [χ^2 (1) = 5.58, $p < 0.05$, Cramer's V = 0.31], with increased random assault cases and decreased domestic violence victims observed during COVID-19 (Figure 5B). Frequencies of the locations of assault injuries by COVID period and stratified by assault subgroup are presented in Table 3.

Table 2. Demographic characteristics between COVID periods across all assault subgroups.

Demographic Variables	Pre-COVID (n = 689) n (%)			COVID Period (n = 543) n (%)		
	Random	Domestic	Prison	Random	Domestic	Prison
All	502 (72.9)	62 (9.0)	125 (18.1)	398 (73.3)	49 (9.0)	96 (17.7)
Sex						
Male	432 (86.1)	16 (25.8)	120 (96)	344 (86.4)	13 (26.5)	91 (94.8)
Female	70 (13.9)	46 (74.2)	5 (4)	54 (13.6)	36 (73.5)	5 (5.2)
Age Group						
18–39	336 (66.9)	38 (61.3)	83 (66.4)	269 (67.6)	35 (71.4)	81 (84.4)
40–59	143 (28.5)	19 (30.6)	40 (32)	118 (29.6)	11 (22.5)	14 (14.6)
60+ [a]	23 (4.6)	5 (8.1)	2 (1.6)	11 (2.8)	3 (6.1)	1 (1)
Nationality						
Australian	301 (60.0)	38 (61.3)	87 (69.6)	234 (58.8)	32 (65.3)	60 (62.5)
Indigenous [b]	25 (8.3)	4 (10.5)	6 (6.9)	30 (12.8)	3 (9.4)	8 (13.3)
Non-Australians	194 (38.6)	24 (38.7)	14 (11.2)	154 (38.7)	16 (32.7)	17 (17.7)
Unknown [c]	7 (1.4)	0 (0)	24 (19.2)	10 (2.5)	1 (2)	19 (19.8)
Alcohol Consumption [d]						
No	147 (55.3)	29 (82.9)	81 (100)	119 (60.1)	22 (75.9)	49 (100)
Yes	95 (35.7)	3 (8.6)	N/A	66 (33.3)	3 (10.3)	N/A
Unknown [c]	24 (9)	3 (8.6)	0 (0)	13 (6.6)	4 (13.8)	0 (0)

[a] Removed in chi-square analysis due to low cell count. [b] Aboriginal and Torres Strait Islanders. Percentages are based on Australian group rather than assault subgroup totals. [c] 'Unknown' subgroup removed from chi-square analyses. [d] Data restricted to one year of pre-COVID (n = 382) as data collection halted one year into the COVID period (n = 276; total n = 658).

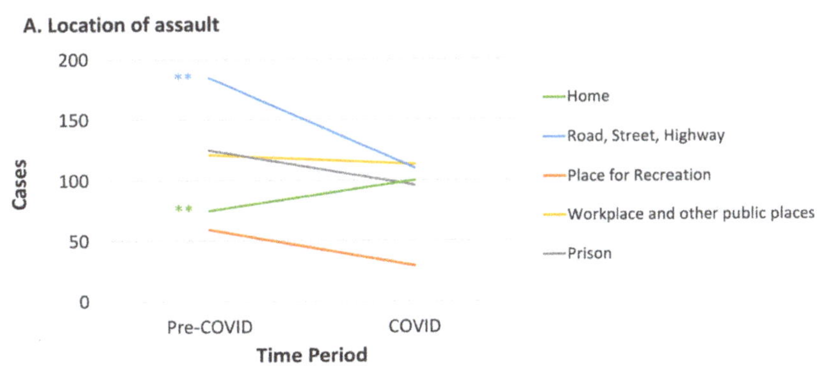

Figure 5. *Cont.*

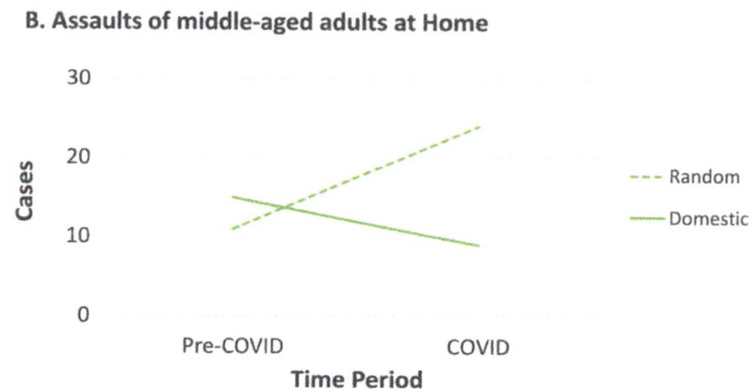

Figure 5. Change in assault-related TBI cases by location of injury between the pre-COVID and COVID periods: (**A**) across all locations of injury (** significant adjusted residuals at $p < 0.05$, FWE corrected); (**B**) across random and domestic assault groups at home in middle-aged (40–59 years old) adults.

Table 3. Assault-related TBI cases by location of injury during the pre-COVID and COVID periods.

Location of Injury	Pre-COVID	COVID Period
Home	75 (10.9)	100 (18.4)
Road/Street/Highway	185 (26.8)	110 (20.2)
Place for Recreation	59 (8.5)	29 (5.3)
Workplace and other public places	121 (17.5)	113 (20.8)
Prison	125 (18.1)	96 (17.6)
Unknown [a]	126 (18.2)	96 (17.6)

[a] 'Unknown' subgroup removed from chi-square analyses.

3.1.3. When Did Victims of Assault-Related TBI Present at the ED during the COVID Pandemic?

The time of day in which assault patients arrive to the ED was unaffected by the COVID pandemic across all assault subgroups ($p > 0.05$). There was also no pandemic effect on whether assault patients arrived at the ED within 24 h ($p > 0.05$). None of the assault subgroups revealed any significant differences in COVID period for these time variables either ($p > 0.05$). Frequencies of time variables by COVID period and stratified by assault subgroup are displayed in Table 4.

Table 4. Time variables between COVID periods across all assault subgroups.

Time Variables	Pre-COVID n (%)			COVID Period n (%)		
	Random	Domestic	Prison	Random	Domestic	Prison
ED Presentation Time						
Morning (6:00–12:00)	83 (16.5)	12 (19.3)	9 (7.2)	68 (17.1)	8 (16.3)	9 (9.4)
Afternoon (12:00–18:00)	124 (24.7)	17 (27.4)	51 (40.8)	103 (25.9)	12 (24.5)	36 (37.5)
Evening (18:00–24:00)	132 (26.3)	19 (30.6)	59 (47.2)	117 (29.4)	17 (34.7)	48 (50)
Night (0:00–6:00)	163 (32.5)	14 (22.6)	6 (4.8)	110 (27.6)	12 (24.5)	3 (3.1)
TOI Reporting > 24 h						
No	236 (47)	25 (40.3)	78 (62.4)	197 (49.5)	23 (46.9)	58 (60.4)
Yes	45 (9)	5 (8.1)	10 (8)	35 (8.8)	7 (14.3)	2 (2.1)
Unknown [a]	221 (44)	32 (51.6)	37 (29.6)	166 (41.7)	19 (38.8)	36 (37.5)

[a] 'Unknown' subgroup removed from chi-square analyses. ED, emergency department; TOI, time of injury.

3.2. Overall Results Independent of COVID-19

As the pandemic effect on assault-TBI was limited to a prison age subgroup and location, we report results after collapsing across both pre-COVID and COVID periods, from 30 July 2018 to 30 October 2021.

3.2.1. Who Were Victims of Assaults with Head Injuries?

Of the 1232 patients with a head injury resulting from an assault, 900 (73.1%) were due to RV assault, 111 (9%) due to DV assault, and 221 (17.9%) were PP victims (see Figure 6 and Supplementary Table S1). Assault victims were predominantly male (n = 1016, 82%), aged between 18–39 years old (n = 842, 68%), and of Australian nationality (n = 743, 60% excluding unknown cases; see below and Supplementary Table S1). Six percent (n = 76) of Australian assault victims were of Indigenous background. A third of the victims reported having consumed alcohol at the time of injury (n = 325, 33% excluding unknown cases).

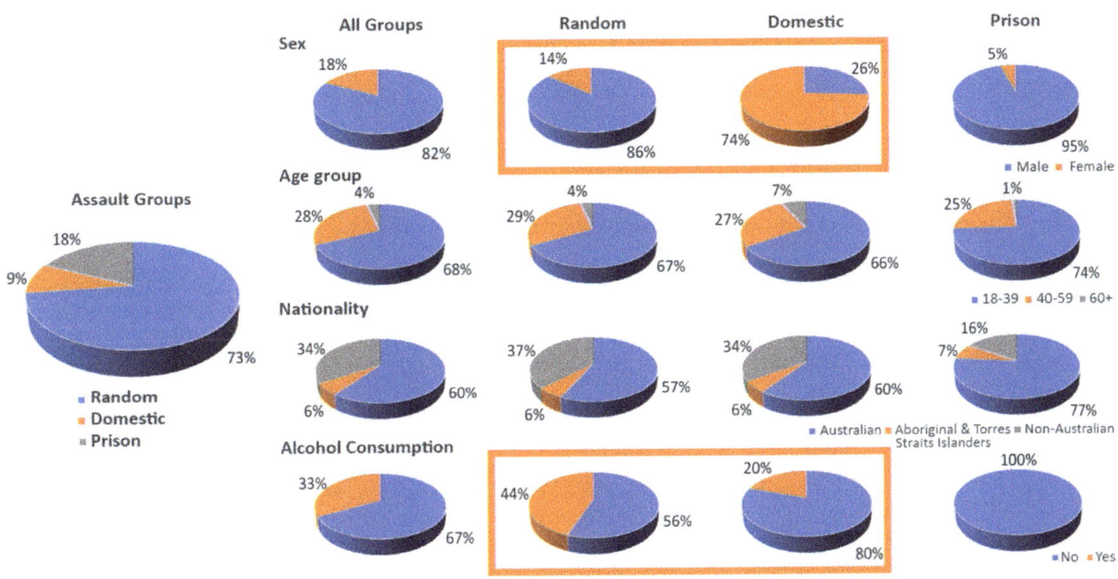

Figure 6. Who was a victim of assault-related TBI in Melbourne, Australia, between 30 July 2018 and 30 October 2021? Left, overall proportion per assault group. Right, breakdown of assault-related TBI by sex, age group, nationality, and alcohol consumption (rows) and assault group (columns). Highlighted in orange squares are noticeably contrasting differences in the proportion of cases between RV and DV assault in terms of sex and alcohol consumption. percentages in nationality and alcohol consumption exclude 'Unknown' cases (see Supplementary Table S1).

There was a clear contrast in the sex of the victim between RV and DV assaults: 86% of the RV assault cases were males, whereas 74% of the DV assault cases were females. Most victims across all groups were young adults (68% overall). In the general population, approximately 60% of victims were Australian and 6% were Aboriginal or Torres Strait Islanders. In the prison population, 74% of the victims were Australian and 7% Aboriginal or Torres Strait Islanders. Another interesting difference between RV and DV assaults related to alcohol consumption, with nearly half (44%) of the RV assault victims reporting alcohol consumption versus a fifth (20%) of DV assault victims.

A total of 19.1% (235) of all cases did not have information regarding alcohol consumption and 5% of all cases (61) did not register their nationality.

3.2.2. Where Were Victims of Assaults with Head Injuries?

Excluding PP victims, the majority of victims were assaulted in the street (38%), followed by the workplace or other public areas (29%), home (22%), and places of recreation (11%) (Figure 7 and Supplementary Table S2). RV assaults followed a similar pattern: the street (41%), followed by the workplace/public areas (33%), then by home and places of recreation (both at 13%). In contrast, DV assaults took place, as expected, overwhelmingly at home (87%), followed by the street (9%) and the workplace/public places (4%), and none taking place in a place of recreation. In addition, the location of 18% (n = 222) of all assaults was unknown (see Supplementary Table S2).

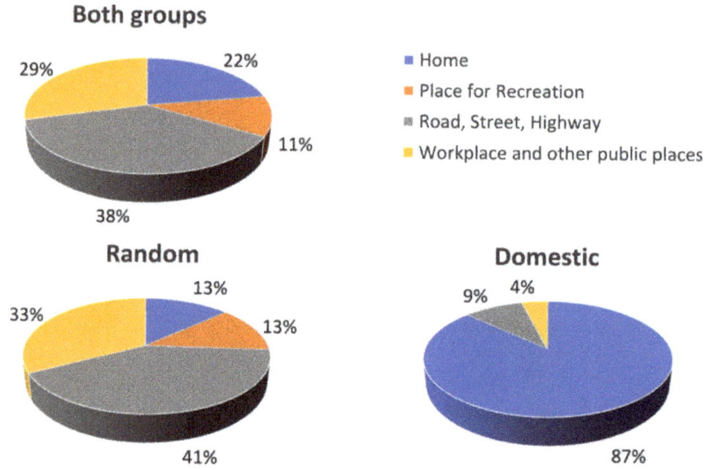

Figure 7. Where were victims of assault-related TBI in Melbourne, Australia, attacked between 30 July 2018 and 30 October 2021 (excludes PP victims)?

3.2.3. When Did Victims of Assault-Related TBI Present at the ED?

The number of victims of assault increased across the morning (6:00–12:00), afternoon (12:00–18:00), and evening (18:00–24:00) periods in all assault subgroups, and it further increased at night (0:00–6:00) for RV assaults, when it peaked (Figure 8 and Supplementary Table S3). In contrast, the number of DV and PP assaults decreased during the night period.

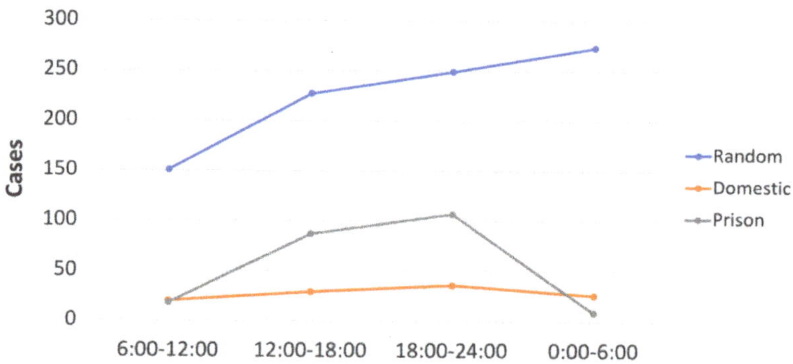

Figure 8. When did victims of assault-related TBI in Melbourne, Australia, present at the ED between 30 July 2018 and 30 October 2021? Shown in the plot are number of cases across morning (6:00–12:00), afternoon (12:00–18:00), evening (18:00–24:00), and night (0:00–6:00) periods for the random, domestic, and prison assault subgroups.

In addition, 85.6% (n = 617) of assault patients reported arriving at the ED within 24 h of the assault and 14.4% (n = 104) reported arriving 24 h after the assault. Time of injury information was unknown for 511 individuals (41% of all cases; see Supplementary Table S3).

4. Discussion

4.1. Effect of the COVID-19 Pandemic

In this paper, we investigated changes in the **Who**, **When,** and **Where** of assault-related TBI brought about by the COVID-19 restrictions in an inner-city hospital in Melbourne, Australia. Overall, we observed a 21% decrease in the number of assault-related TBI. This is in line with Australian [13,25,29] and international trends showing a reduction (and no change is some instances) in rates of assault, overall and regarding random assault [10,11,13–16,19,24,25,28,29]. Our finding of a decrease in domestic assault, on the other hand, adds to the heterogeneity in this category, which is divided between reports of increases and decreases in cases (as can be seen in Supplementary Table S4), with slightly more increases [10–31,38]. For example, Moslehi and colleagues (2021) utilized police data and revealed a decline in domestic assault victims during the lockdown in New South Wales and Victoria [25]. In contrast, an analysis of Victorian health practitioners' responses to a survey revealed that the COVID pandemic has led to an increase in the frequency and severity of violence against women [37]. These mixed findings in the literature may reflect the different methods used to collect the data (e.g., ED admissions, reports of calls to DV shelters, police calls, surveys of health practitioners, crime data). This decrease in assault-related TBI cases is also in accordance with ample studies showing significant declines in ED attendance during the pandemic (in keeping with stay-at-home orders), but also influenced by fear of acquiring COVID-19 or avoiding hospitals [47,48]. The true number during the COVID pandemic is therefore likely underestimated as assault victims might not have sought help [38] or received medical care (including hospital attendance) for their head injury. This can result in assault survivors living with an undiagnosed head injury, which can have devastating long-term health consequences if untreated [49]. This issue has been raised by other studies examining ED presentations during COVID-19 [31]. Besides misclassifications or under-reporting of DV, the random assault-related TBI cases at home could be potential intrafamilial violence. Indeed, in Victoria, 1138 incidents of adolescent family violence were recorded in 2018–19 [50,51], with young aggressor violence increasing by 11.8% over the past five years [50]. We also know that there is under-reporting of this violence due to victims who are family members (mostly women) and feeling protective of the young person and not implicating them in the assault or seeking further help for it [52].

We found no effect of the COVID-19 restrictions on the **Who** and **When** of assault-related TBI. There was therefore no difference in the effect of COVID-19 restrictions between RV, DV, and PP assault groups, or between males and females, or according to age group, nationality, or alcohol consumption. However, we found the COVID-19 pandemic significantly affected the **Where** of assault-related TBI. Specifically, we observed a shift in the location of assaults from the street to the home. The significant increase in intentional head injuries sustained at home during the COVID-pandemic can be explained by theories of aggression [53] in psychology, or strain [54] in criminology. According to the general aggression model (GAM) [53], for example, there are multiple causal proximal factors (including high levels of frustration and stress) and distal factors (such as difficult life conditions) that may result in an increase in assaults in the home environment.

Pandemics requiring quarantining have been shown to bring about a wide range of stressors (e.g., social isolation, diminished physical and daily activity and routines, fears of infection, financial insecurity, job loss, inadequate supplies and information, reduced access to health services) resulting in negative psychological effects (e.g., depression, stress, post-traumatic stress disorder, anger, sleep disorders, and problematic substance use) [55], present also during the COVID-19 pandemic [56]. Together, these stressors and associated psychological effects may amplify the risk of violence [57–59]. In Australia, unemployment rose from 5.2% in March to 6.8% in August 2020 [60]. Additionally, the levels of stress and depression were shown to increase by 25% among Australians in the same year after the onset of the pandemic [61]. The shift of assault to the home during COVID-19 is consistent with previous work revealing that more assault injuries requiring hospital treatment occurred at home during 2020 compared to 2019 in both regional and metropolitan Victoria [31]. Additionally, in line with VISU's findings (VISU, 2020; editions 1–9) of an increase in intentional injuries at home irrespective of sex, we found no difference in the effect of COVID-19 restrictions on assault-related TBI between males and females. Our observed decreases in assault-related TBI cases sustained on the street are in line with findings suggesting fewer injuries were sustained in public spaces during the COVID pandemic [62]. This is also in accordance with opportunity theory and routine activity theory, which predict a fall in levels of crime occurring in public spaces (including assault) due to disruption in daily patterns of mobility of potential victims, guardians, and perpetrators [24,28].

Interestingly, the increase in assault-related TBI cases at home was driven by RV assaults (i.e., physical attack by a stranger or an acquaintance that is not a family member) on middle-aged adults (40–59 years old). While these assaults were classified as random (as opposed to domestic violence or prison assault), this categorisation was based on the testimony provided by patients as recorded by triage nurses in the human intent descriptor and ED presenting complaint comments. Unless explicitly stated by patients, no other information was available indicating the perpetrator of these assaults. Thus, it is possible that these particular assault-related TBI cases (perpetrated by an unspecified assailant) could be domestic assaults otherwise misclassified, due to the lack of accuracy of the self-report by the victims [49]. It is not readily apparent why the shift in the location of assault was driven by middle-age adults, and interpretation is further limited as there were not enough older adults to include in the analysis.

Self-reported history among domestic violence victims may be further confounded by both under- and/or over-reporting of brain injury incidence, due to the potential for misunderstanding specific terminology, emotional avoidance, and poor recall or suppression of event recall. Suppression may flow from the potentially traumatic nature of the experience (e.g., the development of post-traumatic stress disorder (PTSD) symptomatology that may interfere with recall), or lack of awareness of or minimisation of the severity of the injury (e.g., due to fear of potential repercussions of reporting or distrust of authority figures) [49].

Finally, this is the only study reporting on the impact of the pandemic and associated restrictions on the prison population. Our subgroup analysis revealed a significantly lower number of middle-aged prison assault victims during the COVID period compared to the pre-COVID period.

4.2. Overall Results Independent of COVID-19

Looking at the data without partitioning into pre-COVID and COVID periods, we observed noticeably contrasting differences in the proportion of cases between random assault and domestic violence in terms of sex and alcohol consumption. Specifically, 86% of the random assault cases were males, whereas 74% of the domestic assault cases were females. Nearly half (44%) of the random assault victims reported alcohol consumption versus a fifth (20%) of domestic violence victims. These patterns are in line with the general aggression model, which posits alcohol use as a situational risk factor and gender as a biological distal factor that might contribute to aggressive behaviour [53].

Within our domestic assault population, a significantly greater proportion was women (74%). This aligns with prior studies examining brain injury in domestic violence victims [63,64] and reviews of a range of injuries resulting from physical assault, including head, neck, and facial injuries [65]. Although both men and women experience domestic violence [66], women are (i) at greater risk of family, domestic, and sexual violence; (ii) more frequently injured and experience more severe injuries, in comparison to male partners [67]; and (iii) less likely to seek help for their physical and mental health needs [68,69]. The high prevalence rates of violence against women in this study align with other Australian and international studies. For example, globally, one in four ever-partnered women has experienced physical or sexual violence from an intimate partner since the age of 15 years [70]. In Australia, one in six Australian women (compared to 1 in 16 men) has experienced physical or sexual violence from a male relative since the age of 16 years [71]. Domestic violence victims who suffer from head injuries often experience sequelae, such as decreased cognitive functioning, memory loss, and post-traumatic stress disorder [49]. This indicates the urgent need of preventive measures for family and domestic violence that may include a combination of government and nongovernment policy initiatives, and changes in public discourse and practice.

Women are most likely to know the perpetrator (often their current or a previous partner) and the violence usually takes place in their home. In contrast, men are more likely to experience violence from strangers and in a public place [71]. Our results showed that Australian males injured by random assault presented as the group of patients at highest risk of assault TBI across the time periods, which is supported by previous retrospective studies [72–75]. To our knowledge, very little research has been conducted on the extent and impact of head injuries incurred during random assaults [76]. This highlights the need for targeted treatment approaches for this subgroup. Clinicians should be provided with established treatment guidelines and educational resources to improve their awareness of the many types of violence, how to identify and assist victims, and where to refer these patients for follow-up treatment in their community. Particular attention will need to be paid to addressing the treatment barriers faced by male victims that present with assault-related injury. For example, research on patterns of health service use suggests that men utilise healthcare services and engage in treatment follow-up less frequently than women [77,78].

Various internal factors (e.g., embarrassment, masculinity norms, cultural norms, negative attitudes towards help-seeking, etc.) and systemic barriers (e.g., accessibility issues, lack of time, ED waiting times, etc.) have all been reported as obstacles that discourage men from seeking medical help [79–81]. Moreover, innovative public health promotion strategies will need to be developed that aim to improve health literacy and treatment–engagement behaviours in men, and emphasise preventative health measures (i.e., reducing male violence), particularly in male-dominant settings (e.g., pubs, sports bars).

Furthermore, these violence prevention strategies should focus on reduction in alcohol use. Our results showed that alcohol consumption appeared to play an important role in assault-related head injuries in Melbourne. Alcohol was present in 44% of the random assault victims, and 20% of the domestic violence victims. Other retrospective studies have found a similar relationship between alcohol consumption and violence (e.g., Romania [72], Norway [82]). A recent review [83] suggests that brief alcohol intervention programs delivered in emergency department settings can be a cost-reducing approach to treating excessive alcohol consumption and improve heath in the long-term. Another strategy would be to limit drinking hours (and restricting availability of alcohol), which has showed to be effective in some countries [84].

In broad agreement with Australian assault data [85,86], we found for head injury victims in our study that: (i) most were young adults, followed by middle-aged adults, and older adults; (ii) most were born in Australia, rather than overseas; and (iii) were most commonly assaulted in a nonresidential location. The proportion of Aboriginal and Torres Strait Islander peoples in our sample with a head injury in the 2018–2021 period (~10%) was substantially less than the proportion of Aboriginal and Torres Strait Islander peoples hospitalised due to assault in 2019–2020 in the whole of Australia (~31%) [87]. This latter figure can only be considered indicative, as it is a national figure that refers to hospitalisations broadly, rather than solely due to a head injury. One final result that may be of interest for ED practitioners is the time of admission for intentional head injuries, which we found to increase across the day and peak in the evening period for DV and PP assaults. For RV assaults the time of admission similarly increased throughout the day but, in contrast with DV and PP, it peaked in the night period.

4.3. Limitations

While this study provides one of the first reports to examine the effect of the COVID-pandemic on assault-related head injuries in Australia, it has some limitations. Firstly, it is important to keep in mind that in this study we focus on assault-related head injuries. Our findings are therefore indicative of a particularly serious form of violence rather than more broadly being reflective of less severe types of physical violence or alternative forms of violence (like emotional, verbal, or financial abuse). Second, our design was cross-sectional and retrospective. The data retrieved can only suggest but not demonstrate a causal relationship [88]. Future studies examining the impact of a pandemic on intentional head injuries should adopt a prospective, longitudinal design, to allow the identification of risk factors and examination of causal links between variables [89]. These longitudinal studies would also offer great utility for the validation of theories of aggression [53] in psychology, or strain [54] in criminology. Moreover, this study was conducted in a single adult hospital of the inner eastern region of metropolitan Melbourne (St Vincent's Hospital) and this could limit the generalizability of the findings to young populations (including children and adolescents) or to other parts of Australia (including rural and regional areas). Future multicentre studies should endeavour to gather medical record data from a range of emergency departments across age groups and different sites, as was done by Cassell et al. [90]. On the other hand, as detailed in the introduction, there is much variability in the effect of COVID-19 restrictions on interpersonal violence, so studies focusing on specific places and age groups are crucial to understanding this variability.

Another limitation is related to missing data in the medical record database, including detailed clinical characteristics of the head injury (e.g., severity of traumatic brain injury), and this limited the data analysis. In addition, several variables (alcohol consumption, nationality, location of assault) were left unspecified in some cases, which could alter the results. Also introducing a level of uncertainty in our findings is a proportion of assault cases (20%) that were miscategorised and needed to be corrected. Furthermore, patients with multisystem trauma, in addition to trauma to the head, might not have been categorised as having a head injury and could therefore be missing (e.g., chest stabbings with additional head trauma are more likely to not be categorised as TBI). Clinician entries for our sample exist (that were beyond the purview of this study), which could reveal further inconsistencies and help further confirm existing cases. Future work could establish a statewide or national injury registry system and mandatory recording of all clinical characteristics, to manage gaps and sources of uncertainty in the recording of important clinical information. This will be crucial to better understanding the extent of the problem of head injuries in assault victims.

5. Conclusions

In this study, we found the COVID-19 pandemic significantly affected the **Where** of assault-related TBI. We saw assaults causing head injury shifted from the street to the home, with the increase at home being driven by random assaults on middle-aged adults. Our findings provide an understanding of the effects of sustained COVID-19 restrictions on interpersonal violence, with novel insights into assault-related head injuries. It is expected that these findings will guide the development of novel screening tools, targeted preventive measures, and intervention strategies, and by doing so it will inform policy and practice to enhance the mental health outcomes of assault victims living with TBI.

Supplementary Materials: The following supporting information can be downloaded at: https://www.mdpi.com/article/10.3390/ijerph20010063/s1, Table S1: *Who* was a victim of assault-related TBI in Melbourne; Table S2: *Where* were victims of assault-related TBI in Melbourne; Table S3: *When* did victims of assault-related TBI in Melbourne, Australia, present at the ED between 30 July 2018 and 30 October 2021? Table S4: Summary of publications examining the effect of the COVID pandemic on interpersonal violence (according to type of violence and type of data collection).

Author Contributions: Conceptualization, J.F.D.D., H.A., N.R. and K.C.; data curation, J.T. and L.S.; formal analysis, J.T. and J.F.D.D.; funding acquisition, H.A. and K.C.; investigation, J.F.D.D., J.B., L.S., H.A., J.S. and K.C.; methodology, K.C.; project administration, H.A. and K.C.; resources, H.A.; supervision, J.F.D.D., H.A., J.S. and K.C.; visualization, J.F.D.D.; writing—original draft, J.F.D.D., J.B. and K.C.; writing—review and editing, J.F.D.D., L.S., H.A., J.S., N.R. and K.C. All authors have read and agreed to the published version of the manuscript.

Funding: K.C. is supported by a Veski Fellowship. The Victorian Near-miss Award Pilot is administered by Veski for the Victorian Health and Medical Research Workforce Project on behalf of the Victorian Government and the Association of Australian Medical Research Institutes. Funding for the Pilot has been provided by the Victorian Department of Jobs, Precincts and Regions.

Institutional Review Board Statement: This study was conducted in accordance with the Declaration of Helsinki, and approved by the Ethics Committee of St. Vincent's Hospital Melbourne (protocol code 66135, LRR 167/20 and date of approval: 3 September 2020)." for studies involving humans.

Informed Consent Statement: Patient consent was waived as data are emergency department records accessed retrospectively and it was deemed impracticable to re-contact the large number of patients involved to obtain informed consent. These patients are not seen by research or hospital staff on a regular basis or ever and time had elapsed since their hospital attendance. There was, therefore, little or no access to patients or opportunity to seek informed consent. In addition, data were deidentified prior to collection and no individual patient characteristics were referred to in the paper.

Data Availability Statement: The data presented in this study are available on request from the corresponding author.

Acknowledgments: We thank Honey Asal Baseri for assistance with the ethics application and the compilation of the reference list.

Conflicts of Interest: The authors declare no conflict of interest.

References

1. Crimes Act 1958 (Vic), s. 31. Available online: https://www.legislation.vic.gov.au/in-force/acts/crimes-act-1958/294 (accessed on 15 September 2022).
2. Bradbury-Jones, C.; Isham, L. The Pandemic Paradox: The Consequences of COVID-19 on Domestic Violence. *J. Clin. Nurs.* **2020**, *29*, 2047–2049. [CrossRef]
3. United Nations Human Rights Office of the High Commissioner. States Must Combat Domestic Violence in the Context of COVID-19 Lockdowns—UN Rights Expert. Available online: https://www.ohchr.org/en/press-releases/2020/03/states-must-combat-domestic-violence-context-covid-19-lockdowns-un-rights (accessed on 14 September 2022).
4. UN Women. The Shadow Pandemic: Violence against Women during COVID-19. Available online: https://www.unwomen.org/en/news/in-focus/in-focus-gender-equality-in-covid-19-response/violence-against-women-during-covid-19 (accessed on 14 September 2022).
5. Bazyar, J.; Chehreh, R.; Sadeghifar, J.; Karamelahi, Z.; Ahmadimazhin, S.; Vafery, Y.; Daliri, S. Effects of the COVID-19 Pandemic on the Intimate Partner Violence and Sexual Function: A Systematic Review. *Prehospital Disaster Med.* **2021**, *36*, 593–598. [CrossRef]
6. Piquero, A.R.; Jennings, W.G.; Jemison, E.; Kaukinen, C.; Knaul, F.M. Domestic Violence during the COVID-19 Pandemic—Evidence from a Systematic Review and Meta-Analysis. *J. Crim. Justice* **2021**, *74*, 101806. [CrossRef]
7. Lausi, G.; Pizzo, A.; Cricenti, C.; Baldi, M.; Desiderio, R.; Giannini, A.M.; Mari, E. Intimate Partner Violence during the COVID-19 Pandemic: A Review of the Phenomenon from Victims' and Help Professionals' Perspectives. *Int. J. Environ. Res. Public Health* **2021**, *18*, 6204. [CrossRef]
8. Kourti, A.; Stavridou, A.; Panagouli, E.; Psaltopoulou, T.; Spiliopoulou, C.; Tsolia, M.; Sergentanis, T.N.; Tsitsika, A. Domestic Violence During the COVID-19 Pandemic: A Systematic Review. *Trauma Violence Abus.* **2021**, *17*, 15248380211038690. [CrossRef]
9. Thiel, F.; Büechl, V.C.S.; Rehberg, F.; Mojahed, A.; Daniels, J.K.; Schellong, J.; Garthus-Niegel, S. Changes in Prevalence and Severity of Domestic Violence During the COVID-19 Pandemic: A Systematic Review. *Front. Psychiatry* **2022**, *13*, 874183. [CrossRef]
10. Abrams, D.S. COVID and Crime: An Early Empirical Look. *J. Public Econ.* **2021**, *194*, 104344. [CrossRef]
11. Ashby, M.P.J. Initial Evidence on the Relationship between the Coronavirus Pandemic and Crime in the United States. *Crime Sci.* **2020**, *9*, 6. [CrossRef]
12. Bullinger, L.R.; Carr, J.B.; Packham, A. COVID-19 and Crime: Effects of Stay-at-Home Orders on Domestic Violence. *Am. J. Health Econ.* **2021**, *7*, 249–280. [CrossRef]

13. Burgess, A.; Nguyen, H.; Chai, W.; Kelly, S. Police-Recorded Crime Trends in Victoria during the COVID-19 Pandemic: Update to End of December 2020. 2021; pp. 1–26. Available online: https://www.crimestatistics.vic.gov.au/research-and-evaluation/publications/police-recorded-crime-trends-in-victoria-during-the-covid-19-1 (accessed on 18 August 2022).
14. Campedelli, G.M.; Favarin, S.; Aziani, A.; Piquero, A.R. Disentangling Community-Level Changes in Crime Trends during the COVID-19 Pandemic in Chicago. *Crime Sci.* **2020**, *9*, 21. [CrossRef]
15. Campedelli, G.M.; Aziani, A.; Favarin, S. Exploring the Immediate Effects of COVID-19 Containment Policies on Crime: An Empirical Analysis of the Short-Term Aftermath in Los Angeles. *Am. J. Crim. Justice* **2021**, *46*, 704–727. [CrossRef]
16. Balmori de la Miyar, J.R.; Hoehn-Velasco, L.; Silverio-Murillo, A. Druglords Don't Stay at Home: COVID-19 Pandemic and Crime Patterns in Mexico City. *J. Crim. Justice* **2021**, *72*, 101745. [CrossRef]
17. Di Franco, M.; Martines, G.F.; Carpinteri, G.; Trovato, G.; Catalano, D. Domestic Violence Detection amid the COVID-19 Pandemic: The Value of the WHO Questionnaire in Emergency Medicine. *QJM Int. J. Med.* **2021**, *114*, 637–641. [CrossRef]
18. Evans, D.P.; Hawk, S.R.; Ripkey, C.E. Domestic Violence in Atlanta, Georgia Before and During COVID-19. *Violence Gend.* **2021**, *8*, 140–147. [CrossRef]
19. Gerell, M.; Kardell, J.; Kindgren, J. Minor Covid-19 Association with Crime in Sweden. *Crime Sci.* **2020**, *9*, 19. [CrossRef]
20. Gosangi, B.; Park, H.; Thomas, R.; Gujrathi, R.; Bay, C.P.; Raja, A.S.; Seltzer, S.E.; Balcom, M.C.; McDonald, M.L.; Orgill, D.P.; et al. Exacerbation of Physical Intimate Partner Violence during COVID-19 Lockdown. *Radiology* **2021**, *298*, E38–E45. [CrossRef]
21. Hsu, L.C.; Henke, A. COVID-19, Staying at Home, and Domestic Violence. *Rev. Econ. Househ.* **2021**, *19*, 145–155. [CrossRef]
22. Leslie, E.; Wilson, R. Sheltering in Place and Domestic Violence: Evidence from Calls for Service during COVID-19. *J. Public Econ.* **2020**, *189*, 104241. [CrossRef]
23. McCrary, J.; Sanga, S. The Impact of the Coronavirus Lockdown on Domestic Violence. *SSRN Electron. J.* **2021**, *23*, 137–163. [CrossRef]
24. Mohler, G.; Bertozzi, A.L.; Carter, J.; Short, M.B.; Sledge, D.; Tita, G.E.; Uchida, C.D.; Brantingham, P.J. Impact of Social Distancing during COVID-19 Pandemic on Crime in Los Angeles and Indianapolis. *J. Crim. Justice* **2020**, *68*, 101692. [CrossRef]
25. Moslehi, S.; Parasnis, J.; Tani, M.; Vejayaratnam, J. Assaults during Lockdown in New South Wales and Victoria. *Aust. J. Labour Econ.* **2021**, *24*, 199–212.
26. Muldoon, K.A.; Denize, K.M.; Talarico, R.; Fell, D.B.; Sobiesiak, A.; Heimerl, M.; Sampsel, K. COVID-19 Pandemic and Violence: Rising Risks and Decreasing Urgent Care-Seeking for Sexual Assault and Domestic Violence Survivors. *BMC Med.* **2021**, *19*, 20. [CrossRef] [PubMed]
27. Nix, J.; Richards, T.N. The Immediate and Long-Term Effects of COVID-19 Stay-at-Home Orders on Domestic Violence Calls for Service across Six U.S. Jurisdictions. *Police Pract. Res.* **2021**, *22*, 1443–1451. [CrossRef]
28. Nivette, A.E.; Zahnow, R.; Aguilar, R.; Ahven, A.; Amram, S.; Ariel, B.; Burbano, M.J.A.; Astolfi, R.; Baier, D.; Bark, H.M.; et al. A Global Analysis of the Impact of COVID-19 Stay-at-Home Restrictions on Crime. *Nat. Hum. Behav.* **2021**, *5*, 868–877. [CrossRef] [PubMed]
29. Payne, J.L.; Morgan, A.; Piquero, A.R. COVID-19 and Social Distancing Measures in Queensland, Australia, Are Associated with Short-Term Decreases in Recorded Violent Crime. *J. Exp. Criminol.* **2022**, *18*, 89–113. [CrossRef]
30. Rhodes, H.X.; Petersen, K.; Lunsford, L.; Biswas, S. COVID-19 Resilience for Survival: Occurrence of Domestic Violence During Lockdown at a Rural American College of Surgeons Verified Level One Trauma Center. *Cureus* **2020**, *12*, e10059. [CrossRef]
31. The Victorian Injury Surveillance Unit (VISU) Injuries during the COVID-19 Pandemic. 2021. Available online: https://www.monash.edu/muarc/research/research-areas/home-and-community/visu/injuries-during-the-covid-19-pandemic (accessed on 14 September 2022).
32. Leigh, J.K.; Peña, L.D.; Anurudran, A.; Pai, A. "Are You Safe to Talk?": Perspectives of Service Providers on Experiences of Domestic Violence During the COVID-19 Pandemic. *J. Fam. Violence* **2022**, 1–11. [CrossRef]
33. Logan, T.K.; Valente, R. *Who Will Help Me? Domestic Violence Survivors Speak out about Law Enforcement Responses*; National Domestic Violence Hotline: Austin, MN, USA, 2015.
34. Hale, T.; Angrist, N.; Goldszmidt, R.; Kira, B.; Petherick, A.; Phillips, T.; Webster, S.; Cameron-Blake, E.; Hallas, L.; Majumdar, S.; et al. A Global Panel Database of Pandemic Policies (Oxford COVID-19 Government Response Tracker). *Nat. Hum. Behav.* **2021**, *5*, 529–538. [CrossRef]
35. Wade, M.J.; Jacomo, A.L.; Armenise, E.; Brown, M.R.; Bunce, J.T.; Cameron, G.J.; Fang, Z.; Farkas, K.; Gilpin, D.F.; Graham, D.W.; et al. Understanding and Managing Uncertainty and Variability for Wastewater Monitoring beyond the Pandemic: Lessons Learned from the United Kingdom National COVID-19 Surveillance Programmes. *J. Hazard. Mater.* **2022**, *424*, 127456. [CrossRef]
36. Kennedy, E. *"The Worst Year": Domestic Violence Soars in Australia during COVID-19*; The Guardian: London, UK, 2020.
37. Pfitzner, N.; Fitz-Gibbon, K.; True, J. *Responding to the 'Shadow Pandemic': Practitioner Views on the Nature of and Responses to Violence against Women in Victoria, Australia during the COVID-19 Restrictions*; Monash Gender and Family Violence Prevention Centre, Monash University: Victoria, Australia, 2020; pp. 1–28. [CrossRef]
38. Boxall, H.; Morgan, A. *Intimate Partner Violence during the COVID-19 Pandemic: A Survey of Women in Australia*; Australian Institute of Criminology: Canberra, Australia, 2021; pp. 1–54. Available online: https://www.anrows.org.au/publication/intimate-partner-violence-during-the-covid-19-pandemic-a-survey-of-women-in-australia/ (accessed on 18 August 2022).

39. Kwako, L.E.; Glass, N.; Campbell, J.; Melvin, K.C.; Barr, T.; Gill, J.M. Traumatic Brain Injury in Intimate Partner Violence: A Critical Review of Outcomes and Mechanisms. *Trauma Violence Abus.* **2011**, *12*, 115–126. [CrossRef]
40. Bown, D.; Belli, A.; Qureshi, K.; Davies, D.; Toman, E.; Upthegrove, R. Post-Traumatic Stress Disorder and Self-Reported Outcomes after Traumatic Brain Injury in Victims of Assault. *PLoS ONE* **2019**, *14*, e0211684. [CrossRef] [PubMed]
41. Bushnik, T.; Hanks, R.A.; Kreutzer, J.; Rosenthal, M. Etiology of Traumatic Brain Injury: Characterization of Differential Outcomes up to 1 Year Postinjury. *Arch. Phys. Med. Rehabil.* **2003**, *84*, 255–262. [CrossRef] [PubMed]
42. Mathias, J.L.; Harman-Smith, Y.; Bowden, S.C.; Rosenfeld, J.V.; Bigler, E.D. Contribution of Psychological Trauma to Outcomes after Traumatic Brain Injury: Assaults versus Sporting Injuries. *J. Neurotrauma* **2014**, *31*, 658–669. [CrossRef] [PubMed]
43. Department of Health and Aged Care Timelines of Melbourne's Lockdown—Since the Pandemic Began. Lockdown Stats Melbourne. Available online: https://lockdownstats.melbourne/timeline/ (accessed on 14 September 2022).
44. Colarusso, C.A. *Child and Adult Development*; (Critical Issues in Psychiatry); Springer: New York, NY, USA, 1992. [CrossRef]
45. McDonough, A. The Experiences and Concerns of Young Adults (18–40 Years) Living with an Implanted Cardioverter Defibrillator (ICD). *Eur. J. Cardiovasc. Nurs.* **2009**, *8*, 274–280. [CrossRef] [PubMed]
46. Petry, N.M. A Comparison of Young, Middle-Aged, and Older Adult Treatment-Seeking Pathological Gamblers. *Gerontologist* **2002**, *42*, 92–99. [CrossRef] [PubMed]
47. Bullrich, M.B.; Fridman, S.; Mandzia, J.L.; Mai, L.M.; Khaw, A.; Gonzalez, J.C.V.; Bagur, R.; Sposato, L.A. COVID-19: Stroke Admissions, Emergency Department Visits, and Prevention Clinic Referrals. *Can. J. Neurol. Sci.* **2020**, *47*, 693–696. [CrossRef] [PubMed]
48. Mitchell, R.D.; O'Reilly, G.M.; Mitra, B.; Smit, D.V.; Miller, J.P.; Cameron, P.A. Impact of COVID-19 State of Emergency Restrictions on Presentations to Two Victorian Emergency Departments. *Emerg. Med. Australas.* **2020**, *32*, 1027–1033. [CrossRef]
49. Esopenko, C.; Meyer, J.; Wilde, E.A.; Marshall, A.D.; Tate, D.F.; Lin, A.P.; Koerte, I.K.; Werner, K.B.; Dennis, E.L.; Ware, A.L.; et al. A Global Collaboration to Study Intimate Partner Violence-Related Head Trauma: The ENIGMA Consortium IPV Working Group. *Brain Imaging Behav.* **2021**, *15*, 475. [CrossRef]
50. Crime Statistics Agency. Adolescent Family Violence in Victoria. 2020. Available online: https://www.crimestatistics.vic.gov.au/research-and-evaluation/publications/adolescent-family-violence-in-victoria (accessed on 27 November 2022).
51. Phillips, B.; McGuinness, C. Police Reported Adolescent Family Violence in Victoria. Available online: https://files.crimestatistics.vic.gov.au/2021-07/Crime%20Statistics%20Agency%20Data%20Snapshot%201%20Adolescent%20Family%20Violence.pdf (accessed on 27 November 2022).
52. Campbell, E.; Richter, J.; Howard, J.; Cockburn, H. *Positive Interventions for Perpetrators of Adolescent Violence in the Home (AVITH)*; ANROWS: Sydney, Austria, 2020; ISBN 978-1-925925-96-8.
53. Anderson, C.A.; Bushman, B.J. Human Aggression. *Annu. Rev. Psychol.* **2002**, *53*, 27–51. [CrossRef]
54. Agnew, R. *Pressured Into Crime: An Overview of General Strain Theory*; Oxford University Press: New York, NY, USA, 2006.
55. Brooks, S.K.; Webster, R.K.; Smith, L.E.; Woodland, L.; Wessely, S.; Greenberg, N.; Rubin, G.J. The Psychological Impact of Quarantine and How to Reduce It: Rapid Review of the Evidence. *Lancet* **2020**, *395*, 912–920. [CrossRef]
56. Scarpetta, S.; Colombo, F.; Hewlett, E. Tackling the Mental Health Impact of the COVID-19 Crisis: An Integrated, Whole-of-Society Response. Available online: https://www.oecd.org/coronavirus/policy-responses/tackling-the-mental-health-impact-of-the-covid-19-crisis-an-integrated-whole-of-society-response-0ccafa0b/ (accessed on 14 September 2022).
57. Benson, M.L.; Fox, G.L.; DeMaris, A.; Wyk, J.V. Neighborhood Disadvantage, Individual Economic Distress and Violence against Women in Intimate Relationships. *J. Quant. Criminol.* **2003**, *19*, 207–235. [CrossRef]
58. Boden, J.M.; Fergusson, D.M.; Horwood, L.J. Alcohol Misuse and Violent Behavior: Findings from a 30-Year Longitudinal Study. *Drug Alcohol Depend.* **2012**, *122*, 135–141. [CrossRef] [PubMed]
59. Trevillion, K.; Oram, S.; Feder, G.; Howard, L.M. Experiences of Domestic Violence and Mental Disorders: A Systematic Review and Meta-Analysis. *PLoS ONE* **2012**, *7*, e51740. [CrossRef] [PubMed]
60. Australian Bureau of Statistics Labour Force, Australia. July 2022. Available online: https://www.abs.gov.au/statistics/labour/employment-and-unemployment/labour-force-australia/latest-release (accessed on 14 September 2022).
61. Van Rheenen, T.E.; Meyer, D.; Neill, E.; Phillipou, A.; Tan, E.J.; Toh, W.L.; Rossell, S.L. Mental Health Status of Individuals with a Mood-Disorder during the COVID-19 Pandemic in Australia: Initial Results from the COLLATE Project. *J. Affect. Disord.* **2020**, *275*, 69–77. [CrossRef] [PubMed]
62. Figueroa, J.M.; Boddu, J.; Kader, M.; Berry, K.; Kumar, V.; Ayala, V.; Vanni, S.; Jagid, J. The Effects of Lockdown During the Severe Acute Respiratory Syndrome Coronavirus 2 (SARS-CoV-2) Pandemic on Neurotrauma-Related Hospital Admissions. *World Neurosurg.* **2021**, *146*, e1–e5. [CrossRef] [PubMed]
63. Haag, H.; Biscardi, M.; Smith, N.; MacGregor, N.; Colantonio, A.; Pauktuutit Inuit Women of Canada. Traumatic Brain Injury and Intimate Partner Violence: Addressing Knowledge and Service Gaps among Indigenous Populations in Canada. *Brain Impair.* **2019**, *20*, 197–210. [CrossRef]
64. Zieman, G.; Bridwell, A.; Cárdenas, J.F. Traumatic Brain Injury in Domestic Violence Victims: A Retrospective Study at the Barrow Neurological Institute. *J. Neurotrauma* **2017**, *34*, 876–880. [CrossRef]
65. Satyen, L.; Supol, M.; Ranganathan, A.; Toumbourou, J. International and Cross-Cultural Research on Men's Violence against Female Intimate Partners. In *The SAGE Handbook of Domestic Violence*; Sage: Thousand Oaks, CA, USA, 2021; pp. 40–60.

66. Kolbe, V.; Büttner, A. Domestic Violence Against Men—Prevalence and Risk Factors. *Dtsch. Ärzteblatt Int.* **2020**, *117*, 534. [CrossRef]
67. Winstok, Z.; Straus, M.A. Gender Differences in the Link between Intimate Partner Physical Violence and Depression. *Aggress. Violent Behav.* **2014**, *19*, 91–101. [CrossRef]
68. Satyen, L.; Rogic, A.C.; Supol, M. Intimate Partner Violence and Help-Seeking Behaviour: A Systematic Review of Cross-Cultural Differences. *J. Immigr. Minor. Health* **2019**, *21*, 879–892. [CrossRef]
69. Satyen, L.; Toumbourou, J.W.; Heerde, J.; Supol, M.; Ranganathan, A. The Royal Commission into Family Violence: Trends in the Reporting of Intimate Partner Violence and Help-Seeking Behavior. *J. Interpers. Violence* **2021**, *36*, 11009–11034. [CrossRef] [PubMed]
70. World Health Organisation. Violence against Women. Available online: https://www.who.int/news-room/fact-sheets/detail/violence-against-women (accessed on 14 September 2022).
71. Australian Institute of Health and Welfare. *Family, Domestic and Sexual Violence in Australia 2018*; Australian Institute of Health and Welfare: Canberra, Australia, 2018; ISBN 978-1-76054-302-0.
72. Gal, M.; Rus, D.; Peek-Asa, C.; Chereches, Ř.M.; Sįirlincan, E.O.; Boeriu, C.; Baba, Č.O. Epidemiology of Assault and Self-Harm Injuries Treated in a Large Romanian Emergency Department. *Eur. J. Emerg. Med.* **2012**, *19*, 146–152. [CrossRef]
73. Kruse, M.; Brønnum-Hansen, H.; Helweg-Larsen, K.; Sørensen, J. Identifying Victims of Violence Using Register-Based Data. *Scand. J. Public Health* **2010**, *38*, 611–617. [CrossRef]
74. Reilly, J.; Muldoon, O.T.; Byrne, C. Young Men as Victims and Perpetrators of Violence in Northern Ireland: A Qualitative Analysis. *J. Soc. Issues* **2004**, *60*, 469–484. [CrossRef]
75. Steen, K.; Hunskaar, S. Violence in an Urban Community from the Perspective of an Accident and Emergency Department: A Two-Year Prospective Study. *Med. Sci. Monit.* **2004**, *10*, CR75–CR79. [PubMed]
76. Jang, S.H.; Kim, S.H.; Kwon, Y.H. Extensive Traumatic Axonal Injury of Brain Due to Violence: A Case Report. *Medicine* **2018**, *97*, e13315. [CrossRef]
77. Mansfield, A.; Addis, M.; Mahalik, J. "Why Won't He Go to the Doctor?": The Psychology of Men's Help Seeking. *Int. J. Men's Health* **2003**, *2*, 93–109. [CrossRef]
78. Tudiver, F.; Talbot, Y. Why Don't Men Seek Help? Family Physicians' Perspectives on Help-Seeking Behavior in Men. *J. Fam. Pract.* **1999**, *48*, 47–52.
79. Mursa, R.; Patterson, C.; Halcomb, E. Men's Help-seeking and Engagement with General Practice: An Integrative Review. *J. Adv. Nurs.* **2022**, *78*, 1938. [CrossRef]
80. Teo, C.H.; Ng, C.J.; Booth, A.; White, A. Barriers and Facilitators to Health Screening in Men: A Systematic Review. *Soc. Sci. Med.* **2016**, *165*, 168–176. [CrossRef]
81. Yousaf, O.; Grunfeld, E.A.; Hunter, M.S. A Systematic Review of the Factors Associated with Delays in Medical and Psychological Help-Seeking among Men. *Health Psychol. Rev.* **2015**, *9*, 264–276. [CrossRef] [PubMed]
82. Norström, T.; Pape, H. Alcohol, Suppressed Anger and Violence. *Addiction* **2010**, *105*, 1580–1586. [CrossRef] [PubMed]
83. Barbosa, C.; Cowell, A.J.; Dowd, W.N. Alcohol Consumption in Response to the COVID-19 Pandemic in the United States. *J. Addict. Med.* **2021**, *15*, 341. [CrossRef] [PubMed]
84. Middleton, J.C.; Hahn, R.A.; Kuzara, J.L.; Elder, R.; Brewer, R.; Chattopadhyay, S.; Fielding, J.; Naimi, T.S.; Toomey, T.; Lawrence, B. Effectiveness of Policies Maintaining or Restricting Days of Alcohol Sales on Excessive Alcohol Consumption and Related Harms. *Am. J. Prev. Med.* **2010**, *39*, 575–589. [CrossRef] [PubMed]
85. Australian Bureau of Statistics Crime Victimisation, Australia, 2020-21 Financial Year | Australian Bureau of Statistics. Available online: https://www.abs.gov.au/statistics/people/crime-and-justice/crime-victimisation-australia/latest-release (accessed on 14 September 2022).
86. Australian Bureau of Statistics Main Features—Physical Assault. Available online: https://www.abs.gov.au/ausstats/abs@.nsf/Lookup/by%20Subject/4530.0~{}2017-18~{}Main%20Features~{}Physical%20assault~{}4 (accessed on 14 September 2022).
87. Australian Institute of Health and Welfare Injury in Australia: Assault and Homicide. Available online: https://www.aihw.gov.au/reports/injury/assault-and-homicide (accessed on 14 September 2022).
88. Mann, C.J. Observational Research Methods. Research Design II: Cohort, Cross Sectional, and Case-Control Studies. *Emerg. Med. J.* **2003**, *20*, 54–60. [CrossRef]
89. Hammoudeh, S.; Gadelhaq, W.; Janahi, I. Prospective Cohort Studies in Medical Research. In *Cohort Studies in Health Sciences*; IntechOpen: London, UK, 2018; pp. 11–28. [CrossRef]
90. Cassell, E.; Reid, N.; Clapperton, A.; Houy-Prang, K.; Kerr, E. *Assault-Related Injury among Young People Aged 15-34 Years That Occurred in Public Places: Deaths and Hospital-Treated Injury*; Victorian Injury Surveillance Unit: Melbourne, Australia, 2011.

International Journal of
Environmental Research and Public Health

MDPI

Article

Changes in Mental Health, Emotional Distress, and Substance Use Affecting Women Experiencing Violence and Their Service Providers during COVID-19 in a U.S. Southern State

April Schweinhart *, Camila Aramburú, Rachel Bauer, Ashley Simons-Rudolph, Katharine Atwood and Winnie Kavulani Luseno

Pacific Institute for Research and Evaluation, 4061 Powder Mill Road, Suite 350, Beltsville, MD 20705, USA
* Correspondence: aschweinhart@pire.org

Abstract: Research conducted during the COVID-19 pandemic has revealed many unintended consequences of mandated safety precautions, including increased perpetration of intimate partner violence (IPV), increases in substance use, and worsening mental health conditions. We conducted a repeated, cross-sectional survey of survivors of IPV, a longitudinal survey of service providers working in an IPV shelter, and interviews with both. We conducted surveys at the beginning of the pandemic and nearly half a year later to assess mental health and, for clients, substance use. Results showed that two small samples of survivors living in the shelter in 2020 and 2021 experienced both mental health decline and increased use of substances. Qualitative data from in-depth interviews suggest that COVID-19-related restrictions mirrored survivors' experiences of power and control in violent relationships. Further, IPV service providers—essential workers during COVID-19—experienced stress associated with reports of burnout and mental fatigue. This study suggests that community-based organizations can help mitigate the impacts of COVID-19 on survivors of IPV but should avoid adding additional work for staff as service providers experienced mental and emotional stress.

Keywords: intimate partner violence; mental health; substance use; COVID-19; power and control

Citation: Schweinhart, A.; Aramburú, C.; Bauer, R.; Simons-Rudolph, A.; Atwood, K.; Luseno, W.K. Changes in Mental Health, Emotional Distress, and Substance Use Affecting Women Experiencing Violence and Their Service Providers during COVID-19 in a U.S. Southern State. *Int. J. Environ. Res. Public Health* **2023**, *20*, 2896. https://doi.org/10.3390/ijerph20042896

Academic Editors: Krim K. Lacey and Rohan D. Jeremiah

Received: 31 October 2022
Revised: 17 January 2023
Accepted: 3 February 2023
Published: 7 February 2023

1. Introduction

Soon after stay-at-home orders for the COVID-19 pandemic were issued, researchers began studying how these orders, precautions, and the pandemic affected individuals. Many of these studies focused on the effects of the pandemic on mental health and substance use in the general population and found that the unintended consequences of COVID-19-related public health orders include psychological distress, fear of infection, insufficient resources, and income insecurity [1–4]. For example, adults were three times more likely to meet the criteria for depressive and/or anxiety disorders in April and May 2020 than they were in 2019 [5] and eight times more likely to fit the criteria for serious mental distress in 2020 than they were in 2018 [6]. In addition to the increase in mental health conditions, data collected in 2020 show an increase in substance use. More specifically, 13.3% of adults surveyed in 2020 reported that they had started or increased their substance use to cope with stress or emotions related to the pandemic [7]. Impacts on mental health and coping behaviors due to the pandemic were found across all demographic groups, but most significantly among younger people [5–9], female-identifying individuals [8,9], persons with low financial assets [10], persons with children in the household [5], and those identifying as black or Hispanic [7,9]. Additionally, strong predictors of changes to mental health included: pre-pandemic psychiatric diagnoses [7,8,11,12], past victimization [11], job and/or wage loss or high COVID-19 financial stressors [10–12], smoking [12], a higher consumption of alcohol or cannabis [8], and worry about contracting COVID-19 [12].

The effects of COVID-19 on the general population may be compounded for those experiencing violence, as research shows that well-documented co-morbidities of violence include substance misuse and mental health concerns. According to one review, over half of women seeking treatment for mental health had experienced IPV [13,14], and IPV has been associated with depression, PTSD, anxiety, dysthymia, and phobias [15,16]. Research shows that having a diagnosis of serious mental illness indicates a greater likelihood of experiencing violence, but victimization also indicates a greater likelihood of having a serious illness diagnosed [13,14,17–19]. Further, IPV and substance use have a complicated, bi-directional relationship, as substance use might be a response to trauma and/or increase the likelihood of trauma occurring [20–22].

Many have already investigated the relationship between COVID-19 and increasing rates of IPV perpetration that is physical, sexual, or consequential of perpetrator substance use [1,23–29]. Not only have rates of IPV increased, but some researchers have also suggested that violence during COVID-19 may have been more severe, as indicated by the types of injuries sustained [30]. For instance, sexual and physical (as opposed to, for example, emotional) violence increased [29,31]. In a 2021 online survey of 53 individuals experiencing safety concerns related to IPV, more than 40% of the participants reported decreases in safety [32]. Two other studies found that individuals experiencing IPV reported more stress than those in relationships without IPV and that COVID-19 caused loneliness among survivors of IPV [33,34]. A fear of COVID-19 infection was also a reported barrier to seeking help for IPV during the pandemic [35,36]. Authors also cite an underreporting of violence as well as a lack of services available as affecting the impacts of increases in violence perpetration during the pandemic [23,28,37]. These research findings prompted calls to further integrate services across intersecting domains, such as mental healthcare and substance use treatment, to better reach individuals experiencing violence [24,28,31,35,38,39].

Public health directives, such as wearing personal protective equipment (PPE), stay-at-home orders, and social distancing, were essential to mitigating the spread of COVID-19, especially in communal living spaces such as IPV shelters [40]. However, less is understood about how the pandemic and related public health orders affected survivors of IPV. As an example, Welfare-Wilson et al. [41] reported on their own psychological distress from wearing masks as survivors of IPV, as it served as a physical reminder of the abuse they had endured. Fishere et al. [42] examined populations in Egypt, Germany, and Italy with a history of trauma and determined that those who had experienced trauma were more at risk for the negative mental health impacts of the pandemic than participants without past exposure to trauma (most instances of IPV would be considered traumatic by those experiencing them). Often, social isolation is a tactic perpetrators of violence use to separate victims from resources, family, and friends and may be re-experienced by survivors when their government directs them to self-isolate [43]. Further, income insecurity due to employment changes (e.g., unemployment or reduced work hours) during the pandemic was also found to be an instigator of stress in women [3].

While the literature on the impacts of the pandemic on IPV survivors is limited, evidence has been published on the COVID-19 impacts of another vulnerable population, survivors of war. Both during war and during the pandemic, communities have witnessed dramatic decreases in social and tangible support systems [44]. Changes in access to social services can exacerbate the problems of already underserved populations [4,45,46]. Further, Stolow et al. [47] touched on the negative consequences of officials using fear-based approaches to gain compliance from their communities. These approaches can amplify an already stress-inducing event, such as the pandemic, in addition to causing unfavorable reactions and driving a wedge between officials and the community they serve. Survivors of the Holocaust may be retraumatized by public health restrictions such as the lockdown, as they are reminiscent of the wartime controlling of movement, resources, and information [44]. Similarly, survivors of the Bosnian and Herzegovinian genocide reported greater PTSD symptoms and generally greater impacts of the pandemic [48]. Power, manipulation, and fear are all tactics used by perpetrators of violence to control their victims, as is described in Duluth's Model of Power and Control [49], which we have adapted to consider the connection with the impacts of COVID-19 [50]. In sum, these findings seem to suggest public heath orders implemented during the pandemic may retraumatize survivors of violence by triggering previous trauma or replicating experiences and situations similar to violence.

Importantly, the noted decreases in available services for IPV could be related to COVID-19 effects on service providers, including burnout, mental distress, and high turnover rates. Generally, providers labeled as essential workers experienced greater stress, a lack of access to necessary resources (PPE), and greater burnout during COVID-19 than before [40,51–53]. Many social service providers indicated they were unprepared for the professional challenges of COVID-19 [53] and were impacted personally by the pandemic's primary consequences, such as not having enough access to food or healthcare and becoming ill, as well as secondary consequences such as stress [32,53]. Professional support was noted as key for continuing to provide services [51,52,54]. Many providers also experienced increased caseloads, and some researchers found that the additional stress and workloads affected the quality of services provided [55]. The impact of the pandemic on providers of care is important to consider when researching its impact on clients seeking care, because the quality of care may be affected by shared environmental circumstances.

The intersectional relationships between IPV, substance misuse, and mental illness, coupled with an increase in all three during the pandemic, led us to examine changes in substance use and mental health concerns among IPV survivors and service providers. We hypothesized that survivors of violence may be experiencing greater mental health concerns and greater impacts of violence during the pandemic and that service providers working with survivors may be experiencing negative effects of stress similar to those noted among other helping professions. Further, the increased stress in providers may be passed on to survivors if the quality of care provided is affected by the pandemic. The motivation for this study included the need to notify service providers of survivors' mental health and substance use changes so they could better address these concerns with their clients [23,28,31,32] as well as to notify IPV service-providing organizations of the need to support their staff. As part of a larger study examining the intersection of HIV, substance misuse, and violence, we asked survivors living in a domestic violence shelter in a Southern U.S. State and the IPV service providers working in the same shelter about their COVID-19-related experiences. We also conducted in-depth interviews with the same populations to further explain any changes in self-reported mental, physical, or substance use behaviors.

2. Materials and Methods

Our research team used a mixed-methods approach to studying changes in mood and behavior related to the COVID-19 pandemic among survivors residing in an IPV shelter as well as the service-providing staff at the same organization. Quantitative data were collected using a repeated cross-sectional study design for clients and a longitudinal design for service providers. We sampled clients and service providers via convenience sampling and voluntary response sampling. In-depth interviews were conducted to collect qualitative data. All interview and survey questions, summaries of survey data, and interview themes were reviewed by a community advisory board, consisting of seven women with lived violence and/or substance use experience. Consent was obtained for all staff, clients, and community advisory board members to participate in data collection and interpretation efforts.

Original data collection protocols involved in-person, one-on-one interviews and client survey recruitment by the study team. However, the COVID-19 pandemic disrupted in-person data collection efforts. Following state-wide social distancing mandates, the data collection team, in collaboration with IPV shelter staff, developed new protocols for remote data collection methods, specifically the use of online survey platforms (Qualtrics) and web-based conferencing tools (Microsoft Teams) for conducting staff surveys, staff and client in-depth interviews, and community advisory board meetings. All study protocols and instruments were approved by the Pacific Institute for Research and Evaluation's Institutional Review Board (IRB).

2.1. *Quantitative Data Collection (Clients)*

Individuals living through violence and residing at the IPV shelter (clients) were recruited to participate in two rounds of surveys and one in-depth interview. The client surveys included measures near the beginning of the COVID-19 lock down (summer 2020) and at a second time about six months later (spring 2021). These measures asked participants about the impacts and challenges of the COVID-19 pandemic and about changes in their substance use since the pandemic began.

2.1.1. Instrument Development for Clients

Our COVID-19 instruments were based on measures available in the published literature. Nearly all of these published measures have been validated and/or are accessible via the PhenX Toolkit [56–61]. Unique items across instruments were used to identify population-relevant COVID-19 stressors and to measure the impact of COVID-19 on clients' health, well-being, and behaviors at time 1 and time 2. Participants were first asked to indicate (yes = 1, left blank = 0) if they had experienced any of the following COVID-19 stressors:

1. A COVID-19 diagnosis;
2. Worry/anxiety about being infected;
3. Changes in physical health;
4. Not having enough basic supplies (e.g., food, water, medications, or a place to stay);
5. Children experiencing distress;
6. Interpersonal conflict with family members or loved ones;
7. Feeling more depression;
8. Feeling more loneliness;
9. Feeling less safe;
10. Feeling more abused (physically, emotionally, or psychologically).

Participants were also given the option to indicate, "No changes to my life or behavior." For each item above, if individuals reported that they had experienced it, they were then asked to indicate on a 5-point scale (0 = not at all, 1 = a little, 2 = somewhat, 3 = more than some, and 4 = greatly/a lot) how much each experience affected them. Participants were also asked if they engaged in any of the following activities, feelings, or behaviors to overcome COVID-19 stressors (yes = 1, left blank = 0; also developed from the review of COVID-19 instruments):

1. Feeling grateful for the break from usual activities;
2. Connecting with others, including talking with people you trust about your concerns and how you are feeling;
3. Needing more/less sleep or other changes to your normal sleep pattern;
4. Taking breaks from watching, reading, or listening to news stories, including social media;
5. Healthy behaviors such as trying to eat healthy, well-balanced meals, exercising regularly, getting plenty of sleep, or avoiding alcohol and drugs;
6. Engaging in more family activities;
7. Talking with a mental health care provider.

Participants were also given the option to indicate, "None/no changes." If individuals indicated yes to any of the coping mechanisms listed, they were then asked to indicate on a 5-point scale (0 = not at all, 1 = a little, 2 = somewhat, 3 = more than some, and 4 = greatly/a lot) how much each activity, feeling, or behavior helped them cope.

Lastly, clients were asked to report (yes = 1, left blank = 0) if they currently use tobacco (e.g., smoking cigarettes, e-cigs, vapes, or chewing tobacco), alcohol, and/or illicit or illegal substances (e.g., marijuana, prescription drugs not prescribed to you, or meth).

If individuals reported any use, they were then asked to indicate how much their use of the specified substance changed since the COVID-19 pandemic using a 5-point scale (1 = went down a lot, 2 = went down slightly, 3 = stayed the same, 4 = went up slightly, and 5 = went up a lot). The following individual characteristics were also collected via the survey: marital status, age, number of children, gender, level of education, health insurance, employment, and race/ethnicity. Other survey measures were related to HIV knowledge, self-efficacy, and behavior, but they are not the subject of this study.

2.1.2. Survey Administration with Clients

Shelter staff invited residents to complete the 30 min, anonymous paper-and-pencil surveys between 15 July and 21 August 2020 and between 1 March and 13 April 2021. Each recruitment period included completely distinct sets of individuals because residential shelter clients changed between 2020 and 2021. Only female clients that were 18 years or older and residing in the domestic violence shelter during the time of recruitment were eligible to participate. The study team developed flyers, advertisements, and scripts that detailed the study purpose and protocols to assist staff in recruiting participants. If a resident indicated an interest in participating, staff distributed a survey packet including study information and consent forms, the survey, a list of resources for IPV, HIV, and substance use services, and an envelope to seal their survey in once completed.

Shelter residents indicated their consent by completing the survey and returning the sealed envelope to a staff member. Once their survey was completed and returned to the designated staff member, the client received a $15 gift card to a local grocery store. Sealed envelopes with completed surveys were picked up at the shelter weekly by a member of the research team. Survey responses were then entered into an online, password-protected survey development software (Qualtrics) by a trained research associate. Responses were exported to an excel document and merged using SPSS Statistics 27 for analysis.

2.2. Qualitative Data Collection (Clients)

In-depth interviews with clients were held during the fall of 2020. A member of the data collection team that was trained in human-subjects research as well as IPV counseling conducted the interviews to gain insight into clients' thoughts on HIV, HIV testing, and behaviors related to COVID-19.

2.2.1. Interview Guide for Clients

To ensure participants' safety from perpetrators or others who may have been able to overhear interviews, all participants were residing in the shelter at the time of the interview and were escorted to and from a private computer room by shelter staff members. All interviews were conducted using end-to-end encrypted software (Microsoft Teams 1.6) to ensure confidentiality. Our research team developed an interview guide based on the initial responses from quantitative measures indicating that the pandemic was affecting individuals residing in the shelter. The interviewer asked the following questions and prompts:

1. Since COVID-19 is on our minds, I'd like to start by asking about how COVID-19 has or has not impacted the ways that people you know think about their health. How has the virus impacted the way people think about health risks like IPV, HIV, and SUD?
2. How has COVID-19 affected people that you know in their ability to access:
    a. IPV services;
    b. Substance use services;
    c. Services related to your sexual health (exams, testing, etc.);
    d. Other health care services?
3. Is there anything else you would like to tell me about how COVID-19 has impacted people with interpersonal violence in their lives?

Other questions were asked about HIV and risks of violence but are not reported here.

2.2.2. Interview Implementation with Clients

Individuals recruited from the same IPV shelter were recruited for interviews by shelter staff, as described in the preceding section, between 31 August 2020 and 4 November 2020. To ensure client safety and reduce the chances of retraumatization, only individuals residing in the shelter and demonstrating emotional stability at the time of recruitment (as determined by shelter staff) were invited to participate. Additionally, only individuals that were 18 years or older and identifying as female were eligible to participate. Shelter staff distributed interview packets to interested participants. Interview packets included a copy of the consent form, examples of the interview questions, and a resource list with contact numbers for local medical and violence service providers. Interviewees may or may not have also participated in client surveys. Identifying information was not cross checked.

Prior to beginning each interview, the interviewer asked each participant to confirm that they were in a safe, private location, reviewed the consent form, and obtained verbal consent. The interviewer also asked participants if they felt comfortable continuing the interview and if their privacy level changed throughout the interview. Interviews took between 30 and 60 min to complete and explored the impacts of COVID-19, including personal experiences, changes in access to services, and effects of COVID-19 in the context of IPV, HIV, and substance use. After each interview, the participant received a $30 gift card to a local grocery store via email.

The interviewer was trained to identify, respond to, and assess the client's distress; determine the next steps (to conclude or continue the interview); and follow up with IPV service-providing staff to report any distressing incidents (none were reported). In-depth interviews were conducted, recorded, and transcribed using Microsoft Teams. The transcribed files were uploaded to Dedoose, a mixed-methods software (version 8.3.43), to be coded and analyzed.

2.3. Quantitative Data Collection (Staff)

Staff working in the shelter where clients were residing (staff) were invited to participate in a longitudinal survey (i.e., two rounds of data collection) and one close-out interview. These staff surveys included baseline (spring 2020) and follow-up (winter 2021) measures asking participants about the impacts and challenges of the COVID-19 pandemic.

2.3.1. Instrument Development for Staff

Similar to the instruments used with clients, dichotomous and Likert-scale survey items were created based on a mutually exclusive review of available COVID-19 instruments [56–61]. A unique ID was created for each participant to be able to assess their individual changes over time. Participants were first asked to indicate (yes = 1, left blank = 0) if they had experienced any of the following COVID-19 stressors and workplace challenges:

1. Worry/anxiety about being infected;
2. Changes in physical health;
3. Challenges in workplace due to social distancing;
4. Challenges in workplace due to loss of childcare;
5. Challenges in workplace due to technology issues (loss of internet, lack of necessary equipment);
6. Challenges in workplace due to services normally provided impeded by the precautions;
7. Challenges in workplace due to changes to client mental or physical health;
8. Challenges in workplace due to changes to how services are provided to clients.

For each item above, if individuals reported they had experienced it or any workplace challenge, they were then asked to indicate on a 5-point scale (0 = not at all to 4 = greatly/a lot) how much each experience affected them. If participants experienced changes in how they provided services to clients at the IPV shelter, they were also asked to indicate on a 5-point scale (0 = not at all to 4 = greatly/a lot) how confident they felt in administering services in the new way. Additionally, staff were given the option to indicate "yes" or "no" on whether they had experienced other changes to their lives or behaviors due to COVID-19. If a participant indicated "yes," they were encouraged to then list the additional changes to their life or behavior that they had experienced as a result of COVID-19. Other items in the survey asked about HIV knowledge and having the self-confidence to ask clients about sexual safety planning, but they are not the subject of this study.

2.3.2. Survey Administration to Staff

All shelter staff, including, but not limited to, advocates, therapists, group leaders, supervisors/directors, and service coordinators, were invited by the study team and encouraged by leadership at the shelter to complete the 25 min, confidential, online baseline survey between 1 June and 30 July 2020 and the follow-up survey between 18 January and 9 March 2021. The study team and leadership introduced the purpose of the survey during an all-staff meeting. Afterward, an email was sent to each staff member reintroducing the study and inviting them to participate, followed by personalized links to the survey developed by Qualtrics, and distributed to each of the staff via email. Staff received three email reminders during the survey administration period. To enhance staff participation, the study team followed up with department leads to encourage their team members to complete the survey, and staff who completed the survey were entered into a drawing to win one of four $50 Visa gift cards. The winners were randomly selected using Excel. Survey responses were exported to an excel document and merged using SPSS for analysis.

2.4. *Qualitative Data Collection (Staff)*

In-depth interviews with staff were held as project close-out interviews during the summer of 2021. Three members of our team that were trained in data collection with human subjects conducted the in-depth interviews to gain insight into the staff's thoughts on implemented program activities regarding HIV, HIV testing, and behaviors related to COVID-19.

2.4.1. Interview Guide for Staff

All interviews were conducted using end-to-end encrypted software (Microsoft Teams 1.6) to ensure confidentiality. Our research team developed an interview guide based on responses from quantitative measures and activities conducted as part of the larger project. The interviewers, all qualitative methods-trained researchers, asked the following questions and prompts:

1. While we are really proud of our work together on this project, one thing we found is that staff report that they still struggle with conversations with clients about substance use, HIV, and IPV. What are your thoughts about this? (Probe: What do you think might be keeping staff (or you) from having conversations about substance use, HIV, IPV?)
2. Some IPV shelter clients have taken advantage of the opportunity to get a free, confidential HIV test in shelter. Others have not. Some of these clients have chosen to go elsewhere to get tested. Why do you think women are not getting tested in shelter?
3. Thinking back, what did you appreciate about this project? (Activities included training on HIV, training on how to talk to clients about HIV and make sexual safety plans, new protocols for HIV testing in shelter and for non-residential clients, and surveys of staff and clients).
4. What would you have done differently?
5. Anything else that we should know as we wrap up the project and write up our lessons learned for other IPV advocate service agencies?

2.4.2. Interview Implementation with Staff

Staff from the same IPV shelter were recruited for interviews via emails sent from project researchers between 1 October and 4 November 2021 (interviews took place from 8 October to 4 November). Prior to beginning each interview, the interviewer reviewed the consent form and obtained verbal consent from the participant. The interviews were recorded and transcribed for analysis. After each interview, the participant was emailed a $10 gift card. Although none of the interview questions for staff asked anything specifically about experiences with COVID-19, some staff responses were relevant as explained in Section 3.

2.5. Data Analysis

2.5.1. Survey Data Analysis

A trained statistician cleaned the data and removed any identifying information before conducting descriptive analyses on the survey responses. Many participants seemed confused by the presentation of the questions that asked them to both indicate if an experience had happened and then rate how much it had affected them. To correct for any confusion, frequencies of experiences include any response of "yes," indicating the experience happened, and any response to the level of affectedness that was greater than zero. That is, if a participant did not respond to the item asking if the event happened, but did rate it as having affected them, that item was counted as a positive response to the experience having happened.

Our research team discussed the descriptive results, including the means, standard deviations, and frequencies of responses, before determining final analysis plans. Further analyses included conducting paired and independent tests for differences in means (Student's *t*-test), correlations between survey response items (Spearman's r-test), and non-parametric measures of sample differences (Mann–Whitney U-test).

2.5.2. Interview and Open-Ended Response Data Analysis

The qualitative data from the client interviews were segmented to develop a coding scheme using an iterative and inductive approach. After the initial coding scheme was developed, the data were exported by the software and catalogued in a codebook. Another member of the project team completed a preliminary review of the coding scheme and findings to further organize and hone themes into more descriptive categories as well as to ensure uniformity across all aspects of the analysis. Both primary analysts conducted additional reviews of the thematic analysis to reach a consensus on the main themes and to identify significant findings. After the initial review, the findings were presented to the larger team for discussion and review to finalize themes. Findings were also shared with the project's community advisory board, who championed the idea and helped to construct a conceptual model that aligns with Duluth's Model Power and Control Wheel [49] (see Results). These findings were first presented at the 14th Annual InWomen's Conference [50].

Staff interviews were similarly analyzed using a grounded theory approach [62] by one reviewer that was trained in qualitative methodology, and codes were reviewed by the project director (first author). Like those of client interviews, the results of staff interviews were shared with the community advisory board. Open-ended responses from staff surveys were iteratively reviewed and segmented into themes and thematically coded using a grounded theory approach as well.

3. Results

3.1. Quantitative Results (Clients)

During the first data collection period, a total of 19 clients completed the surveys. A different set of 15 clients completed the same surveys 5–7 months later, at time 2. The demographics for clients who participated in the surveys (time 1 and time 2) are listed in Table 1. The frequency and percent response rates for each COVID-19 experience, as well as the average response scores for how much each item affected clients, are listed in Table 2. Some of the frequency responses between clients selecting a COVID-19 experience and rating their level of affect may differ due to missing data. No clients at time 1 and only two clients at time 2 reported that they had experienced "no changes to [their] life or behavior."

Table 1. Clients' demographic characteristics.

Items						
	Time 1 (n = 19)			**Time 2 (n = 15)**		
	Minimum	**Maximum**	**Mean**	**Minimum**	**Maximum**	**Mean**
Age	21	61	38.8	29	57	38.3
Number of Children	0	4	1.87	1	5	2.80

Items	**Response Frequencies**			
	Time 1		**Time 2**	
Relationship Status	*n*	%	*n*	%
Married	3	15.8	1	7.1
Dating > 1 person	0	–	1	7.1
Dating 1 person	0	–	2	14.3
Dating 1 person in a serious relationship	1	5.3	3	21.14
Single	15	78.9	7	50.0
Total	19	100.0	14	100.0
Gender Identity	*n*	%	*n*	%
Female	16	84.2	12	80.0
Male	1	5.3	2	13.3
Other (transgender, other, or preferred not to answer)	2	10.6	1	6.7
Total	19	100.0	15	100.0
Highest Level of Education	*n*	%	*n*	%
Some college	8	42.1	5	33.3
Some high school	4	21.1	4	26.7
College degree	0	–	3	20.0
High-school graduate or GED	4	21.1	2	13.3
Less than high school	3	15.8	1	6.7
Total	19	100.0	15	100.0
Health Insurance Status	*n*	%	*n*	%
No health insurance	2	10.5	1	6.7
Private insurance	2	10.5	1	6.7
Public insurance (Medicaid, Medicare)	14	73.7	13	86.7
Total	18	100.0	15	100.0
Employment Status	*n*	%	*n*	%
Not currently working	13	68.4	13	86.7
Working full or part time or a student	5	26.4	2	13.3
Total	18	100.0	15	100.0
Race	*n*	%	*n*	%
White/Caucasian	9	47.4	8	53.3
Black or African American	5	26.3	5	33.3
American Indian	4	21.2	3	20.0
Other [a]	9	47.4	2	6.7
Total	18	100.0	15	100.0

[a] American Indian; American Indian, White/Caucasian; Black or African American, Native Hawaiian or Other Pacific Islander; Bosnian/Eastern European.

All items related to COVID-19 were experienced by a majority of the participants at time 1, including 68% indicating that they had experienced a COVID-19 diagnosis and/or had changes to their physical health (Table 2). By time 2, no clients indicated experiencing COVID-19 diagnoses, and around one-third indicated worry about being infected (33%), changes in physical health (33%), not having enough basic supplies (40%), or their children experiencing distress (33%). However, although the percentage scores decreased for the following items from time 1 to time 2, a majority of clients still indicated experiencing interpersonal conflict (53%), feeling more depression and loneliness (60%), feeling less safe (60%), and feeling more abused (67%). Moreover, average scores for how clients were affected by these last five items increased between clients surveyed at time 1 and those surveyed at time 2. To determine if these increases were significant, we conducted an independent-samples *t*-test on the clients' reported affectedness for each item, using Bonferroni correction for multiple analyses. As captured in Table 2, none of the changes from time 1 to time 2 were significant, indicating that clients at each time reported the same level of affectedness for these experiences.

Table 2. Clients' COVID-19 experiences.

Experiences	**Response Frequencies**				**Level of Affectedness**				**Significance**	
	Time 1 (n = 19)		**Time 2 (n = 15)**		**Time 1 (n = 19)**		**Time 2 (n = 15)**			
	n	%	n	%	n	**Mean** [a]	n	**Mean** [a]	**(df) t**	p
COVID-19 diagnosis	13	68.4	0	0	13	0.15	0	0	–	–
Worry/anxiety about being infected	18	94.7	5	33.3	17	1.88	8	1.83	(27) 0.08	0.93
Changes in physical health	13	68.4	5	33.3	12	0.75	6	0.91	(21) −0.34	0.74
Not having enough basic supplies	16	84.2	6	40.0	15	2.47	8	2.09	(24) 0.57 [b]	0.58
Children experiencing distress	14	73.7	5	33.3	14	1.5	4	1.33	(21) 0.27 [b]	0.79
Interpersonal conflict with family or loved ones	18	94.7	8	53.3	16	2.38	8	2	(25) 0.62	0.54
Feeling more depression	19	100.0	9	60.0	17	2.65	10	2.42	(27) 0.45	0.66
Feeling more loneliness	19	100.0	9	60.0	17	2.76	10	2.5	(27) 0.47 [b]	0.65
Feeling less safe	17	89.5	9	60.0	15	2.27	10	2.31	(26) −0.07	0.95
Feeling more abused	17	89.5	10	66.7	16	2.25	10	2.83	(26) −1.07	0.29
No changes to my life or behavior	0	0	2	13.3	–	–	–	–	–	–
Coping Strategies	n	%	n	%	n	**Mean** [a]	n	**Mean** [a]	**(df) t** [c]	p
Feeling grateful for the break from usual activities	12	63.2	13	86.7	12	0.54	5	1.0	(23) 0.92	0.37
Connecting with others, including talking with people you trust about your concerns and how you are feeling	15	78.9	10	66.7	14	1.17	9	1.25	(24) 1.37	0.18
Needing more/less sleep or other changes to your normal sleep pattern	16	84.2	8	53.3	14	2.54	11	1.5	(25) −0.44	0.67
Taking breaks from watching, reading, or listening to news stories, including social media	16	84.2	9	60.0	15	3.0	10	1.4	(25) −2.65	0.01
Healthy behaviors like trying to eat healthy, well-balanced meals, exercising regularly, getting plenty of sleep, or avoiding alcohol and drugs	14	73.7	10	66.7	14	2.0	10	1.75	(24) 0.21	0.84
Engaging in more family activities	12	63.2	13	86.7	12	1.55	6	1.5	(21) −0.34	0.74
Talking with a mental health care provider.	17	89.5	8	53.3	15	1.92	10	1.5	(25) 0.14	0.89

[a] Scale: 0 = not at all to 4 = greatly/a lot. [b] Where indicated, Levene's test for equal variances was significant, and reported *t*-test and significance levels reflect an assumption for unequal variances. [c] Equal variances assumed for all items.

Table 2 also depicts results of the coping strategies clients used. At time 1, only two clients (11%) indicated that they had experienced none of these coping strategies, and at time 2, zero clients indicated that they had not used any of these coping strategies. Like with COVID-19 experiences, most clients reported using all the listed coping strategies at time 1, and fewer indicated using these strategies 5–7 months later; exceptions include "feeling grateful for the break from usual activities" and "engaging in more family activities," both of which increased in prevalence by time 2. We also conducted independent-samples *t*-tests for how much each of the coping strategies affected clients and found no differences between time 1 and time 2 (corrected alpha of 0.006).

Table 3 shows changes in clients' substance use from time 1 to time 2. Most clients at time 1 indicated that their use of alcohol (90%), illegal substances (58%), and tobacco (68%) had changed. In the interviews 5–7 months later, fewer clients indicated that their use of alcohol (73%), illegal substances (27%), and tobacco (33%) had changed. Earlier in the pandemic (time 1), clients, on average, reported that their substance use for all three categories had increased (scores > 3). By 5–7 months later, clients reported using less alcohol and tobacco (scores < 3), but still more illegal drugs since the start of COVID-19 as well as since time 1, although these reported changes in the amount of use were non-significant (Table 3).

Table 3. Clients' substance use.

Substance (Change in Use)	**Response Frequencies**				**Change in Use**				**Significance**	
	Time 1 (n = 19)		**Time 2 (n = 15)**		**Time 1 (n = 19)**		**Time 2 (n = 15)**			
	n	%	n	%	n	**Mean** [e]	n	**Mean** [e]	**(df) t** [f]	p
Alcohol	17	89.5	11	73.3	10	3.56	5	2.90	(13) −0.37	0.72
Illicit or illegal substances (e.g., marijuana, prescription drugs not prescribed to you, or meth).	11	57.9	4	26.7	12	3.10	4	3.40	(14) 0.96	0.32
Tobacco use (e.g., smoking cigarettes, e-cigs, vapes, or chewing tobacco).	13	68.4	5	33.3	16	3.58	10	2.75	(24) 1.26	0.22

[e] Scale: 1 = went down a lot, 2 = went down slightly, 3 = stayed the same, 4 = went up slightly, and 5 = went up a lot; Equal variances assumed for all items. [f] Levene's test for equal variances was significant, and reported *t*-test and significance levels reflect an assumption for unequal variances.

We also conducted Spearman's rank-order correlations to determine if reports of survivors' experiences of more loneliness, depression, and abuse were related to reports of greater substance use. Again, we used a Bonferroni correction (alpha rate of 0.006) as a conservative correction to account for running multiple correlations. At time 1, feeling more loneliness was associated with feeling more depression and feeling more abused. At time 2, the relationships changed such that depression was associated with feeling more loneliness, less safe, and more abused. Table 4 shows the complete results of these analyses.

Table 4. Correlations between clients' experiences.

	Time 1 (n = 19)				**Time 2 (n = 15)**			
Clients' Experience		r	p	n		r	p	n
Depression	Loneliness *	0.697	0.002	17	Loneliness *	0.924	<0.001	12
	Less safe	0.508	0.053	15	Less safe *	0.712	0.009	12
	More abused	0.561	0.029	15	More abused *	0.74	0.006	12
	Tobacco use	0.216	0.458	14	Tobacco use	0.411	0.272	9
	Alcohol use	0.557	0.152	8	Alcohol use	0.738	0.262	4
	Illicit use	0.269	0.451	10	Illicit use	0	1	3

Table 4. *Cont.*

	Time 1 (n = 19)				Time 2 (n = 15)			
Clients' Experience		r	p	n		r	p	n
Loneliness	Less safe	0.493	0.062	15	Less safe	0.668	0.018	12
	More abused *	0.717	0.003	15	More abused	0.508	0.092	12
	Tobacco use	0.085	0.772	14	Tobacco use	0.32	0.402	9
	Alcohol use	0.6	0.115	8	Alcohol use	0.258	0.742	4
	Illicit use	−0.073	0.842	10	Illicit use	−0.5	0.667	3
Less safe	More abused	0.449	0.093	15	More abused	0.47	0.123	12
	Tobacco use	0.099	0.749	13	Tobacco use	0.41	0.273	9
	Alcohol use	0.478	0.231	8	Alcohol use	0.703	0.185	5
	Illicit use	−0.453	0.188	10	Illicit use	0	1	4
More abused	Tobacco use	0.022	0.941	14	Tobacco use	0.187	0.63	9
	Alcohol use	0	1	9	Alcohol use	0.775	0.225	4
	Illicit use	−0.393	0.231	11	Illicit use	1.000		3

* Denotes significance.

3.2. *Qualitative Results (Clients)*

Interviews were conducted with six clients receiving services in the IPV resident shelter. We conducted a thematic coding of the client interviews, which yielded three primary themes related to COVID-19: (1) IPV survivors experienced impacts of COVID-19 on their mental and physical health, (2) survivors shared the effects of stay-at-home orders on support system/services access and financial security, and (3) COVID-19-related experiences were retraumatizing for clients because they mirrored how abusers use power and control to perpetrate aspects of IPV. These identified themes were mapped onto most of the elements of the Duluth Model Power and Control Wheel of IPV [49] presented in Figure 1 and present a substantial overlap. Figure 2 depicts the relationship between COVID-19 experiences reported by survivors interviewed in this study and the traditional elements of power and control used by violent perpetrators, as well as exemplary quotes from survivors relating to each element.

3.2.1. COVID-19 Impacts on Clients' Physical and Mental Health

Participants reported that their physical health was at risk during the pandemic given the increased risk of infection of COVID-19 in addition to the postponing of needed healthcare as a result of navigating care in an overburdened healthcare system. Medical professionals' focus on COVID-19 infections also meant there was less focus on other health needs, such as HIV and IPV care, according to participants. Broadly, clients described increased stress levels relative to changes in income, access to services and support systems, and worry and uncertainty about COVID-19 testing and screening. Further, participants shared the compounding effects of having a history of trauma with the emotional impacts of the pandemic. One participant described this by saying, "People feel like they are not going to make it [emotionally]. There is a heaviness like a burden." An increased engagement in negative coping mechanisms, such as substance use, and a decrease in resiliency was also identified.

Figure 1. The Duluth Models Power and Control Wheel [49]. Reprinted with written permission from Domestic Abuse Intervention Programs (DAIP) of Duluth, MN.

3.2.2. COVID-19 Limited Access to Support Systems/Services and Financial Security

Like a violent partner, COVID-19 restrictions limited access to supportive systems such as family and friends because guidance included avoiding contact with anyone outside of one's household. While this separation could mitigate the spread of infection, clients indicated that it led to stress, a loss of social connectedness and feelings of support, and other negative mental health issues. Additionally, clients were affected by COVID-19 regulations around health care providers' offices, including longer wait times, providers not accepting new patients, offices disallowing supportive health advocates, stifling personal protective equipment requirements, the burden of following public health guidelines (e.g., having to shout personal information through a plastic screen), and a fear of COVID-19 infection. Participants also shared challenges related to sexual healthcare, safe-sex supplies, and contraception choices, all of which can also be made difficult to obtain or use appropriately when in a violent relationship. Financial instability was also posed given changes in employment status.

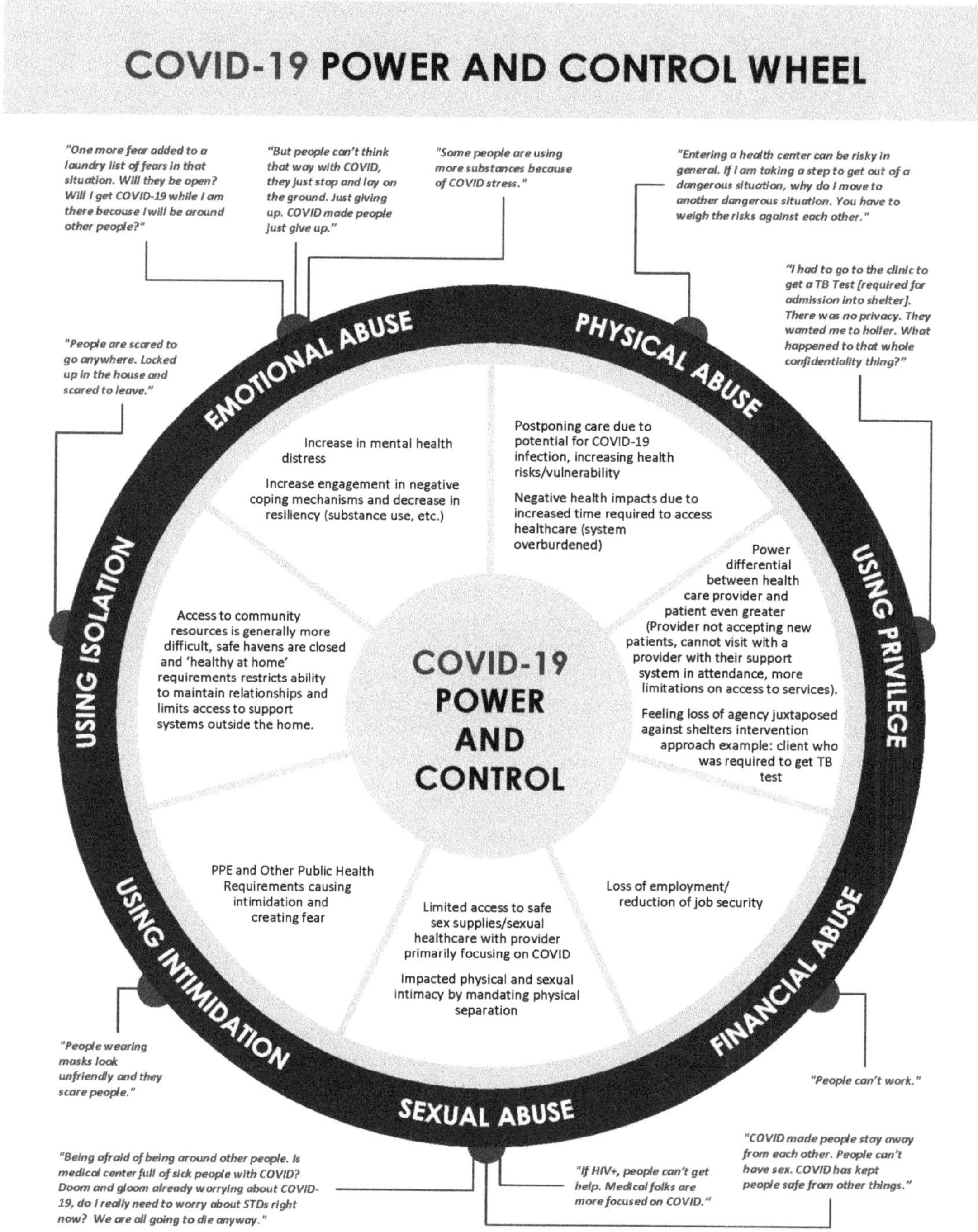

Figure 2. COVID-19 power and control wheel. Duluth's Power and Control Wheel [49] was used as a framework to show how COVID-19 emphasized and provided new examples of IPV. This adaptation was first presented by Bauer et al. [50] at the 14th Annual InWomen's Conference.

3.2.3. Clients Were Retraumatized by COVID-19 Restrictions

Interviews suggested the pattern of COVID-19-related health directives was similar to how perpetrators of violence use power to control their partners. Our findings suggest that the virus, in addition to government-sanctioned control over bodily autonomy (mask mandates) and restrictions to movement, was retraumatizing for survivors. Further, participants indicated that wearing personal protective equipment made individuals appear menacing. Power differentials (privilege) between clients and their providers were also described as being exacerbated given changes to healthcare access and strict protocols for accessing services. Feelings of lost agency imposed by the shelter's policies were also described by a participant who was required to have a tuberculosis test before being allowed to reside in the shelter.

3.3. *Quantitative Results (Staff)*

During the four-week baseline data collection period, a total of 59 staff members participated in the survey. In the follow-up survey, 40 staff members participated. Of those 40, 35 also took the baseline survey. The demographics of all staff who participated in the surveys (baseline and follow up) are listed in Table 5.

Table 5. Staff's demographics.

Items	**Baseline (n = 59)**			**Follow Up (n = 40)**		
	Minimum	**Maximum**	**Mean**	**Minimum**	**Maximum**	**Mean**
Age	21	61	38.8	29	57	38.3
Professional Experience						
Months worked at the center	2	300	46.72	1	228	47.7
Months worked with people who have experienced IPV	0	300	54.72	0	420	79.0
Items	**Response Frequencies**					
	Baseline (n = 59)		**Follow Up (n = 40)**			
Gender Identity	n	%	n	%		
Female	46	79.3	31	83.8		
Male	6	10.3	4	10.8		
Nonbinary/prefer not to say	6	3.4	1	2.7		
Total	58	100.0	37	100.0		
Highest Level of Education	n	%	n	%		
High-school graduate or GED	1	1.7	1	2.7		
Some college	5	8.6	1	2.7		
College degree	34	58.6	23	62.2		
Post-graduate degree	18	31	12	32.4		
Total	58	100.0	37	100.0		
Current Job Title	n	%	n	%		
Advocate	28	49.1	23	62.2		
Administrative positions	13	22.8	4	10.8		
Supervisor	4	7.0	4	10.8		
Counselor/Therapist	3	5.3	2	5.4		
Prevention Coordinator	2	3.5	–	–		
Director	2	3.5	2	5.4		
Other [a]	5	8.8	2	5.4		
Total	57	100.0	37	100.0		
Race/Ethnicity	n	%	n	%		
Hispanic/Latino	2	3.5	0	0		
White/Caucasian	42	73.7	25	62.5		

Table 5. *Cont.*

Items	Baseline (n = 59)			Follow Up (n = 40)		
	Minimum	Maximum	Mean	Minimum	Maximum	Mean
Black or African American	9		15.8	11		27.5
Asian, Native Hawaiian, or other Pacific Islander	1		1.8	1		2.5
American Indian	1		1.8	0		0
Other	2		3.4	1		2.5
Total	57		100.0	38		100.0

[a] Intern Therapist/Coordinator, Volunteer Coordinator, Art Therapist, Building Services, Coordinator, Outreach Coordinator, DV Housing Coordinator.

The frequency and percentage response rates for each COVID-19 experience, as well as the average response scores for how much each item affected the staff, are listed in Table 6. Some of the frequency responses between staff selecting a COVID-19 experience and rating their level of affect may differ due to missing data. Only two staff at baseline and no staff at follow up reported that they had experienced "none of the above" changes to their lives or behaviors, but both sets of staff indicated that they had experienced other changes that were not listed. Most COVID-19-related experiences were reported at similar rates by staff at baseline and follow up. Worry about being infected, changes in physical health, social distancing, and changes in how staff provided services to clients all slightly decreased from baseline to follow up. The reported loss of childcare, services provided by them being made more difficult, and changes in their mental or physical health all increased from baseline to follow up. To determine if these changes were significant, we conducted paired-samples t-tests on staff's reported affectedness by each item, using Bonferroni correction for multiple analyses. As captured in Table 6, none of the changes from baseline to follow up were significant, indicating that staff also reported the same level of affectedness for these experiences at follow up as they did at baseline.

Table 6. Staff's COVID-19 experiences.

Experience	Response Frequencies				Average Affected Score				Significance [b]	
	Baseline (n = 59)		Follow Up (n = 40)		Baseline (n = 59)		Follow Up (n = 40)		(n = 35)	
	n	%	n	%	n	Mean [a]	n	Mean [a]	(df) t	p
Worry/anxiety about being infected	49	83.1	32	80.0	49	2.86	31	2.74	(20) −0.33	0.75
Changes in physical health	19	32.2	12	30.0	18	2.44	12	2.75	(5) 0.00	1.00
Challenges in your workplace due to:	n	%	n	%	n	Mean [a]	n	Mean [a]	(df) t	p
Social distancing	44	74.6	29	72.5	44	3.00	28	2.79	(14) 0.52	0.61
Loss of childcare	7	11.9	5	12.5	7	3.29	5	2.20	(1) −0.33	0.80
Technology issues (e.g., loss of internet)	17	28.8	12	30.0	17	2.24	12	2.08	(4) 0.54	0.62
Services you provide were made difficult by the precautions	32	54.2	22	55.0	32	2.66	21	2.57	(9) −0.56	0.60
Changes in client mental and/or physical health	26	44.1	27	67.5	26	2.88	26	3.00	(11) −2.70	0.02
Changes in how you provide services to your clients	42	71.2	24	60.0	42	2.95	23	2.74	(15) −0.22	0.83
If yes, how confident do you feel in administering services this new way?	–	–	–	–	40	2.90	23	2.83	(14) 1.83	0.09
None of the above	2	3.4	0	0	–	–	–	–	–	–
Have there been other changes to your life or behavior due to COVID-19?	36	61.0	21	55.3	–	–	–	–	–	–

[a] Scale: 0 = not at all to 4 = greatly/a lot. [b] Significance tests represent paired t-tests.

3.4. Qualitative Results (Staff)

The final staff survey question included an open-ended response option for staff to report other changes in their lives or behaviors. These open-ended responses from the baseline and follow-up surveys were reviewed and thematically coded (see Table 7). The coders agreed on 11 primary themes from these responses. The remaining responses that did not fit into these 11 categories included limited food and supplies in stores, online classes, an appreciation for well-being, and struggles in faith.

Table 7. Staff's open-ended responses of COVID-19 experiences.

Themes	Response Frequencies			
	Baseline (*n* = 36; 75 Responses)		Follow Up (*n* = 21; 36 Responses)	
	n	%	*n*	%
Changes to spending time with family or friends and/or challenges with not seeing or being physically close to family or friends	15	20.0	5	13.9
Changes to self-care plans/coping strategies, including hobbies and/or recreational activities	13	17.3	3	8.3
Mental health challenges and/or emotional distress	12	16.0	12	33.3
Mental health challenges and/or emotional distress specifically due to work changes or challenges	5	6.7	4	11.1
Work changes and challenges (e.g., longer hours, staff capacity, or telecommuting)	11	14.7	6	16.7
Concerns and/or worries about oneself or others being infected, including increased safety precautions	8	10.7	4	11.1
Changes in schedules, routines, or roles	4	5.3	–	–
Competing professional and parental responsibilities, including child's schoolwork; difficulty with time management	3	4.0	2	5.6
Difficulty planning for future	2	2.7	–	–
Personal loss	2	2.7	3	8.3
Financial challenges and/or budgeting changes	2	2.7	1	2.8
Other	3	4.0	2	5.6

Although none of the interview questions for staff asked anything specifically about experiences with COVID-19, staff still mentioned difficulties associated with the pandemic during interviews. Across ten interviews with participating staff from the IPV shelter, seven staff explicitly mentioned COVID-19. The primary theme regarding COVID-19-related responses was that work related to the project and in general was made particularly difficult by the pandemic. Staff indicated that COVID-19 restrictions and near daily changes to safety protocols changed how they interacted with clients. Two of the interviewees specifically suggested that COVID-19 affected everyone working in the helping field because "we cannot do in-person contact" as usual. The inability to work face-to-face with clients changed how staff were able to interact with clients. Most staff also indicated that they desired more in-person service to resume.

4. Discussion

Our findings are relevant as the effects of COVID-19 continue and the potential for future global health crises rises. We describe survivors' mental health and substance use changes related to the COVID-19 pandemic as well as provider responses to the pandemic so that service providers can better address these concerns with their clients and better support their staff. Both clients and staff reported multiple affecting experiences related to

COVID-19. In fact, of the nearly 100 persons we surveyed, only two individuals indicated that COVID-19 had not affected their lives or behaviors. Both clients and service providers indicated that the unintended consequences of the pandemic and related health regulations included not being able to meet their basic needs for food and supplies in addition to financial challenges and mental and emotional health changes. When preparing for the next public health emergency, it will be important that the plans used in 2020 are revised to better meet individuals' basic needs.

Many of the effects of COVID-19 reported by survivors of violence, such as contracting COVID-19 and worrying about infection, may have been experienced by anyone during the pandemic. Importantly, these results indicate that survivors of violence were also reporting potentially more serious or retraumatizing outcomes such as increased feelings of loneliness, depression, and abuse. The changes from time 1 to time 2 across these more concerning items were not significant, indicating that the clients surveyed at time 1 reported the same level of affectedness for these experiences as those surveyed at time 2. Due to our limited sample size, we also ran nonparametric tests (Mann–Whitney U-tests) for significance on these measures, which revealed the same conclusions. These conclusions were, namely, that survivors reported an increase in negative mental and physical health outcomes because of COVID-19 and related public health regulations, which did not get better even after nearly half a year. These results suggest that mental health will also be a primary concern during the next public health emergency. Providers, communities, and policy makers must work together to address current workforce shortages in mental health and wellness, and researchers and practitioners should further investigate virtual methods of treatment so that we are better prepared in the future.

Furthermore, clients reported an increase in substance misuse in the early pandemic. Although fewer survivors surveyed in the spring of 2021 reported an increase in their alcohol or tobacco use as a result of COVID-19-related experiences, the changes over time were not significant. The survivors surveyed at time 2 also represent a different, independent set of participants which may have behaved differently at time 1. Worryingly, survivors reported pandemic-related increases in illicit drug use, including marijuana, prescription drug misuse, and methamphetamines, both early in the pandemic (summer 2020) and almost half a year later. Although fewer survivors reported an increase in using illegal substances at time 2, scores relating to survivors' amount of use did not significantly change over time, indicating that the increase in use was similar for survivors who were using at both time points. As the effects of the COVID-19 pandemic continue, those working with survivors of violence need to be aware of the possibility that substance use is common among survivors and may have increased since 2020. This study draws further attention to the need for multisector and co-located services for survivors of violence that include mental and behavioral healthcare and, specifically, trauma-informed substance use treatment and recovery.

Our correlational analysis suggests that feelings of loneliness, depression, safety, and abuse are positively related. The relationship between these negative mental health outcomes and abuse is not surprising given that previous research has found associations between experiencing IPV and depression, PTSD, anxiety, and dysthymia [32,33]. Changes in mental health seem to co-occur with experiences of violence and all changes remained mostly consistent over time, indicating that survivors may not have experienced relief as COVID-19 restrictions have lapsed. Some of these mental health effects could also be related to changes in service provisions and provider capacities as service providers were also suffering from stress due to the pandemic. The clients' reports of feeling more abused and less safe may be related to actual increases in violence perpetration and/or the retraumatizing effects of COVID-19-related regulations as described in client interviews. It was indeed some of these findings related to the COVID-19 experiences of survivors that led us to add questions related to COVID-19 to our interviews with survivors. Sharing these results may help future researchers and service providers work together to develop preemptive interventions for survivors that combat the tendency for public health measures to retraumatize survivors.

The interview results suggested that COVID-19 may be perceived as mirroring the power and controlling aspects of IPV. We present a substantial overlap between the emotional abuse perpetrated by a controlling partner and the impact of public health guidance and fears of infection from COVID-19 (see Figure 2). Comparable to the bodily harm of physical violence, postponing healthcare due to a fear of infection or acquiring care in an over-burdened healthcare system can result in adverse physical health effects. Power differentials (privilege) between clients and providers are intensified given restrictions on healthcare access and strict protocols for accessing services. Like a violent perpetrator, COVID-19 restrictions limit access to sexual healthcare, safe-sex supplies, and contraception choices. Support system access is limited by 'healthy at home' ordinances. Other commonalities include the menacing appearance of PPE and a lack of control of finances with employment disruptions. Retraumatization may further exacerbate the psychological and physical impacts brought on by the pandemic in addition to triggering survivors of IPV. These findings suggest that the Duluth Model of Power and Control [49] may be useful as a framework through which practitioners can understand and more directly address the possibility of re-occurring trauma due to COVID-19 and future pandemics and which offers the following tangible suggestions for service providers [63,64]:

- Reduce the menacing appearance of PPE by making your name easily readable or attaching a photograph of yourself;
- Openly share changes in practice due to COVID-19 and communicate an understanding of how the pandemic and new protocols can be retraumatizing;
- Include the client's voice when developing a care/services plan to maintain their autonomy;
- Reduce accessibility barriers by offering telehealth services.

Our results related to staff experiences may help explain some of the loneliness, depression, and safety concerns experienced by clients. Staff also experienced the expected outcomes of living through a pandemic, including a lack of access to basic needs, financial instability, and worry about infection. Staff also experienced negative mental health outcomes and reported that they made changes to how they worked with clients because of COVID-19 experiences. This study confirms that IPV service providers, like others in the helping field, were greatly affected by the pandemic. It is highly likely that staff experiencing such stressors were unable to provide pre-pandemic levels of attentiveness and care, despite their best intentions. Some pre-pandemic services, such as shelter capacity and face-to-face counseling, also decreased or ceased entirely during the pandemic to meet COVID-19-related safety precautions. These changes in quality or perceived quality of care could provide some reasoning as to why survivors were experiencing worsening mental health and seeking other coping mechanisms, such as substance misuse. Other themes that have come out of working and talking with IPV service providers include challenges due to low retention of staff, a lack of hazard pay, and a general lack of workforce available and willing to take on the demanding work involved with supporting survivors of violence. Furthermore, staff desired to see services return to pre-pandemic methods, especially to connect more in person with clients. Charitable and government funders should consider providing additional support and extending incentives so that service providers working with this population can be paid equitably relative to the risks and difficulties of this work.

The primary limitation of this study is its sample size. Our sample of survivors at time 1 was small ($n = 19$) and at time 2 even smaller ($n = 15$). Further, a limitation of all cross-sectional research is the possibility that the differences in individuals participating over time may impact the outcomes being studied. Our sampling method is also subject to sampling and self-selection bias, another limitation of this work. Additionally, interviews were conducted with only six survivors and all data collection was limited to a sample of individuals living in the same Southern state and receiving residential services from the same provider. Our staff sample was larger and enabled a repeated-measures analysis but was still limited in size ($n = 35$) and geographic location and by the fact that all staff were employed by the same service-providing organization. Given the limitations of this study, including sample size and all participants residing in the same shelter, we caution against generalizing these results to the wider population. Future research should be conducted to confirm these findings and test its applicability for other kinds of trauma-informed care.

Our results are also limited by the fact that survivors' and staff's changes in mental/physical health and changes in substance misuse by survivors are both self-reported. Future work could confirm physical changes, such as COVID-19 diagnoses, as well as emotional changes by measuring depression and anxiety using validated instruments. Although two of our reference sources for instrument creation have not been validated, they have been used by other researchers and come from reputable sources (i.e., the Harris Poll). Our interviews with clients and staff were also limited by individual availability and the capacity of our partner IPV service-providing organization. Due to the challenges of the pandemic, including a lack of workforce and PPE, staff were unable to recruit and schedule interviews with more than six clients residing in the shelter in the summer of 2020. The turnover of staff at the organization was also very high (at least 44 staff members left the organization between 2020 and 2021), which limited our ability to conduct paired analyses and recruit for staff interviews. Finally, staff interviews were not designed to measure COVID-19-related information. Adding COVID-19-related questions to staff interviews would allow for further investigation of the challenges and changes related to COVID-19.

5. Conclusions

COVID-19 has been and continues to be devastating for many reasons. The impacts and ramifications of this pandemic have yet to be fully understood; however, it has also shed light on the compounding effects that trauma like IPV has on individuals in ways not previously recognized. The data reported here show that survivors indeed reported experiencing changes in mental health (feelings of depression, loneliness, abuse, and lowered perceptions of safety) and substance use (changes in tobacco, alcohol, and illicit substance use) related to the pandemic. Our findings are interpreted in the context of qualitative data from in-depth interviews suggesting that COVID-19-related movement restrictions and stay-at-home orders mimic survivors' experiences of power and control in violent relationships. Community-based organizations, such as violence shelters, can help mitigate the ongoing impacts of COVID-19 and provide an important voice in developing more nuanced public health efforts for survivors while continuing to maintain essential health and safety protocols. Service-providing organizations should also be cautious about adding to the existing workload of their staff, as this study also shows that service providers were adversely affected by the pandemic, including in their ability to provide needed services to survivors of IPV. To our knowledge, the parallels between COVID-19 public health measures and IPV have not been explored, and these findings offer a new theoretical framework to the field. Our results also provide opportunities for systems to engage in greater empathy and multifaceted support to mitigate the impacts of IPV on survivors in their recovery.

Author Contributions: Conceptualization, A.S. and R.B.; conceptualization of the COVID-19 Power and Control Wheel, R.B.; methodology, A.S., C.A., R.B., A.S.-R., K.A. and W.K.L.; validation, A.S. and C.A.; formal analysis, A.S., C.A., R.B. and A.S.-R.; writing—original draft preparation, A.S., C.A. and R.B.; writing—review and editing, A.S., C.A., R.B. and A.S.-R.; project administration, A.S.; funding acquisition, A.S., K.A., A.S.-R. and W.K.L. All authors have read and agreed to the published version of the manuscript.

Funding: This research was funded by the U.S. Department of Health and Human Services, Office of Women's Health, FAIN 1-ASTWH190075-01-00.

Institutional Review Board Statement: This study was conducted in accordance with the Declaration of Helsinki and approved by the Institutional Review Board (or Ethics Committee) of the Pacific Institute for Research and Evaluation (protocol code 1574457; last protocol approval 29 September 2021).

Informed Consent Statement: Informed consent was obtained from all subjects involved in this study, which included consent to publish papers resulting from research findings.

Data Availability Statement: The data presented in this study are available on request from the corresponding author. The data are not publicly available due to confidentiality concerns for IPV staff and survivors of violence.

Acknowledgments: The authors wish to acknowledge the contributions of the community advisory board in reviewing and providing feedback on all data collection instruments and protocols, and research findings. Additionally, we would like to thank the Duluth team for meeting with us to discuss our findings further. We would also like to acknowledge the local IPV and HIV service providers who collaborated on the project design and contributed to data collection efforts.

Conflicts of Interest: The authors declare no conflict of interest. The funders had no role in the design of the study; in the collection, analyses, or interpretation of data; in the writing of the manuscript; or in the decision to publish the results.

References

1. Boserup, B.; Mckenney, M.; Elkbuli, A. Alarming trends in US domestic violence during the COVID-19 pandemic. *Am. J. Emerg. Med.* **2020**, *38*, 2753–2755. [CrossRef]
2. Brooks, S.K.; Webster, R.K.; Smith, L.E.; Woodland, L.; Wessely, S.; Greenberg, N.; Rubin, G.J. The psychological impact of quarantine and how to reduce it: Rapid review of the evidence. *Lancet* **2020**, *395*, 912–920. [CrossRef] [PubMed]
3. Beland, L.P.; Brouder, A.; Haddad, J.; Mikola, D. Covid-19, family stress and domestic violence: Remote work, isolation and bargaining power. *IZA Discuss. Pap.* **2021**, *47*, 439–459. [CrossRef]
4. Chadan, J.S.; Taylor, J.; Bradbury-Jones, C.; Nirantharakumar, K.; Kane, E.; Bandyopadhyay, S. COVID-19: A public health approach to manage domestic violence is needed. *Lancet Public Health* **2020**, *5*, e309. [CrossRef]
5. Twenge, J.M.; Joiner, T.E. Mental distress among U.S. adults during the COVID-19 pandemic. *J. Clin. Psychol.* **2020**, *76*, 2170–2182. [CrossRef]
6. Twenge, J.M.; Joiner, T.E. U.S. Census Bureau-assessed prevalence of anxiety and depressive symptoms in 2019 and during the 2020 COVID-19 pandemic. *Depress. Anxiety* **2020**, *37*, 954–956. [CrossRef] [PubMed]
7. Czeisler, M.E.; Lane, R.I.; Petrosky, E.; Wiley, J.F.; Christensen, A.; Njai, R.; Weaver, M.D.; Robbins, R.; Facer-childs, E.R.; Barger, L.K.; et al. Mental Health, Substance Use, and Suicidal Ideation During the COVID-19 Pandemic—United States. *Morb. Mortal. Wkly. Rep.* **2020**, *69*, 1049. [CrossRef] [PubMed]
8. Holingue, C.; Kalb, L.G.; Riehm, K.E.; Bennett, D.; Kapteyn, A.; Veldhuis, C.B.; Johnson, R.M.; Fallin, M.D.; Kreuter, F.; Stuart, E.A.; et al. Mental distress in the United States at the beginning of the COVID-19 pandemic. *Am. J. Public Health* **2020**, *110*, 1628–1634. [CrossRef]
9. Breslau, J.; Finucane, M.L.; Locker, A.; Baird, M.D.; Roth, E.A.; Collins, R.L. A longitudinal study of psychological distress in the United States before and during the COVID-19 pandemic. *Prev. Med.* **2021**, *143*, 106362. [CrossRef] [PubMed]
10. Ettman, C.K.; Abdalla, S.M.; Cohen, G.H.; Sampson, L.; Vivier, P.M.; Galea, S. Low assets and financial stressors associated with higher depression during COVID-19 in a nationally representative sample of US adults. *J. Epidemiol. Community Health* **2021**, *75*, 501–508. [CrossRef]
11. Holman, A.E.; Thompson, R.R.; Garfin, D.R.; Cohen, R.S. The unfolding COVID-19 pandemic: A probability-based, nationally representative study of mental health in the United States. *Sci. Adv.* **2020**, *6*, eabd5390. [CrossRef]
12. Parcesepe, A.M.; Robertson, M.; Berry, A.; Maroko, A.; Zimba, R.; Grov, C.; Westmoreland, D.; Kulkarni, S.; Rane, M.; Salgado-You, W.; et al. The relationship between anxiety, health, and potential stressors among adults in the United States during the COVID-19 pandemic. *medRxiv* **2020**, *10*, 20221440.
13. Gearon, J.S.; Kaltman, S.I.; Brown, C.; Bellack, A.S. Traumatic life events and PTSD among women with substance use disorders and schizophrenia. *Psychiatr. Serv.* **2003**, *54*, 523–528. [CrossRef] [PubMed]
14. Oram, S.; Trevillion, K.; Feder, G.; Howard, L. Prevalence of experiences of domestic violence among psychiatric patients: Systematic review. *Br. J. Psychiatry* **2013**, *202*, 94–99. [CrossRef] [PubMed]
15. Ludermir, A.B.; Schraiber, L.B.; D'Oliveira, A.; Franca-Junior, I.; Jansen, H.A. Violence against women by their intimate partner and common mental disorders. *Soc. Sci. Med.* **2008**, *66*, 1008–1018. [CrossRef] [PubMed]
16. Sullivan, T.P.; Holt, L.J. PTSD symptom clusters are differentially related to substance use among community women exposed to intimate partner violence. *J. Trauma. Stress Off. Publ. Int. Soc. Trauma Stress Stud.* **2008**, *2*, 173–180. [CrossRef]
17. Mason, R.; Mont, J.D. Advancing our knowledge of the complexity and management of intimate partner violence and co-occurring mental health and substance abuse problems in women. *F1000Prime Rep.* **2015**, *7*, 65. [CrossRef]
18. Lipsky, S.; Caetano, R. Impact of intimate partner violence on unmet need for mental health care: Results from the NSDUH. *Psychiatr. Serv.* **2007**, *58*, 822–829. [CrossRef]
19. GIlbert, A.R.; Morrissey, J.P.; Domino, M.E. Service utilization patterns as predictors of response to trauma-informed integrated treatment for women with co-occurring disorders. *J. Dual Diagn.* **2011**, *7*, 117–129. [CrossRef] [PubMed]

20. Smith, P.H.; Homish, G.G.; Leonard, K.E.; Cornelius, J.R. Intimate partner violence and specific substance use disorders: Findings from the National Epidemiological Survey on Alcohol and Related Conditions. *Psychol. Addict. Behav.* **2012**, *26*, 236. [CrossRef] [PubMed]
21. Schneider, R.; Burnette, M.L.; Ilgen, M.A.; Timko, C. Prevalence and correlates of intimate partner violence victimization among men and women entering substance use disorder treatment. *Violence Vict.* **2009**, *24*, 744–756. [CrossRef]
22. Brabete, A.; Wolfson, L.; Stinson, J.; Poole, N.; Allen, S.; Greaves, L. Exploring the Linkages between Substance Use, Natural Disasters, Pandemics, and Intimate Partner Violence against Women: A Rapid Review in the Context of COVID-19. *Sexes* **2021**, *2*, 509–522. [CrossRef]
23. Baidoo, L.; Zakrison, T.L.; Feldmeth, G.; Lindau, S.T.; Tung, E.L. Resources During the 2020 COVID-19 Stay-at-Home Order in Chicago, Illinois. *JAMA Netw. Open* **2021**, *9*, e2122260. [CrossRef] [PubMed]
24. Evans, D.P.; Hawk, S.R.; Ripkey, C.E. Domestic Violence in Atlanta, Georgia Before and During COVID-19. *Violence Gend.* **2021**, *8*, 140–147. [CrossRef] [PubMed]
25. Hsu, L.-C.; Henke, A. COVID-19, staying at home, and domestic violence. *Rev. Econ. Te Househ.* **2021**, *19*, 145–155. [CrossRef]
26. McNeil, A.; Hicks, L.; Yalcinoz-Ucan, B.; Browne, D.T. Prevalence & Correlates of Intimate Partner Violence During COVID-19: A Rapid Review. *J. Fam. Violence* **2022**, *38*, 241–261. [PubMed]
27. Nix, J.; Richards, T.N. The immediate and long-term effects of COVID-19 stay-at-home orders on domestic violence calls for service across six U.S. jurisdictions. *Police Pract. Res.* **2021**, *22*, 1443–1451. [CrossRef]
28. Lyons, M.; Brewer, G. Experiences of intimate partner violence during lockdown and the COVID-19 pandemic. *J. Fam. Violence* **2021**, *37*, 969–977. [CrossRef]
29. Gresham, A.M.; Peters, B.J.; Karantzas, G.; Cameron, L.D.; Simpson, J.A. Examining associations between COVID-19 stressors, intimate partner violence, health, and health behaviors. *J. Soc. Perosnal Relatsh.* **2021**, *38*, 2291–2307. [CrossRef]
30. Gosangi, B.; Park, H.; Thomas, R.; Gujrathi, R.; Bay, C.P.; Raja, A.S.; Seltzer, S.E.; Balcom, M.C.; McDonald, M.L.; Orgill, D.P.; et al. Exacerbation of Physical Intimate Partner Violence during COVID-19 Lockdown. *Radiology* **2020**, *298*, E38–E45. [CrossRef]
31. Jetelina, K.K.; Knell, G.; Moslberry, R.J. Changes in intimate partner violence during the early stages of the COVID-19 pandemic in the USA. *Inj. Prev.* **2021**, *27*, 93–97. [CrossRef] [PubMed]
32. Wood, L.; Baumler, E.; Schrag, R.V.; Guillot-Wright, S.; Hairston, D.; Temple, J.; Torres, E. "Don't Know where to Go for Help": Safety and Economic Needs among Violence Survivors during the COVID-19 Pandemic. *J. Fam. Violence* **2021**, *37*, 959–967. [CrossRef]
33. Buttell, F.; Cannon, C.; Ferreria, R.; Rose, K. COVID-19 and intimate partner violence: Prevalence of resilience and perceived stress during a pandemic. *Traumatology* **2021**, *27*, 20–28. [CrossRef]
34. Goodman, L.A.; Epstein, D. Loneliness and the COVID-19 Pandemic: Implications for Intimate Partner Violence Survivors. *J. Fam. Violence* **2020**, *37*, 767–774. [CrossRef] [PubMed]
35. Sanchez, O.R.; Diama, V.B.; Rodrigues, L.; Surita, F.G. Violence against women during the COVID-19 pandemic: An integrative review. *Int. J. Gynecol. Obstet.* **2020**, *151*, 180–187. [CrossRef] [PubMed]
36. Rossi, F.S.; Shankar, M.; Buckholdt, K.; Bailey, Y.; Israni, S.T.; Iverson, K.M. Trying Times and Trying Out Solutions: Intimate Partner Violence Screening and Support for Women Veterans During COVID-19. *J. Gen. Intern. Med.* **2020**, *35*, 2728–2731. [CrossRef]
37. Kofman, Y.B.; Garfin, D.R. Home is not always a haven: The domestic violence crisis amid the COVID-19 pandemic. *Psychol. Trauma Theory Res. Pract. Policy* **2020**, *12*, S199–S201. [CrossRef]
38. Rieger, A.; Blackburn, A.M.; Bystrynski, J.; Garthe, R.C. The impact of the COVID-19 pandemic on gender-based violence in the United States: Framework and policy recommendations. *Psychol. Trauma Theory Res. Pract. Policy* **2022**, *14*, 471. [CrossRef]
39. Holland, K. Trends in U.S. Emergency Department visits for mental health, overdose, and violence outcomes before and during the COVID-19 Pandemic. *JAMA Psychiatry* **2021**, *78*, 372–379. [CrossRef]
40. Nnawilezi, N.; Hacskaylo, M. Identifying and responding to the complex needs of domestic violence housing practitioners at the onset of the COVID-19 pandemic. *J. Fam. Violence* **2021**, *37*, 915–925. [CrossRef]
41. Welfare-Wilson, A.; Adley, L.; Bell, Z.; Luby, R. COVID-19 and how the wearing of face coverings can affect those with an experience of trauma. *J. Psychiatr. Ment. Health Nurs.* **2021**, *28*, 777–782. [CrossRef]
42. Fishere, M.; Bartoli, E. COVID-19 and risk of retraumatization in adults with a past exposure to potentially traumatic events: A cross-cultural exploration across Egypt, Germany, and Italy. *J. Community Psychol.* **2022**, *50*, 2578–2596. [CrossRef] [PubMed]
43. Sharma, A.; Borah, B. Covid-19 and domestic violence: An indirect path to social and economic crisis. *J. Fam. Violence* **2022**, *37*, 759–765. [CrossRef]
44. Lubel. The Loneliness of the Long-Distance Holocaust Survivor. Reuters, 21 April 2020. Available online: https://news.trust.org/item/20200421123555-jp10m. (accessed on 7 March 2022).
45. Bergman, S.; Bjørnholt, M.; Helseth, H. Norwegian shelters for victims of domestic violence in the COVID-19 pandemic–navigating the new normal. *J. Fam. Violence* **2021**, *37*, 927–937. [CrossRef] [PubMed]
46. Olding, J.; Zisman, S.; Olding, C.; Fan, K. Penetrating trauma during a global pandemic: Changing patterns in interpersonal violence, self-harm and domestic violence in the Covid-19 outbreak. *Surgeon* **2021**, *19*, e9–e13. [CrossRef]
47. Stolow, J.A.; Moses, L.M.; Lederer, A.M.; Carter, R. How fear appeal approaches in COVID-19 health communication may be harming the global community. *Health Educ. Behav.* **2020**, *47*, 531–535. [CrossRef] [PubMed]

48. Jeftić, A.; Ikizer, G.; Tuominen, J.; Chrona, S.; Kumaga, R. Connection between the COVID-19 pandemic, war trauma reminders, perceived stress, loneliness, and PTSD in Bosnia and Herzegovina. *Curr. Psychol.* **2021**, *22*, 1–13. [CrossRef] [PubMed]
49. Pence, E.; Paymer, M. *Education Guide for Men Who Batter: The Duluth Model*; Springer: New York, NY, USA, 1993.
50. Bauer, R.; Simons-Rudolph, A.; Schweinhart, A.; Atwood, K.; Aramburú, C.; Luseno, W. COVID-19 Through the Lens of IPV Survivors: Parallels in Experiences of Power and Control between a Global Pandemic and an Abusive Partner. In Proceedings of the 14th Annual International InWomen's Conference, Minneapolis, MN, USA, 10 June 2022.
51. Morse, G.A.; Dell, N.A. The well-being and perspectives of community-based behavioral health staff during the COVID-19 pandemic. *Soc. Work. Health Care* **2021**, *60*, 117–130. [CrossRef] [PubMed]
52. Miller, J.J.; Niu, C.; Moody, S. Child welfare workers and peritraumatic distress: The impact of COVID-19. *Child. Youth Serv. Rev.* **2020**, *119*, 105508. [CrossRef]
53. Blevins, D.; Henry, B.F.; Sung, M.; Edelmen, J.; Black, A.C.; Dawes, M.; Molfenter, T.; Hagle, H.; Drexler, K.; Cates-Wessel, K.; et al. Well-being of health care professionals treating opioid use disorder during the COVID-19 pandemic: Results from a national survey. *Psychiatr. Serv.* **2022**, *73*, 374–380. [CrossRef]
54. Garcia, R.; Henderson, C.; Randell, K.; Villaveces, A.; Katz, A.; Abioye, F.; DeGue, S.; Premo, K.; MIller-Wallfish, S.; Chang, J.C.; et al. The impact of the COVID-19 pandemic on intimate partner violence advocates and agencies. *J. Fam. Violence* **2022**, *37*, 893–906. [CrossRef]
55. Sapire, R.; Ostrowski, J.; Maier, M.; Samari, G.; Bencomo, C.; McGovern, T. COVID-19 and gender-based violence service provision in the United States. *PloS ONE* **2022**, *17*, e0263970. [CrossRef]
56. Nikolaidis, A.; Paksarian, D.; Alexander, L.; Derosa, J.; Dunn, J.; Nielson, D.M.; Droney, I.; Kang, M.; Douka, I.; Bromet, E.; et al. The Coronavirus Health and Impact Survey (CRISIS) reveals reproducible correlates of pandemic-related mood states across the Atlantic. *Sci. Rep.* **2020**, *11*, 8139. [CrossRef]
57. Kazak, A.E.; Alderfer, M.; Enlow, P.T.; Lewis, A.M.; Vega, G.; Barakat, L.; Kassam-Adams, N.; Pai, A.; Canter, K.S.; Hildenbrand, A.K.; et al. COVID-19 Exposure and Family Impact Scales: Factor Structure and Initial Psychometrics. *J. Pediatr. Psychol.* **2021**, *46*, 504–513. [CrossRef] [PubMed]
58. Harkness, A.; Behar-Zusman, V.; Safren, S.A. Understanding the Impact of COVID-19 on Latino Sexual Minority Men in a US HIV Hot Spot. *AIDS Behav.* **2020**, *24*, 2017–2023. [CrossRef] [PubMed]
59. Harris Poll COVID-19 Survey Wave 9. 2020. Available online: https://theharrispoll.com/briefs/covid-19-tracker-wave-9/ (accessed on 14 September 2020).
60. CDC. *COVID-19 Community Survey Question Bank (Draft)*; Center for Disease Control: Atlanta, GA, USA, 2020.
61. Grasso, D.J.; Briggs-Gowan, M.J.; Ford, J.D.; Carter, A.S. *The Epidemic—Pandemic Impacts Inventory (EPII)*; University of Connecticut School of Medicine: Farmington, CT, USA, 2020.
62. CDC. National Library of Medicine Form: CDC COVID-19 Community Survey Question Bank (DRAFT). 1 April 2020. Available online: https://cde.nlm.nih.gov/formView?tinyId=Kcceysolt. (accessed on 1 May 2020).
63. Locke, K. The grounded theory approach to qualitative research. In *Measuring and Analyzing Behavior in Organizations: Advances in Measurement and Data Analysis*; Drasgow, F., Schmitt, N., Eds.; Jossey-Bass: San Francisco, CA, USA, 2002; pp. 17–43.
64. Hall, S.; White, A.; Ballas, J.; Saxton, S.N.; Dempsey, A.; Saxer, K. Education in Trauma-Informed Care in Maternity Settings Can Promote Mental Health During the COVID-19 Pandemic. *J. Obs. Gynecol. Neonatal Nurs.* **2021**, *50*, 340–351. [CrossRef] [PubMed]

International Journal of
Environmental Research and Public Health

MDPI

Article

Women Tell All: A Comparative Thematic Analysis of Women's Perspectives on Two Brief Counseling Interventions for Intimate Partner Violence

Danielle R. Shayani [1,*], Sara B. Danitz [1], Stephanie K. Low [1], Alison B. Hamilton [2,3] and Katherine M. Iverson [1,4,*]

1 Women's Health Sciences Division of the National Center for PTSD, VA Boston Healthcare System, Boston, MA 02130, USA; sara.danitz@va.gov (S.B.D.); stephanie.low@va.gov (S.K.L.)
2 VA Center for the Study of Healthcare Innovation, Implementation and Policy, VA Greater Los Angeles Healthcare System, Los Angeles, CA 90073, USA; alisonh@ucla.edu
3 Department of Psychiatry and Biobehavioral Sciences, Los Angeles Greffen School of Medicine, University of California, Los Angeles, CA 90095, USA
4 Department of Psychiatry, Boston University School of Medicine, Boston, MA 02118, USA
* Correspondence: danielleshayani@gmail.com (D.R.S.); katherine.iverson@va.gov (K.M.I.)

Abstract: Background: Intimate partner violence (IPV) is a significant public health problem that is commonly experienced by women and associated with psychosocial health issues. Recovering from IPV through Strengths and Empowerment (RISE) is a brief, clinician-administered, variable-length (1–6 sessions), modular, individualized psychosocial counseling intervention developed for women experiencing IPV. We present qualitative feedback and quantitative helpfulness ratings from women patients of the Veterans Health Administration who completed a randomized clinical trial (RCT) comparing RISE to a clinician-administered advocacy-based Enhanced Care as Usual (ECAU; a single structured session consisting of psychoeducation, safety-planning, resources, and referrals). Methods: 58 participants ($_{M}$age = 39.21) completed post-intervention semi-structured qualitative interviews, including helpfulness ratings, at two follow-up assessments (10- and 14-weeks post-enrollment) to assess the acceptability, usefulness, and perceived fit of the interventions for women's needs. Interviews were transcribed and analyzed using a hybrid deductive-inductive analytic approach. Results: While both the RISE and ECAU interventions were deemed helpful (interventions were rated as 'highly helpful' by 77% of RISE and 52% of ECAU participants), differences were identified in perceived impacts of the intervention, application of content, approach to patient-centeredness, and implementation recommendations. Conclusions: Findings shed light on women Veterans' experiences and preferences for IPV psychosocial counseling interventions. Such knowledge can inform evidence-based, trauma-informed, and individualized care for women Veterans who experience IPV and may have relevance to other populations of women who experience IPV.

Keywords: intimate partner violence; patient preferences; qualitative research; treatment; women veterans

Citation: Shayani, D.R.; Danitz, S.B.; Low, S.K.; Hamilton, A.B.; Iverson, K.M. Women Tell All: A Comparative Thematic Analysis of Women's Perspectives on Two Brief Counseling Interventions for Intimate Partner Violence. *Int. J. Environ. Res. Public Health* **2022**, *19*, 2513. https://doi.org/10.3390/ijerph19052513

Academic Editors: Krim K. Lacey, Rohan D. Jeremiah and Ko-Ling Chan

Received: 14 November 2021
Accepted: 18 February 2022
Published: 22 February 2022

1. Introduction

Intimate partner violence (IPV), including physical, sexual, and psychological violence, is a complex population health problem. IPV is the most prevalent form of violence against women globally, with recent data from the World Health Organization (WHO) demonstrating that IPV is prevalent across the globe, with more than 640 million women worldwide who experience IPV during their lifetime [1]. According to estimates from the WHO, more than one in four (27%) women have been subjected to physical and/or sexual violence by an intimate partner during their lifetime while one in ten women have experienced physical and/or sexual violence within the past year [1]. The impact of such violence on the physical, mental, and social health of women has been well-documented in the literature [2–4]. For example, IPV is associated with numerous emotional and mental health issues including reduced self-efficacy and quality of life, and increased depression, anxiety, posttraumatic stress symptoms, suicidal ideation, and suicide attempts [5–9]. As a result of the multitude of health issues and stress associated with IPV, women who experience IPV often have increased healthcare utilization in both single and multi-country studies [9–12]. These clinical encounters, regardless of their purpose, provide important opportunities for clinicians to safely and sensitively inquire about IPV and provide therapeutic clinical responses [13,14].

Although routine screening for IPV in the healthcare setting is effective in identifying patients who experience IPV [15], it is critical that screening and response practices include offering referrals to interventions that can appropriately support women following their IPV disclosures. A systematic review by Bair-Merritt and colleagues (2014) reported that promising healthcare-based counseling interventions for women experiencing IPV typically contain elements of advocacy, safety planning, and linkages with community-based resources [16]. Little is known, however, about women's perceptions of such interventions and the extent to which IPV interventions meet their unique needs and preferences. Some advocacy-based interventions and mental health treatments have been shown to have benefits for women experiencing IPV primarily using quantitative methods [16–18]. Quantitative outcomes from randomized clinical trials are certainly critical to evaluating the clinical utility of different interventions, but they are not the only form of evidence. Patient experience and preferences are another important source of evidence [19], but there has been little published about women's more personal experiences with more structured IPV interventions, including their perceptions of the helpfulness, fit and acceptability of these interventions and recommendations for modifying the interventions or their implementation characteristics based on their personal experiences with the interventions. Investigating qualitative outcomes serves to fill this gap and can inform recommendations for enhancing IPV interventions to better fit and address women's needs. Although there are many studies examining women's experiences and preferences for IPV screening and response procedures [20], there is much less research on women's experiences regarding clinician-administered structured and/or manualized IPV psychosocial counseling interventions.

The need to understand women's nuanced experiences of these types of IPV interventions comes at an important juncture in the fields of medicine and IPV, intersecting with the integration of patient-centered care [21] and survivor-centered practice [22,23]. These overlapping models of care both emphasize that interventions should be responsive to individual patient/client preferences, goals and values, and individualized needs. Similarly, both patient- and survivor-centered care emphasize personalized positive outcomes–as opposed to focusing primarily on symptom reduction and violence cessation. Thus, in addition to evaluating psychosocial counseling interventions for IPV via traditional examinations of change over time in researcher-selected quantitative measures, it is equally important to also understand the perspectives of the end-users in order to enhance the likelihood of successful uptake of new interventions into routine care [24,25]. It is, therefore, timely to gather women's perceptions of and feedback on IPV interventions to understand the extent to which structured clinician-administered psychosocial interventions meet their needs as well to inform enhancements in clinical practice and program development to better address IPV.

One group of end-users that is particularly relevant to study are women who have served in the military. Women Veterans are an important population for IPV treatment research as they are at high risk for experiencing IPV, with past-year estimates ranging from 19–37% [26–29]. Within the United States, women Veterans are more likely to have experienced IPV during their lifetime relative to women who never served in the military [30], and there is evidence that IPV is prevalent among military populations [31–33]. Although the field does not yet have a comprehensive understanding of why women Veterans are at heightened risk for IPV, military sexual trauma (i.e., sexual assault and sexual harassment during military services), increases risk for IPV [26]. Moreover, recent IPV is known to contribute to women Veterans' current health needs above and beyond the impact of other stressors that are prevalent among women Veterans (e.g., military sexual trauma and deployment-related exposures) [34–37]. Due to the high prevalence of IPV and its negative impacts on health, some Veterans' healthcare organizations are moving towards integrating care for IPV within existing health services. Within the United States, the Veterans Health Administration is actively implementing screening and intervention for IPV. Understanding women Veterans' perspectives on IPV interventions is therefore important for informing these efforts.

The current study begins to fill the aforementioned gaps in the literature by incorporating qualitative methods along with helpfulness ratings to assess women Veterans' IPV treatment experiences within the context of a larger randomized clinical trial (RCT) study. This RCT targeted women Veterans of the United States Armed Services who were patients of the Veterans Health Administration (VHA) and compared a new empowerment-focused modular-based brief counseling intervention (described in more detail in the Methods section) to an advocacy-based Enhanced Care as Usual (ECAU) intervention [38]. The present study examines post-treatment semi-structured interview data from the parent RCT to understand women Veterans' perceptions of the IPV interventions with respect to usefulness, acceptability, and perceived impact, and to gather feedback for informing future implementation of IPV counseling programs. Through collecting and reporting on these qualitative interview findings, in tandem with examining participants' ratings of overall treatment usefulness, there is potential to more thoroughly understand women's experiences with IPV interventions in a way that is attuned to women's unique perspectives and preferences. The current study has potential to advance the IPV psychosocial counseling intervention literature by focusing specifically on women Veterans' experiences with treatment based on their verbal feedback, as opposed to relying on traditional quantitative outcomes alone, as has frequently been the case in prior studies examining new psychosocial counseling interventions for women who experience IPV (e.g., [18,39–41]).

2. Materials and Methods

2.1. Design and Participants

We conducted semi-structured interviews with participants 10- and 14-weeks following enrollment in a RCT comparing the Recovering from Intimate Partner Violence through Strengths and Empowerment (RISE) brief counseling intervention to an ECAU comparison condition for women Veterans VHA patients who experienced past-year IPV (registered in ClinicalTrials.gov; NCT03261700). The larger RCT and primary quantitative findings have been described elsewhere [38]. In brief, the study took place at an urban VHA medical center in the New England region of the US between October 2018 and November 2020. Data was collected with approval from the VA Boston Healthcare System's Institutional Review Board (IRB #3078).

In total, 60 women VHA patients participated in the larger RCT. Participants were recruited via flyers posted in the hospital, self-referrals, clinician referrals, and recruitment letters mailed to VHA patients. Flyers defined IPV and described the treatment study. Recruitment letters broadly described a Women's Treatment Preferences study taking place at the local VHA medical center. Interested women were screened by phone for eligibility criteria, in which a trained research assistant (DS) administered a five-item IPV screener that has been validated with women Veterans [26] and asked basic demographics and mental health questions. Women were included if they reported: (1) past-year IPV (i.e., one or more instances of physical, sexual, and/or psychological IPV on the Revised Conflict Tactics Scale (CTS-2) [42], (2) past-year VHA care, (3) being at least 18 years of age, and (4) willingness to have sessions audio recorded. Women were excluded if they endorsed active past-month symptoms of mania or psychosis and/or homicidal or suicidal ideation warranting hospitalization.

2.2. Procedures

The recruitment, intervention, and analysis team included trained individuals from a variety of educational backgrounds. More details are provided throughout the manuscript. For the RCT, trained bachelor-level research assistants and a doctoral-level clinical psychologist conducted screening, consent, and assessment procedures. Women who were eligible following a phone screening scheduled an in-person enrollment session, and those who were ineligible were provided with appropriate alternative resources. At the enrollment session, women provided written informed consent and filled out a packet of questionnaires for their pre-treatment assessment. They were randomized to receive RISE or ECAU, which they received immediately following their pre-treatment assessment (for additional details on primary and secondary quantitative measures and findings, see Iverson et al.) [38]. Most participants ($n = 50$) received sessions and assessments in person at a local VHA medical center as was intended with the original study design, and 10 participants received one or more sessions and/or assessments via telehealth due to the COVID-19 pandemic. There were no significant differences in pretreatment sociodemographic characteristics for the ten participants who had telehealth sessions versus those who did not as part of the larger study (all p-values > 0.05). The study's randomization procedures remained the same following the onset of COVID-19 and resulted in an even distribution of participants to each of the two intervention conditions. Participants completed follow-up assessments 10- and 14-weeks following enrollment, which included semi-structured qualitative interviews at each time point. Participants were compensated $25, $50, and $75, respectively, at each of the three assessment timepoints. The compensation was commensurate with the amount of time required to complete the assessments and was approved by the Institutional Review Board. Participant flow throughout the study is shown in Figure 1. The current study focuses on helpfulness ratings and qualitative findings from the post-intervention semi-structured interviews conducted at both the 10- and 14-week follow-up assessments.

2.3. Intervention: Recovering from IPV through Strengths and Empowerment (RISE)

RISE is a variable-length, modular-based, survivor-centered and trauma-informed intervention that ranges from 1–6 sessions and was administered over the course of 10 weeks in the current study. RISE is rooted in principles of Motivational Interviewing [43] and empowerment, and consists of six modules, namely: (A) Safety Planning, (B) Education on Health Effects of IPV and Warning Signs, (C) Improving Coping and Self-Care, (D) Enhancing Social Support, (E) Making Difficult Decisions, and (F) Connecting with Resources and Moving Forward (see Iverson, Danitz et al., 2021 [44] for more information regarding the RISE modules). During the initial session, RISE clinicians provided an overview of RISE and its structure, introduced the concept of self-efficacy, and invited the woman to share her experiences with IPV and her goals for treatment. Next, the participant selected a module to focus on during the remainder of the session and set a behaviorally-specific goal related to the module to focus on following the session. Subsequent sessions focused on a safety check-in, self-efficacy tracking, goal review, and additional module selection and goal setting. Each module includes specific handouts, exercises, and related goal setting. Modules do not need to be conducted sequentially, nor do all modules need to be completed, and modules can be repeated, as determined by the woman receiving RISE. Participants chose how many RISE sessions to receive, up to the six-session limit. Participants were connected to other VHA and community services, as desired. Additional information regarding the RISE philosophy, content, and structure are reported elsewhere [44].

2.4. Intervention: Enhanced Care as Usual Condition (ECAU)

ECAU is an advocacy-based intervention that incorporates best-practice recommendations for addressing IPV in VHA. Participants in the ECAU condition received a one-time, 60-min intervention with a provider. At the start of the session, participants were given VHA's IPV educational brochure to provide psychoeducation about different forms of IPV, prevalence rates of IPV, and the effects of IPV on physical, mental, and social health. ECAU provides information about safety planning, including an optional brief safety plan that can be completed with the provider. Participants in the ECAU condition receive information about local and national resources, including both VHA and community resources, and have the opportunity to connect with these resources and receive referrals as relevant and requested by the woman.

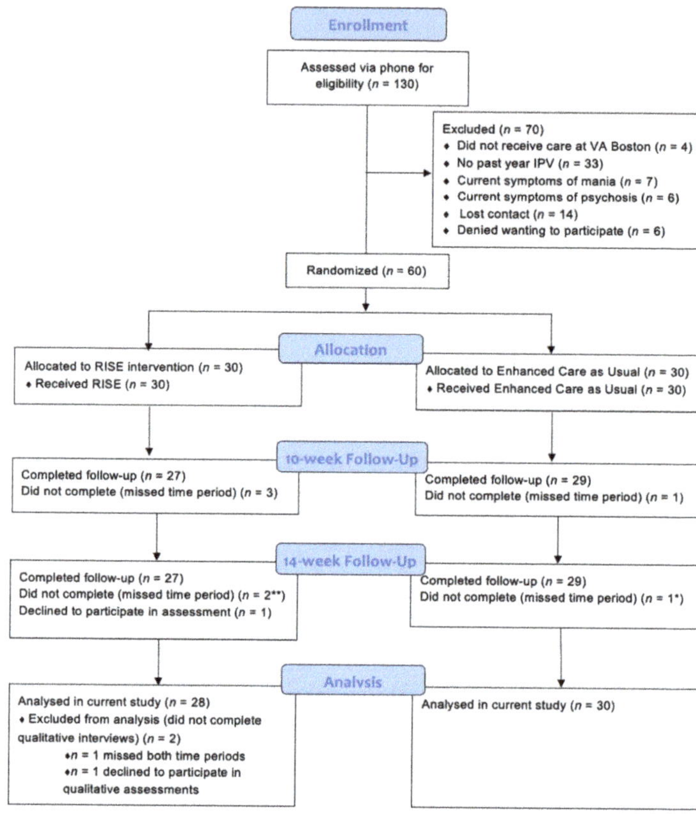

Figure 1. Participant flow through the study, including qualitative interview for analysis. Note. * In the Enhanced Care as Usual (ECAU) condition, the participant who missed the 10-week assessment was not the same participant who missed the 14-week assessment. Thus all 30 ECAU participants had interview data analyzed in the current study. ** Of the RISE participants, one of the three participants with missing data missed only one of the two assessments. Thus 28 RISE participants had interview data analyzed in the current study.

2.5. Interventionists

Interventionists were VHA clinical providers, including one social worker and three clinical psychologists, with relevant clinical experience and expertise in trauma-informed care; all were women. Providers delivered both interventions within a primary-care setting and an outpatient mental health clinic. Providers participated in weekly consultation with the RISE intervention developer, and both RISE and ECAU sessions were reviewed by the study principal investigator (KI) and discussed to ensure fidelity to the respective treatments.

2.6. Approach

Semi-structured audio recorded interviews were conducted at the 10- and 14-week post-treatment assessments by qualitatively-trained study staff. The interviews were conducted at both timepoints, as it was possible that women's perspectives or recommendations could be different at the 14-week assessment because they have had more time to try out what they learned in the interventions. Author AH, a medical anthropologist and implementation scientist, provided oversight and overarching guidance for data collection and analysis. An interview guide was developed based on the treatment development and implementation literature, and Veteran and clinician stakeholder input. Interview questions were semi-structured in nature, with a focus on elucidating participant experiences and attitudes about their respective intervention. Of note, the interview guide had been piloted and refined during a pilot study [44]. All interviews were conducted by the project manager (SD), a doctoral level female psychologist with training in qualitative interviewing, or the research assistant (DS), a bachelor's level female with training in qualitative interviewing. The interview guide included questions querying their overall experiences with acceptability of the intervention (e.g., "What did you like about the intervention?", "What didn't you like about the intervention?"), perceived impacts of the intervention (e.g., "How, if at all, do you think participating in the intervention has impacted you?"), application of content (e.g., "how, if at all, do you use the information from the intervention in your everyday life?"), modifications needed to enhance acceptability and helpfulness of the intervention (e.g., "What do you wish you could have changed about the intervention to make it more useful to you?"), and additional implementation recommendations (e.g., "Is there anything you'd like us to change about how the intervention is delivered?"). We added items about experiences with treatment during the COVID-19 pandemic (e.g., "To what extent, if at all, has the current COVID-19 pandemic impacted your ability to participate in this intervention?"). In addition to these open-ended questions, the interviewer asked women to rate "how helpful [they] found the intervention" on a 5-point Likert scale (1 = highly helpful, 2 = somewhat helpful, 3 = neither helpful nor unhelpful, 4 = somewhat unhelpful, and 5 = highly unhelpful). Interviews (mean = 18 min) were transcribed verbatim.

2.7. Data Analysis Strategy

Interviews were analyzed using a hybrid deductive-inductive analytic approach, following an established multi-step approach for efficient and effective identification of key findings from the interviews. The analysis team was trained and led by AH and consisted of two doctoral-level clinical psychologists and a bachelor's level research assistant (KI, SD, and DS). The multi-step approach followed common rapid analytic methods in intervention development and implementation research [45,46]. First, a template was developed deductively with topics from the interview guide questions (i.e., 1–2 topics per primary interview question). Each analyst independently summarized the same three transcripts, to test out the template and to establish consistency of summaries across analysts. Summaries were compared to one another, and refinements were made to the template and the summarizing process. Then, all transcripts were summarized using the template, generating one summary per transcript that contained key content points and exemplary quotations (as well as other observations when relevant, i.e., any content that fell outside of the deductively derived topics) from the transcript. Interview transcripts and summaries were reviewed by the qualitative lead, who provided regular feedback regarding completeness and consistency.

Next, the team compiled the summaries into matrices, one matrix each for the RISE and ECAU participants, and used matrix analysis [47] to display content and explore themes inductively within and across conditions at the 10- and 14-week assessments. Themes for the 10- and 14-week assessments were found to be consistently similar within both the RISE and ECAU conditions and findings for the two timepoints were subsequently merged. Findings were then summarized for each condition, highlighting similarities and differences in perceptions across the two conditions. Research assigned participant numbers accompany exemplary quotes to protect participant confidentiality.

3. Results

Of the 60 participants from the RCT, 58 (28 = RISE, 30 = ECAU) participants completed the interviews at the 10- and/or 14-week follow-up assessments and are included in the analysis (RISE: $n = 1$ did not complete either the 10- or 14-week assessment and $n = 1$ did not complete the interview portion at either assessment point, resulting in $n = 28$; ECAU: $n = 2$ did not complete 10- or 14-week assessment but because these were different participants, there was interview data at one of these timepoints for all 30 ECAU participants). Figure 1 provides a summary of participant flow throughout the study. Table 1 describes the baseline sociodemographic characteristics and IPV characteristics of the current sample by condition. A higher percentage of participants in the RISE condition were employed full-time. There were no other group differences in sociodemographic or IPV characteristics (all *p*-values > 0.05). Three interviews were not transcribed due to recording not being feasible and two interviews from each condition were accidently deleted prior to being transferred and transcribed. In these instances, we relied on memos and written notes for these participants.

Table 1. Baseline Participant Characteristics by Condition ($N = 58$).

Sociodemographic Characteristics [a]	RISE ($n = 28$)	ECAU ($n = 30$)	Statistic	*p*-Value
Age, *M (SD)*	38.0 (11.0)	40.5 (13)	$t = 0.79$	0.44
Race/Ethnicity			$\chi^2 = 4.60$	0.47
Black	7 (25.0)	5 (16.7)		
White/Caucasian	19 (67.9)	16 (53.3)		
Asian	1 (3.6)	2 (6.7)		
Native American	0 (0)	1 (3.3)		
Other Race	0 (0)	3 (10)		
Multiple Races	1 (3.6)	4 (13.3)		
White Non-Hispanic	27 (96.4)	25 (83.3)	$\chi^2 = 0.21$	0.64
Non-White/Hispanic	1 (3.6)	5 (16.7)		
Sexual Orientation			$\chi^2 = 2.24$	0.53
Heterosexual	18 (64.3)	24 (80)		
Lesbian/Gay	3 (10.7)	1 (3.3)		
Bisexual	5 (17.9)	4 (13.3)		
Pansexual	2 (7.1)	1 (3.3)		
Relationship Status			$\chi^2 = 6.13$	0.29
Married/Cohabitating	7 (25)	5 (16.7)		
LT/NM	7 (25)	5 (16.7)		
NM/NLT	3 (10.7)	1 (3.3)		
Single	7 (25.0)	8 (26.7)		
Separated	2 (7.1)	9 (30)		
Other	2 (7.1)	2 (6.7)		
Income			$\chi^2 = 8.59$	0.28
Less than $15,000	2 (7.1)	4 (13.3)		
$15,000–$24,999	2 (7.1)	4 (13.3)		
$25,000–34,999	3 (10.7)	3 (10)		
$35,000–$44,999	5 (17.9)	2 (6.7)		
$45,000–$54,999	3 (10.7)	6 (20)		
$55,000–$64,999	2 (7.1)	5 (16.7)		
$65,000–$74,999	3 (10.7)	0 (0)		
$75,000 or more	8 (28.6)	5 (16.7)		

Table 1. *Cont.*

Sociodemographic Characteristics [a]	RISE (n = 28)	ECAU (n = 30)	Statistic	p-Value
Employment Status			$\chi^2 = 28.15$	0.001
Employed Full Time *	16 (57.1)	8 (27.6)		
Employed Part Time	5 (17.9)	4 (13.8)		
Student Full Time	4 (14.3)	7 (24.1)		
Student Part Time	2 (6.9)	1 (3.4)		
Unpaid Volunteer	3 (10.7)	7 (23.3)		
Retired or Other	5 (19.9)	4 (13.8)		
Education			$\chi^2 = 3.48$	0.63
Vocational/Tech College	3 (10.7)	5 (16.7)		
Some College/Associate	14 (50)	16 (53.3)		
Bachelor's Degree	6 (21.4)	4 (13.3)		
Master's/Doctoral Degree	5 (17.9)	5 (16.7)		
Military Branch			$\chi^2 = 4.40$	0.49
Army	15 (53.6)	16 (53.3)		
Navy	3 (10.7)	4 (13.3)		
Air Force	5 (17.9)	2 (6.7)		
Marine Corps	4 (14.3)	4 (13.3)		
Years of Military Service *M* (*SD*)	6.9 (5.6)	7.1 (8.9)	$t = 0.09$	0.93
IPV Experience			$\chi^2 = 3.31$	0.19
Past-Year Psychological IPV	28 (100)	30 (100)		
Past-Year Physical IPV	16 (57.1)	24 (80)		
Past-Year Sexual IPV	15 (53.6)	11 (36.7)		
Length of IPV in Relationship			$\chi^2 = 3.00$	0.81
Less than 6 months	6 (21.4)	3 (10)		
Between 6 months and 1 year	6 (21.4)	5 (16.7)		
Between 1 and 3 years	6 (21.4)	6 (20.0)		
Between 3 and 5 years	4 (14.3)	5 (16.7)		
Between 5 and 7 years	2 (7.1)	2 (6.7)		
Between 7 and 9 years	0 (0)	1 (3.3)		
10+ years	4 (14.3)	7 (23.3)		

Note. * In the Enhanced Care as Usual (ECAU) condition, the participant who missed the 10-week assessment was not the same participant who missed the 14-week assessment. Thus all 30 ECAU participants had interview data analyzed in the current study. [a] All values are n (%) unless otherwise specified. Percentages may not equate to 100% because of rounding and/or missing data for participant characteristics. Military characteristics are for Veteran participants (n = 55; condi-tions did not differ in proportion of non-Veteran participants; p = 0.16). Abbreviations: RISE = Recovering from IPV through Strengths and Empowerment, ECAU = enhanced care as usual, LT/NM = living together/not married, NM/NLT = not married/not living together.

In the ECAU condition, all participants (n = 30) received a one-session intervention. In the RISE condition (n = 28), 23 women (82.1%) completed at least two sessions, 21 (75%) completed at least three sessions, 17 (60.7%) completed at least four sessions, 14 (50%) completed at least five sessions, and nine (32%) completed all six sessions. The percentage of RISE participants selecting each module were as follows: Improving Coping and Self-Care (75%), Education on Health Effects of IPV and Warning Signs (57.1%), Enhancing Social Support (57.1%), Connecting with Resources and Moving Forward (57.1%), Making Difficult Decisions (50%), and Safety Planning (35.7%).

In terms of quantitative ratings of overall helpfulness (on a Likert scale of 1–5, with 1 = highly helpful, 2 = somewhat helpful, 3 = neither helpful nor unhelpful, 4 = somewhat unhelpful, 5 = highly unhelpful), none of the participants reported less than adequate levels of perceived helpfulness (i.e., no ratings of 3 or higher). The majority of RISE participants (76.9%) and just over half of ECAU participants (51.7%) rated the intervention as 'highly helpful.' The remaining participants in both groups rated the intervention as 'somewhat helpful' (23.1% for RISE and 48.3% for ECAU).

Similarly, qualitative results indicated that all participants, regardless of their condition, were appreciative of having an intervention available to them; the majority were not aware of other alternative counseling interventions for IPV. Both interventions were perceived as generally acceptable, although several differences were identified in terms of perceived impact, application of content, patient-centeredness, and recommendations for implementation.

3.1. Perceived Impact of the Intervention

Women in both conditions reported that they found the intervention to be helpful, but the specific ways in which the interventions were perceived as helpful tended to differ between the two conditions. RISE participants shared more positive impacts on emotional health and psychosocial well-being, whereas the ECAU participants tended to highlight more practical impacts. Specifically, women in the RISE group reported the intervention impacted the way they felt about themselves, including feeling more empowered, confident, and independent than when they started the intervention. For example, women in RISE shared that they felt more confident to think about their relationships and their personal needs differently and take a more active role in improving various areas of their life, including their relationships, and prioritizing their physical and mental health. For instance, a RISE participant described,

> *"RISE has empowered me to take much more control over the interpersonal relationships in my life (RISE, 101)".*

While discussing making the decision to leave her relationship during the study, another participant shared,

> *"It's definitely made me realize and get some self-worth back and feel more empowered by my decisions (RISE, 102)".*

Similarly, another woman in RISE shared that,

> *"I didn't realize I wasn't taking care of myself or advocating for myself much. RISE gave me that confidence to start doing that (RISE, 103)".*

Confidence and independence were increased through independent thinking and decision-making. As noted by a RISE participant when discussing her desire to be more financially independent,

> *"In the past I wanted to be separated from him, but I realized I couldn't do that. Now I am working towards that financial independence (RISE, 104)".*

These types of benefits were not typically noted among women in the ECAU group.

In terms of potential mechanisms of these changes, women in the RISE group, many of whom opted to participate in multiple RISE sessions (mean sessions received was 3.8 sessions), shared that reflecting over time with their RISE provider and engaging in exercises within specific modules, setting goals related to the module, and practicing between sessions helped them acknowledge their strengths and restore self-esteem,

> "[RISE] *opened my eyes and after every session, I would think about what the session was about. When I'm driving or when I have a quiet period, I would realize, 'oh yeah, I do have this quality' or 'oh yes, I've been able to handle this problem.' So, it made me see that I wasn't as awful as I thought I was or as inadequate as I thought I was. It made me realize I've accomplished a lot more than I had realized (RISE, 104)".*

Women in the ECAU group described the intervention as having helpful impacts too, particularly in terms of increasing their overall knowledge about IPV and the variety of resources they could potentially make use of now or in the future. In terms of knowledge, multiple women discussed the value of learning about and paying homage to the different forms of IPV and their impacts on health, which helped them to validate their IPV experiences. One woman stated,

> "[the intervention] *covered all bases including every aspect of abuse in a relationship: physical, sexual, and emotional. I feel as though emotional abuse can be more detrimental than physical sometimes (ECAU, 105)".*

Another woman noted,

> *"It impacted me by teaching me that I'm not responsible and I don't deserve specific treatment, like abuse. Whether it's physical, emotional, mental (ECAU, 106)".*

This information was typically perceived as normalizing and helped women understand they were not alone in their experiences. Notably, the ECAU participants consistently commented on the impact of the breadth of information provided within the brochure that was used to help facilitate the information sharing and elicit discussion during the session,

> *"The wealth of information and contact information for resources in the pamphlet I took it home, and I poured over it for days. I googled every single thing, whether I thought I needed it or not. Stuff like that. But that whole thing made me feel not alone in this (ECAU, 107)".*

The intervention and brochure in particular led this participant to seek out additional information and resources.

3.2. Application of Content

Participants in both conditions reported that they applied tools and resources provided through the interventions. However, women in RISE endorsed more active changes in their daily lives through incorporating self-care, activating social support, and being more assertive in relationships, whereas women in ECAU applied tools specifically from the informational session and brochure, such as accessing IPV-relevant services and increasing awareness of IPV-related health impacts.

RISE participants identified several topics and handouts that they directly applied and utilized in their daily lives. Some notable applications were self-care, using decisional balance exercises from the Making Difficult Decisions module and applying strategies from the Enhancing Social Support and Safety Planning modules. For example, when asked about intervention applications, one participant shared,

> *"I still have and use the handouts, especially the self-care handout. Sometimes it's hard for me to do self-care, but with handouts it reminds me that I don't have to do anything major. It can be something simple, like aromatherapy. Even if I don't have the funds to go out. Just little things. It definitely adds up (RISE, 103)".*

Another participant described utilizing an exercise that is part of the Making Difficult Decisions module after participating in RISE:

> *"I have been weighing my pros and cons sometimes before I make difficult decisions (RISE, 108)".*

Increased skills around making decisions led to more confidence in her ability to make good decisions for herself.

Moreover, other RISE participants elaborated on the importance of social support as a mechanism of coping and maintaining safety. During and following the receipt of RISE, women engaged with social support, noting:

> "[RISE] *led me to reach out to a couple people just to make sure we were covered in case I had to use my safety plan. For me, that was a little bit more of going outside of my norm to ask for help, especially for the relationship situation (RISE, 109)".*

Likewise, another woman described utilizing content and concepts from the Education on Health Effects of IPV and Warning Signs module to improve her physical and mental health, noting:

> "[RISE] *really impacted my physical health so much. I try to make plans to workout more or exercise or do things that were more towards my physical wellness. Emotionally, RISE kind of helped me to stabilize my emotional roller coaster on some days (RISE, 110)".*

These examples of applying RISE concepts, resources, and skills emphasize some of the RISE intervention's unique mechanisms of helpfulness, appropriateness, and usability.

Participants in ECAU also provided examples of applying what they had learned from the intervention, although the applications were somewhat less concrete and mostly involved the information and resources discussed in the session and the associated brochure. An ECAU participant noted,

> *"I liked that she gave me the pamphlet and went through it with me during the session. It was helpful. She gave me resources to help me and places to go in the VA for certain things (ECAU, 111)".*

She elaborated that her provider helped connect her with case management, and she had since been utilizing their services which she found valuable in moving towards practical goals.

The sentiment that the pamphlet was a helpful tool resounded amongst many participants in ECAU. Another ECAU participant echoed that,

> *"just to have that information was comforting (ECAU, 112)".*

This participant emphasized that the statistics about other women experiencing IPV, as well as the normalization of common reactions and health consequences of IPV, also played a role in providing social connectedness, as it made her feel comforted and not alone. Participants in both interventions often disclosed that they did not fully comprehend the seriousness of the abuse in their relationship or that they were not to blame for the abuse. Similarly, another ECAU participant poignantly appreciated the brochure and gave credit to the intervention for impacting the decision to leave her partner, stating:

> *"I felt like I had resources within the brochure. You gave me a lot of resources to use to feel better and get help to leave. So that was good (ECAU, 113)".*

Participants in ECAU utilized the pamphlet to better understand their situation:

> *"I've been evaluating my situation more clearly with information from the brochure (ECAU, 114)".*

This participant reflected that the validating nature of their provider helped normalize her IPV experiences and therefore enabled her to be more open to recognizing the corresponding health impacts.

3.3. Patient-Centered Approach

Participants in both the RISE and ECAU conditions expressed appreciation for the patient-centered nature of the interventions. Further, RISE participants noted that they appreciated the flexible yet structured and contained nature of RISE,

> *"I liked that we had a menu. Every week I got to pick because then I don't have to sit there and wonder, 'okay, what do I want to talk about today.' She gave me options. If I didn't want to deal with the feelings today and instead deal with coping with stress, that option and choice was very good for me (RISE, 108)".*

Similarly, another participant described how selecting the focus of her session was empowering because it gave her agency in her own treatment, noting:

> *"I got to pick the topic based on what I was going through. That was very good. It helped me to think, 'okay do I need to focus on this area a little bit more or that area.' So, I liked that I was choosing myself but talking to somebody with expertise at the same time (RISE, 110)".*

Another RISE participant echoed this sentiment, stating:

> *"I liked the menu items in the beginning that we covered. It gave me a chance to figure out where I was currently at in my mental state, and where I am at in that relationship. So, I really liked that. It definitely catered to what I needed instead of, this is what we are going to do today regardless of what I feel. So, I liked that (RISE, 115)".*

In both groups, participants liked that the interventions were tailored to them as women Veterans who experienced IPV. In particular, they valued that the interventions had general resources as well as specific resources related to their identities as women and as Veterans. An ECAU participant further describes this in reference to a referral that she was provided to a Post-9/11 social worker:

> *"It is tailored to us, which is more specific, it's more beneficial than just some random* [other resource]*... oh there's an actual office just for Veterans like me, and you should go there (ECAU, 116)".*

The participant reflects how targeting women Veterans specifically and individualizing the intervention to assist in their explicit needs contributed to her high level of satisfaction with the intervention. This may encourage women to feel more comfortable utilizing follow-up services as they reflect on their individual needs. Another ECAU participant emphasized the value of utilizing a women's space within the VHA. She stated,

> *"I wasn't aware there was a space for us women with partner issues. I was very happy that I was able to get that information because I want to say that I haven't received that anywhere. Then, after the session, I felt like I had a space to do so (ECAU, 117)".*

3.4. Implementation Recommendations

Participants were asked to describe any changes they would make to how the intervention was delivered that would have improved their overall experience with the intervention or that might help other women experiencing IPV. Across both conditions, there was a desire for more sessions; however, this desire was more common and pronounced for ECAU participants, and the rationale for wanting more sessions differed between groups. The RISE participants who wanted more sessions indicated a desire to continue to further their progress, as they had experienced initial positive impacts from the intervention, and they wanted to continue their growth. For example, one woman in the RISE group shared,

> *"I wish that it could have been more thorough and longer. Like if it became a permanent thing, I am sure that would fix the problem, but just the one a week and because it did have such a big impact on me, there wasn't enough of it because now here I am, and now I'm on the other side of that, and there's still a lot of work that needs to be done (RISE, 102)".*

This suggests that RISE might be more impactful if participants had the option to engage in more sessions. Later in the interview, she described in detail why it would have been helpful for her to have more sessions,

> *"I wanted to do all the topics and there were six, but there were only six sessions. I wish it could have been longer. Some weeks I really wanted to go back over one topic, but then I wouldn't be able to, I'd have to cut one out (RISE, 102)".*

Another RISE participant indicated that she wanted several more sessions

> *"because that really helps you set goals and then it helps you keep them. To go back and look at the first goal that you set, you know, 20 weeks prior, would be extremely helpful to kind of just remind yourself like you made this progress, don't let go of it. Just to kind of build habits so it is not like something that you do once, and you move on and you don't do it again (RISE, 118)".*

This suggests that including more RISE sessions might further instill the skills and applications implemented in RISE.

The ECAU participants wanted more sessions because they wanted the opportunity to further reflect on their IPV experiences and gain more in-depth benefits from the intervention. ECAU focused primarily on providing information and resources, validation, and safety planning. Although the intervention was generally deemed acceptable, many ECAU participants expressed that they wished they had a designated time and space to reflect on their IPV experiences and its impact on their lives in more detail, and wished they had more sessions to reflect on things that arose or were triggered during their ECAU session. One participant stated that she would have benefitted from *"more time to process things (ECAU, 112)"*.

This participant went on to mention that having more sessions could have strengthened the impact of the supportive messaging that is part of the intervention:

"I feel like if I had more sessions, the more stuff would stick. Just being reassured that things weren't my fault or things like that would stick more (ECAU, 112)".

Although ECAU participants appreciated and utilized the informational and resources-based intervention, a number of participants reported feeling emotionally triggered or overwhelmed by the extensive information provided in a single session:

"I think that the brochure she showed was really good, but with the brochure, I noticed after being here, I had a really hard day after that, and the day after. I think it was because of the brochure and how simplified it was (ECAU, 119)".

This participant recommended that some women may appreciate an offer for a scheduled phone or in-person check-in following the session to validate, problem solve, and answer questions. Another ECAU participant echoed,

"Just, it just seemed a little overwhelming. I actually feel like, hmm, maybe to have a couple more sessions so you don't feel so stressed (ECAU, 120)".

This participant recommended breaking up the ECAU intervention into multiple sessions to give participants the opportunity to consume the IPV information at a more manageable pace, hence reducing their stress and enhancing their ability to benefit more from the intervention. Another ECAU participant voiced that having multiple sessions would have helped her feel more comfortable and open with her clinician. She stated,

"I definitely would have said maybe a couple more sessions to get it all out to that one person and see that one person a few times and start to kind of build a relationship (ECAU, 121)".

This participant suggests that having more sessions might have facilitated a stronger therapeutic relationship which might have led to higher acceptability of the treatment.

An additional domain related to implementation recommendations was the desire for telehealth options. Prior to the COVID-19 pandemic, both interventions were delivered in person. Due to the COVID-19 pandemic, RISE and ECAU were converted to telehealth for the final 10 participants in the study. Before the COVID-19 pandemic, women in both interventions consistently expressed interest in utilizing telehealth as an option to limit barriers to care that are common among women with recent IPV experiences. As detailed here by a participant in the RISE group,

"Maybe doing telecommunication or skype videos. Cause I think that would have a greater impact...you could reach a lot more people. If they can't get to you, they can literally just use their phone or computer and still talk to that person as long as they are in a safe space. And maybe they don't feel comfortable [in the medical center] *and they feel comfortable in their house talking (RISE, 122)"*.

Once the interventions were adapted to telehealth, interview questions were modified to inquire about their experience of receiving an IPV intervention during the pandemic. One woman who transitioned from in-person RISE sessions to telehealth suggested that telehealth was a better option for her as she could more easily attend sessions (in this case, avoid transportation barriers with getting to the medical center),

"I almost think it's better over the phone because I am in my own comfortable space. I am not rushing to get into a hospital. Getting through traffic. I was resistant to doing therapy over the phone, but now, I have adapted to it, and I actually prefer it more (RISE, 123)".

Another participant in the RISE condition shared that she experienced an unanticipated problem with telehealth related to privacy:

"I was completely comfortable with telehealth. The only time I wasn't was when I was at my boyfriend's mom's house. I was like in my car doing it. It was my own fault for forgetting that I had the session, but my window was down, I think someone might have overheard me. But normally if I am home, I am completely comfortable (RISE, 118)".

Although some participants were hesitant to participate in teletherapy originally, as some had difficulty locating a private space, most women ultimately found it more palatable and feasible since it cut down time constraints and other barriers to care.

4. Discussion

Women who have experienced IPV and seek IPV treatment have a variety of unique needs and preferences [24,48,49]. Through qualitative exit-interviews conducted in the context of a larger RCT of a new brief counseling intervention, the women Veterans in this study provided insightful feedback that can inform IPV programs and clinical practice with women Veterans who experience IPV and may have relevance to other populations who experience IPV. Both interventions were deemed as generally acceptable, as demonstrated by both quantitative helpfulness ratings and women's subjective experiences and feedback regarding the counseling interventions received. Findings across conditions highlighted women's preferences for, and benefits of, receiving tangible resources, a sense of social-connectedness, patient-centeredness, flexibility, and a sense of empowerment surrounding their treatment plan and goals.

Our findings add to prior qualitative work investigating IPV survivors' experiences with disclosing and discussing IPV in general mental health contexts [11,50] by adding the perspective of women Veterans with past-year IPV experiences who participated in structured psychosocial counseling interventions during an RCT. Sorrentino and colleagues [11] gathered qualitative feedback regarding IPV screening, disclosure, and response within the VHA healthcare setting from women Veterans who had lived experience with IPV and received past or ongoing mental health care (not necessarily for IPV) [11]. Results from the current study demonstrate that women's experience of RISE replicates and extends several of Sorrentino's [11] findings, including the importance of patient-centered IPV treatment that includes respect for clients' self-determination and flexibility (i.e., content focus and number of sessions included in the intervention) and promoting safety and access to outside resources. In the present study, women particularly appreciated RISE's flexibility, patient centeredness, and tailored resource provision (i.e., discussing in detail those resources that most map on to the concerns and stated needs of women). Current study findings suggest that clinicians addressing IPV would benefit from utilizing these principles in the context of psychosocial counseling for IPV and in the context of identifying IPV in the context of mental health care. Overall, participants who received RISE appreciated being able to choose the total number of sessions attended (between 1 and 6) and each session's focus (i.e., personalized module selection). This finding aligns with the growing evidence base supporting patient preferences for flexible and modular mental health treatment models [51,52].

Interviews in the current study revealed that the additional flexibility during the COVID-19 pandemic (i.e., receiving the intervention via telehealth) across both interventions was important, feasible, acceptable, and safe. Trauma-informed telehealth strategies (use of headphones for participants; environmental safety checks that included yes/no questions to assess for presence of another adult or child over 2 years of age; participant use of code words to change the subject if a partner or other person enters the room or is in earshot) were applied to bolster women's privacy, confidentiality, safety, and comfort addressing IPV via telehealth [53,54]. We also brainstormed with women, when relevant, locating private and safe locations for participating in IPV intervention sessions. Women sometimes took calls or videos from their (parked) cars which we endearingly referred to 'counseling in cars' [53,54]. This demonstrates support for delivering RISE and other IPV interventions face-to-face and via telehealth, which is important not only in the context of a pandemic or other public health crisis and is often compatible with patients' busy and often hectic lives [55]. It also provides another way to explicitly offer choice and voice in IPV care.

Women across both intervention conditions shared during the interviews that they utilized a number of additional resources and services as a result of direct linkages from the intervention. IPV screening and response literature confirms the importance of tangible IPV resources [56–59], and our study extends this by highlighting concrete resources and applications that are important in formal IPV counseling. Women Veterans in the current study across both conditions noted that it was helpful that providers had a comprehensive list of relevant services at hand as well as help clients personally connect with outside resources in the community (i.e., making a call together), which may have contributed to client follow through. Additionally, echoing findings from Dyer and colleagues (2020), women in this study across both intervention conditions valued the gender tailoring and the importance and attention placed on women Veterans within the treatment (e.g., resources specific to women, and to Veterans) and suggest that this type of tailoring is important in IPV counseling [60].

A number of the participants across the groups spoke about the importance of the IPV interventions for enhancing a sense of social-connectedness and social support. The literature reveals that social support is instrumental in fostering quality-of-life and healing, including in the context of abuse and IPV [61–63]. Women in both intervention groups noted that they felt comforted and supported through learning about the wide prevalence of IPV (e.g., by not feeling alone in their experiences), while women in RISE shared that they reached out to their support systems and the people they listed on their safety plan to feel connected. It is possible that RISE's "Enhancing Social Support" module and accompanying worksheets encouraged women to reach out to support systems including friends and family members in a more concrete way than women in the ECAU condition, perhaps contributing to positive quantitative psychosocial outcomes and more overall satisfaction with the RISE intervention observed in the parent study [38].

Participants in both intervention conditions endorsed a preference for being offered multiple sessions and the perceived benefits of reflecting weekly and engaging in exercises/practice between sessions (e.g., to process things that were triggering in the prior session, to engage in at-home application of skills learned, etc.). Participants in previous studies have emphasized that discussing IPV-related events is highly personal and understandably upsetting [50]; as such, it may be important to offer multiple sessions to allow for processing the difficult emotions that are often activated when discussing IPV and related situations. RISE's multi-session format and client-centered strategies are aligned with trauma-informed counseling and other multi-session evidence-based trauma focused therapies (e.g., Prolonged Exposure [PE]) [64] that include between session practice to consolidate and further treatment gains. RISE was designed not to elicit trauma-focused details from survivors of IPV, but instead to provide a trauma-informed, non-judgmental intervention where women can discuss their IPV history in broad strokes while focusing on developing skills to prevent future IPV experiences, and enhancing empowerment and self-efficacy, both of which are primary factors that may be associated with long-term benefits in the lives of women [38].

Limitations of the Study

Our findings must be interpreted in light of its limitations. First, the study's modest sample size and relatively brief and limited follow-up assessments (10- and 14-weeks following enrollment) are limitations. The brief timeframe for the follow-up assessments makes it impossible to know if the usefulness and acceptability of the interventions persist over time. It is possible women may have different perceptions of the interventions' strengths and weaknesses over time and that the 4 weeks between the two follow-up assessments was not long enough to capture such experiences. Future studies should include longer term follow-up assessments that include both qualitative and quantitative outcomes. Additionally, by design, there is variation in the uptake of the number of

RISE sessions received and in the modules selected by participants. In the present study, the qualitative interviews were designed to assess participants' experience with the RISE and advocacy-based ECAU interventions overall. The present study did not examine individual differences in how participants were impacted by the interventions and thus findings should not be interpreted to imply that all participants were affected the same by the intervention. Future studies of RISE should assess more specific feedback about the individual modules, ordering of the modules, and length of the RISE intervention. Although we found strong support among this sample for the identified themes, the findings are not necessarily universal, and the findings should not be assumed to apply to all women who experience IPV. Rather, these findings might highlight the importance of these themes as they relate to women Veterans and some themes may not be as transferrable to other clinical populations. Indeed, in addition to IPV, women Veterans tend to experience more trauma exposures over the lifespan and have additional mental and physical health needs as compared to their civilian counterparts [65,66]. Additionally, women Veterans who use the VHA often have mental and physical health conditions [67]. This is an important consideration since all participants were current VHA patients. Finally, the sample was limited to women, and future studies would benefit from including men and non-binary gender identities, who also experience IPV.

5. Conclusions

Understanding women's experiences and preferences for psychosocial counseling interventions for IPV is critical to providing evidence-based and trauma-informed care for this prevalent issue. Our study focused on women Veterans. The current findings reinforce the notion that women want flexibility and a sense of empowerment surrounding the length and content of their IPV treatment. Additionally, it is important for clinicians to provide social and logistical support (tailored resources, concrete skills, and tools to apply in their daily lives), which helps women feel less alone in their IPV experiences. These are practical suggestions that can be implemented into clinical practice with women Veterans who experience IPV and are likely applicable to other populations of women experiencing IPV.

Author Contributions: D.R.S., S.B.D., A.B.H. and K.M.I. contributed to the conceptualization and methodology of the manuscript. D.R.S., S.B.D., A.B.H. and K.M.I. contributed to the investigation, interpretation, and analysis of the data. D.R.S. and S.K.L. contributed to the writing—original draft preparation and resources, and all authors contributed to writing—review and editing. All authors have read and agreed to the published version of the manuscript.

Funding: This research was supported by the Department of Veterans Affairs (VA) Office of Research and Development Health Services Research & Development Services [IIR 16-062; Iverson].

Institutional Review Board Statement: Data collection was approved by the VA Boston Healthcare System's Institutional Review Board.

Informed Consent Statement: Informed consent was obtained from all subjects involved in the study.

Data Availability Statement: The datasets generated during and/or analyzed during the current study are not publicly available due to Human Studies protections placed upon them by the Boston VA Healthcare System Institutional Review Boards. Data are available from the authors upon reasonable request, which would also involve obtaining permission from the VA Boston Healthcare System Institutional Review Board.

Acknowledgments: The authors are grateful to Stephanie Kaplan, Laura Brennan, Jessica Chmielewski, Alessandra Grillo, and Isabella Gabrielson, for their assistance with treatment delivery and project implementation for this study. None of these individuals reported a conflict of interest regarding their participation in the implementation of this study.

Conflicts of Interest: The authors declare no conflict of interest.

Trial Registration: ClinicalTrials.gov Identifier: NCT03261700.

References

1. World Health Organization. *Violence Against Women Prevalence Estimates, 2018: Global, Regional and National Prevalence Estimates for Intimate Partner Violence against Women and Global and Regional Prevalence Estimates for Non-Partner Sexual Violence Against Women*; WHO: Geneva, Switzerland, 2021.
2. Smith, S.G.; Zhang, X.; Basile, K.C.; Merrick, M.T.; Wang, J.; Kresnow, M.-J.; Chen, J. *The National Intimate Partner and Sexual Violence Survey: 2015 Data Brief–Updated Release*; Centers for Disease Control and Prevention: Atlanta, GA, USA, 2018.
3. Thompson, R.S.; Bonomi, A.E.; Anderson, M.; Reid, R.J.; Dimer, J.A.; Carrell, D.; Rivara, F.P. Intimate Partner Violence: Prevalence, Types, and Chronicity in Adult Women. *Am. J. Prev. Med.* **2006**, *30*, 447–457. [CrossRef] [PubMed]
4. Ellsberg, M.; Jansen, H.A.; Heise, L.; Watts, C.H.; Garcia-Moreno, C.; WHO Multi-country Study on Women's Health and Domestic Violence against Women Study Team. Intimate partner violence and women's physical and mental health in the WHO multi-country study on women's health and domestic violence: An observational study. *Lancet* **2008**, *371*, 1165–1172. [CrossRef]
5. Benight, C.C.; Bandura, A. Social cognitive theory of posttraumatic recovery: The role of perceived self-efficacy. *Behav. Res. Ther.* **2004**, *42*, 1129–1148. [CrossRef] [PubMed]
6. Dardis, C.M.; Dichter, M.E.; Iverson, K.M. Empowerment, PTSD and revictimization among women who have experienced intimate partner violence. *Psychiatry Res.* **2018**, *266*, 103–110. [CrossRef]
7. Johnson, D.M.; Worell, J.; Chandler, R.K. Assessing Psychological Health and Empowerment in Women: The Personal Progress Scale Revised. *Women Health* **2005**, *41*, 109–129. [CrossRef]
8. McLean, C.; Follette, V.M. Acceptance and Commitment Therapy as a Non-Pathologizing Intervention Approach for Survivors of Trauma. *J. Trauma Dissociation* **2015**, *17*, 138–150. [CrossRef]
9. Potter, L.C.; Morris, R.; Hegarty, K.; García-Moreno, C.; Feder, G. Categories and health impacts of intimate partner violence in the World Health Organization multi-country study on women's health and domestic violence. *Int. J. Epidemiol.* **2021**, *50*, 652–662. [CrossRef]
10. Bonomi, A.E.; Anderson, M.L.; Rivara, F.P.; Thompson, R.S. Health Care Utilization and Costs Associated with Physical and Nonphysical-Only Intimate Partner Violence. *Health Serv. Res.* **2009**, *44*, 1052–1067. [CrossRef]
11. Sorrentino, A.E.; Iverson, K.M.; Tuepker, A.; True, G.; Cusack, M.; Newell, S.; Dichter, M.E. Mental health care in the context of intimate partner violence: Survivor perspectives. *Psychol. Serv.* **2021**, *18*, 512–522. [CrossRef]
12. Musa, A.; Chojenta, C.; Geleto, A.; Loxton, D. The associations between intimate partner violence and maternal health care service utilization: A systematic review and meta-analysis. *BMC Women's Health* **2019**, *19*, 1–14. [CrossRef]
13. Miller, E.; McCaw, B. Intimate Partner Violence. *N. Engl. J. Med.* **2019**, *380*, 850–857. [CrossRef] [PubMed]
14. Curry, S.J.; Krist, A.H.; Owens, D.K.; Barry, M.J.; Caughey, A.B.; Davidson, K.; Doubeni, C.A.; Epling, J.W.; Grossman, D.C. Screening for Intimate Partner Violence, Elder Abuse, and Abuse of Vulnerable Adults: US Preventive Services Task Force final recommendation statement. *JAMA J. Am. Med. Assoc.* **2018**, *320*, 1678–1687. [CrossRef]
15. Feltner, C.; Wallace, I.; Berkman, N.; Kistler, C.E.; Middleton, J.C.; Barclay, C.; Higginbotham, L.; Green, J.T.; Jonas, D.E. Screening for Intimate Partner Violence, Elder Abuse, and Abuse of Vulnerable Adults: Evidence report and systematic review for the US Preventive Services Task Force. *JAMA J. Am. Med. Assoc.* **2018**, *320*, 1688–1701. [CrossRef] [PubMed]
16. Bair-Merritt, M.H.; Lewis-O'Connor, A.; Goel, S.; Amato, P.; Ismailji, T.; Jelley, M.; Lenahan, P.; Cronholm, P. Primary Care–Based Interventions for Intimate Partner Violence: A systematic review. *Am. J. Prev. Med.* **2014**, *46*, 188–194. [CrossRef]
17. Johnson, D.M.; Zlotnick, C.; Hoffman, L.; Palmieri, P.A.; Johnson, N.L.; Holmes, S.C.; Ceroni, T.L. A Randomized Controlled Trial Comparing HOPE Treatment and Present-Centered Therapy in Women Residing in Shelter With PTSD From Intimate Partner Violence. *Psychol. Women Q.* **2020**, *44*, 539–553. [CrossRef]
18. Iverson, K.M.; Shenk, C.; Fruzzetti, A.E. Dialectical behavior therapy for women victims of domestic abuse: A pilot study. *Prof. Psychol. Res. Pract.* **2009**, *40*, 242–248. [CrossRef]
19. Blackwood, J.; Armstrong, M.J.; Schaefer, C.; Graham, I.D.; Knaapen, L.; Straus, S.E.; Urquhart, R.; Gagliardi, A.R. How do guideline developers identify, incorporate and report patient preferences? An international cross-sectional survey. *BMC Health Serv. Res.* **2020**, *20*, 1–10. [CrossRef]
20. Tarzia, L.; Bohren, M.A.; Cameron, J.; Garcia-Moreno, C.; O'Doherty, L.; Fiolet, R.; Hooker, L.; Wellington, M.; Parker, R.; Koziol-McLain, J.; et al. Women's experiences and expectations after disclosure of intimate partner abuse to a healthcare provider: A qualitative meta-synthesis. *BMJ Open* **2020**, *10*, e041339. [CrossRef]
21. Greene, S. A Framework for Making Patient-Centered Care Front and Center. *Perm. J.* **2012**, *16*, 49–53. [CrossRef]
22. Goodman, L.A.; Thomas, K.; Cattaneo, L.B.; Heimel, D.; Woulfe, J.; Chong, S.K. Survivor-Defined Practice in Domestic Violence Work: Measure development and preliminary evidence of link to empowerment. *J. Interpers. Violence* **2016**, *31*, 163–185. [CrossRef]
23. Kulkarni, S. Intersectional Trauma-Informed Intimate Partner Violence (IPV) Services: Narrowing the Gap between IPV Service Delivery and Survivor Needs. *J. Fam. Violence* **2019**, *34*, 55–64. [CrossRef]
24. Grillo, A.R.; Danitz, S.B.; Dichter, M.E.; Driscoll, M.A.; Gerber, M.R.; Hamilton, A.B.; Wiltsey-Stirman, S.; Iverson, K.M. Strides Toward Recovery From Intimate Partner Violence: Elucidating Patient-Centered Outcomes to Optimize a Brief Counseling Intervention for Women. *J. Interpers. Violence* **2019**, *36*, 8431–8453. [CrossRef] [PubMed]
25. Lyon, A.R.; Koerner, K. User-centered design for psychosocial intervention development and implementation. *Clin. Psychol. Sci. Pract.* **2016**, *23*, 180–200. [CrossRef] [PubMed]

26. Iverson, K.M.; King, M.W.; Gerber, M.R.; Resick, P.A.; Kimerling, R.; Street, A.E.; Vogt, D. Accuracy of an Intimate Partner Violence Screening Tool for Female VHA Patients: A Replication and Extension. *J. Trauma. Stress* **2015**, *28*, 79–82. [CrossRef] [PubMed]
27. Kimerling, R.; Iverson, K.M.; Dichter, M.E.; Rodriguez, A.L.; Wong, A.; Pavao, J. Prevalence of Intimate Partner Violence among Women Veterans who Utilize Veterans Health Administration Primary Care. *J. Gen. Intern. Med.* **2016**, *31*, 888–894. [CrossRef]
28. Murdoch, M. Women veterans' experiences with domestic violence and with sexual harassment while in the military. *Arch. Fam. Med.* **1995**, *4*, 411–418. [CrossRef]
29. Iverson, K.M.; Vogt, D.; Dichter, M.E.; Carpenter, S.L.; Kimerling, R.; Street, A.E.; Gerber, M.R. Intimate Partner Violence and Current Mental Health Needs Among Female Veterans. *J. Am. Board Fam. Med.* **2015**, *28*, 772–776. [CrossRef]
30. Dichter, M.E.; Cerulli, C.; Bossarte, R.M. Intimate Partner Violence Victimization Among Women Veterans and Associated Heart Health Risks. *Women's Health Issues* **2011**, *21*, S190–S194. [CrossRef]
31. Ortabag, T.; Ozdemir, S.; Bebis, H.; Ceylan, S. Perspectives of Young Adult Men Regarding Violence against Women: A Cross-sectional Study from Turkey. *J. Fam. Violence* **2014**, *29*, 665–674. [CrossRef]
32. Dighton, G.; Roberts, E.; Hoon, A.E.; Dymond, S. Gambling problems and the impact of family in UK armed forces veterans. *J. Behav. Addict.* **2018**, *7*, 355–365. [CrossRef]
33. Zamorski, M.A.; Wiens-Kinkaid, M.E. Cross-sectional prevalence survey of intimate partner violence perpetration and victimization in Canadian military personnel. *BMC Public Health* **2013**, *13*, 1019. [CrossRef] [PubMed]
34. Dichter, M.E.; Sorrentino, A.; Bellamy, S.; Medvedeva, E.; Roberts, C.B.; Iverson, K.M. Disproportionate Mental Health Burden Associated With Past-Year Intimate Partner Violence Among Women Receiving Care in the Veterans Health Administration. *J. Trauma. Stress* **2017**, *30*, 555–563. [CrossRef] [PubMed]
35. Iverson, K.M.; Vogt, D.; Maskin, R.M.; Smith, B.N. Intimate Partner Violence Victimization and Associated Implications for Health and Functioning Among Male and Female Post-9/11 Veterans. *Med. Care* **2017**, *55*, S78–S84. [CrossRef] [PubMed]
36. Portnoy, G.A.; Relyea, M.R.; Street, A.E.; Haskell, S.G.; Iverson, K.M. A Longitudinal Analysis of Women Veterans' Partner Violence Perpetration: The Roles of Interpersonal Trauma and Posttraumatic Stress Symptoms. *J. Fam. Violence* **2019**, *35*, 361–372. [CrossRef]
37. Bartlett, B.A.; Iverson, K.M.; Mitchell, K.S. Intimate partner violence and disordered eating among male and female veterans. *Psychiatry Res.* **2018**, *260*, 98–104. [CrossRef] [PubMed]
38. Iverson, K.M.; Danitz, S.B.; Shayani, D.R.; Vogt, D.; Stirman, S.W.; Hamilton, A.B.; Mahoney, C.T.; Gerber, M.R.; Dichter, M.E. Recovering from Intimate Partner Violence through Strengths and Empowerment: Findings from a Randomized Clinical Trial. *J. Clin. Psychiatry* **2021**, *83*, 38188. [CrossRef]
39. Teague, A.K.; Hahna, N.D.; McKinney, C.H. Group Music Therapy with Women who have Experienced Intimate Partner Violence. *Music Ther. Perspect.* **2006**, *24*, 80–86. [CrossRef]
40. Cort, N.A.; Cerulli, C.; Poleshuck, E.L.; Bellenger, K.M.; Xia, Y.; Tu, X.; Mazzotta, C.M.; Talbot, N.L. Interpersonal psychotherapy for depressed women with histories of intimate partner violence. *Psychol. Trauma Theory Res. Pract. Policy* **2014**, *6*, 700–707. [CrossRef]
41. Johnson, D.M.; Zlotnick, C.; Perez, S. Cognitive behavioral treatment of PTSD in residents of battered women's shelters: Results of a randomized clinical trial. *J. Consult. Clin. Psychol.* **2011**, *79*, 542–551. [CrossRef]
42. Straus, M.A.; Hamby, S.L.; Boney-McCoy, S.; Sugarman, D.B. The Revised Conflict Tactics Scales (CTS2) development and preliminary psychometric data. *J. Fam. Issues* **1996**, *17*, 283–316. [CrossRef]
43. Miller, W.R.; Rollnick, S. *Motivational Interviewing: Helping People Change*; Guilford Press: New York, NY, USA, 2012.
44. Iverson, K.M.; Danitz, S.B.; Driscoll, M.; Vogt, D.; Hamilton, A.B.; Gerber, M.R.; Stirman, S.W.; Shayani, D.R.; Suvak, M.K.; Dichter, M.E. Recovering from intimate partner violence through Strengths and Empowerment (RISE): Development, pilot testing, and refinement of a patient-centered brief counseling intervention for women. *Psychol. Serv.* **2021**. [CrossRef] [PubMed]
45. Hamilton, A.B.; Finley, E.P. Qualitative methods in implementation research: An introduction. *Psychiatry Res.* **2019**, *280*, 112516. [CrossRef] [PubMed]
46. Lewinski, A.A.; Crowley, M.J.; Miller, C.; Bosworth, H.B.; Jackson, G.L.; Steinhauser, K.; White-Clark, C.; McCant, F.; Zullig, L.L. Applied Rapid Qualitative Analysis to Develop a Contextually Appropriate Intervention and Increase the Likelihood of Uptake. *Med. Care* **2021**, *59*, S242–S251. [CrossRef] [PubMed]
47. Averill, J.B. Matrix Analysis as a Complementary Analytic Strategy in Qualitative Inquiry. *Qual. Health Res.* **2002**, *12*, 855–866. [CrossRef] [PubMed]
48. Chang, J.C.; Cluss, P.A.; Ranieri, L.; Hawker, L.; Buranosky, R.; Dado, D.; McNeil, M.; Scholle, S.H. Health care interventions for intimate partner violence: What women want. *Women's Health Issues* **2005**, *15*, 21–30. [CrossRef] [PubMed]
49. Iverson, K.M.; Stirman, S.W.; Street, A.E.; Gerber, M.R.; Carpenter, S.L.; Dichter, M.E.; Bair-Merritt, M.; Vogt, D.; Carpenter, L.S. Female veterans' preferences for counseling related to intimate partner violence: Informing patient-centered interventions. *Gen. Hosp. Psychiatry* **2016**, *40*, 33–38. [CrossRef]
50. Trevillion, K.; Hughes, B.; Feder, G.; Borschmann, R.; Oram, S.; Howard, L.M. Disclosure of domestic violence in mental health settings: A qualitative meta-synthesis. *Int. Rev. Psychiatry* **2014**, *26*, 430–444. [CrossRef]
51. Chorpita, B.F.; Daleiden, E.L.; Weisz, J.R. Modularity in the design and application of therapeutic interventions. *Appl. Prev. Psychol.* **2005**, *11*, 141–156. [CrossRef]

52. Palinkas, L.A.; Weisz, J.R.; Chorpita, B.F.; Levine, B.; Garland, A.F.; Hoagwood, K.E.; Landsverk, J. Continued Use of Evidence-Based Treatments After a Randomized Controlled Effectiveness Trial: A Qualitative Study. *Psychiatr. Serv.* **2013**, *64*, 1110–1118. [CrossRef]
53. Gerber, M.R.; Elisseou, S.; Sager, Z.S.; Keith, J.A. Trauma-Informed Telehealth in the COVID-19 Era and Beyond. *Fed. Pract.* **2020**, *37*, 302–308. [CrossRef]
54. Rossi, F.S.; Shankar, M.; Buckholdt, K.; Bailey, Y.; Israni, S.T.; Iverson, K.M. Trying Times and Trying Out Solutions: Intimate Partner Violence Screening and Support for Women Veterans During COVID-19. *J. Gen. Intern. Med.* **2020**, *35*, 2728–2731. [CrossRef]
55. Moring, J.C.; Dondanville, K.A.; Fina, B.A.; Hassija, C.; Chard, K.; Monson, C.; LoSavio, S.T.; Wells, S.Y.; Morland, L.A.; Kaysen, D.; et al. Cognitive Processing Therapy for Posttraumatic Stress Disorder via Telehealth: Practical Considerations During the COVID-19 Pandemic. *J. Trauma. Stress* **2020**, *33*, 371–379. [CrossRef] [PubMed]
56. Rivas, C.; Ramsay, J.; Sadowski, L.; Davidson, L.L.; Dunnes, D.; Eldridge, S.; Hegarty, K.; Taft, A.; Feder, G. Advocacy Interventions to Reduce or Eliminate Violence and Promote the Physical and Psychosocial Well-Being of Women who Experience Intimate Partner Abuse: A Systematic Review. *Campbell Syst. Rev.* **2016**, *12*, 1–202. [CrossRef]
57. Chamberlain, L.; Levenson, R. Addressing intimate partner violence, reproductive and sexual coercion. In *A Guide for Obstetric, Gynecologic and Reproductive Health Care Settings*, 2nd ed.; Futures Without Violence: San Francisco, CA, USA, 2012; Volume 1. [CrossRef]
58. Ghandour, R.M.; Campbell, J.C.; Lloyd, J. Screening and Counseling for Intimate Partner Violence: A Vision for the Future. *J. Women's Health* **2015**, *24*, 57–61. [CrossRef] [PubMed]
59. Iverson, K.M.; Huang, K.; Wells, S.Y.; Wright, J.D.; Gerber, M.; Wiltsey-Stirman, S. Women Veterans' Preferences for Intimate Partner Violence Screening and Response Procedures Within the Veterans Health Administration. *Res. Nurs. Health* **2014**, *37*, 302–311. [CrossRef]
60. Dyer, K.E.; Moreau, J.L.; Finley, E.; Bean-Mayberry, B.; Farmer, M.M.; Bernet, D.; Kress, A.; Lewis, J.L.; Batuman, F.K.; Haskell, S.G.; et al. Tailoring an evidence-based lifestyle intervention to meet the needs of women Veterans with prediabetes. *Women Health* **2020**, *60*, 748–762. [CrossRef]
61. Anderson, K.M.; Renner, L.M.; Danis, F.S. Recovery: Resilience and growth in the aftermath of domestic violence. *Violence Against Women* **2012**, *18*, 1279–1299. [CrossRef]
62. Beeble, M.L.; Bybee, D.; Sullivan, C.M.; Adams, A.E. Main, mediating, and moderating effects of social support on the well-being of survivors of intimate partner violence across 2 years. *J. Consult. Clin. Psychol.* **2009**, *77*, 718–729. [CrossRef]
63. Ogbe, E.; Harmon, S.; Van den Bergh, R.; Degomme, O. A systematic review of intimate partner violence interventions focused on improving social support and/ mental health outcomes of survivors. *PLoS ONE* **2020**, *15*, e0235177. [CrossRef]
64. Foa, E.B.; Rothbaum, B.O. *Treating the Trauma of Rape: Cognitive Behavioral Therapy for PTSD*; Guilford: New York, NY, USA, 1998.
65. Gerber, M.R.; Iverson, K.M.; Dichter, M.E.; Klap, R.; Latta, R.E. Women Veterans and Intimate Partner Violence: Current State of Knowledge and Future Directions. *J. Women's Health* **2014**, *23*, 302–309. [CrossRef]
66. McCauley, H.L.; Blosnich, J.R.; Dichter, M.E. Adverse Childhood Experiences and Adult Health Outcomes Among Veteran and Non-Veteran Women. *J. Women's Health* **2015**, *24*, 723–729. [CrossRef] [PubMed]
67. Frayne, S.M.; Saechao, F.; Maisel, N.C.; Friedman, S.A.; Finlay, A.; Berg, E.; Balasubramanian, V.; Dally, S.K.; Ananth, L.; Romodan, Y.; et al. Sociodemographics, utilization, costs of care, and health profile. In *Sourcebook: Women Veterans in the Veterans Health Administration*; Department of Veterans Affairs: Washington, DC, USA, 2014; Volume 3.

International Journal of
Environmental Research and Public Health

MDPI

Systematic Review

The Effectiveness of Culturally Specific Male Domestic Violence Offender Intervention Programs on Behavior Changes and Mental Health: A Systematic Review

Lata Satyen *, Ashlyn Hansen, Jane Louise Green and Laura Zark

School of Psychology, Deakin University, Burwood, VIC 3125, Australia
* Correspondence: lata@deakin.edu.au

Abstract: The objective of domestic violence intervention programs is to address perpetrator behavior. However, the suitability and effectiveness of these programs in confronting problematic behavior for ethnically diverse groups is unclear. Therefore, the aim of this systematic review was to cohesively examine whether such programs are effective in reducing recidivism, changing perpetrator behavior, and addressing mental health issues for culturally diverse groups. Several databases were searched for peer-reviewed articles that included culturally specific components or ethnically diverse cohorts in offender intervention programs. 10 articles met the inclusion criteria. The findings demonstrate greater effectiveness of programs with greater cultural engagement: through culturally trained facilitators, addressing the cultural and patriarchal norms relevant to the specific client group, and discussion of gender roles and attitudes to gender equality specific to the cultural context. Such programs achieved some positive outcomes including: reduced recidivism, improved mental health, and better attitudes to gender equality. However, the findings are limited to a few ethnically diverse groups, and not all studies measured all outcomes listed above. This review suggests the development and implementation of suitable offender intervention programs that address perpetrator behavior and mental health in ethnically diverse client groups. When culturally relevant and effective programs are implemented, it could lead to men's modification of perpetrating behavior and create safer family relationships.

Keywords: domestic violence; perpetrator; intervention; behavior modification; mental health; culture; ethnicity

Citation: Satyen, L.; Hansen, A.; Green, J.L.; Zark, L. The Effectiveness of Culturally Specific Male Domestic Violence Offender Intervention Programs on Behavior Changes and Mental Health: A Systematic Review. *Int. J. Environ. Res. Public Health* **2022**, *19*, 15180. https://doi.org/10.3390/ijerph192215180

Academic Editors: Krim K. Lacey and Rohan D. Jeremiah

Received: 18 September 2022
Accepted: 10 November 2022
Published: 17 November 2022

1. Introduction

With the ongoing increase in rates of violence against women, it is necessary to develop effective interventions to change perpetrator behavior. This violence continues despite the range of policies, prevention and intervention programs, and funding allocated to address the issue. We know that globally, one in four ever-partnered women have experienced physical or sexual violence from a male intimate partner since the age of 15 years [1]. There is also evidence that some communities are at higher risk of women experiencing violence from a male intimate partner, with the highest prevalence rate in low-income regions [1,2]. These regions tend to have populations with increased cultural diversity and ethnic minority groups, and associated intersectional risk factors including trauma, discrimination, social and economic deprivation, social isolation and pre and post-migration stress [3]. The violence is caused by individual factors and social systems that influence perpetrators to commit physical, psychological, sexual, financial, spiritual, social abuse [4], and a pattern of coercive control. Given the serious and long-lasting physical, social, and mental health consequences of intimate partner violence (IPV), the World Health Organization (WHO) [5] has called for higher quality intervention and prevention strategies to reduce the prevalence and impact of IPV. While acknowledging that IPV occurs in diverse partnerships, this review focuses on male perpetration towards their female partners. While no community is showing decreasing levels of violence against women, we need to examine the effectiveness of existing violence prevention and intervention programs in reducing rates of violence in cultural minority and non-Anglo-Saxon groups. This will help us identify universal and unique factors that can be implemented to achieve the goal of behavior change to reduce recidivism rates, improve mental health and ensure women are able to live in a safer society.

1.1. Interventions for Perpetrators

A range of mechanisms have been developed to address male perpetration of intimate partner violence. The most commonly used perpetrator intervention strategies to date include mandatory arrest, feminist sociocultural programs (e.g., the Duluth model) [6], and cognitive-behavioral therapy (CBT) [7]. Feminist sociocultural programs focus on addressing gender-related attitudes, encouraging accountability and personal responsibility for abusive behavior, and promoting gender-equal attitudes and behaviors [8]. The emphasis placed by feminist sociocultural programs on male perpetrators' choice to be violent means that to benefit from these programs, perpetrators must be motivated to alter their notions of power and control [9]. However, a recent, comprehensive review asserted that if perpetrators are unwilling to actively participate in programs to alter violent behavior, feminist principles may be of little use in facilitating change [10]. We therefore need to examine alternate approaches to maladaptive patterns of thinking.

A few programs focus on psychotherapy and identifying individual causes of violence including behavioral deficits or psychopathology [11]. Although CBT can address individual behavioral issues, most CBT-related perpetrator programs are administered in a group setting that focus on skills training for anger management, better communication, assertiveness, and relaxation [8]. Further, CBT assumes that clients are motivated to change their behavior and capable of altering their cognitive or behavioral patterns [12]. However, research shows that many abusive men do not have the capacity to engage in treatment methods, or to alter their cognitions related to power and control, and increase their empathy for their partners and children [13]. The literature therefore suggests that feminist and cognitive-behavioral approaches may be ineffective because men are either not willing or able to change their thinking and/or behavior. This leads us to examine what successes existing CBT-focused behavior intervention programs are achieving.

The Duluth model was originally implemented with feminist and sociocultural underpinnings and using the constructs of power and control [6]; it has since been adapted to apply a combination of cognitive-behavioral techniques and feminist approaches [14]. It aims to both challenge men's sense of power and control and teach them alternative skills to reduce conflict in their relationships and reduce their perpetration of violence towards their partners [14]. This approach is one of the few that has been applied to male perpetrators of African American, Native American, and Latino descent, apart from Ango-Saxons [10]. In spite of some of its positive facets, it is limited in its acknowledgement of men's issues related to racism and discrimination; further, it does not address immigration-related challenges and their relationship to perpetration, and has not been evaluated for its effectiveness with other ethnic groups [15,16]. Thus, despite the development and implementation of a range of domestic and family violence perpetrator intervention programs, the adequacy and efficacy of these programs appears to be lacking.

Evaluations of intervention programs have shown that group treatments for IPV perpetrators have limited success in altering the cycle of violence [8,17]. Indeed, irrespective of the strategy adopted, one in three perpetrators exhibit a new abusive pattern of IPV within 6 months of a victim's report [8]. A few reasons have been elucidated about the challenges to treating this part of the population. Most perpetrators present a combination of being child victims of family violence [18,19] and characteristics such as impulsivity, psychological entitlement, poor regulation of anger, and empathy impairment as well as narcissistic and antisocial behavior [20,21] along with substance abuse problems [22]. Such behavioral risk factors associated with adverse childhood experiences can lead to enduring negative effects on brain development and thus, are difficult to address as part of behavioral modifications [23].

Traditional IPV treatment models based on the principles of CBT or the Duluth model have been shown in systematic reviews to have little to no effect on recidivism [11,24,25], although significant methodological issues and high attrition rates preclude clear conclusions on their effectiveness. These findings also vary considerably across populations and settings [11,24]. Additionally, Chang and Saunders [26] highlight the elevated risk of attrition from these programs amongst minority groups. The majority of research evaluating the effectiveness of these models has been conducted in the North American context [27] and a number of studies have found that these programs may be inappropriate or ineffective for ethnic and cultural minority groups [16,28]. Thus, research demonstrates mixed findings in relation to the adequacy of intervention programs to address perpetrator behavior and reduce the rates of violence against women in the community.

1.2. Theoretical Perspectives of Perpetrator Intervention Programs

The theoretical premises on which perpetrator intervention programs have been developed include ecological, cognitive-behavioral, feminist, and intersectional approaches. Ecological approaches [29] attempt to address the individual, relational, and societal level factors that might influence a perpetrator's abusive behavior; while cognitive-behavioral approaches endeavor to restructure beliefs regarding gender and gendered violence and teach skills for effective communication and self-regulation, particularly with regard to regulation of anger [7]. Feminist-focused intervention programs aim to instill gender-positive attitudes and challenge hierarchical patriarchal structures [9,30]. Programs that utilize an intersectional approach posit that gender-based violence cannot be understood without exploring the interactions between gender inequality and other forms of marginalization, such as those based on race and class (e.g., Crenshaw, 1989) [31]. This approach considers the different experiences of groups who occupy positions of privilege and of marginalization on the basis of multiple intersecting identities [3,10,32,33].

In the context of working with minority ethnic groups and non-Anglo-Saxon communities, program practitioners need to be culturally sensitive and ensure that the impact of culture is not minimized or misunderstood, particularly as most treatment systems are guided by dominant White-centric theories [32]. 'Culture' should also not be an "added-on" feature of programs [32]. Rather, practitioners need to develop an in-depth knowledge of cultural norms of the communities they are engaging with, including the practices of dowry, arranged marriage, and female genital mutilation. Importantly, practitioners must not assume that violence against women is "culturally normative" [32].

1.3. Ethnicity and Intimate Partner Violence Perpetrator Programs

Research on culturally specific interventions to reduce IPV remains scant [24,34]. These interventions have not been thoroughly evaluated or have been evaluated using different measures of success. Examining the evidence for the use of such programs, and particularly their application in ethnic minority and non-Anglo-Saxon groups, is necessary for developing and implementing appropriate program protocols for these groups. Turhan [10] recently conducted a narrative review of current approaches to IPV perpetrator intervention to evaluate their suitability for marginalized ethnic subpopulations. He found variations in the degree to which 'culture' was applied across existing intervention programs. For example, some paradigms associated domestic violence with social issues such as traditional patriarchal and gender roles, spirituality, and immigration-related stressors [32,35] while others [10,36] found structural issues such as practitioners' knowledge of racism and discrimination to influence the success of the program.

Client-related issues can also impact engagement with an intervention. For example, Turhan [10] found that program participants' knowledge of the premise of therapy, language barriers, and awareness of the issue of domestic violence could lead to increased program engagement and reduced attrition. The importance of the establishment of rapport and trust between the client and program facilitator were also highlighted as important factors in creating a positive therapeutic environment [10]. This was in addition to practitioners being able to apply appropriate techniques that address men's needs in their social and cultural contexts [10].

Program developers need to identify and address various risk factors for men from ethnic minority backgrounds. Studies illustrate that hardship, trauma, and psychological distress, as well as acculturation and shifts in cultural beliefs and values, can contribute to family conflict [37,38]. Migration-related stressors such as financial and employment pressures, loss of informal supports, lack of access to health and social services, and exposure to discrimination in the host country may also act as cumulative risk factors for IPV amongst ethnic and cultural minority groups [39–43]. Programs that incorporate ways of discussing these issues and intervening in culturally relevant ways have a greater chance of being successful. Migration-related stressors also call for social justice systems to be more supportive and for communities to create better social supports for families in abusive relationships.

Given the close relationship of 'culture' to the constructs of family and gender roles, which are the focus of current IPV treatment models [11,44,45], it is necessary to develop culturally appropriate approaches for IPV perpetrators from ethnic minority and non-Anglo-Saxon groups. A failure to provide culturally informed interventions presents a risk to such groups, who may not benefit from dominant IPV perpetrator treatment models [46]. Indeed, integrative programs that are community-driven and foster culturally sensitive discussions about gender, power, and violence have greater acceptability and effectiveness for promoting non-violent behavior in cultural and ethnic minority communities [45–47]. To date, there is no comprehensive review of culturally specific IPV perpetrator programs for ethnic minority and non-Anglo-Saxon populations to measure recidivism and other program outcomes. Therefore, the aim of this review was to systematically examine the evidence for the effectiveness of culturally specific interventions for male perpetrators of domestic and family violence to achieve positive behavior change and address mental health issues.

2. Materials and Methods

2.1. Search Strategy

Studies were identified by systematically searching thirteen electronic databases for the period 1993–2022, with the final search of all databases being conducted on 9 August 2022: Academic Search Complete, AMED, CINAHL Complete, Criminal Justice Abstracts with Full Text, E-Journals, Health Source: Nursing/Academic Edition, MEDLINE, MEDLINE Complete, PsycARTICLES, PsycEXTRA, Psychology and Behavioural Sciences Collection, PsycINFO, and Social Work Abstracts. The effective combination of search terms was designed and set up by one reviewer according to the PRISMA statement [47] and different terms and rules of each database. Reference lists of retrieved studies were then hand-searched and papers citing these relevant studies in Google Scholar were screened to identify any additional studies that may have been overlooked. Specific keywords and free text terms for perpetrators of intimate partner violence, interventions and culture were used for each database (Supplementary Materials S1). Only studies with key terms in their title or abstract were included for review.

2.2. Study Selection

Any peer-reviewed journal article that evaluated the effectiveness of culturally specific interventions for adult male perpetrators of intimate partner violence and was written in the English language and published between January 1993–August 2022, was considered for review. Studies were excluded if any participants were identified as female or under the age of 18 years; or if the intervention program was not culturally specific. Furthermore, studies that did not measure outcomes related to the effectiveness of the intervention, such rates of recidivism and re-assaults; changes to psychopathological symptoms related to perpetration including anger, empathy, impulsivity, self-esteem and inadaptation; attitudes towards gender and sexuality; and satisfaction with intervention engagement, were excluded. Studies not published in the English language were also excluded.

2.3. Screening and Data Extraction

One researcher (A.H.) screened titles and abstracts of studies which were identified through electronic database searches, following the removal of duplicate references using EndNote X8.2 software (Clarivate, London, UK). Full text articles of potentially relevant studies were then assessed independently by three co-authors (A.H., L.S. and L.Z). Discrepancies in eligibility assessment were resolved through discussion between all four co-authors.

Key study characteristics and outcomes were then extracted as indicated in Supplementary Materials S2. Study characteristics included: risk of bias, country of participant population, inclusion and exclusion criteria, demographics of participants, sample size, format and description of culturally specific intervention component, type and description of comparison condition. Study outcomes extracted included: intervention effect on recidivism and re-assaults; changes to psychopathological symptoms related to perpetration including anger, empathy, impulsivity, self-esteem and inadaptation; attitudes towards gender and sexuality; and satisfaction with intervention engagement.

As a result of our initial search, 2851 studies were identified, reduced to 1612 after the removal of duplicates. After reviewing titles and abstracts to determine whether articles were relevant to the scope of the current study, 58 articles remained to be screened in full text. Of the 58 articles screened, an additional 48 were excluded (see Figure 1 for exclusion reasons). The reference lists of the remaining 10 articles were then screened, which revealed no additional article that met criteria for inclusion. A final total of 10 articles were included for review. The studies have been summarized to describe study quality, characteristics and outcomes.

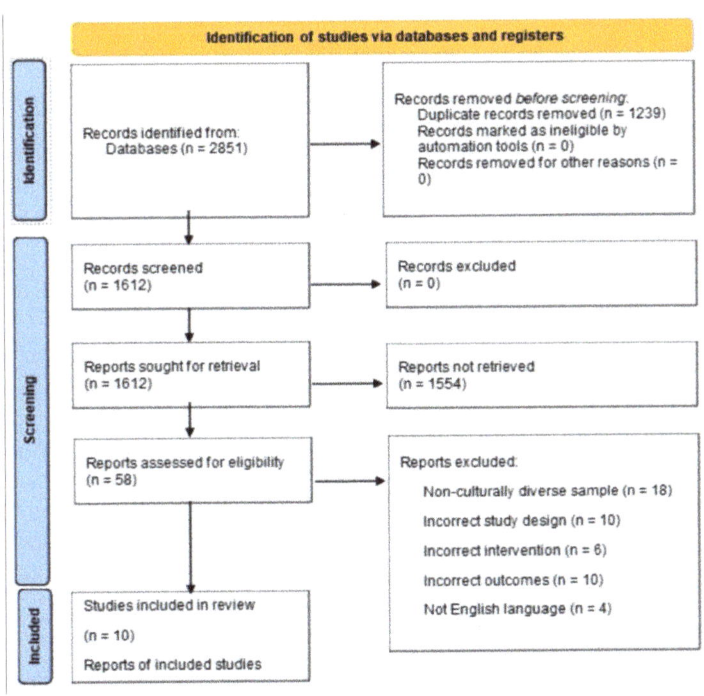

Figure 1. Preferred Reporting Items for Systematic Reviews and Meta-Analyses (PRISMA) flow diagram for study selection. Adapted from Page et al. (2021) [48].

2.4. Study Design Characteristics

Among the 10 studies that were included for review, six were conducted in North America, three in Europe and one in Asia. Four of the studies used post-intervention qualitative evaluations. Of the remaining six quantitative studies, three utilized a pre/post-test design without a control group, one utilized a randomized controlled trial design, one a case series design and one utilized a case–control design.

2.5. Quality Assessment

Qualitative studies were appraised by two reviewers (L.S. and J.G.) for methodological quality using the Critical Appraisal Skills Programme (CASP) Qualitative Checklist [49]. A value of 'Yes',' No' or 'Can't determine' was assigned to each requirement. Results of this appraisal are captured in Table 1. Quantitative studies were assessed using the National Heart, Blood and Lung Institute's (NHLBI) Quality Assessment Tools for Before-After Studies With No Control Group, Controlled Intervention Studies, Case-Control Studies, and Case Series Studies [50]. The findings of this assessment are captured in Table 2.

2.6. Sample

Reported sample sizes of included studies ranged from N = 12–792 (M = 253.29), with an approximate total of N = 1950. Two studies [16,51] did not report the sample size. Study samples across the 10 included studies comprised a number of ethnic minority and non-Anglo-Saxon groups including: African American FV (family violence) perpetrators [28], Hispanic/Latina FV perpetrators [16,52–54], Canadian Aboriginal FV perpetrators [51,55], Vietnamese FV perpetrators [56], Swedish FV perpetrators [57], and an 'immigrant' group which included European, African, American and Asian ethnic groups [58]. Amongst these, three studies [52,56,57] examined non-Anglo-Saxon majority populations, whilst the remaining seven [16,28,51,53–55,58], examined sub-ethnic groups within broader populations.

Table 1. Quality assessment of included qualitative studies.

Reference (Year)	Criteria										Overall Assessment of Methodological Quality
	1	2	3	4	5	6	7	8	9	10	
Hancock & Sui (2009) [16]	+	+	+	+	+	+	+	+	+	+	No or very minor concerns
Parra-Cardona et al. (2013) [53]	+	+	+	+	+	+	+	+	+	+	No or very minor concerns
Welland & Ribner (2010) [54]	+	+	+	+	+	+	+	+	−	+	No or very minor concerns
Hoang, Quach & Tran (2013) [56]	+	+	+	+	+	+	+	−	+	+	No or very minor concerns

Note. Criteria: 1 = Was there a clear statement of the aims? 2 = Was a qualitative methodology appropriate? 3 = Was the research design appropriate? 4 = Was the recruitment strategy appropriate? 5 = Was the method of data collection appropriate? 6 = Was the relationship between the researcher and participant adequately considered? 7 = Were ethical issues taken into consideration? 8 = Was the data analysis sufficiently rigorous? 9 = Was there a clear statement of the findings? 10 = Was the value of the research discussed? Symbols: + =yes; − = no.

Table 2. Quality assessment of included quantitative studies.

Authors (Year)		Criteria														Quality Rating
		1	2	3	4	5	6	7	8	9	10	11	12	13	14	
Gondolf (2004) [14]	Assessed with Quality Assessment Tool for Controlled Intervention Studies (Criteria B)	+	+	−	?	?	+	+	−	+	+	+	+	+	+	Fair
Zellerer (2003) [51]	Assessed with Quality Assessment Tool for Before-After (Pre-Post) Studies with No Control Group (Criteria A)	+	+	+	?	?	+	−	/	?	?	−	−			Fair
Echeburúa (2006) [52]	Assessed with Quality Assessment Tool for Before-After (Pre-Post) Studies with No Control Group (Criteria A)	+	+	+	+	−	+	+	/	+	+	−	/			Good

Table 2. *Cont.*

Authors (Year)		Criteria														Quality Rating
		1	2	3	4	5	6	7	8	9	10	11	12	13	14	
Puchala et al. (2010) [55]	Assessed with Quality Assessment Tool for Case Series Studies (Criteria D)	+	+	+	+	+	+	+	+	+						Good
Haggård et al. (2015) [57]	Assessed with Quality Assessment Tool of Case Controlled Studies (Criteria C)	+	+	+	+	+	+	/	−	+	+	+	+			Good
Echauri et al. (2013) [58]	Assessed with Quality Assessment Tool for Before-After (Pre-Post) Studies with No Control Group (Criteria A)	+	+	+	+	+	+	+	/	+	+	+	/			Good

Note. Quantitative studies were assessed using the Quality Assessment Tools published by the National Heart, Lung and Blood Institute (NHLBI) [50]. The criteria for each of the utilised tools have been fully explained in Supplementary Materials S3. Symbols: + = yes; − = no; ? = unclear; / = not applicable.

3. Results

3.1. Culturally Specific Interventions

All studies included for review, with the exception of one [58], evaluated intervention programs delivered in group sessions and not individually. Languages of program delivery included English [28,51,55], Spanish [16,52–54,58], Swedish [57], and Vietnamese [56]. In addition to delivery in non-English languages, culturally distinct components of intervention programs also included: the use of culturally knowledgeable facilitators (i.e., those who either spoke the language preferred by the clients, were from the same cultural background, or had training in delivering services to a specific cultural group) [16,28,51,53,55], discussion of culturally diverse expressions of masculinity [16,28,53,55,56], use of cultural healing traditions [52,56], and recognition of cultural issues and challenges faced by the men [16,28,51,53,56].

3.2. Measures of Recidivism

Four studies included some measure of violent recidivism or further violence as a metric of program effectiveness in their evaluation of the culturally specific program [28,56–58]. Data on reoffending were collected either through self-report [56,58], partner report [28], or government-managed crime registries [57].

3.3. Key Findings

3.3.1. Recidivism

The key qualitative and quantitative findings of the studies are presented in Supplementary Materials S2. The table demonstrates that of the 10 included studies, all studies (with the exception of one [57]), showed positive outcomes associated with engagement in culturally specific interventions. Outcome measures varied between the studies, however, six studies [16,28,51,55,56,58] reported either a complete absence or reduction in episodes of abuse. Echauri et al. [57] found that in 85.9% of cases, treatment was effective in reducing physical and psychological perpetration of abuse, with success rates increasing to 87% at the 12-month follow up period. These findings were consistent across immigrant and national populations. Gondolf [28] found that re-assault rates, as reported by the men's partners, increased from 32% in the first 15 months following treatment, to 42% at 48 months following treatment, which was adjusted to 47% for underreporting using arrest records and men's self-report. However, when using a retrospective approach from the end of the follow-up period to allow for the intervention to take effect, only 10% of men had re-assaulted their partners in the previous year and over two-thirds of women reported an improvement in their quality of life. Similarly, Hoang et al. [56] reported following engagement with the Responsible Men's Club, almost 70% of men had not perpetrated any violence, and of the remaining 30% there had been only one episode of violence in the last six months, compared to between two and six episodes in the pre-intervention survey. Of the people that engaged with traditional healing elders ($n = 76$), 49 people reported drastic reductions in domestic violence during their engagement, 9 reported no change in the violence, and 11 reported a continued escalation in violence or they were lost to follow up. 29 of the 49 individuals reported that the violence had completely stopped. Qualitative findings from both Hancock and Siu [16] and Zellerer [51] indicate that men who engaged in the intervention programs believed the programs had helped them to understand and control their violence [51] and they were able to provide suggestions to other participants on how to avoid abusive strategies [16]. However, these results do not in themselves indicate a reduction in violence.

3.3.2. Psychopathology

An improvement in psychopathological symptoms as a result of engaging in culturally specific intervention programs were reported by six studies [16,51,52,54,55,58]. Echauri et al. [58] defined treatment success as a complete disappearance of abuse and a reduction in psychopathological symptoms. Pathological symptoms were measured using the Symptom Checklist 90 Revised (SCL-90-R) and State-Trait Anger Expression Inventory-2 (STAXI-2) at pre and post and at a 12-month follow-up. The SCL-90-R is a self-report measure of psychopathology that includes measures of depression, anxiety, hostility, psychosis, somatization, obsessive compulsive behavior, interpersonal sensitivity, phobic anxiety, and paranoid ideation [59]. The STAXI-2 measures the intensity of state and trait anger expression. Echauri et al. [58] reported significant improvement in all of the variables for both immigrant and national samples, with most participants further improving between posttreatment and the 12-month follow-up. Similarly, Echeburua et al. [52] reported an overall reduction in psychopathological symptomatology in the posttreatment assessment, as measured in the SCL-90-R and a reported increase in overall emotional stability. In the Puchala et al. study [55], pre and post assessment of psychopathological complaints including anxiety, fear, sleep problems and sadness, indicated a reduction in overall distress as assessed by the MYMOP2 (Measure Your Medical Outcome Profile 2) measure. Self-reported reductions in anxiety were also identified in Welland and Ribner [54], and a reduction in aggressiveness was observed by staff among participants in the Zellerer study [51].

3.3.3. Gender-Related Attitudes

A change in cognitive biases and beliefs about women and gender roles, were reported in four studies [16,52,54,56]. Echeberua et al. [52] reported a lower score on The Inventory of Distorted Thoughts About Women at the posttreatment assessment, indicating fewer cognitive distortions in relation to men's attitudes toward women. Similarly, a pre and posttreatment measure in the Hoang et al. study [56] indicated that men's attitudes towards gender roles and masculine identities had improved significantly. In addition, men reported learning from thinking about situations from their partners points of view and their marital relationships. Similarly, participants in the Welland and Ribner study [54], discussed a shift in their attitudes towards gender roles, including a recognition of their partners rights and agency, which they reported as positive for both them and their partners. Most participants reported the concept of gender equality as new to them and all participants appeared to accept new ideas about gender roles. A participant in the Hancock and Siu study [16] reported that engagement in the program had helped to change his view of women from objects to persons.

3.3.4. Family Communication

Improvements in communication and alternative coping strategies to the use of violence were discussed in four of the studies [16,51,54,56]. In two of the studies [54,56], improved communication and strategies also supported improved parenting styles, and in one study [51], communication among peers was observed to improve during the treatment. Improved communication styles included 'time-out' strategies to help men recognise the changes in their emotions and physical state when entering conflict [56]; making 'I rather than you' statements to express their feelings in a non-violent manner [56]; using role plays to practice conflict resolutions [16]; and learning to be honest, developing respectful communication skills and to communicate with other men [54].

3.3.5. Program Satisfaction

Participant satisfaction with engaging in interventions was reported as an outcome in four of the studies [51–54]. Reports of satisfaction varied, with qualitative studies indicating that satisfaction was derived from an ability to explore their cultural and spiritual heritage [51], learning how to be nurturing fathers [54], and establishing close interpersonal relationships between participants and group facilitators [53]. Echeburua et al. [52] incorporated The Questionnaire of Satisfaction with Treatment measure. However, no pre or post measures were provided. Participant satisfaction was instead assumed through the high levels of engagement, with 92% completing the program. Three other studies reported completion rates as an outcome of the intervention program [16,28,57].

One study found no positive outcomes associated with the interventions [57]. In this study, the rates of violent recidivism were higher among the treatment group in comparison to the control group, and rates of intimate partner violence recidivism were consistent across the two groups.

4. Discussion

This systematic review shows that there is hope for behavior change to occur through culturally relevant male perpetrator intervention programs for intimate partner violence. This is the first systematic review to methodically examine the current evidence in relation to the effectiveness of male behavior modification programs for domestic violence offenders that have incorporated a 'cultural' aspect or have included clients from ethnic minority and/or non-Anglo-Saxon backgrounds. Our review examined features of intervention programs that determine their unique applicability to ethnic minority populations and outcomes relevant to behavior change, a reduction in recidivism, improved mental health, and client introspection of transformations of gender related attitudes.

While the outcome measures varied, most studies in this review showed positive outcomes as a result of perpetrators' engagement with the culturally specific intervention. The men in 6 [16,28,51,55,56,58] of the 10 studies did not repeat the overall abuse or reduced their incidences of abuse; these findings are in contrast to previous studies [11,24,25] that found treatment programs had almost a nil effect on recidivism. It is to be noted that in these past studies, participant attrition from the from was high that prevented any distinct conclusions being drawn about program effectiveness. Furthermore, one study [58] in the present review demonstrated effectiveness in reducing physical and psychological abuse even at the 12-month follow up period. However, not all studies though demonstrated long-term improvements. Previous studies that offered group treatments to IPV perpetrators had limited success in reducing the cycle of violence, thus demonstrating the importance of individualized, tailored intervention approaches.

Upon close examination of the specific aspects of the reviewed programs that may have led to successful outcomes, we found that programs implemented in languages relevant to the client group were fundamental to their success; these programs also benefited from bi-cultural facilitators. They also specifically measured recidivism to determine the role of their program in addressing re-offending behavior. It is recommended that other programs also incorporate such aspects and monitor clients' behavior over the long term to succeed. These findings align with intervention program objectives to address recidivism.

The review shows that cultural engagement could enhance client participation and reduce their attrition, a problem highlighted by Chang and Saunders [26] among minority groups. For example, Hoang et al. [56] enabled clients to interact with traditional healing elders; they believed that increased engagement with community leaders from the community could be one reason for a reduction in domestic violence in over half the participants. While previous studies have not specifically examined the influence of traditional healing elders, the importance of practitioners applying techniques addressing the social and cultural contexts have been explored [10]. We, however, need to further understand the training required for traditional healers to be part of behavior modification programs and appraise their pre-existing notions of gender equality and issues relevant to reducing violence against women prior to involving them in intervention programs.

Studies [16,51,52,54,55,58] that showed successful treatment of clinical symptoms, including improvements in psychopathology, anger, emotional stability, distress, and anxiety, had evaluated programs that had the following defining cultural features: diversity in language/s used, facilitators training cultural nuances or facilitators from the same background or a combination of these with cultural healing traditions [55]. These findings reiterate the guidance provided by Almeida and Dolan-Delvecchio [32] that program practitioners should be culturally sensitive and that treatment systems are culturally comprehensive and not only developed and implemented with dominant, White-centric theories.

Fewer than half the studies reviewed found alterations in thinking patterns and beliefs about women and gender norms. However, those [16,52,54,56] that were successful focused on adopting culturally relevant strategies to address masculinity and promote gender equal attitudes [56]. Empowerment, usually used to facilitate women's growth after a negative event, was recognized as an essential component of behavior modification by Hoang et al. [56] who indicated that men could use their agency to challenge traditional notions of unequal power relations and deconstruct and reconstruct their notions of masculinity. They applied this framework to their participants in Vietnam and asked men to re-think their traditional social roles and what it meant to be a man in the Vietnamese society. This study showed success in creating alternative narratives for men by using existing narratives and using culturally appropriate knowledge to deconstruct them. Similarly, Welland and Ribner [54] demonstrated that when Latino participants in their study realized that being *machista*, a term commonly used in Latin American cultures to describe male chauvinist behavior, was not useful in the context of their personal relationships, they changed their attitudes towards gender roles. These align with some aspects of the Duluth model that uses a feminist approach to challenge men's sense of power and control and educates them with alternative skills to reduce conflict in their relationships and their violence towards their partners [14]. Thus, the model adopted by Hoang et al. [56] and Welland and Ribner [54], when well-resourced and applied in a culturally relevant way in each cultural context, could lend itself to a program to advance practitioners' understanding of cultural norms and address perpetrators' behaviors successfully [32].

This review also shows that perpetrator behavior modification programs could assist with improved communication skills. Four studies [16,51,54,56] demonstrated that their clients were able to communicate better to their partners/ex-partners and peers after intervention. They conducted their program in a language suitable to their client group and addressed challenges faced by the men that were relevant to their cultural background and demographic characteristics. For example, Welland and Ribner [54] addressed the importance of *respeto*, which is traditionally regarded as respectful behavior to high status individuals; participants in their program identified the importance of this mannerism of communication in an intimate relationship. Participants recognized that they had previously lacked empathetic communication in their personal relationships due to the male socialization in their society, and therefore had not been exposed to childhood experiences of positive role models [54]. Removing language barriers therefore could lead to an improvement in relationship transactional skills. This could also pave the way for better parenting skills [54].

Another outcome measured in four studies [51–54] was client satisfaction with program engagement. These were mainly introspective measures. Those programs that had high levels of engagement such as discussing participants' cultural and spiritual heritage, learning to be develop their parenting skills, or where a close interpersonal relationship was fostered between participants and facilitators led to lower client attrition; this outcome is essential as previous studies [10,26] have shown a high participant attrition, especially those from minority communities, from perpetrator intervention programs. Thus, when perpetrators of IPV are engaged and continue to participate, they are more likely to benefit from the program and can modify their behavior.

Limitations

There are however caveats to the positive findings illustrated in this review. First, this review could only find 10 studies that met the inclusion criteria; most of these were conducted in North America and they examined various minority ethnic and non-Anglo-Saxon groups. Therefore, the applicability of the present findings to the multicultural diversity in this world, is limited. There was also only one study that examined an Indigenous group; this underscores the necessity of examining the effectiveness of domestic violence perpetrator intervention programs for other Indigenous groups. Nonetheless, there are some cultural norms that are similar across several minority groups, therefore, the findings would still have applicability. Another limitation is that success of the perpetrator intervention program was measured in a variety of ways and not consistently across the studies. This allows for minimal integration of the factors that could lead to the determination of an efficacious program. Future studies should incorporate some common measures of behavioral outcomes and evaluate them in the short and long-term. A main limiting factor that reduces the deduction of the findings is that most studies examined perpetrators' reports of successful outcomes and not the men's partners' perspectives of behavior change, reduced recidivism, or demonstration of gender-related attitudes within the family. Without such an examination, it is difficult to ascertain whether participants and program facilitators have the same introspection and observation of behavioral changes that those who were abused consider. Future studies must make an effort to assess changes through other external assessments.

5. Conclusions

Despite the limitations, this review is valuable in providing a systematic overview of what works for perpetrators from minority ethnic groups to alter their behavior for the better through behavior modification intervention programs. We have demonstrated the factors that lead to successful outcomes in male domestic violence perpetrator intervention programs including: client-associated language programs, facilitators who are culturally trained and/or bicultural facilitators who have an advanced knowledge of the cultural norms of the client group, developing and implementing programs that suit the cultural background of the clients (with an in-depth understanding of cultural norms and nuances relevant to interpersonal communication), discussion of patriarchal norms such as *machismo* that underpin and reinforce male domination and female subordination, discussions of gender roles and attitudes to gender equality specific to each cultural context; and greater culturally relevant client engagement. With the incorporation of such culturally relevant strategies, the studies included in this review have demonstrated that positive outcomes including improved mental health, reduced recidivism, behavior change, and better attitudes to gender equality could be achieved for perpetrators and their families.

This review thus contributes to the body of literature that examines the effectiveness of male domestic violence perpetrator intervention programs. It has examined the unique and universal factors relevant to diverse cultural groups that could assist with improved outcomes to reduce violence against women. Further research is required to examine what works for different cultural groups. Dominant White-centric models should not be applied to perpetrator clients who are from minority ethnic backgrounds or from non-Anglo-Saxon groups. Rather, program developers and facilitators could recognize the cultural nuances of their client group and then incorporate the successful approaches utilized by the studies examined in this review. This will lead to greater client engagement and a possibility of success. This will ultimately lead to men altering their maladaptive behaviors and making relationships safer for women and their families.

Supplementary Materials: The following supporting information can be downloaded at: https://www.mdpi.com/article/10.3390/ijerph192215180/s1, Supplementary Materials S1, Systematic Review Search Strategy; Supplementary Materials S2, Table S1: Methodological characteristics and key findings of the included studies; Supplementary Materials S3, Criteria for the Quality Assessment Tools (NHLBI).

Author Contributions: Conceptualization, L.S. and A.H.; Data curation (selection and review of articles), L.S., A.H., J.L.G. and L.Z.; Qualitative assessment, L.S. and J.L.G.; Writing—original draft preparation, L.S., A.H. and J.L.G.; Writing—review and editing, L.S., A.H., J.L.G. and L.Z. All authors have read and agreed to the published version of the manuscript.

Funding: This research received no external funding.

Institutional Review Board Statement: Not required for a systematic review.

Informed Consent Statement: Not applicable.

Data Availability Statement: Not applicable.

Acknowledgments: We wish to thank Louisa Sher, the Deakin University librarian who assisted us with developing our search terms for this review.

Conflicts of Interest: The authors declare no conflict of interest.

References

1. World Health Organization. Violence against Women Prevalence Estimates, 2018: Global, Regional and National Prevalence Estimates for Intimate Partner Violence against Women and Global and Regional Prevalence Estimates for Non-Partner Sexual Violence against Women: Executive Summary. 2021. Available online: https://www.who.int/publications/i/item/9789240026681 (accessed on 12 July 2021).
2. Garcia-Moreno, C.; Jansen, H.A.; Ellsberg, M.; Heise, L.; Watts, C.H. Prevalence of intimate partner violence: Findings from the WHO multi-country study on women's health and domestic violence. *Lancet* **2006**, *368*, 1260–1269. [CrossRef]
3. Pease, B.; Rees, S. Theorising men's violence towards women in refugee families: Towards an intersectional feminist framework. *Just Policy: A J. Aust. Soc. Policy* **2008**, *47*, 39–45.
4. Satyen, L.; Supol, M.; Ranganathan, A.; Toumbourou, J. International and cross-cultural research on men's violence against female intimate partners. In *The SAGE Handbook of Domestic Violence*; Shackelford, T.K., Ed.; SAGE Publications Ltd.: New York, NY, USA, 2021; pp. 40–60. [CrossRef]
5. World Health Organization. Global Plan of Action: Health Systems Address Violence against Women and Girls. 2016. Available online: https://apps.who.int/iris/handle/10665/251664 (accessed on 7 July 2021).
6. Pence, E.; Paymar, M.; Ritmeester, T. *Education Groups for Men Who Batter: The Duluth Model*; Springer Publishing Company: Berlin/Heidelberg, Germany, 1993.
7. Murphy, C.M.; Eckhardt, C.I. *Treating the Abusive Partner: An Individualized Cognitive-Behavioral Approach*; Guilford Press: New York, NY, USA, 2005.
8. Condino, V.; Tanzilli, A.; Speranza, A.M.; Lingiardi, V. Therapeutic interventions in intimate partner violence: An overview. *Res. Psychother. Psychopathol. Process Outcome* **2016**, *19*, 79–88. [CrossRef]
9. Healy, K.M.; Smith, C.; O'Sullivan, C.S. *Batterer Intervention: Program Approaches and Criminal Justice Strategies*; DIANE Publishing: Darby, PA, USA, 1998.
10. Turhan, Z. Improving approaches in psychotherapy and domestic violence interventions for perpetrators from marginalized ethnic groups. *Aggress. Violent Behav.* **2020**, *50*, 101337. [CrossRef]
11. Eckhardt, C.I.; Murphy, C.M.; Whitaker, D.J.; Sprunger, J.; Dykstra, R.; Woodard, K. The Effectiveness of Intervention Programs for Perpetrators and Victims of Intimate Partner Violence. *Partn. Abus.* **2013**, *4*, 196–231. [CrossRef]
12. Young, J.E. *Cognitive Therapy for Personality Disorders: A Schema-Focused Approach*; Professional Resource Press/Professional Resource Exchange: Cambridge, MA, USA, 1999.
13. Dobash, R.P.; Cavanagh, K.; Lewis, R. A Research Evaluation of British Programmes for Violent Men. *J. Soc. Policy* **1999**, *28*, 205–233. [CrossRef]
14. Gondolf, E.W. Theoretical and research support for the Duluth Model: A reply to dutton and corvo. *Aggress. Violent Behav.* **2007**, *12*, 644–657. [CrossRef]
15. Emezue, C.N.; Williams, O.J.; Bloom, T.L. Culturally-Differentiated Batterer Intervention Programs for Immigrant Male Batterers (IMB): An Integrative Review. *J. Aggress. Maltreat. Trauma* **2021**, *30*, 907–930. [CrossRef]
16. Hancock, T.U.; Siu, K. A Culturally Sensitive Intervention with Domestically Violent Latino Immigrant Men. *J. Fam. Violence* **2009**, *24*, 123–132. [CrossRef]
17. Eckhardt, C.I.; Samper, R.E.; Murphy, C.M. Anger Disturbances Among Perpetrators of Intimate Partner Violence. *J. Interpers. Violence* **2008**, *23*, 1600–1617. [CrossRef]

18. Capaldi, D.M.; Langhinrichsen-Rohling, J. Informing Intimate Partner Violence Prevention Efforts: Dyadic, Developmental, and Contextual Considerations. *Prev. Sci.* **2012**, *13*, 323–328. [CrossRef] [PubMed]
19. Gortner, E.T.; Gollan, J.K.; Jacobson, N.S. Psychological Aspects of Perpetrators of Domestic Violence and Their Relationships with the Victims. *Psychiatr. Clin. N. Am.* **1997**, *20*, 337–352. [CrossRef]
20. Holtzworth-Munroe, A.; Stuart, G.L. Typologies of male batterers: Three subtypes and the differences among them. *Psychol. Bull.* **1994**, *116*, 476–497. [CrossRef] [PubMed]
21. Jackson, M.A.; Sippel, L.M.; Mota, N.; Whalen, D.; Schumacher, J.A. Borderline personality disorder and related constructs as risk factors for intimate partner violence perpetration. *Aggress. Violent Behav.* **2015**, *24*, 95–106. [CrossRef]
22. Singh, V.; Tolman, R.; Walton, M.; Chermack, S.; Cunningham, R. Characteristics of Men Who Perpetrate Intimate Partner Violence. *J. Am. Board Fam. Med.* **2014**, *27*, 661–668. [CrossRef]
23. Teicher, M.H. Scars That Won't Heal: The Neurobiology of Child Abuse. *Sci. Am.* **2002**, *286*, 68–75. [CrossRef]
24. Babcock, J.C.; Green, C.E.; Robie, C. Does batterers' treatment work? A meta-analytic review of domestic violence treatment. *Clin. Psychol. Rev.* **2004**, *23*, 1023–1053. [CrossRef]
25. Corvo, K.; Dutton, D.; Chen, W.-Y. Toward Evidence-Based Practice with Domestic Violence Perpetrators. *J. Aggress. Maltreatment Trauma* **2008**, *16*, 111–130. [CrossRef]
26. Chang, H.; Saunders, D.G. Predictors of Attrition in Two Types of Group Programs for Men Who Batter. *J. Fam. Violence* **2002**, *17*, 273–292. [CrossRef]
27. Smedslund, G.; Dalsbø, T.K.; Steiro, A.K.; Winsvold, A.; Clench-Aas, J. Cognitive behavioural therapy for men who physically abuse their female partner. *Campbell Syst. Rev.* **2011**, *7*, 1–25. [CrossRef]
28. Gondolf, E.W. Evaluating batterer counseling programs: A difficult task showing some effects and implications. *Aggress. Violent Behav.* **2004**, *9*, 605–631. [CrossRef]
29. Bronfenbrenner, U. *The Ecology of Human Development: Experiments by Nature and Design*; Harvard University Press: Cambridge, MA, USA, 1979.
30. Shepard, M.F.; Pence, E.L.; Weisz, A.N. Coordinating Community Responses to Domestic Violence: Lessons From Duluth and Beyond. *Violence Vict.* **2000**, *15*, 351–352. [CrossRef]
31. Crenshaw, K. Demarginalizing the intersection of race and sex: A Black feminist critique of antidiscrimination doctrine, feminist theory, and antiracist politics [1989]. In *Feminist Legal Theory*; Bartlett, K., Kennedy, R., Eds.; Routledge: London, UK, 2018; pp. 57–80.
32. Almeida, R.V.; Dolan-Delvecchio, K. Addressing Culture in Batterers Intervention. *Violence Against Women* **1999**, *5*, 654–683. [CrossRef]
33. Turhan, Z. The Lived Experiences of Turkish Perpetrators' Engagement in Domestic Violence Interventions. Ph.D. Thesis, Goldsmiths, University of London, London, UK, 2019. [CrossRef]
34. Akoensi, T.D.; Koehler, J.A.; Lösel, F.; Humphreys, D.K. Domestic Violence Perpetrator Programs in Europe, Part II. *Int. J. Offender Ther. Comp. Criminol.* **2012**, *57*, 1206–1225. [CrossRef] [PubMed]
35. Nedegaard, R. Intimate Partner Violence in Muslim Communities. *Arts Soc. Sci. J.* **2014**, *1*, 2–8. [CrossRef]
36. Gill, A.K. Patriarchal violence in the name of 'honour'. *Int. J. Crim. Justice Sci.* **2006**, *1*, 1–12.
37. Kim, C.; Sung, H.E. The Effects of Acculturation on Intimate Partner Violence Among Chinese Immigrants in New York City. *J. Fam. Violence* **2015**, *31*, 325–336. [CrossRef]
38. Lindhorst, T.; Tajima, E. Reconceptualizing and Operationalizing Context in Survey Research on Intimate Partner Violence. *J. Interpers. Violence* **2008**, *23*, 362–388. [CrossRef]
39. Keller, E.M.; Brennan, P.K. Cultural Considerations and Challenges to Service Delivery for Sudanese Victims of Domestic Violence: Insights from Service Providers and Actors in the Criminal Justice System. *Int. Rev. Vict.* **2007**, *14*, 115–141. [CrossRef]
40. Paat, Y.-F. Risk and Resilience of Immigrant Women in Intimate Partner Violence. *J. Hum. Behav. Soc. Environ.* **2014**, *24*, 725–740. [CrossRef]
41. West, C.M. African Immigrant Women and Intimate Partner Violence: A Systematic Review. *J. Aggress. Maltreat. Trauma* **2016**, *25*, 4–17. [CrossRef]
42. Rai, A.; Choi, Y.J. Socio-cultural risk factors impacting domestic violence among South Asian immigrant women: A scoping review. *Aggress. Violent Behav.* **2018**, *38*, 76–85. [CrossRef]
43. Sasseville, N.; Maurice, P.; Montminy, L.; Hassan, G.; St-Pierre, E. Cumulative Contexts of Vulnerability to Intimate Partner Violence Among Women with Disabilities, Elderly Women, and Immigrant Women: Prevalence, Risk Factors, Explanatory Theories, and Prevention. *Trauma Violence Abus.* **2020**, *23*, 88–100. [CrossRef]
44. Ellsberg, M.; Arango, D.J.; Morton, M.; Gennari, F.; Kiplesund, S.; Contreras, M.; Watts, C. Prevention of violence against women and girls: What does the evidence say? *Lancet* **2014**, *385*, 1555–1566. [CrossRef]
45. Heise, L. What Works to Prevent Partner Violence? An Evidence Overview. STRIVE Research Consortium. 2011. Available online: http://strive.lshtm.ac.uk/system/files/attachments/What%20works%20to%20prevent%20partner%20violence.pdf (accessed on 7 July 2021).
46. Becker, K.D.; Mathis, G.; Mueller, C.W.; Issari, K.; Atta, S.S.; Okado, I. Barriers to Treatment in an Ethnically Diverse Sample of Families Enrolled in a Community-Based Domestic Violence Intervention. *J. Aggress. Maltreat. Trauma* **2012**, *21*, 829–850. [CrossRef]

47. Thandi, G.; Lloyd, B. *'This Is a Man's Problem': Strategies for Working with South Asian Male Perpetrators of Intimate Partner Violence*; Justice Institute of British Columbia: New Westminster, BC, Canada, 2011. Available online: https://www.jibc.ca/sites/default/files/research/pdf/This-is-a-man%27s-problem_REPORT.pdf (accessed on 18 July 2021).
48. Page, M.J.; McKenzie, J.E.; Bossuyt, P.M.; Boutron, I.; Hoffmann, T.C.; Mulrow, C.D.; Shamseer, L.; Tetzlaff, J.M.; Akl, E.A.; Brennan, S.E.; et al. The PRISMA 2020 statement: An updated guideline for reporting systematic reviews. *PLoS Med.* **2021**, *18*, e1003583. [CrossRef] [PubMed]
49. Critical Appraisal Skills Programme. Critical Appraisal Skills Programme Qualitative Checklist. 2019. Available online: https://casp-uk.net/casp-tools-checklists/ (accessed on 7 July 2021).
50. National Institutes of Health. Quality Assessment Tools. 2014. Available online: https://www.nhlbi.nih.gov/health-pro/guidelines/in-develop/cardiovascular-risk-reduction/tools/cohort (accessed on 18 July 2021).
51. Zellerer, E. Culturally Competent Programs: The First Family Violence Program for Aboriginal Men in Prison. *Prison J.* **2003**, *83*, 171–190. [CrossRef]
52. Echeburúa, E.; Fernández-Montalvo, J.; Amor, P.J. Psychological Treatment of Men Convicted of Gender Violence. *Int. J. Offender Ther. Comp. Criminol.* **2006**, *50*, 57–70. [CrossRef]
53. Parra-Cardona, J.R.; Escobar-Chew, A.R.; Holtrop, K.; Carpenter, G.; Guzmán, R.; Hernández, D.; Zamudio, E.; Ramírez, D.G. En el Grupo Tomas Conciencia (In Group You Become Aware). *Violence Against Women* **2013**, *19*, 107–132. [CrossRef]
54. Welland, C.; Ribner, N.; Christauria, W.; Neil, R. Culturally Specific Treatment for Partner-Abusive Latino Men: A Qualitative Study to Identify and Implement Program Components. *Violence Vict.* **2010**, *25*, 799–813. [CrossRef]
55. Puchala, C.; Paul, S.; Kennedy, C.; Mehl-Madrona, L. Using Traditional Spirituality to Reduce Domestic Violence within Aboriginal Communities. *J. Altern. Complement. Med.* **2010**, *16*, 89–96. [CrossRef] [PubMed]
56. Hoang, T.-A.; Quach, T.T.; Tran, T.T. 'Because I am a man, I should be gentle to my wife and my children': Positive masculinity to stop gender-based violence in a coastal district in Vietnam. *Gend. Dev.* **2013**, *21*, 81–96. [CrossRef]
57. Haggård, U.; Freij, I.; Danielsson, M.; Wenander, D.; Långström, N. Effectiveness of the IDAP Treatment Program for Male Perpetrators of Intimate Partner Violence. *J. Interpers. Violence* **2017**, *32*, 1027–1043. [CrossRef] [PubMed]
58. Echauri, J.A.; Fernández-Montalvo, J.; Martínez, M. Effectiveness of a treatment programme for immigrants who committed gender-based violence against their partners. *Psicothema* **2013**, *25*, 49–54. [CrossRef] [PubMed]
59. Olsen, L.R.; Mortensen, E.L.; Bech, P. The SCL-90 and SCL-90R versions validated by item response models in a Danish community sample. *Acta Psychiatr. Scand.* **2004**, *110*, 225–229. [CrossRef]

International Journal of
Environmental Research and Public Health

MDPI

Article

Using Mindfulness to Improve Mental Health Outcomes of Immigrant Women with Experiences of Intimate Partner Violence

Ashley Vroegindewey and Bushra Sabri *

Johns Hopkins University School of Nursing, Baltimore, MD 21205, USA
* Correspondence: bsabri1@jhu.edu; Tel.: +1-410-955-7105

Abstract: Immigrant women are disproportionately affected by intimate partner violence (IPV), which poses risk for mental health problems, such as PTSD and depression. Post-migration barriers limit immigrant women's access to supportive services, which can further debilitate their mental health symptoms and their safety. The Being safe, Healthy, and Positively Empowered (BSHAPE) digital intervention was designed to address physical safety and healthcare needs of immigrant women through a multi-component approach that integrated mindfulness-based stress reduction (MBSR) practices. This paper reports qualitative feedback findings from eighteen Black immigrant women with recent IPV exposure and co-occurring mental health symptoms, who participated in the mindfulness sessions of BSHAPE. We identified elements of mindfulness that women perceived as beneficial in their healing. Women's feedback indicated healing and empowerment through positive appraisals and coping strategies. The benefits were noted for mindfulness elements promoting self-compassion, self-actualization, intentionality of moving forward in life, and developing positivity or a sense of optimism. Other helpful elements were relaxation, self-care and reflection, self-awareness, self-control and focused thinking. Our findings show that incorporating mindfulness practices in interventions can be beneficial for promoting the healing and empowerment of immigrant women in abusive relationships.

Keywords: intimate partner violence; immigrant women; mental health; PTSD; coping; mindfulness; mindfulness-based stress reduction

check for updates

Citation: Vroegindewey, A.; Sabri, B. Using Mindfulness to Improve Mental Health Outcomes of Immigrant Women with Experiences of Intimate Partner Violence. *Int. J. Environ. Res. Public Health* **2022**, *19*, 12714. https://doi.org/10.3390/ijerph191912714

Academic Editors: Rohan D. Jeremiah and Krim K. Lacey

Received: 18 August 2022
Accepted: 2 October 2022
Published: 5 October 2022

1. Introduction

Immigrant women in the US, including immigrant women of African descent [1], are disproportionately affected by intimate partner violence (IPV). The friction between maintaining traditional cultural gender roles and new gender roles in Western society upon immigration contributes to greater vulnerability to IPV among immigrant women. For example, West African women face multiple instances of abuse post-migration and a sense of frustration with the existing options for assistance [2]. Other post-migration factors include partner or husband's lack of employment and resulting feelings of disempowerment [3]. Stressors, such as language barriers, limited access to economic and community resources, limited or lack of knowledge of legal services and rights, adherence to traditional gender roles, social isolation and discrimination, and lack of cultural awareness by service providers, can place immigrant women at high risk for multiple health issues [1–5]. These barriers also inhibit immigrant women survivors from obtaining the appropriate trauma-informed help and attention that they need.

A traumatic experience, such as IPV, for marginalized women (e.g., immigrant) can greatly disrupt proper cognitive–emotion regulation and manifest as posttraumatic stress disorder (PTSD) or depressive symptoms [6,7]. In addition to mental health symptoms such as shock, confusion, guilt, self-blame, withdrawal, flashbacks, or insomnia, women manifest symptoms in the form of hypervigilance, avoidance, intense fear, or anxiety related to disclosure of IPV [8–10]. Traumatic life experiences, such as IPV also negatively impact the body's stress regulation mechanism and immune response, which can develop into "toxic stress" and trigger a sequalae of various physical health problems, including an increased risk for morbidity [11,12]. The likelihood of stress becoming toxic and affecting women's physical health is associated with immigrant women in abusive relationships facing continued and repeated IPV with a lack of options for breaking free from abuse. Immigrant women are at risk for continued and repeated exposures to IPV due to risk factors at multiple levels of the social ecology [13]. These include patriarchal cultural norms at the societal level, dependency on the abusive partner for immigration status at the relationship level, lack of community support or limited access to resources for support at the community level, and poverty, low education, poor mental health, social isolation, and lack of knowledge of resources at the individual level [13]. Factors such as social isolation and stigma related to IPV and mental health in immigrant communities can be barriers to seeking help for immigrant women [13,14]. The immigrant woman's exposure to the first instances of abuse or violence offers no protective factors to another abusive incident if there are no supportive structures, culturally informed safety action plans, or strong coping mechanisms in place [13].

A chronic state of stress, fear, and poor mental health due to living in an abusive environment potentiate illness burden and the use of maladaptive coping strategies (e.g., substance abuse). The existence of comorbid health conditions inhibit women's help seeking and leaving an abusive relationship [7,15]. Unaddressed needs for care may place immigrant women survivors of IPV at greater risk of harm and isolation rendered by IPV. Consequentially, effective mental health and stress management interventions are incredibly important to appropriately address the care needs of immigrant women with exposures to violence and trauma [6,7,15]. However, immigrant women with mental health problems face numerous barriers to accessing mental health care. These include language barriers or stigma associated with mental health or mental health counseling. Other barriers include dependence on an abusive partner, a controlling partner who restricts access to services, or lack of available culturally sensitive practices for mental health care [14]. Abusive relationships exacerbate these barriers for immigrant women. Mindfulness practices can be alternative approaches to support immigrant women with mental health problems who are unable to access stress management and mental health care services due to immigration, stigma, religious, cultural, socio-economic, or partner-related barriers.

Evidence shows that mindfulness approaches can lead to significant improvement in mental health [16–18]. Mindfulness is defined as "awareness of one's moment-to-moment experience nonjudgmentally and with acceptance" [16] (p. 2). The practice of non-passive acceptance reinforces attention on the present moment experience whenever the mind wanders by shifting from trauma-related stimuli to the present experience [9,16]. Mindfulness practices encourage the individual to focus on and accept the consciousness or emotional experience rather than revert to negative coping mechanisms often associated with PTSD symptoms, such as suppression, over-engagement, numbness, or avoidance [9,16,19,20]. Attention control exercises, such as alternative breathing or open monitoring, train women survivors to be present in the moment with non-judgement and acceptance while simultaneously targeting positive cognitive reappraisal [16,19,21]. Possessing a nonjudgmental stance toward traumatic experiences encourages positive cognitive changes, such as desensitization, as well as decreased rumination and perceived stress [20,21]. Thus, mindfulness practices can lead to decreased symptoms of PTSD through improved emotion and stress regulation, increased attention, and non-judgmental acceptance [9,16,19].

Decentering, another component of mindfulness, helps in navigating trauma-associated negative emotions and alterations in arousal by increasing awareness of one's sensory, cognitive, and affective responses that do not necessarily require exposure to one's trauma [18,19,21]. Decentering one's thoughts and emotions and perceiving them as passing sensations or mental events rather than identifying them to be accurate representations of reality increases metacognitive awareness and attention [19]. Decentering may predict better clinical outcomes, leading to lower rates of depressive relapses [16]. Thus, various components of mindfulness components can lead to improvement in mental health symptoms among immigrant women with experiences of IPV.

The impact of mindfulness in promoting the healing of IPV survivors can be explained by the Taylor and Aspinwall's Psychosocial model (1996). According to this model, life stressors can indirectly affect psychosocial outcomes based on how the individual perceives or accepts the stressor and how an individual copes [22]. Appraisal is defined as cognitive evaluation and interpretation of an experience that influences the perception of the stressful experience [22]. Coping is the conscious and voluntary management of stress in response to the negative experience with the expectation to reduce stress and build resiliency [23]. Mindfulness-based stress reduction activities can enhance women's internal strengths as resources and promote adaptive appraisals (e.g., positive self-actualization) and coping (e.g., relaxation), which can lead to positive outcomes (e.g., empowerment) and promote the path to healing. Such approaches can especially be beneficial for marginalized populations, such as immigrant women, who are unable to access mental health care due to stigma, shame, transportation, and economic issues [13,14]. Mindfulness-based approaches can be utilized in women's homes daily without the need for an in-person visit to a provider. Thus, additional research is needed to build evidence for the beneficial effects of mindfulness approaches for marginalized women with mental health issues related to IPV and other stressors in their lives.

Rationale and Significance

Although studies examined the impact of in-person mindfulness-based stress reduction (MBSR) approaches for improving mental health symptoms of diverse populations [9,18,20], including that of US-born survivors of interpersonal violence or IPV [17,19,21], studies are yet to explore the impact of remote phone-delivered mindfulness approaches on the mental health of immigrant women with experiences of IPV. Further, studies are yet to explore how elements of mindfulness delivered over the phone could promote healing among immigrant women with co-occurring IPV and mental health problems. Remotely delivered trauma-informed mindfulness can be a useful approach for addressing stress reduction and the mental health care needs of immigrant women in a stigma-free environment. The approach can be especially beneficial for women who voluntarily or involuntarily are unable to access mental health care services due to poverty, lack of insurance for mental health care, stigma, socio-cultural, religious, or other reasons. The format of remote delivery can be useful for women who face transportation barriers, or stigma and shame in sharing sensitive experiences face-to-face, as well as for those who are impacted by challenges related to situations such as the COVID-19 pandemic. Digital interventions, such as phone applications, coupled with safety strategies, have the potential to reach women who are unable to attend traditional in-person interventions due to fear or control of the abuser by providing privacy per the woman's convenience and safety [24]. Using a sample of Black immigrant women, this study explored the impact of mindfulness in improving women's mental health, as well as the components or elements of mindfulness that women perceived as beneficial in their healing. For this study, "Black immigrant" refers to foreign-born immigrant women coming from Africa or immigrant women of African descent. The findings can be informative for practitioners as to which elements to emphasize in mindfulness interventions for women with IPV exposures and those with comorbid PTSD symptoms or depression.

2. Materials and Methods

2.1. BSHAPE Design and Development

The Being Safe, Healthy, and Positively Empowered (BSHAPE) intervention was designed to address the physical safety and mental health needs of immigrant women through a multi-component approach that integrated mindfulness, or mindfulness-based stress reduction (MBSR), in its intervention. While BSHAPE addressed other needs through components such as strengths-based feedback, psychoeducation on HIV risk reduction, or education on immigration-related resources, the mindfulness combined with weekly behavioral activation homework assignments focused on stress reduction, mental health, and safety. The BSHAPE pilot trial focused on Black immigrant women because many Black women in the US migrate from conflict-affected regions, with some forced to flee their home countries as refugees [25]. Thus, they are more likely to have lifetime cumulative exposures to violence, such as war or the imminent threat of harm. However, the intervention was designed to be adaptable for immigrant women from other racial/ethnic backgrounds.

Components of the BSHAPE intervention included an assessment and participation in a phone-delivered strengths-based feedback session, followed by online psychoeducational modules and MBSR phone sessions with a facilitator. The details of the intervention are provided elsewhere [25]. The phone-based MBSR component of BSHAPE consisted of weekly half-hour sessions between the woman and a trained masters-level graduate student facilitator for four weeks. Facilitators of the mindfulness sessions were trained masters-level graduate students who received training in mindfulness using a MBSR curriculum. Facilitators completed two days of in-person or virtual training on MBSR and were given a standardized mindfulness curriculum manual with audio recordings of the meditation's practices. The MBSR curriculum was designed by Tawanna Kane, a certified and experienced mindfulness instructor with experience working with diverse and underserved populations [26], and was an adaptation of Jon Kabat Zinn's MBSR program [25,27].

The MBSR sessions were designed to be individualized, self-guided, and exploratory, prompting one to think about daily life stresses and triggers. The one-on-one sessions between mindfulness facilitators and women allowed open dialogue and expression of feelings, thoughts, and perceptions of safety and security in their own words, especially on sensitive topics, without them feeling like their privacy was invaded. The facilitators introduced different stress reduction techniques to the woman, which included alternative breathing methods, promoting weekly pleasurable activities, body scans, or "lovingkindness" meditations. The weekly sessions also allowed for the woman to express any concerns that she had, including weekly safety check-ins with the woman and discussing a safety plan in any event that the woman felt unsafe and provided information about supportive services. Upon completion of each session, facilitators documented the woman's fidelity to the intervention's activities and her response [25]. All study procedures were approved by the home institution of the study's principal investigator (blinded for review).

2.2. Recruitment

BSHAPE research assistants recruited women via emails, listservs (subscribers on an electronic mailing list), flyers posted in community locations, study information posted periodically in the organization's newsletters, social media platforms through a social media ad campaign, snowball sampling, and word-of-mouth throughout the United States through assistance from universities and colleges, student associations, immigrant/refugee agencies, or churches. Women who were interested answered the screening questions to determine eligibility on the study website. The research team reviewed eligible women's registration information and contacted them by phone to obtain informed consent, to enroll them into the study, and to set up an appointment for their remote baseline survey and assessment. To be eligible, women had to be (a) 18 to 55 years of age, (b) a foreign-born immigrant woman born in Africa or a Black immigrant born in any other region outside the U.S., (c) in a current or past intimate partner relationship, (d) report lifetime exposures to violence, with clinically significant symptoms of PTSD (scores higher than 2.5) [25,28]; and/or depression (score of 10 or higher) [25,29] and (e) report at least one sexual HIV risk behavior (e.g., multiple sexual partners).

2.3. Participants

In the BSHAPE study, 42 out of 144 women reported recent (within past 12 months) experiences of IPV. This paper reports findings from 18 women randomized to the intervention arm of BSHAPE, who were recent IPV survivors and participated in the remote BSHAPE mindfulness sessions. IPV in this study included physical, sexual, and/or psychological abuse. The average age of women with recent IPV was 35.39 (SD = 8.96). A total of 47% (n = 8) were married, 17.6% (n = 3) were separated, and others were either in non-marital relationship or were partnered or divorced. Seventy-five percent (n = 12) were in a heterosexual relationship with two identifying as asexual and others in the bisexual or queer category. Approximately 44% (n = 8) were recent immigrants were in the US for four years or less than four years. Education was high, with most women having a bachelors or master's degree (71%, n = 12). Most women (89%, n = 16) were born in Africa, followed by those born in other regions outside the U.S. Fifty percent (n = 9) indicated moderate or moderately severe depressive symptoms, with fifty percent of women reporting severe depressive symptoms (n = 9) and/or co-occurring clinically significant PTSD symptoms (sixty-seven percent, n = 12). Among lifetime trauma exposures, besides family violence or IPV, a large percentage of women reported experiences of collective identity trauma (e.g., racism and war experience) (89%, n = 16), personal identity trauma (i.e., events challenging the self, such as bullying and sexual abuse) (94.4%, n = 17), attachment trauma (e.g., abandonment by parent) (83.3%, n = 15) and survival trauma (83.3%, n = 15) (e.g., exposures to torture, accidents, or disasters) [30].

2.4. Measures and Data Collection

Qualitative data were collected and tracked from women weekly through fidelity forms. The fidelity forms included documentation of how the trained mindfulness facilitator rated the fidelity of each session to the script and core components of the MBSR intervention. Every week, the facilitator documented the women's adherence to home practices, their perceptions of safety during safety check-ins, mindfulness components covered during the session, facilitator's reflection, and the women's evaluation. The forms documented the women's evaluation of the overall session verbatim and their ratings of the overall quality of the facilitator's delivery of mindfulness. Fidelity was also ensured through weekly supervision with the expert investigator on the team.

Adherence to the completion of the phone-based sessions and its weekly interventions were also tracked and documented as measurable outcomes. Upon completion of the four-week phone sessions, a feedback survey was given to the women, asking them to share their overall feedback (what was helpful, what they liked most, and if there was anything that could be improved or added), any barriers they faced in active, consistent participation, and whether they would continue the home practices beyond the four weeks. Additionally, women were asked about the needs for additional resources that would support them in continuing their practice.

2.5. Data Analysis

For this study, a qualitative descriptive approach [31] was used for comprehensively capturing immigrant women survivors' experiences and stories in their own words. Data were analyzed using the qualitative content analysis procedure [25,32]. The process involved coding and categorizing the feedback into themes using the questions in the feedback guide, followed by additional coding of content not covered by the feedback guide. The analysis was conducted by two members of the research team (the principal investigator and the graduate student), with members agreeing to the content and meaning of each theme, summarizing based upon the frequency of each theme and refining them further into sub-themes. Pseudonyms were used to present participant's quotes.

3. Results

Women shared how mindfulness practices were beneficial for their health and well-being. The key benefits were illustrated as healing and empowerment through positive appraisals and coping. The beneficial effects were noted for elements promoting self-love, self-actualization, intentionality of moving forward, and possessing a positive attitude towards life. Women also reported utilizing coping strategies, such as relaxation, self-care and reflection, self-awareness, self-control, and focus. In our analysis of quantitative data, women in the intervention arm also reported improvement in PTSD and depressive symptoms. The findings of the quantitative data are reported elsewhere [25].

3.1. Healing and Empowerment

The BSHAPE sessions were designed to enhance coping skills (e.g., nonjudgmental acceptance) to better counteract negative perceptions of stress, and to promote healing and positive mental health outcomes. Self-empowerment was the overarching theme found and can be defined as the state when the individual learns to "observe a feeling rather than be the feeling ... With this comes a new internal freedom. The individual becomes less reactionary and can make a conscious choice in how to respond to internal states" [33] (p. 74). One woman described feeling "empowered" perfectly in her own way, while simultaneously representing how survivors of IPV can attain a sense of achievement, self-worth, and peace in life:

> *[I feel] at peace, exhilarated ... felt like I achieved a lot for quite some time, and felt like I deserved this. I feel at peace doing this as a reward* (Tina, 32 years old).

3.2. Positive Appraisal

Positive self-appraisals were highlighted in survivors' feedback on their engagement in mindfulness practices. Mindfulness practices promoted self-actualization, lovingkindness, intentions of moving forward in life, and developed positive attitudes.

3.2.1. Self-Compassion or Lovingkindness

The "loving-kindness" meditative component of mindfulness promotes compassion or love towards oneself and others in addition to adapting a non-judgmental mindful existence [9,18]. Some survivors ($n = 3$) shared that acknowledging and accepting their past and present, without avoiding or self-condemning, helped them to develop a stronger sense of self-compassion and lovingkindness towards themselves and others. This is fundamental for women survivors of IPV, as many women struggle to show self-compassion without judgement, which could propitiate severe PTSD symptoms, such as avoidance [19,21]. One woman who was married reported finding peace in everyday moments, such as washing the dishes, because she realized that she could replace self-inflicted suffering with lovingkindness towards herself and others:

> *Lovingkindness ... is our way to do good, in world, first have peace within me, then show love to people; and everything follows. Love comes at end of everything. To reduce stress, love self. Don't need to suffer any more* (Sara, 38 years old).

3.2.2. Self-Actualization

Some women survivors ($n = 4$) reported making significant self-realizations. They felt more affirmed in their self-worth and in their strengths and potentiality to do things beyond what they thought they were capable of before the mindfulness session. One woman who liked listening to music and prayer, said:

> *I think it is a good thing to do lovingkindness meditation because it ... allowed me to go back far away and see some good things from the past, it was a good session, and I liked to do it again; Closing my eyes and going somewhere, imagining to be somewhere and when I come back, the bell ringing; Feeling like I'm far away, made me think of a lot of things ... that was helpful* (Shahana, 36 years old).

Another woman survivor, who was a busy mother and aspiring nurse, expressed her potential in becoming a nurse:

I don't like seeing blood and people in pain; but it is a good job. Nurses are working. I can be good at it (Linda, 37 years old).

3.2.3. Intentionality of Moving Forward

Some survivors (n = 4) decided to take a step further in moving beyond the suffering of pain and being under the control of their abuser. This re-appraisal of control in one's own life proved to be a pivotal moment for many of the IPV survivors, as it empowered them to make choices or take opportunities that are better for themselves [8] and for others.

For example, one woman, who was married with two teenage children, recently immigrated to the US and was trying to obtain a green card and learn a new language. She was striving to make life easier for her children despite her own pain and loss:

I am trying to work on my English and my marriage. I don't want my kids to suffer or to have the pain (Cindy, 40 years old).

Another woman, who was married to an American citizen, expressed her intention in taking more control of her life by being true to herself through the practice of journaling:

My intention is to not let other people control my life . . . I aspire to be truthful to myself. . . (Libby, 31 years old).

3.2.4. Positive Attitude towards Life

Six women (n = 6) expressed developing a positive attitude, or a sense of optimism, from the mindfulness sessions. They viewed the sessions as beneficial and with an overall sense of feeling "positive" at the end of the sessions. This is contrary to what most survivors of IPV feel about themselves and their outlook on life, as most feel the despondency related to depression or PTSD [21]. From this change in perspective, some women were able to see some good things from the past, which propelled them towards a more optimistic approach to the present moment and future. One survivor who was a student and enjoyed the positive affirmations of the sessions, shared:

It [mindfulness session] was just a positive experience; All those things that I was feeling . . . I was able to conquer with a more positive attitude and outlook (Karla, 22 years old).

3.3. Positive Coping

Women reported benefits of mindfulness sessions in terms of promoting engagement in coping strategies, such as relaxation, self-care and self-reflection, faith-based practices and prayer, self-awareness, and practicing self-control or focused thinking.

3.3.1. Relaxation

Many women (n = 9) felt relaxed either mentally and/or physically after engaging in mindfulness practices. For most women, relaxation was a sense of letting go or emptying oneself from daily stress or worries that may be especially triggering for those with experiences of IPV. For some women, relaxation provided a sense of "calmness" or "peace", especially with the body scans or alternative breathing exercises. One woman, who enjoyed listening to music and taking naps, demonstrated how relaxation lifted a mental load from her, freeing herself from worries. It also manifested itself physically:

Mind is even lighter than earlier, especially laying down; not thinking about worrisomethoughts, they're not on my mind; . . . I feel more relieved in chest/head- no more burden (Susan, 39 years old).

Relaxation of the mind and body can help regulate the cognitive–emotional function and minimize "toxic stress", physiological stress often associated with intrusive symptoms of PTSD [19,21]. As one woman who practiced breathing exercises and mindfulness on her walks shared:

> *I feel very relaxed . . . needed a break from work and the kids; I feel very calm and relaxed; I had a very hectic couple of weeks. This was helpful . . . reduction sessions helped me calm down, which is something I need now* (Briana, 32 years old).

3.3.2. Self-Care and Reflection, including Faith-Based Practices

Twelve women ($n = 12$) shared that mindfulness sessions enhanced their motivation towards self-care. The sessions helped them realize the importance of health and happiness in their daily lives. The act of giving back to themselves validated their own worth, especially when many IPV survivors feel as though abuse took something away from them. These small practices of self-management are also good daily coping mechanisms to counteract the cumulative stress that could be toxic to mental health [21]. Women reported reduced stress when practicing self-care activities. One woman highlighted the importance of self-care in her life despite her busy schedule:

> *I liked how I can take some time and do these mindfulness activities; Usually I get very stressed and tension builds up with my work emails. I take deep breaths and do some breathing exercises which helps me when I am in my thoughts. Pleasurable activities for me would be to exercise, be more active, go on walks* (Briana, 32 years old).

For another woman, her self-care practices included self-reflection by taking the time to journal:

> *I actually followed your advice and started to write it out. It helps like crazy, but at first, a little awkward . . . Once you start writing it feels really good* (Libby, 31 years old).

Faith was a significant part of some women's lives and beliefs, especially since it proved to be a stronghold during times of trauma. The sessions encouraged the women to continue faith practices, as it helped in stress reduction. These practices included praying (or being present with God), journaling, or meditation of Scripture. One woman survivor of the Christian faith said that she regularly prays and meditates, is her chosen way to cope through difficult circumstances:

> *I've been doing more of other meditation, before you called, that is one of the things I've done and was journaling. I take a scripture, think through it quiet myself and get to the spirit behind that space. I just take my time, so far about 30 min, sometimes an hour* (Ruth, 30 years old).

3.3.3. Self-Awareness

Self-awareness of body and mind was identified as another helpful component of mindfulness practices. Focusing on sensations and consciousness at the present moment helped strengthen attention control or cognitive–emotion regulation, thereby reducing physiological and mental stress related to IPV [19,21]. Dissociative symptoms were also targeted and mitigated by increased connection to the self and a greater awareness of internal and external experiences [9]. Overall, women shared positive feedback in being more in-tune and present with their bodies and minds. Five women ($n = 5$) reported feeling certain sensations in some areas of their bodies, in their breathing, or in their thoughts.

> *Mindful sessions help when mind is wandering everywhere. It helps me calm down and make me aware of the environment. I really needed that today; the body scan audio made me focus on my breathing* (Briana, 32 years old).

3.3.4. Self-Control and Focused Thinking

The mindfulness phone sessions introduced different stress reduction techniques (e.g., "STOP" or alternative breathing) that encouraged them ($n = 8$) to take control over how they responded to daily stresses in life. Women shared that they were able to first recognize their ability to focus their thinking without distraction and use self-control by not letting the feelings of the stressors control them. These are good practices for strengthening reappraisal, which further reinforces sustained focused attention on unfolding present experiences. Cognitive reappraisal decreases dissociative or ruminating symptoms often found in survivors of IPV and can lead to positive mental health outcomes [19,21]. One woman who regularly practiced "STOP" (a technique taught to re-evaluate the stressful situation before responding to it) when disciplining her children and enjoyed helping people in her spare time, said:

> *STOP is like a solution within your reach; STOP, it's easy to remember. I should use it everyday with my children; I tried it to take my mind away while doing things that I enjoy doing* (Charlene, age unknown).

Another survivor shared:

> *My head isn't as scattered as before. Before, my brain was thinking many things at a time, but now I am thinking calmly and slowly* (Sara, 38 years old).

4. Discussion

Women with recent IPV experiences in BSHAPE reported positive outcomes after participating in mindfulness sessions. The findings are in line with our quantitative analysis of data [25] where women who participated in the BSHAPE intervention reported significant reduction in stress, improved ability to manage stress, reduced PTSD and depression symptoms, and overall empowerment at post-intervention [25]. Based on the qualitative feedback on the mindfulness component of BSHAPE, we found that mindfulness activities were beneficial in developing positive appraisals and adaptive coping among survivors of IPV. Women highlighted some helpful elements of BSHAPE mindfulness sessions. These included: lovingkindness, self-actualization, intentionality, positivity, relaxation, enhanced motivation towards self-care or reflection, self-awareness, and self-control or focused thinking. Mindfulness encourages the individual to focus on coping strategies and problem solving without having to focus on triggering trauma-related content by sharpening trauma-related cognitions with purposeful acceptance and decentering [9,19].

Research shows that IPV often erodes women's self-esteem or confidence about their own personal value and worth [8,34]. Thus, interventions are needed to enhance their self-esteem and confidence, and promote self-empowerment [8]. The strategies include helping women understand the effects of trauma on their health and well-being, addressing their negative beliefs or unhealthy coping mechanisms, encouraging personal empowerment and establishing safety in an individualized approach. Women in our study expressed feelings of self-worth as an outcome of engaging in mindfulness practices, as opposed to apathy or negative beliefs about oneself. Mindfulness meditation can teach empathy skills or sensitivity toward oneself and others while cultivating an attitude of love and compassion among survivors of interpersonal violence [18]. With these mindsets and self-actualizations, women are encouraged and self-empowered to move forward in their lives with a renewed positive sense of purpose and self-confidence, while overcoming personal barriers and negative self-perceptions.

In our study, mindfulness activities (e.g., body scan and meditations) stimulated the relaxation and self-awareness of women's physical and mental states, and further encouraged them to adopt activities of daily care into their lives to better manage stress. This reinforces health benefits to the body and mind while mitigating the debilitating impacts of toxic stress from IPV [18,19,21]. Additionally, women reported feeling encouraged using individualized strategies, such as engaging in faith-based practices or adopting a more hopeful and intentional paradigm of life. This is invaluable for survivors living with PTSD, as it strengthens their coping mechanisms and provides opportunity for positive change, even when they cannot change their external circumstances [16]. Women in our study not only shared having more self-control in their responses to stress, but also indicated using cognitive restructuring strategies (i.e., reappraisal of experiences) without being distracted by prehistoric triggering stressful experiences. This is supported by other research that identified the positive impacts of mindfulness meditation on cognitive attention and concentration in addition to motivational drives [18]. Furthermore, in line with research on women survivors of violence [8,17,21,25], self-empowerment was an overarching theme. In a recent systematic review and meta-analysis of interventions for survivors of IPV, empowerment was found to play a vital role in improving PTSD and depressive symptoms among survivors [34]. Thus, empowerment is a key component of intervention for survivors of IPV with PTSD and/or depressive symptoms.

4.1. Recommendations of Mindfulness in the Clinical, Non-Clinical, and Faith-Based Settings

BSHAPE is a culturally tailored and trauma-informed intervention that could be well-applied in diverse clinical and non-clinical settings. According to Borrell-Carrió et al. (2004), a holistic response to a patient's suffering considers the biological, psychological, and social dimensions of the patient, individualizes the patient's situation, and gives the patient "a sense of being understood", while establishing a therapeutic and trusting relationship between the client and the provider [35] (p. 576). This holistic, therapeutic response is especially important for underserved and marginalized racial minorities with a complex history of trauma and IPV [15]. Our feasibility and acceptability evaluation identified the need for additional tailoring of the mindfulness practices to survivor's needs [25]. Care should be individualized to the woman while prioritizing and supporting her goals in creating a safety plan that she would be able to follow-up with [8,25,35,36]. This not only sets realistic and attainable personal goals for the client, but further empowers her in her decision making and life, while further strengthening her coping mechanisms and healing.

Phone-based mindfulness interventions may be an appropriate method of communication between the facilitator and IPV survivor, as it allows the woman convenience and privacy in her own home without feeling as though she is being the subject under examination. It also encourages a woman to communicate without judgement [25]. There is also compelling evidence that MBSR works, but it cannot work in a vacuum [8,17,18,21,34]. For example, one study recommended providing logistical support with childcare, food, and transport in the MBSR intervention [21], in addition to psychoeducation resources [8,17,21,34]. Mindfulness can be integrated in diverse treatment settings, such as at a substance abuse treatment facility for women [18]. In addition to mindfulness, the BSHAPE intervention integrates strengths-based assessments, feedback, psychoeducation, safety planning, and referrals. These integrated components are needed to assess and strengthen effective coping skills for stressors in women's daily lives, empowering them step by step, and building long-lasting resilience [37]. Remote mindfulness practices can be beneficial for women immigrant survivors of IPV who face numerous barriers, such as stigmatization and language, in accessing services. Especially in non-mental health settings, mindfulness practices can be implemented in a cost-effective manner, making it more acceptable and feasible for underserved and marginalized populations [18,21], such as Black immigrant women survivors of IPV [25].

Some women in BSHAPE expressed a faith-based background (e.g., Christianity or Islam) in which they regularly practiced and congregated with others of the same faith. Contrary to hesitant perceptions of Christianity or other religions toward Buddhist-associated practices, mindfulness may prove to be a beneficial component of faith-based therapies. It could even strengthen certain values (e.g., forgiveness and compassion) and practices of faith (e.g., cultivating a life of mindful prayer, being present with God, or having a posture of gratitude or awe and wonder toward the beauty of life) without further compromising core beliefs and values [25,33]. Thus, such practices could be linked to faith-based beliefs when working with survivors for whom faith is a fundamental part of their lives.

4.2. Recommendations for Further Research

Most studies to date for IPV survivors examined the impact of in-person individual or group-based therapeutic approaches, such as cognitive behavioral therapy. Additional research is needed on the usefulness of remote, individual, and cost-effective approaches to care for immigrant women survivors of IPV who face numerous barriers to accessing standard care services. Studies are needed to examine if mindfulness can be effective as a stand-alone intervention or in combination with other mental health therapeutic approaches.

4.3. Limitations

There were several limitations to this study. This preliminary evaluation and feedback is based on a relatively small sample of IPV survivors. Additional research using a large sample size of diverse groups of immigrant survivors of IPV can strengthen our study findings. The feedback given by the women was self-reported, which may have biased the results. Although the phone calls were more feasible in a pandemic setting due to COVID-19, they were less conducive to a setting where women were multi-tasking or were in a distractive environment. Only English speakers were included in this small pilot study, which limited the generalizability of the study's findings to non-English speaking immigrant women in the United States. The next iteration of the BSHAPE trial will incorporate multiple languages and more tailored approaches with diverse groups of immigrant survivors of IPV.

5. Conclusions

Immigrant women with IPV experiences in the US face an understated number of external obstacles and internal suffering, which negatively affect their mental health and well-being. Culturally sensitive mindfulness practices may help alleviate women's daily physical and mental stress, as well as enhance positive coping and empowerment. Mindfulness practices can offer women an opportunity to reappraise their own lives during stressful experiences by equipping them with the tools and skills they need to overcome and heal in a way that is meaningful to them.

Author Contributions: Conceptualization, B.S.; Formal analysis, A.V. and B.S.; Funding acquisition, B.S.; Investigation, B.S.; Methodology, B.S.; Project administration, B.S.; Supervision, B.S.; Validation, B.S.; Writing—original draft, A.V. and B.S.; Writing—review & editing, B.S. All authors have read and agreed to the published version of the manuscript.

Funding: This research was funded by the Eunice Kennedy Shriver National Institute of Child Health & Human Development grant numbers K99HD082350; R00HD082350. The content is solely the responsibilities of the authors and does not necessarily represent the official views of the National Institutes of Health.

Institutional Review Board Statement: This research was approved by Johns Hopkins School of Medicine Institutional Review Board.

Informed Consent Statement: Informed consent was obtained from all subjects involved in the study.

Data Availability Statement: The data generated for this article is presented in the results of the study.

Conflicts of Interest: The authors declare no conflict of interest.

References

1. Mose, G.B.; Gillum, T.L. Intimate Partner Violence in African Immigrant Communities in the United States: Reflections from the IDVAAC African Women's Round Table on Domestic Violence. *J. Aggress. Maltreatment Trauma* **2016**, *25*, 50–62. [CrossRef]
2. Akinsulure-Smith, A.M.; Chu, T.; Keatley, E.; Rasmussen, A. Intimate Partner Violence among West African Immigrants. *J. Aggress. Maltreatment Trauma* **2013**, *22*, 109–126. [CrossRef] [PubMed]
3. West, C.M. African Immigrant Women and Intimate Partner Violence: A Systematic Review. *J. Aggress. Maltreatment Trauma* **2016**, *25*, 4–17. [CrossRef]
4. Corley, A.; Sabri, B. Exploring African Immigrant Women's Pre- and Post-Migration Exposures to Stress and Violence, Sources of Resilience, and Psychosocial Outcomes. *Issues Ment. Health Nurs.* **2021**, *42*, 484–494. [CrossRef] [PubMed]
5. Ting, L.; Panchanadeswaran, S. Barriers to Help-Seeking Among Immigrant African Women Survivors of Partner Abuse: Listening to Women's Own Voices. *J. Aggress. Maltreatment Trauma* **2009**, *18*, 817–838. [CrossRef]
6. Pemberton, J.V.; Loeb, T.B. Impact of Sexual and Interpersonal Violence and Trauma on Women: Trauma-Informed Practice and Feminist Theory. *J. Fem. Fam. Ther.* **2020**, *32*, 115–131. [CrossRef]

7. Sabri, B.; Stockman, J.K.; Bertrand, D.R.; Campbell, D.W.; Callwood, G.B.; Campbell, J.C. Victimization Experiences, Substance Misuse, and Mental Health Problems in Relation to Risk for Lethality Among African American and African Caribbean Women. *J. Interpers. Violence* **2013**, *28*, 3223–3241. [CrossRef]
8. Stockman, J.K.; Hayashi, H.; Campbell, J.C. Intimate Partner Violence and Its Health Impact on Ethnic Minority Women. *J. Women's Health* **2015**, *24*, 62–79. [CrossRef]
9. Boyd, J.E.; Lanius, R.A.; McKinnon, M.C. Mindfulness-Based Treatments for Posttraumatic Stress Disorder: A Review of the Treatment Literature and Neurobiological Evidence. *J. Psychiatry Neurosci.* **2018**, *43*, 7–25. [CrossRef]
10. Post-Traumatic Stress Disorder. National Institute of Mental Health (NIMH). Available online: https://www.nimh.nih.gov/health/topics/post-traumatic-stress-disorder-ptsd (accessed on 8 August 2022).
11. Sabri, B.; Granger, D.A. Gender-Based Violence and Trauma in Marginalized Populations of Women: Role of Biological Embedding and Toxic Stress. *Health Care Women Int.* **2018**, *39*, 1038–1055. [CrossRef]
12. Woods, A.B.; Page, G.G.; O'Campo, P.; Pugh, L.C.; Ford, D.; Campbell, J.C. The Mediation Effect of Posttraumatic Stress Disorder Symptoms on the Relationship of Intimate Partner Violence and IFN-γ Levels. *Am. J. Community Psychol.* **2005**, *36*, 159–175. [CrossRef] [PubMed]
13. Sabri, B.; Nnawulezi, N.; Njie-Carr, V.P.S.; Messing, J.; Ward-Lasher, A.; Alvarez, C.; Campbell, J.C. Multilevel Risk and Protective Factors for Intimate Partner Violence Among African, Asian, and Latina Immigrant and Refugee Women: Perceptions of Effective Safety Planning Interventions. *Race Soc. Probl.* **2018**, *10*, 348–365. [CrossRef] [PubMed]
14. DeSa, S.; Gebremeskel, A.T.; Omonaiye, O.; Yaya, S. Barriers and Facilitators to Access Mental Health Services among Refugee Women in High-Income Countries: A Systematic Review. *Syst. Rev.* **2022**, *11*, 62. [CrossRef]
15. Sabri, B.; Bolyard, R.; McFadgion, A.L.; Stockman, J.K.; Lucea, M.B.; Callwood, G.B.; Coverston, C.R.; Campbell, J.C. Intimate Partner Violence, Depression, PTSD, and Use of Mental Health Resources Among Ethnically Diverse Black Women. *Soc. Work. Health Care* **2013**, *52*, 351–369. [CrossRef] [PubMed]
16. Keng, S.-L.; Smoski, M.J.; Robins, C.J. Effects of Mindfulness on Psychological Health: A Review of Empirical Studies. *Clin. Psychol. Rev.* **2011**, *31*, 1041–1056. [CrossRef]
17. Kelly, A.; Garland, E.L. Trauma-Informed Mindfulness-Based Stress Reduction for Female Survivors of Interpersonal Violence: Results from a Stage I RCT: TI-MBSR for IPV Survivors. *J. Clin. Psychol.* **2016**, *72*, 311–328. [CrossRef]
18. Lee, M.Y.; Zaharlick, A.; Akers, D. Impact of Meditation on Mental Health Outcomes of Female Trauma Survivors of Interpersonal Violence with Co-Occurring Disorders: A Randomized Controlled Trial. *J. Interpers. Violence* **2017**, *32*, 2139–2165. [CrossRef]
19. Gallegos, A.M.; Heffner, K.L.; Cerulli, C.; Luck, P.; McGuinness, S.; Pigeon, W.R. Effects of Mindfulness Training on Posttraumatic Stress Symptoms from a Community-Based Pilot Clinical Trial among Survivors of Intimate Partner Violence. *Psychol. Trauma Theory Res. Pract. Policy* **2020**, *12*, 859–868. [CrossRef]
20. Lindsay, E.K. Mindfulness Interventions for Offsetting Health Risk Following Early Life Stress: Promising Directions. *Brain Behav. Immun. Health* **2021**, *17*, 100338. [CrossRef]
21. Dutton, M.A.; Bermudez, D.; Matás, A.; Majid, H.; Myers, N.L. Mindfulness-Based Stress Reduction for Low-Income, Predominantly African American Women with PTSD and a History of Intimate Partner Violence. *Cogn. Behav. Pract.* **2013**, *20*, 23–32. [CrossRef]
22. Kafetsios, K. Taylor and Aspinwall Psychosocial Stress Model. In *Encyclopedia of Quality of Life and Well-Being Research*; Michalos, A.C., Ed.; Springer: Dordrecht, The Netherlands, 2014; pp. 6591–6593. [CrossRef]
23. Algorani, E.B.; Gupta, V. Coping Mechanisms. In *StatPearls*; StatPearls Publishing: Treasure Island, FL, USA, 2022.
24. Sabri, B.; Saha, J.; Lee, J.; Murray, S. Conducting Digital Intervention Research among Immigrant Survivors of Intimate Partner Violence: Methodological, Safety and Ethnical Considerations. *J. Fam. Violence* **2022**. [CrossRef] [PubMed]
25. Sabri, B.; Vroegindewey, A.; Hagos, M. Development, Feasibility, Acceptability and Preliminary Evaluation of the Internet and Mobile Phone-Based BSHAPE Intervention for Immigrant Survivors of Cumulative Trauma. *Contemp. Clin. Trials* **2021**, *110*, 106591. [CrossRef] [PubMed]
26. Kane, T. Inner Resources Project. Available online: http://www.innerresourcesproject.com/about-tawanna (accessed on 9 September 2022).
27. Kabat-Zinn, J. Mindfulness Training. Available online: https://mbsrtraining.com/jon-kabat-zinn-mindfulness (accessed on 9 September 2022).
28. Mollica, R.F.; Caspi-Yavin, Y.; Bollini, P.; Truong, T.; Tor, S.; Lavelle, J. The Harvard Trauma Questionnaire: Validating a Cross-Cultural Instrument for Measuring Torture, Trauma, and Posttraumatic Stress Disorder in Indochinese Refugees. *J. Nerv. Ment. Dis.* **1992**, *180*, 111–116. [CrossRef] [PubMed]
29. Kroenke, K.; Spitzer, R.L.; Williams, J.B.W. The PHQ-9: Validity of a Brief Depression Severity Measure. *J. Gen. Intern. Med.* **2001**, *16*, 606–613. [CrossRef]
30. Kira, I.A.; Fawzi, M.H.; Fawzi, M.M. The Dynamics of Cumulative Trauma and Trauma Types in Adults Patients with Psychiatric Disorders: Two Cross-Cultural Studies. *Traumatology* **2013**, *19*, 179–195. [CrossRef]
31. Kim, H.; Sefcik, J.S.; Bradway, C. Characteristics of Qualitative Descriptive Studies: A Systematic Review. *Res. Nurs. Health* **2017**, *40*, 23–42. [CrossRef]
32. Hsieh, H.F.; Shannon, S.E. Three Approaches to Qualitative Content Analysis. *Qual. Health Res.* **2005**, *15*, 1277–1288. [CrossRef]

33. Symington, S.H.; Symington, M.F. A Christian Model of Mindfulness: Using Mindfulness Principles to Support Psychological Well-Being, Value-Based Behavior, and the Christian Spiritual Journey. *J. Psychol. Christ.* **2012**, *31*, 71–77.
34. Karakurt, G.; Koç, E.; Katta, P.; Jones, N.; Bolen, S.D. Treatments for Female Victims of Intimate Partner Violence: Systematic Review and Meta-Analysis. *Front. Psychol.* **2022**, *13*, 793021. [CrossRef]
35. Borrell-Carrio, F. The Biopsychosocial Model 25 Years Later: Principles, Practice, and Scientific Inquiry. *Ann. Fam. Med.* **2004**, *2*, 576–582. [CrossRef]
36. Anyikwa, V.A. Trauma-Informed Approach to Survivors of Intimate Partner Violence. *J. Evid. -Inf. Soc. Work.* **2016**, *13*, 484–491. [CrossRef] [PubMed]
37. Sabri, B.; Gielen, A. Integrated Multicomponent Interventions for Safety and Health Risks Among Black Female Survivors of Violence: A Systematic Review. *Trauma Violence Abus.* **2019**, *20*, 720–731. [CrossRef] [PubMed]

International Journal of
Environmental Research and Public Health

MDPI

Article

The Post-Traumatic Growth Journey of Women Who Have Survived Intimate Partner Violence: A Synthesized Theory Emphasizing Obstacles and Facilitating Factors

Hulda S. Bryngeirsdottir *, Denise Saint Arnault and Sigridur Halldorsdottir

School of Health Sciences, University of Akureyri, Solborg v/Nordurslod, 600 Akureyri, Iceland; starnaul@med.umich.edu (D.S.A.); sigridur@unak.is (S.H.)
* Correspondence: hulda@unak.is

Abstract: Suffering intimate partner violence (IPV) is a devastating personal experience and post-traumatic growth (PTG) is a positive, psychological change in a person, following trauma such as IPV. There is a gap in the literature when it comes to theories on PTG after surviving IPV. The aim of this theory development was to synthesize an approach to understanding the PTG journey of female IPV survivors. According to our theory, their PTG journey includes eight main components: 1. The women's early experience of trauma, 2. The consequences of that trauma, 3. Their experiences of IPV, 4. The consequences of IPV, 5. The facilitating factors to PTG, 6. The hindering factors to PTG, 7. Their experience of PTG, and 8. The lingering effects of IPV. According to our findings, PTG is a real possibility for female IPV survivors, and it is likely to improve their mental health, well-being, and quality of life, as well as that of their children, loved ones, and communities, thereby decreasing the damaging effects of IPV. The theory can be useful for professionals when guiding female survivors of IPV to promote their recovery and healing. Due to the lack of research in this field, additional research is needed to further develop this theory.

Keywords: post-traumatic growth (PTG); intimate partner violence (IPV); gender-based violence (GBV); mental health; trauma recovery; rehabilitation; women's health; public health; theory development; theory synthesis

check for updates

Citation: Bryngeirsdottir, H.S.; Arnault, D.S.; Halldorsdottir, S. The Post-Traumatic Growth Journey of Women Who Have Survived Intimate Partner Violence: A Synthesized Theory Emphasizing Obstacles and Facilitating Factors. *Int. J. Environ. Res. Public Health* **2022**, *19*, 8653. https://doi.org/10.3390/ijerph19148653

Academic Editor: Liliana Dell'Osso

Received: 26 May 2022
Accepted: 14 July 2022
Published: 16 July 2022

Publisher's Note: MDPI stays neutral with regard to jurisdictional claims in published maps and institutional affiliations.

1. Introduction

Gender-based violence (GBV) is a serious, societal problem [1–5], affecting approximately one in three women all around the world [1–3]. The forms of GBV vary and the causes are multidimensional, including social, cultural, economic, and political [5,6]. Intimate partner violence (IPV) is the most common type of violence against women [1–3,5,7] and includes physical and psychological aggression, controlling behaviour and/or sexual coercion, the perpetrator most often being a current or former intimate partner [2,7]. Global research has revealed that women are more likely to be assaulted, injured, raped, or killed by their male spouse or male ex-spouse than by anyone else [8–10]. Even though the typologies of IPV vary [11–13], the consequences of suffering IPV are often serious, affecting the woman's physical and psychological health in a destructive way [2,5,14–19] and even resulting in her being murdered by the perpetrator [15,20]. Suffering IPV also affects the victim's social wellbeing in a negative way [4,5,9,21], as well as that of her children [4,5,7,9,21,22] and loved ones [5,9,21,23]. Women who have suffered IPV endure a higher illness burden, their comorbidity is high, they are more likely to be diagnosed with mental illness and are in increased danger of substance use disorders than women who have not experienced IPV or abuse [7,15,24].

Violence against women is now widely considered a serious public health problem [7,21,25] which concerns all sectors of society and violates human rights [2,7,21,26,27]. According to WHO's study on women's health and domestic violence against women, conducted in fifteen settings in ten countries, sociodemographic factors, such as age, marital status, and educational status, did not explain the differences found between the settings of the research [21]. GBV, including IPV, has severe economic costs not only for the victims of violence, but also for their community. These costs are due to expenditures on service provision because of violence, lost income for the women suffering GBV/IPV and their families, decreased productivity, as well as the destructive impacts on future human capital formation, affecting the economic growth in a negative way [27]. Economic abuse is a unique form of abuse, well-known within intimate partner relationships, which negatively affects the victim's life in an extensive way, i.e., her mental health and psychological well-being, family formations, parenting practices, children's behavior, and youth outcomes [28].

A considerable proportion of people experience psychological trauma sometime in their lives. The key aspects of psychological trauma are life threat, uncontrollability, and unpredictability [29,30]. Even though a traumatic experience can lead to various psychological problems [31–33], most trauma survivors show enormous adaptability when coping with their experience [34,35]. The development of post-traumatic outcomes depends on the physical and emotional proximity to the traumatic event [33,36–38]. Suffering IPV is a complex traumatic experience [39,40], in which the perpetrator has forced the victim into survival mode by taking over the control of her life [39]. Therefore, making the decision of staying in or leaving a violent relationship is also complex [41,42]. Leaving such a relationship means profound changes in the life of the female survivor of IPV, since the woman moves from survival mode to starting a new life where she is in control [39]. In a qualitative online survey, 665 female survivors of IPV described their experiences and definitions of their long-term recovery following IPV. When defining their recovery, the women focused on their lived experience of the phenomenon instead of psychological and academic concepts commonly used by researchers. The five themes they used to describe their definition of recovery were safety and survival, having their freedom, moving on, having a better life, and issues with children and parenting. Many of them also described relapses, digressions, and highs and lows as a part of their recovery. The themes described were woven together in their description of their journey to recovery. According to these findings, recovery following IPV can take a long time and is both individual and multidimensional in nature, requiring a great deal of support [43].

Post-traumatic growth (PTG) has been described as a positive, psychological change in a person, following traumatic events and severe difficulties, where the person focuses on the possible positive outcomes of the trauma instead of focusing on the negative consequences [44]. PTG consists of five main components, i.e., the person experiences positive spiritual change, sees new possibilities in life, appreciates life more, experiences increased personal strength, and has better relations to other people [44,45]. Research has shown that many people who have had symptoms of PTSD following trauma, have described these extensive positive changes in their lives [46–54]. When estimating PTG, all these components are considered [50–55]. We identified a gap in the literature since most PTG work has been undertaken on a variety of trauma and little is known about PTG after IPV. The general nature of PTG theory can be criticized when being used for various groups of trauma survivors, such as for female survivors of IPV and, therefore, trauma-specific PTG theories are needed.

Recognizing IPV as a major social problem that negatively affects public health has progressively changed attitudes toward IPV against women [25,56]. This has resulted in an increased interest in the research area of IPV [25,56], leading to an international, steady increase in the number of publications on the subject over the last 20 years [25]. Research on PTG has been conducted in various fields of the literature of trauma, such as transportation accidents or other accidental injuries [57–59], natural disasters [60–65], interpersonal experiences [66–78], medical problems [79–86], and other life experiences [87–90]. Even so, when it comes to research on PTG following IPV among female survivors, there seems to be a severe lack of literature [91]. Since PTG has been shown to improve quality of life in multiple ways, the possibility of PTG among female survivors of IPV is important.

Purpose of the Theory Development and the Main Question

This theory development is part of a larger research project aimed at exploring the post-traumatic growth of female IPV survivors. The first study in the research project was a phenomenological study about the experience of PTG among people who had suffered various traumas [92], and the following two phenomenological studies examined the facilitators [93] and obstacles to female survivors' PTG journey following IPV [94]. The main aim of the present theory development is identifying and describing the main components of the PTG journey of female IPV survivors. Our full team consisted of two professors (one Icelandic and one American) as well as one Icelandic doctoral student. The Icelandic team conducted the phenomenological and theoretical analysis. We developed the theory through theory synthesis using the key concepts and key statements reported in our already published papers, our rich databases on the subject, as well as published material pertaining to PTG in IPV survivors. When organizing existing knowledge into a framework about a certain phenomenon, combining it with databases of the phenomena of interest to develop a theory on the subject, theory synthesis is an appropriate and well-known methodological strategy [95]. Therefore, when developing this theory, the theory synthesis method was used. The purpose of the theory development was to identify, describe, and explain the main components on the PTG journey of Icelandic female IPV survivors. The main question of the theory development was: What are the main components of the PTG journey of female IPV survivors?

2. Materials and Methods

2.1. Design of the Theory Development

After pulling together available knowledge on the components of the PTG journey of female IPV survivors in our already published studies, our databases of the subject, as well as published material pertaining to PTG in IPV survivors, key concepts, and key statements were organized into a synthesized theory, mainly by using abstract thought processes, e.g., critical, conceptual, and creative thinking, as well as inductive and deductive reasoning. Since only a part of our research data has already been published, we have access to a large amount of data that we have collected on the phenomenon, which gave us the opportunity to present an even deeper understanding of the PTG journey of female IPV survivors. However, we only use findings where more than half of the twenty-two participants in the databases of the studies [92–94] reported a key component. When undertaking various studies on the same phenomena from different angles, researchers can gain more insight on the research data by using the research results from the new studies, which is the aim of theory synthesis [95].

2.2. The Method of Theory Synthesis

The method of theory synthesis involves three steps, where, in step one, the key concepts and key statements of the synthesized theory are specified. In step two, the literature is reviewed to identify factors that relate to the key concepts and key statements. In step three, the key concepts and key statements are then organized into an integrated description of the phenomena [95]. The three main steps of the theory synthesis, and the way it was used in this theory development, are described further in Table 1.

Table 1. Theory synthesis: an overview of the method and how it was used in this theory development.

Step	Description	Overview of What We Did
Step 1	The key concepts and key statements from the studies and the databases, used to develop the theory, are specified and explained.	We used our own studies and extensive databases (see Tables 2 and 3) and analyses of them in the theory synthesis. These contain information about how female survivors of IPV who had reached PTG described their journey to PTG, how they perceived their PTG, and how the lingering effects of their former traumatic experience influenced their PTG.

Table 1. *Cont.*

Step	Description	Overview of What We Did
Step 2	The key concepts and key statements used to develop the theory are compared to the literature, to identify and define their relation to other factors.	The key concepts and key statements identified in step one were used when comparing the main concepts used in the theory to the literature of PTG among female survivors of IPV. Most of the articles from the literature were partially related to the women's journey to PTG, their experience of PTG, and the lingering effects of their prior traumatic experience in life on their experience of PTG.
Step 3	The key concepts and key statements of the theory and their relations are presented in text, figure(s), or table(s).	After comparing the detailed descriptions of female survivors' journey to PTG following IPV, their experience of the facilitators and the obstacles on the journey as well as of PTG and the lingering effects of their prior traumatic experience on their PTG. We present the results in text, figures, and tables.

Table 2. The published studies used to develop the theory in step I.

Authors and Date	Title	Published
Bryngeirsdottir and Halldors-dottir, 2021 [92]	The Challenging Journey from Trauma to Post-Traumatic Growth: Experiences of Facilitating and Hindering Factors	Scandinavian Journal of Caring Sciences 00, 1–17
Bryngeirsdottir and Halldors-dottir, 2022 [93]	"I'm a Winner, Not a Victim": The Facilitating Factors of Post-Traumatic Growth among Women Who Have Suffered Intimate Partner Violence	International Journal of Environmental Research and Public Health 19, 1342. Special Issue: Environment and Behavior
Bryngeirsdottir and Halldors-dottir, 2022 [94]	Fourteen Main Obstacles on the Journey to Post-Traumatic Growth as Experienced by Female Survivors of Intimate Partner Violence	International Journal of Environmental Research and Public Health 19, 5377. Special Issue: Violence against Women as an Interdisciplinary Challenge in Public Health

Table 3. Summary of research data collected by the first author, used to develop the theory in step I.

Research Data	Number of Interviews	Main Criteria for Participation	Word Count
Qualitative interviews	13	Icelandic men and women who self-reported PTG following traumas	90.172 (M = 6.936)
Qualitative interviews	22	Icelandic female IPV survivors who self-reported PTG following traumas caused by IPV	199.386 (M = 9.063)
SUMMARY	35 interviews		289.558 (M = 8.273)

2.3. Steps in the Theory Synthesis

Step 1. The bases of the theory are the lived experiences of female survivors on their journey to PTG following IPV. When describing their PTG journey, they reported their traumatic experiences earlier in life, as well as the facilitators and obstacles affecting their journey to PTG. The women's experience of PTG and the lingering effects of IPV on their growth were also reported. An overview of the studies and research data used in the first step of the theory synthesis can be found in Tables 2 and 3.

Step 2. After working through the evidence base constructed in the first step of the theory synthesis, we analyzed the results of the studies, along with the academic writing used to form the literature background in our own studies in the field of post-traumatic growth following intimate partner violence. To deepen the understanding of the phenomena, we repeatedly examined our research data on the subject. This process was undertaken so that we could come to a joint conclusion about the female survivors' journey to PTG following IPV, including the influencing factors on that journey and the lingering effects of IPV on their PTG. By conducting this analysis, we found confirmation of our findings in step 1. We found that PTG is possible for IPV survivors, despite their lived experience of IPV. Former experience of traumatic events earlier in life should, however, be considered when processing the experience of IPV, aiming for PTG, as well as the facilitators and obstacles met by the survivors of IPV that affect their journey to PTG. It is likely that when a female survivor of IPV reaches PTG, she also experiences some lingering, negative effects of her experience of IPV, even if enjoying PTG.

Step 3. In this last step, we present the results using methods that are the most appropriate for the subject. We chose to present the theory by using text, figures, and tables.

3. Results

The primary question our theory answers is "What are the main components of the PTG journey of female IPV survivors"? When presenting the results, we begin with identifying and defining the main concepts of the theory, i.e., trauma, intimate partner violence (IPV), facilitators of PTG, obstacles to PTG, post-traumatic growth (PTG), and lingering effects of IPV (see Table 4). Secondly, we describe and explain the essence of the theory through the eight major components of the PTG journey of female IPV survivors, identified by the authors i.e., 1. Life before IPV, 2. Wounded or adapted? 3. The experience of IPV, 4. IPV's consequences, 5. Main facilitating factors on the PTG journey, 6. Main obstacles on the PTG journey, 7. The experience of post-traumatic growth and, finally, 8. The lingering effects of IPV. We used text, tables, and figures to present the theory. These are presented in Sections 3.1.1–3.1.8.

Table 4. The main concepts of the theory—defined by the authors for the theory.

Concepts	Definitions
Trauma	An unexpected and threatening event experienced by an individual that he or she cannot stop, control, or influence in any way. Trauma negatively affects the basic experience of living in a safe and predictable world and can even negatively affect the individual's worldview.
Intimate Partner Violence (IPV)	Controlling, dominating and/or violent behaviors in an intimate relationship that causes the victim physical, psychological, sexual, financial, or social harm.
Facilitators of PTG	Personal, social and/or systematic constructive components that are likely to be beneficial to the progress of PTG among female survivors of IPV. For example, these may be internal factors of the woman, i.e., personal abilities, mindset, social wellbeing, former experience of trauma; the attitude and reaction of the woman, the perpetrator, children, loved ones, and other people; and environmental factors, i.e., personal social support, systematic social support, and organized supporting resources.
Obstacles to PTG	Personal, social, and/or systematic destructive components, which are likely to cause a delay in, or prevent, the progress of PTG among female survivors of IPV. These are, for example, feelings of shame; suicidal thoughts; fragile self-identity; insecurity; feeling alone and isolated; triggers; mixed negative feelings; emotional connection to others; physical and psychological health; personal circumstances and social surroundings; the perpetrator; the children; and law and the institutional social system.
Post-Traumatic Growth (PTG)	Following the experience of trauma and through the individual's internal need for change, the woman has managed to process the suffering caused by the trauma. The personal changes experienced include confronting one's own feelings more freely, consciously nourishing inner strength, having deeper relations to others, experiencing personal growth, living a more wholesome life, and having deeper self-knowledge as well as a stronger self-image. Furthermore, the individual enjoys increased social activity, positivity, and patience and has feelings of freedom, power, and energy, without any regrets. Moreover, the individual feels like a winner in life, is less stressed, more appreciative of one's own self, others, and life in general, seeing new possibilities in life, having found a new vision as well as deeper inner peace and wisdom. Even though the negative influences of trauma can be present, the positive factors of post-traumatic growth are dominant. Post-traumatic growth can be likened to a personal resurrection in life following psychological trauma.
Lingering Effects of IPV	The negative, long-term effects of traumatic experience are intertwined with one's PTG. The person becomes aware of these effects, learns to accept them and how to endure them, responding to them in the best and most suitable way, knowing that the effects will pass and/or everything will be all right.

3.1. Description of the Theory

This theory aims to answer the main question by explaining main components of the PTG journey among female survivors of IPV. The theory includes the effects of the trauma and violence they endured early in life, and how that experience served as a certain preparation for their later life experiences. The women's experience of IPV, as well as the consequences they suffered because of it, are considered when theorizing about the PTG journey, as well as the facilitators and obstacles. Some women enjoy more facilitators on their journey, while others meet more obstacles, affecting their possibilities of reaching PTG. The theory includes the survivors' experience of PTG while considering the lingering effects of IPV on their lives after reaching PTG. Though pictured as a one-way process, PTG is a nonlinear, fluid state and regression, e.g., due to triggers, should be considered. Even so, a woman enjoying PTG seems to know how to react to regression in her PTG. She seems to be aware of the possibility of regression, knowing what to be aware of in that matter. She also seems to know the best ways to react to her regression, being aware of that she will overcome this bad feeling and regain her wellbeing, enjoying her PTG. A woman enjoying PTG is also aware of the importance of maintaining it. An overview of the theory is shown in Figure 1.

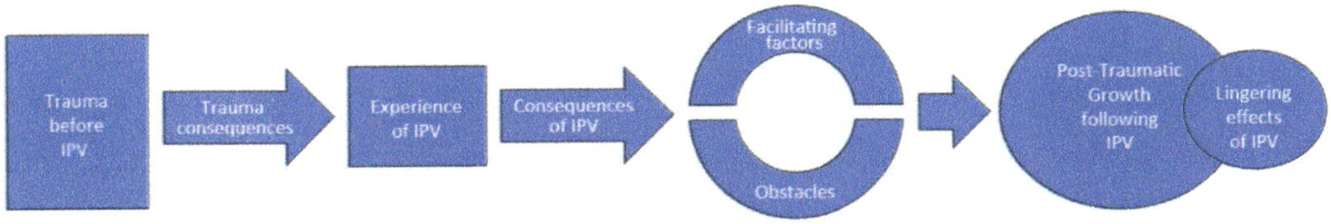

Figure 1. The eight main components of the post-traumatic growth journey by female survivors of intimate partner violence. *Note.* The figure, developed by the authors for the present theory, introduces the eight main components of the PTG journey as experienced by female IPV survivors. 1. Trauma before IPV. 2. Trauma consequences. 3. Experience of IPV. 4. Consequences of IPV. 5. Obstacles on the PTG journey. 6. Facilitating factors on the PTG journey. 7. Post-traumatic growth following IPV. 8. Lingering effects of IPV. Part of the facilitating factors are likely to be part of the women's PTG, while part of the obstacles is likely to remain as part of the negative effects of IPV lingering into her PTG. Though pictured as a one-way, linear process, PTG is a nonlinear, fluid state, where regression, e.g., due to triggers, should be considered. Even so, a female survivor of IPV is likely to be aware of the possibility of regression in her PTG, as well as knowing the best ways for her to respond to such regression. According to this, reaching PTG is not a permanent condition, but requires the woman enjoying it to constantly maintain and nourish her growth.

3.1.1. Component 1: Trauma before IPV

We theorize, based on the aforementioned findings, that a substantial majority of women who suffer IPV have already suffered traumatic events, as children and/or young adults. When experiencing violence and traumas as a child, an adolescent, or a young adult, the female victim has neither the power nor the control in her life, as she would have as an adult, making her more vulnerable and fragile. She, however, reacts in the best way she can, to survive. Suffering traumas early in life is likely to produce serious long-term effects on the victim's selfhood, resulting in fragile boundaries and vulnerability. Some women, however, seem to adapt to their traumatic situation and their experience of suffering trauma early in life, feeling as if they wear a certain shield for their protection. The feeling of being protected by a shield seems to result in their avoidance in confronting demanding situations, instead ignoring them, accepting them as their unchangeable reality. In some cases, however, the 'snowball' effects of previous traumas that have not been processed; this can gradually make survivors of traumas more vulnerable as the size of the 'ball' grows, resulting in a traumatic break-down. We theorize from our findings that if traumatic experiences are not processed in a constructive way, they are likely to undermine the future reaction of the woman when facing further trauma and violence, such as IPV, leaving her more vulnerable than before.

3.1.2. Component 2: Influences of Former Traumas on the Experience of IPV

We theorize, based on the aforementioned findings, that the results of traumatic experiences early in life appear as the victims move on with their lives, either through carrying their vulnerable selfhood and deconstructed boundaries, or through having adapted, feeling stronger, better protected, and even better prepared for life. We theorize that in both cases, the women's personal boundaries have been moved, twisted, damaged, or broken, leaving their personhood fragile. Even if prior experience of traumatic events can motivate and increase the inner strength of the survivors, we propose that whether the woman feels vulnerable or adapted, she is more likely to experience difficulties in confronting traumas and violence later in life, thus being in great danger of being violated in many ways as an adult, including IPV.

An overview of the traumas the women had suffered prior to their experience of IPV and their long-term negative consequences are shown in Table 5.

Table 5. *Component 2*: Overview of the former traumas the participants in the studies had experienced and their long-term negative consequences.

Former Traumas as a Child or Young Adult	Negative Results of Former Traumas	Influence of Former Traumas on Reacting to Traumatic Situations	Influences of Former Traumas on IPV
As a child Neglect, poverty, sexual abuse, bullying, witnessing IPV at home, alcohol abuse by parents, illness, or death of a relative, dependent atmosphere at home, parents' divorce, apathetic and absent parents, demanding parents, stigmatization by community (i.e., because of adverse conditions at home), taking on too much responsibility for their age, difficulties at school. As a young adult Violent relationship, rape, bullying, assault, oppression, threats, property damage, breach of confidentiality, infidelity, divorce, custody dispute, neglect of children, post-partum depression, sickness of loved ones, death of loved ones, financial concerns, accidents, loss of health, codependence, drug abuse by herself or former spouse, alcohol abuse by the survivor or former spouse, bankruptcy.	Fragile self-image, lower feelings of self-worth, shift in personal boundaries, depressed defensive responses, diminished trust in other people, dependence, excessive feeling of responsibility, shame, anxiety, perfectionism, rebelliousness, forbidden to complain, having to succeed no matter what, insecurity, feeling of rejection, grief, suicidal attempts, muscle tension, fear, stress, feeling of guilt, sleep problems, reticence, nervous breakdown.	Destructive reaction to traumas, trouble in processing trauma in a constructive way. Feeling vulnerable or adapted to traumatic situations avoiding confronting the real situations. Snowball-effects of past and current traumas sometimes ending in traumatic breakdown.	Increased danger of being abused, reducing possibilities of leaving violent and life-threatening situations.

3.1.3. Component 3: Experience of IPV

We theorize, based on the aforementioned findings, that the woman in a violent relationship often feels trapped. To survive, she gradually moves her personal boundaries, resulting in the man gaining full power over her life. We theorize that the woman often denies that she is in a violent relationship, hiding what is really going on, thus does not seek help and, therefore, no one is able to help her. Female survivors' experiences of IPV according to the theory are described in Table 6.

Table 6. Component 3: Overview of experiencing IPV.

	The Female Survivors' Lived Experience of IPV: A Summary
Female IPV Survivors	We theorize, based on the aforementioned findings, that being a female victim of IPV can be compared to being held as a hostage in a violent relationship against your will. The woman feels captured and dependent on the perpetrator, where most things are conditional, him deciding what is "right" and what is "wrong", and her "bad behavior" having serious, unpredictable consequences. The woman often feels like she is being silenced, since her opinion does not matter, her words do not have meaning, her needs are ignored, and her will and reactions to the situation seem not to be relevant. Due to the perpetrator's gaslighting, as well as his unpredictable mood and behaviour, the woman often becomes exhausted when trying to please the perpetrator. She seems to continuously move and reset her personal boundaries, losing a small piece of her self-identity every time she does so. In the end, her boundaries are likely to be completely shattered; the woman experiences complete vulnerability and hopelessness, and gives up. Often, she cannot choose whom she meets, she cannot confide in anyone, and there is no one left to back her up or defend her. The perpetrator often has full access to her whenever he wants, threatening her and abusing her in the ways he pleases. Even though the woman is likely to be terrified, she cannot expect anyone to come and rescue her since the violent situation is frequently concealed; the woman may feel like she has been sworn to secrecy and that no one can know of the violence. The woman's physical and psychological health is often systematically threatened as well as her wellbeing. In the end, she is likely to suffer serious health problems if the situation is either long-term or even permanent.

3.1.4. Component 4: Consequences of IPV

We theorize, based on the aforementioned findings, that IPV negatively affects the woman's well-being, health, and life. The trauma process is unique and individual, not only influencing the survivor, but also her children, her loved ones, and her community. Leaving a violent relationship is a complicated, exhausting, and time-consuming process, the completion of it taking place gradually over time. After leaving the perpetrator, the woman often confronts various negative feelings, as well as health problems and poor social status due to her experience of IPV. All this can result in her loss of working capacity, which again leads to loss of routine, loss of social interaction with others, and loss of income. Thus, the post-IPV trauma effects involve various negative influences on the woman's physical and mental health, as well as her social wellbeing, leaving her even more vulnerable. An overview of the consequences of IPV according to the theory is shown in Table 7.

Table 7. Component 4: Overview of the intrapersonal and interpersonal consequences of IPV, according to the women participating in the studies.

Intrapersonal Consequences of IPV	Interpersonal Consequences of IPV
Experiences feelings of fear, grief, anger, shame, helplessness, and betrayal. Feeling of not being herself anymore, having been conquered, defeated, and overpowered. Experiences fear of acknowledging the violence. Easily triggered, feels tired, stressed, suicidal, feels like she has lost so much, and feels uncertain about the future. Suffers insomnia due to anxiety and fear, never knows what will happen next, feels insecure, lacks appetite, suffers pain due to physical injuries. Feels like someone is constantly watching her, feels ashamed of letting the relationship go on for so long. Experiences difficulties in performing usual activities of daily life.	Experiences social isolation, has stopped seeing friends, has stopped seeing family, and has stopped communicating with other people. Does not know how to behave, fakes her feelings, fakes her wellbeing, and pretends to be happy. Feels emotionally absent to other people, experiences lack of interest in sex, as well as lack of interest in romantic relationships

3.1.5. Component 5: Obstacles on the PTG Journey

We theorize, based on the aforementioned findings, that the experience of IPV generally has severe, destructive effects on the survivor's life, creating various obstacles on their PTG journey [94]. We propose that women often suffer negative and diverse feelings towards themselves, experience fear or have been conditioned through their experience of being in a violent relationship, which often prevents them from reporting the violence and seeking appropriate help and support, serving as an obstacle in their PTG. This said, help-seeking is a complex and multifaceted phenomenon, and we do not want to oversimplify it. Women who have survived IPV are often easily triggered; those who have children often suffer on behalf of their children. The perpetrator is likely to keep on abusing and harassing them and their children in various ways, they often feel lonely, tend to overreact, and frequently experience difficulties in emotional connection to other people. All these factors are likely to influence their health and well-being in negative ways, serving as obstacles on their PTG journey. Being in a relationship where the perpetrator is in charge and constantly needs to be pleased is a lot of work. This often results in the woman not taking care of her health; she cannot rest and constantly feels anxious and alert, resulting in a constant decline in her wellbeing. After being in such long-term, stressful situations of a violent relationship, many female survivors of IPV suffer severe long-term or chronic consequences. After being in the stressful situations of a violent relationship for a long-term period, many female survivors of IPV suffer severe health problems, often leading to a loss of working capacity, thus undermining their social welfare and creating obstacles on their PTG journey. The perpetrator often continues harassing the woman after their relationship has ended. Having the perpetrator constantly reminding her of his presence can be very confusing for the woman, reducing her chances of being able to let go of him and depriving her of the peace to recover, serving as an obstacle to her PTG.

According to our theory, many female survivors of IPV feel powerless when it comes to the laws, regulations, and social system; they may experience that the perpetrator holds all the power of the social system in his hands, as well as of the laws and regulations. If not divorced, the woman does not receive the benefits nor the financial support that she is entitled to by law as a single mother, even though she is providing for the children. The perpetrator has many ways in which to use the law, regulations, and social system to delay the separation or divorce, as well as the division of assets and custody of children. Since the woman is forced by law to let the perpetrator meet with the children, even against the children's will, the perpetrator often uses the children to control the woman. Waiting to have the power over their lives, having the perpetrator continuously harassing them in various ways, as well as experiencing the feeling of powerlessness towards laws, regulations, and the social system, affect the woman's mental and physical health in a negative way, often leaving them in an even more vulnerable position towards the perpetrator than before, thus serving as an obstacle on the women's PTG journey. An overview of the obstacles on the journey to PTG following IPV is shown in Table 8.

3.1.6. Component 6: Facilitators on the PTG Journey

We theorize, based on the aforementioned findings, that there are various facilitators for the women's PTG journey following IPV [93]. Survivors who demonstrate positive personal competence, along with personal skills they have advanced through their experiences in life, seem to be better qualified to process their experience of IPV and move along their way to PTG. When a woman makes an independent decision of changing her circumstances for the better and seeks help, it serves as a facilitator of her PTG. When doing so, she is likely to reconsider her perspective to herself, work on her courage, confront and process her experiences of IPV, and set goals for a better future, which are likely to facilitate her PTG. To live in secure circumstances, enjoying social welfare, being able to meet her and her children's basic needs, is an essential facilitating factor in the woman's PTG, since it gives her the opportunity to concentrate on other things than mere survival. Possessing earlier experience of trauma can serve as a helpful preparation for some survivors of IPV. When followed by effective trauma processing, the former experience of trauma can serve as a promoter, increasing the woman's inner personal coping skills as well as her strength, which is likely to facilitate her PTG.

Table 8. Component 5: Overview of the main obstacles on the women's PTG journey following IPV according to the theory.

Main Obstacles	Examples
Negative feelings towards own self	Feels ashamed, blames herself, feeling of being less worthy, experiences self-stigmatization, suicidal thoughts, injured self-identity, disrupted body image, insecurity, anger, and loneliness.
Triggers	Incidents related to the experience of IPV that negatively affect the woman's feelings and wellbeing, e.g., sees a car that resembles the perpetrator's car, reads a column in the paper that diminishes victims of IPV.
Conflicting states of mind	Experiences relief vs. regret, strength vs. vulnerability, joy vs. misery, and comfort vs. displeasure.
Negative feelings on behalf of their children	Feels sad because of what the children have endured due to the violent relationship. Feels angry because of continuing destructive behavior of the perpetrator towards the children.
Problems in connecting to other people	Experiences lack of trust, avoidance of emotional connections, fear of romantic relations and loss of own social standards. Often overreacts to other people's behaviours, actions, words, mimics, tone of voice and body posture.
Health issues	Feels tired, in pain, has trouble sleeping, feels tense, depressed, anxious, endures physical diseases, physical and/or mental breakdown, and burnout.
Challenging personal circumstances	Experiences lack of housing, financial problems, loss of working capability, and social isolation.
Self-destructive behaviour	Talks to herself in a hostile and hurtful way. Blames herself for her situation.
The perpetrator	Continues harassing, stalking, showing threatening, frightening, violent behaviour, financial abuse, and escalating psychological violence.
Mixed feelings towards the perpetrator	Has nightmares, experiences flashbacks and fear, finds it hard to let go. Can be obsessed with the man.
Negative feelings towards laws, regulations, and the social support system	Feels powerless within 'the system', the divorce/separation takes a long time, the division of assets is unfair, the man stays in control, the woman is forced to settle with the perpetrator about their assets and children, she is forced to send the children to the perpetrator against their will, experiences fear of child protection services taking her children away, the perpetrator uses the children to blackmail the woman, while still married to the perpetrator or cohabitated with him, by law, the woman does not receive the support and benefits that she is entitled to as a single mother.

We theorize, based on the aforementioned findings, that it is most effective when the woman herself decides where to seek help, taking the time she needs to work on her task, being self-compassionate while doing so, and reviewing her attitudes towards herself and the ways she treats herself. One of the facilitators on the PTG journey seems to be for the woman to consider and work on her perspectives regarding her loved ones and other people, setting boundaries as well as encouraging good relations where possible. By considering her perspectives to her loved ones and other people, and vice versa, the woman can analyze the patterns of communication with others, deciding if her relations with others are healthy and helpful for her or if she needs to set some boundaries to be in control of her life. The woman setting boundaries to the perpetrator is also an important task for her, to seize and hold on to the control of her own life, serving as a facilitator of her PTG. We theorize that the woman experiencing personal support from her surroundings, as well as from other resources, when building a better life following IPV is a valuable facilitating component on her PTG journey. According to our theory, the most valuable support provided is the support that meets the personal needs of the woman; getting the help she needs, when she needs it, as well as communicating with kind, respectful, and supportive people when dealing with the consequences of IPV and working her way towards PTG. This personal support can be in various forms: informal, formal, or organized resources, or all these types. The absence of the health care system in most of the participating women's accounts reflects their experience that they did not expect the health care system to intervene to facilitate their PTG.

Overview of the facilitators on the journey to PTG following IPV is shown in Table 9.

Table 9. Component 6: Overview of the main facilitators on the women's PTG journey following IPV, according to the theory.

Main Facilitators	Examples
Personal competence and skills	Positive attitude, personal strength, and resilience.
State of mind	Confronting the experience of violence. Rejecting current situation. Deciding to seek help. Setting goals for a better life and PTG. Taking control of own life. Deciding not to be a victim.
Social welfare	Safe living conditions. Safe place to live. Financial security. Professional support.
Previous experience of trauma	Earlier experiences of processing trauma, resulting in increased inner strength
Self-perspective	Chooses where to seek help. Has self-compassion. Gives herself the time needed. Treats herself right
Perspective to loved ones and other people	Considers behaviour towards others and the behaviour from others. Encourages good relations. Sets boundaries.
Perspective to the perpetrator	Sets boundaries. Prevents him from being in control.
Various personal support	Informal support. Systematic support. Organized resources.

3.1.7. Component 7: Post-Traumatic Growth Following IPV

We theorize based on the before-mentioned findings that suffering and surviving terrible violence like IPV can result in various positive outcomes for female survivors, the women being able to view themselves, their lives, and their prospects in a more positive and constructive way than before. Their experience of PTG following IPV is described by various explanatory concepts, most of them being intrapersonal, i.e., existing or occurring within themselves or in their minds, while only a few of the concepts used in describing PTG are interpersonal, i.e., occurring between persons, or are both intrapersonal and interpersonal. When perceiving PTG, the women sense their increased inner strength and self-respect, where they appreciate themselves more and set boundaries to self and others to guard their self-identity. The women seem to know themselves better and are more tolerant towards other people, feeling free, complete, and happy at the same time. They appear to take good care of themselves, looking forward to their future and want to do good by using their experience to help other survivors of IPV. The women are likely to feel resilient and in charge of their lives, not hesitating in seeking appropriate help when they need it and seem to be fully aware of what they need and what they want for themselves. An overview of the experience of PTG by female survivors of IPV is shown in Figure 2.

3.1.8. Component 8: Lingering Effects of IPV in PTG

We theorize, based on the aforementioned findings, that PTG is not a permanent condition but needs to be continuously nourished and maintained by the woman enjoying it. Despite all the positive effects of PTG on the woman's life, the complicated effects of IPV often appear to be long-lasting, serving as lingering negative effects on the PTG of female IPV survivors. While enjoying PTG, many survivors seem to continue experiencing various triggers, bringing back the memories of the violent situation that they were stuck in, causing them "heavy days" and discomfort. Ongoing communication with the perpetrator as well as experiencing their children's suffering because of the violent relationship are also likely to have negative lingering effects on their PTG, as well as their various health problems following the violent relationship, which often have an extensive negative effect on their quality of life. After suffering IPV, women often lose confidence and trust in other people, causing them difficulties in establishing and maintaining relationships with others, also negatively affecting romantic relationships, even after having reached PTG.

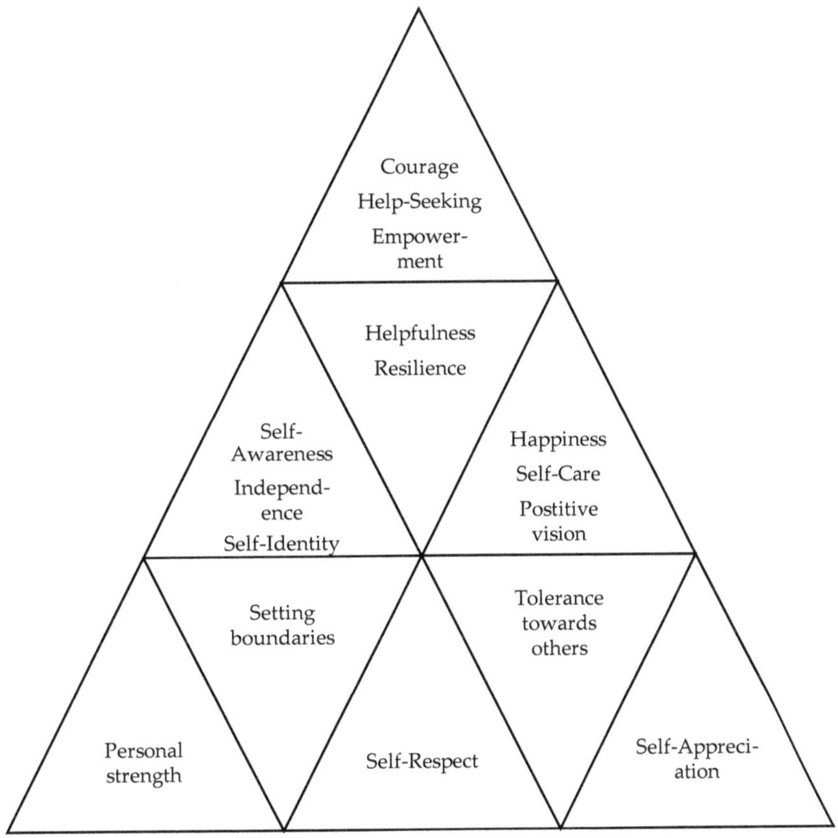

Figure 2. Experience of post-traumatic growth by female survivors of intimate partner violence. *Note.* The figure, developed by the authors as part of the present theory, shows the main concepts the women used to describe their experience of PTG following IPV. The most common concepts are at the bottom of the triangle, serving as a foundation for the descriptive concepts above. The second most common concepts used to illustrate PTG following IPV are in the next row above, building an additional support for the next row above, etc. In accordance with this figure, most of these descriptive concepts are intrapersonal, illustrating that women who enjoy PTG following IPV see themselves in a positive way and have respectful attitudes towards themselves. The figure also contains some interpersonal concepts, referring to the women being respectful of themselves and helpful to others as part of their PTG.

We theorize, based on the aforementioned findings, that female survivors of IPV who have reached PTG are aware of the lingering effects of IPV on their PTG. Having reached PTG, they are likely to be aware that these negative effects of IPV can appear, but they seem to know how to react to them, and are aware that these lingering effects of IPV on their PTG are not permanent. The women seem to be aware of their capability to process the lingering effects of IPV without letting go of their PTG. An overview of the lingering negative effects of IPV in female survivors' PTG is shown in Figure 3.

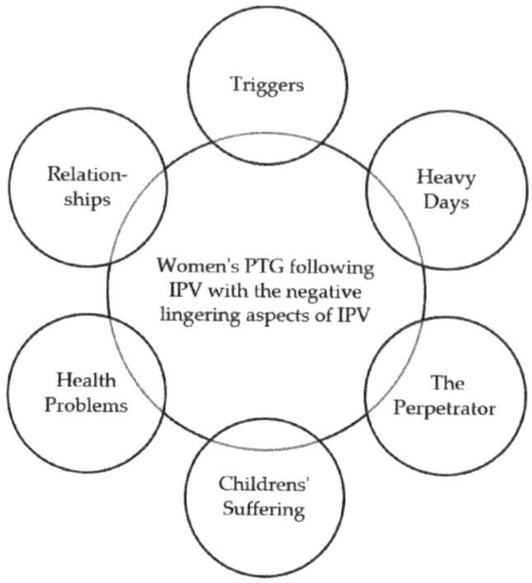

Figure 3. Component 8: An overview of the lingering effects of IPV in female survivors' PTG. *Note*: The figure, developed by the authors for the present theory, shows the negative lingering effects of IPV affecting female survivors' PTG. The figure illustrates women's PTG following IPV in the middle of the figure, where the effects of IPV are lingering from the sides into the area of PTG. Despite the lingering effects of IPV, the survivors' PTG seems to be strong, since the women enjoying PTG are not letting the effects of IPV overtake their PTG. They are aware of the lingering effects of IPV, know how to handle the situation, and are still enjoying PTG.

4. Discussion

Our theory introduced in this article is a valuable contribution to the field of research on PTG and IPV. The purpose of our theory development was to answer the main question, what are the main components of the PTG journey of female IPV survivors? by identifying, describing, and explaining the main components of the PTG journey of female IPV survivors. We theorize that the PTG journey of female survivors of IPV consists of eight main components, as explained in the findings.

When reflecting on people's reaction to suffering personal traumas, research results have revealed various risk factors, as well as protective factors. These influencing factors have been divided into three categories: pre-traumatic, i.e., former experience of trauma; peritraumatic, i.e., severity of the trauma; and post-traumatic, i.e., the person's reaction to the trauma as well as the reaction of his or her surroundings. Social support is helpful in all these stages [96,97]. Our theory is in accordance with this division of influencing factors regarding the reaction to trauma supports, where the woman's life before IPV influences both the probability of her entering a violent relationship as well as her experiences of the violence and how she reacts to the violent situation. According to our theory, the most important facilitating factors on the woman's PTG journey are her intrapersonal attributes, even though social support is always helpful.

According to our theory, the woman's life as a child and/or a young adult is likely to affect the way she is prepared for life. Experiencing trauma and violence early in life, either leaves her vulnerable, where she must move or deconstruct her boundaries to survive; or she adapts to her traumatic situation, resulting in her avoiding confronting difficult situations, but accepting them instead, feeling strong. Either way, to survive, the woman is likely to have changed and deconstructed her basic human rights, leaving her more vulnerable than before. If she is fortunate, she comes to know and interact with genuine and good people in life, but we note that women with prior traumatic experience are in danger of becoming the perfect prey for perpetrators of violence and abuse. Accumulated loads of prior traumas can result in a "building block effect", thus increasing the probability of negative psychological outcomes in victims of traumas [98,99]. Accordingly, the characters and future defenses to traumatic events as adults, as well as their psychological outcomes, can be linked to the women's childhood experiences of trauma. Notably, the results of a recent study of adverse childhood experiences (ACE) and mental health among women experiencing IPV, suggest that IPV survivors are more likely to have multiple and severe ACEs [100].

Research results suggest that, when suffering more than one kind of trauma, it is more likely to affect the victim's mental and physical wellbeing in a negative way, than when suffering one kind of trauma [101]. However, the severity of the consequences depends on how personal the traumatic event is and how intimate the perpetrator is with the victim [33,36–38,101]. Accordingly, being violated against and traumatized by one's intimate partner has a great negative effect on the person's welfare, and repeated violent behaviour is likely to gradually decrease the victim's well-being, health, and quality of life. Each female survivor of IPV suffers and processes her trauma in an individual and unique way [43], which not only influences the surviving woman, but also her children, her loved ones, and her community.

According to our theory, female survivors of IPV meet various obstacles as well as facilitating factors on their PTG journey. Those with more facilitators and less obstacles are more likely to move forward on the PTG journey. Loss of working capacity is one of the reasons behind the financial problems that are very common among female survivors of IPV, leading to various other problems, such as lack of housing and other necessities, undermining their welfare [28]. The experience of financial problems is not only due to the loss of the women's working capacity, but to the financial abuse during their violent relationship, which often continues even if the relationship has ended, sometimes resulting in long-term poverty and even the woman's bankruptcy [28].

Our theory supports the findings of a recent qualitative study; 18 Australian women in the age range of 50–69, who had left an abusive relationship, were interviewed about their experiences of IPV at different stages of their lives. They reported that being in the violent relationship directly affected their physical, psychological, and financial wellbeing in an extensive way. During the period of separation, many women experienced continuing abuse as well as stress due to housing, legal matters, and financial difficulties. After the separation they felt lonely and traumatized, their economy was weak, and they had problems due to damaged relationships with other people [102]. In a recent mini-review of gender-based violence during the COVID-19 pandemic, the research results revealed that the legislatures and services available for victims of IPV are often insufficient, thus worsening their situations [103].

The absence of the health care system in the findings may suggest a need for improvement in that system.

The theory is in line with the results of a recent systematic review of the facilitators of the recovery from GBV, that showed that to recover it is important for the woman to reconnect with themselves, their surroundings, and the world in general, by having support from both formal and informal networks, as well as from other people. According to this systematic review, it is important not to blame the woman, to emphasize the possibilities for her to change her situation, and to address and work on her reflection to affect intimate relationships [104].

PTG has been defined as positive, psychological change in a person, focusing on the possible positive outcomes following traumatic experience [44,73]. According to our theory, suffering and surviving IPV can result in various positive outcomes for the woman, such as reaching PTG. We suggest that a great part of PTG in female IPV survivors emerges in their personal, inner growth and the reconstruction of themselves. The foundation of their PTG is intrapersonal, i.e., possessing positive feelings and respectful attitudes towards themselves and taking the actions needed to preserve that attitude and to be in control of their lives. When enjoying PTG, the women seem to know themselves better and experience various positive feelings towards themselves, feeling resilient and in charge of their lives. They seem to know what they want, know what they need and seek appropriate support when needed. Although their experience of PTG is likely to increase tolerance towards other people, they do not hesitate to set boundaries at the same time, to protect their self-identity and the control of their own lives.

According to our theory, proposed here, even though reaching PTG following the experience of IPV is a great achievement for female survivors, it is neither a simple nor a permanent condition. Life goes on, with its ups and downs, and the survivors' life is not always perfect. Survivors of IPV have experienced serious traumas and their being has been systematically undermined in their violent relationships [1] and the effects of IPV linger into their PTG. The 'triggers' seem to be all around in their environment and many of the women endure 'heavy days' in between, where they are feeling down, going through complicated and negative feelings and discomfort in relation to their experience of IPV.

We theorize that, the frequently continuing harassment of the perpetrator is making their life hard, the women often suffer on behalf of their children's endurance of the former and often ongoing violence, and the women's health problems are likely to extensively affect their lives in a negative way [102]. In addition to all these factors, female survivors of IPV often have trouble trusting other people, which diminishes the possibilities of them having healthy romantic relationships. According to our theory, these negative effects of IPV are likely to linger into their PTG; however, having reached PTG, survivors of IPV seem to be able to recognize these lingering effects of IPV and find the best ways to process them without losing their PTG.

4.1. Limitation of the Theory Development

In step 1 of the theory development we theorized from our three published papers [92–94]. Moreover, we used dense raw data consisting of approximately 300,000 words. However, a large part of that data is unpublished, which is a limitation.

4.2. Future Research and Theory Development Directions

Due to the lack of research in the field of PTG among female IPV survivors, more research is needed to further develop the theory. More research would not only advance the theory but also its specific components. Those undertaking studies requiring a theory as a research framework could use this theory as a framework. Finally, new theories are needed on the PTG journey of IPV survivors, e.g., from the perspective of men and intersex people.

5. Conclusions

When it comes to theory development in the field of PTG among female IPV survivors, there is a gap in the literature. Our research contributes to that field in an important way by undertaking theory development on the eight main components of the PTG journey of female IPV survivors, emphasizing the main obstacles and facilitators on that journey. According to our theory, PTG is a real possibility for female survivors of IPV, which is likely to result in their increased wellbeing and quality of life, as well as the wellbeing of their children and loved ones, and the community as whole, minimizing the destructive effects of IPV. Due to the high prevalence and serious consequences of IPV, it is important to provide some potential of a better life for the survivors. The absence of the health care system in the findings may suggest a need for improvement in that system. Aiming for PTG after suffering IPV is important. The information provided in the theory could be useful for the public and professionals when guiding female IPV survivors on the path to better lives, promoting their recovery and healing, aiming for PTG.

Author Contributions: Conceptualization, H.S.B. and S.H.; methodology, H.S.B. and S.H.; software, H.S.B.; validation, S.H. and D.S.A.; formal analysis, H.S.B. and S.H.; investigation, H.S.B.; resources, H.S.B. and S.H.; data curation, H.S.B.; writing—original draft preparation, H.S.B.; writing—review and editing, S.H., D.S.A. and H.S.B.; visualization, H.S.B.; supervision, S.H. and D.S.A.; project administration, S.H.; funding acquisition, S.H. and H.S.B. All authors have read and agreed to the published version of the manuscript.

Funding: We gratefully acknowledge that this research was funded by The Icelandic Gender Equality Fund (grant number 190174-0551 and 200264-5501) and The Science Fund of the Icelandic Nurses' Association (no number available).

Institutional Review Board Statement: The studies used in the theory development were conducted according to the guidelines of the Declaration of Helsinki and approved by the National Bioethics Committee (reference no: VSN-19-166).

Informed Consent Statement: Informed consent was obtained from all subjects involved in the studies used for the theory development.

Data Availability Statement: The data presented in this theory development are with the corresponding author. Because of anonymity as well as ethical and personal reasons, the raw data are not available, but the published data are all available in open-access format.

Acknowledgments: The authors gratefully acknowledge Rhonda M. Johnson, for her constructive feedback and support. Special gratitude to the Directorate of Equality in Iceland for invaluable help in the data collection phase. Finally, special gratitude to all the people and associations who fight against violence in Iceland and assisted us in reaching participants for the studies.

Conflicts of Interest: The authors declare no conflict of interest. The funders had no role in the design of the studies; in the collection, analyses, or interpretation of data; in the writing of the manuscripts; or in the decision to publish the results of the theory development.

References

1. D'Amore, C.; Martin, S.L.; Wood, K.; Brooks, C. Themes of Healing and Posttraumatic Growth in Women Survivors' Narratives of Intimate Partner Violence. *J. Interpers. Violence* **2021**, *36*, NP2697–NP2724. [CrossRef] [PubMed]
2. World Health Organization. Violence against Women. 2021. Available online: https://www.who.int/en/news-room/fact-sheets/detail/violence-against-women (accessed on 2 May 2022).
3. World Health Organization. *Violence against Women: Intimate Partner and Sexual Violence against Women*; World Health Organization: Geneva, Switzerland, 2019. Available online: https://apps.who.int/iris/bitstream/handle/10665/329889/WHO-RHR-19.16-eng.pdf?ua=1 (accessed on 18 April 2022).
4. Russo, N.F.; Pirlott, A. Gender-Based Violence: Concepts, Methods, and Findings. *Ann. N. Y. Acad. Sci.* **2006**, *1087*, 178–205. [CrossRef] [PubMed]
5. Krahé, B. Violence against women. *Curr. Opin. Psychol.* **2018**, *19*, 6–10. [CrossRef] [PubMed]
6. Sanjel, S. Gender-Based Violence: A Crucial Challenge for Public Health. *Kathmandu Univ. Med J.* **2015**, *11*, 179–184. [CrossRef] [PubMed]
7. Stewart, D.E.; Vigod, S.; Riazantseva, E. New Developments in Intimate Partner Violence and Management of Its Mental Health Sequelae. *Curr. Psychiatry Rep.* **2016**, *18*, 4. [CrossRef]
8. World Health Organization. *Researching Violence against Women: Practical Guidelines for Researchers and Activists*; World Health Organization: Geneva, Switzerland, 2005. Available online: https://apps.who.int/iris/bitstream/handle/10665/42966/9241546476_eng.pdf (accessed on 18 April 2022).
9. World Health Organization. *Global and Regional Estimates of Violence against Women: Prevalence and Health Effects of Intimate Partner Violence and Non-Partner Sexual Violence*; World Health Organization: Geneva, Switzerland, 2013. Available online: https://apps.who.int/iris/bitstream/handle/10665/85239/?sequence=1 (accessed on 18 April 2022).
10. Stark, L.; Ager, A. A Systematic Review of Prevalence Studies of Gender-Based Violence in Complex Emergencies. *Trauma Violence Abus.* **2011**, *12*, 127–134. [CrossRef]
11. Ali, P.A.; Dhingra, K.; McGarry, J. A literature review of intimate partner violence and its classifications. *Aggress. Violent Behav.* **2016**, *31*, 16–25. [CrossRef]
12. Johnson, M.P. Gender and types of intimate partner violence: A response to an anti-feminist literature review. *Aggress. Violent Behav.* **2011**, *16*, 289–296. [CrossRef]
13. McHugh, M.C.; Frieze, I.H. Intimate Partner Violence: New Directions. *Ann. N. Y. Acad. Sci.* **2006**, *1087*, 121–141. [CrossRef]
14. Mijatovic-Jovanovic, V.; Cankovic, S.; Milijasevic, D.; Ukropina, S.; Jovanovic, M.; Cankovic, D. Health consequences of domestic violence against women in Serbia. *Vojn. Pregl.* **2020**, *77*, 14–21. [CrossRef]
15. Heise, L.; Ellsberg, M.; Gottmoeller, M. A global overview of gender-based violence. *Int. J. Gynecol. Obstet.* **2002**, *78*, S5–S14. [CrossRef]
16. Campbell, J.C. Health consequences of intimate partner violence. *Lancet* **2002**, *359*, 1331–1336. [CrossRef]
17. Yim, I.S.; Kofman, Y.B. The psychobiology of stress and intimate partner violence. *Psychoneuroendocrinology* **2019**, *105*, 9–24. [CrossRef] [PubMed]
18. Monahan, K. Intimate Partner Violence (IPV) and Neurological Outcomes: A Review for Practitioners. *J. Aggress. Maltreatment Trauma* **2019**, *28*, 807–825. [CrossRef]

19. Loxton, D.; Dolja-Gore, X.; Anderson, A.E.; Townsend, N. Intimate partner violence adversely impacts health over 16 years and across generations: A longitudinal cohort study. *PLoS ONE* **2017**, *12*, e0178138. [CrossRef]
20. Zara, G.; Gino, S. Intimate Partner Violence and its Escalation Into Femicide. Frailty thy Name Is "Violence against Women". *Front. Psychol.* **2018**, *9*, 1777. [CrossRef]
21. World Health Organization. *Multi-Country Study on Women's Health and Domestic Violence against Women: Summary Report of Initial Results on Prevalence, Health Outcomes and Women's Responses*; World Health Organization: Geneve, Switzerland, 2005; Mise en page 1; Available online: ceid.org.tr (accessed on 18 April 2022).
22. Chiesa, A.E.; Kallechey, L.; Harlaar, N.; Ford, C.R.; Garrido, E.F.; Betts, W.R.; Maguire, S. Intimate partner violence victimization and parenting: A systematic review. *Child Abus. Negl.* **2018**, *80*, 285–300. [CrossRef]
23. Van Heugten, K.; Wilson, E. Witnessing intimate partner violence: Review of the literature on coping in young persons. *Aotearoa New Zealand Soc. Work* **2008**, *20*, 52–62. [CrossRef]
24. Kishton, R.; Sinko, L.; Ortiz, R.; Islam, N.; Fredrickson, A.; Sheils, N.E.; Buresh, J.; Cronholm, P.F.; Matone, M. Describing the Health Status of Women Experiencing Violence or Abuse: An Observational Study Using Claims Data. *J. Prim. Care Community Health* **2022**, *13*. [CrossRef]
25. Wu, Y.; Chen, J.; Fang, H.; Wan, Y. Intimate Partner Violence: A Bibliometric Review of Literature. *Int. J. Environ. Res. Public Health* **2020**, *17*, 5607. [CrossRef]
26. Elghossain, T.; Bott, S.; Akik, C.; Obermeyer, C.M. Prevalence of intimate partner violence against women in the Arab world: A systematic review. *BMC Int. Health Hum. Rights* **2019**, *19*, 29. [CrossRef] [PubMed]
27. Duvvury, N.; Callan, A.; Carney, P.; Raghavendra, S. Intimate partner violence: Economic costs and implications for growth and development. In *Women's Voice, Agency, and Participation Research Series*; World Bank: Washington, DC, USA, 2013. Available online: https://openknowledge.worldbank.org/handle/10986/16697 (accessed on 15 May 2022).
28. Stylianou, A.M. Economic Abuse within Intimate Partner Violence: A Review of the Literature. *Violence Vict.* **2018**, *33*, 3–22. [CrossRef] [PubMed]
29. Weathers, F.W.; Keane, T. The criterion a problem revisited: Controversies and challenges in defining and measuring psychological trauma. *J. Trauma. Stress* **2007**, *20*, 107–121. [CrossRef] [PubMed]
30. Cai, W.; Ding, C.; Tang, Y.-L.; Wu, S.; Yang, D. Effects of social supports on posttraumatic stress disorder symptoms: Moderating role of perceived safety. *Psychol. Trauma Theory Res. Pract. Policy* **2014**, *6*, 724–730. [CrossRef]
31. Boals, A.; Riggs, S.A.; Kraha, A. Coping with Stressful or Traumatic Events: What Aspects of Trauma Reactions are Associated with Health Outcomes? *Stress Health* **2012**, *29*, 156–163. [CrossRef]
32. Brown, R.C.; Berenz, E.C.; Aggen, S.H.; Gardner, C.O.; Knudsen, G.P.; Reichborn-Kjennerud, T.; Kendler, K.S.; Amstadter, A.B. Trauma exposure and Axis I psychopathology: A cotwin control analysis in Norwegian young adults. *Psychol. Trauma Theory Res. Pract. Policy* **2014**, *6*, 652–660. [CrossRef]
33. Dar, M.A.; Wani, R.A.; Margoob, M.A.; Hussain, A.; Rather, Y.H.; Chandel, R.K.; Malla, A.A. Trauma and traumatic stress: The long-term effects of childhood traumatic stress. *Malays. J. Psychiatry Ejournal* **2015**, *23*, 114–123. Available online: http://www.mjpsychiatry.org/index.php/mjp/article/viewFile/327/240 (accessed on 15 May 2022).
34. Anderson, K.M.; Renner, L.M.; Danis, F.S. Recovery: Resilience and growth in the aftermath of domestic violence. *Violence Women* **2012**, *18*, 1279–1299. [CrossRef]
35. Olff, M.; Langeland, W.; Gersons, B.P.R. The psychobiology of PTSD: Coping with trauma. *Psychoneuroendocrinology* **2005**, *30*, 974–982. [CrossRef]
36. Wozniak, J.D.; Caudle, H.E.; Harding, K.; Vieselmeyer, J.; Mezulis, A.H. The effect of trauma proximity and ruminative response styles on posttraumatic stress and posttraumatic growth following a university shooting. *Psychol. Trauma Theory Res. Pract. Policy* **2020**, *12*, 227–234. [CrossRef]
37. May, C.L.; Wisco, B.E. Defining trauma: How level of exposure and proximity affect risk for posttraumatic stress disorder. *Psychol. Trauma Theory Res. Pract. Policy* **2016**, *8*, 233–240. [CrossRef] [PubMed]
38. Pooley, J.A.; Cohen, L.; O'Connor, M.; Taylor, M. Posttraumatic stress and posttraumatic growth and their relationship to coping and self-efficacy in Northwest Australian cyclone communities. *Psychol. Trauma Theory Res. Pract. Policy* **2013**, *5*, 392–399. [CrossRef]
39. Sinko, L.; James, R.; Hughesdon, K. Healing After Gender-Based Violence: A Qualitative Metasynthesis Using Meta-Ethnography. *Trauma Violence Abus.* **2021**, 1524838021991305. [CrossRef]
40. Pico-Alfonso, M.A. Psychological intimate partner violence: The major predictor of posttraumatic stress disorder in abused women. *Neurosci. Biobehav. Rev.* **2005**, *29*, 181–193. [CrossRef]
41. Reisenhofer, S.; Taft, A. Women's journey to safety—The Transtheoretical model in clinical practice when working with women experiencing Intimate Partner Violence: A scientific review and clinical guidance. *Patient Educ. Couns.* **2013**, *93*, 536–548. [CrossRef] [PubMed]
42. Kim, J.; Gray, K.A. Leave or Stay? Battered women's decision after intimate partner violence. *J. Interpers. Violence* **2008**, *23*, 1465–1482. [CrossRef]
43. Carman, M.J.; Kay-Lambkin, F.; Burgman, I. Long-Term Recovery from Intimate Partner Violence: Definitions by Australian Women. *J. Fam. Violence* **2022**, 1–14. [CrossRef]

44. Calhoun, L.G.; Tedeschi, R.G. The foundations of post-traumatic growth: An expanded framework. In *Handbook of Posttraumatic Growth: Research and Practice*, 2nd ed.; Calhoun, L.G., Tedeschi, R.G., Eds.; Routledge: London, UK, 2014; pp. 1–23.
45. Tedeschi, R.G.; Calhoun, L. Posttraumatic growth: A new perspective on psychotraumatology. *Psychiatr. Times* **2004**, *21*, 58–60.
46. Abel, L.; Walker, C.; Samios, C.; Morozow, L. Vicarious posttraumatic growth: Predictors of growth and relationships with adjustment. *Traumatology* **2014**, *20*, 9–18. [CrossRef]
47. Barton, S.; Boals, A.; Knowles, L. Thinking about Trauma: The Unique Contributions of Event Centrality and Posttraumatic Cognitions in Predicting PTSD and Posttraumatic Growth. *J. Trauma. Stress* **2013**, *26*, 718–726. [CrossRef]
48. Coroiu, A.; Körner, A.; Burke, S.; Meterissian, S.; Sabiston, C.M. Stress and posttraumatic growth among survivors of breast cancer: A test of curvilinear effects. *Int. J. Stress Manag.* **2017**, *23*, 84–97. [CrossRef]
49. De Castella, R.; Simmonds, J.G. "There's a deeper level of meaning as to what suffering's all about": Experiences of religious and spiritual growth following trauma. *Ment. Health Relig. Cult.* **2013**, *16*, 536–556. [CrossRef]
50. Jin, Y.; Xu, J.; Liu, H.; Liu, D. Posttraumatic Stress Disorder and Posttraumatic Growth among Adult Survivors of Wenchuan Earthquake After 1 Year: Prevalence and Correlates. *Arch. Psychiatr. Nurs.* **2014**, *28*, 67–73. [CrossRef] [PubMed]
51. Purc-Stephenson, R.J. The Posttraumatic Growth Inventory: Factor structure and invariance among persons with chronic diseases. *Rehabil. Psychol.* **2014**, *59*, 10–18. [CrossRef]
52. Stagg, R. The nadir experience: Crisis, transition, and growth. *Transpers. Psychol. Rev.* **2014**, *46*, 72–91.
53. Su, Y.-J.; Chen, S.-H. Emerging posttraumatic growth: A prospective study with pre- and posttrauma psychological predictors. *Psychol. Trauma Theory Res. Pract. Policy* **2015**, *7*, 103–111. [CrossRef]
54. Taku, K.; Cann, A.; Tedeschi, R.G.; Calhoun, L.G. Core beliefs shaken by an earthquake correlate with posttraumatic growth. *Psychol. Trauma Theory Res. Pract. Policy* **2015**, *7*, 563–569. [CrossRef]
55. Tedeschi, R.G.; Calhoun, L.G. The posttraumatic growth inventory: Measuring the positive legacy of trauma. *J. Trauma. Stress* **1996**, *9*, 455–471. [CrossRef]
56. Gracia, E.; Lila, M.; Santirso, F.A. Attitudes toward Intimate Partner Violence against Women in the European Union: A Systematic Review. *Eur. Psychol.* **2020**, *25*, 104–121. [CrossRef]
57. Nishi, D.; Matsuoka, Y.; Kim, Y. Posttraumatic growth, posttraumatic stress disorder and resilience of motor vehicle accident survivors. *Biopsychosoc. Med.* **2010**, *4*, 7. [CrossRef]
58. Han, K.-M.; Park, J.Y.; Park, H.E.; An, S.R.; Lee, E.H.; Yoon, H.-K.; Ko, Y.-H. Social support moderates association between posttraumatic growth and trauma-related psychopathologies among victims of the Sewol Ferry Disaster. *Psychiatry Res.* **2019**, *272*, 507–514. [CrossRef] [PubMed]
59. Salter, E.; Stallard, P. Posttraumatic growth in child survivors of a road traffic accident. *J. Trauma. Stress* **2004**, *17*, 335–340. [CrossRef] [PubMed]
60. Bernstein, M.; Pfefferbaum, B. Posttraumatic Growth as a Response to Natural Disasters in Children and Adolescents. *Curr. Psychiatry Rep.* **2018**, *20*, 37. [CrossRef]
61. Amiri, H.; Nakhaee, N.; Nagyova, I.; Timkova, V.; Okhovati, M.; Nekoei-Moghadam, M.; Zahedi, R. Posttraumatic growth after earthquake: A systematic review and meta-analysis. *Int. J. Soc. Psychiatry* **2021**, *67*, 867–877. [CrossRef] [PubMed]
62. Sattler, D.N.; Claramita, M.; Muskavage, B. Natural Disasters in Indonesia: Relationships among Posttraumatic Stress, Resource Loss, Depression, Social Support, and Posttraumatic Growth. *J. Loss Trauma* **2018**, *23*, 351–365. [CrossRef]
63. Chan, C.S.; Rhodes, J.E. Religious coping, posttraumatic stress, psychological distress, and posttraumatic growth among female survivors four years after Hurricane Katrina. *J. Trauma. Stress* **2013**, *26*, 257–265. [CrossRef]
64. Zavala, C.; Waters, L.; Arslan, G.; Simpson, A.; del Prado, P.N.; Gargurevich, R. The role of strength-based parenting, posttraumatic stress, and event exposure on posttraumatic growth in flood survivors. *Psychol. Trauma Theory Res. Pract. Policy* **2022**. [CrossRef]
65. Subandi, M.A.; Achmad, T.; Kurniati, H.; Febri, R. Spirituality, gratitude, hope and post-traumatic growth among the survivors of the 2010 eruption of Mount Merapi in Java, Indonesia. *Aust. J. Emerg. Manag.* **2014**, *18*, 19–26.
66. Pan, Y.; Zhao, H.; Xu, H.; Rn, Y.H.; Dong, C.; Rn, Y.P.; Rn, H.Z.; Rn, H.X.; Rn, C.D.P. Post accidental injury: Mediating roles of emotional expressivity, rumination, and posttraumatic growth. *Nurs. Health Sci.* **2022**, *24*, 236–244. [CrossRef]
67. Lee, D.; Yu, E.-S.; Kim, N.H. Resilience as a mediator in the relationship between posttraumatic stress and posttraumatic growth among adult accident or crime victims: The moderated mediating effect of childhood trauma. *Eur. J. Psychotraumatol.* **2020**, *11*, 1704563. [CrossRef]
68. Mutisya, S.S.; Owuor, B. Counseling as a predictor of posttraumatic growth among the Garissa University terrorist attack survivors. *Afr. J. Clin. Psychol.* **2018**, *1*, 1–22.
69. Tsai, J.; El-Gabalawy, R.; Sledge, W.H.; Southwick, S.M.; Pietrzak, R.H. Post-traumatic growth among veterans in the USA: Results from the National Health and Resilience in Veterans Study. *Psychol. Med.* **2015**, *45*, 165–179. [CrossRef] [PubMed]
70. Veronese, G.; Pepe, A.; Massaiu, I.; De Mol, A.-S.; Robbins, I. Posttraumatic growth is related to subjective well-being of aid workers exposed to cumulative trauma in Palestine. *Transcult. Psychiatry* **2017**, *54*, 332–356. [CrossRef] [PubMed]
71. McLean, C.P.; Handa, S.; Dickstein, B.D.; Benson, T.A.; Baker, M.T.; Isler, W.C.; Peterson, A.L.; Litz, B.T. Posttraumatic growth and posttraumatic stress among military medical personnel. *Psychol. Trauma Theory Res. Pract. Policy* **2013**, *5*, 62–68. [CrossRef]
72. Semeijn, J.; Van Ruysseveldt, J.; Vonk, G.; Van Vuuren, T. In flight again with wings that were once broken; effects of post-traumatic growth and personal resources on burnout recovery. *Int. J. Work. Health Manag.* **2019**, *12*, 387–403. [CrossRef]

73. Ulloa, E.; Guzman, M.L.; Salazar, M.; Cala, C. Posttraumatic Growth and Sexual Violence: A Literature Review. *J. Aggress. Maltreat. Trauma* **2016**, *25*, 286–304. [CrossRef]
74. Kılıç, C.; Magruder, K.M.; Koryürek, M.M. Does trauma type relate to posttraumatic growth after war? A pilot study of young Iraqi war survivors living in Turkey. *Transcult. Psychiatry* **2016**, *53*, 110–123. [CrossRef]
75. Yılmaz, G.; Üstün, B.; Günüşen, N.P. Effect of a nurse-led intervention programme on professional quality of life and post-traumatic growth in oncology nurses. *Int. J. Nurs. Pr.* **2018**, *24*, e12687. [CrossRef]
76. Waugh, A.; Kiemle, G.; Slade, P. What aspects of post-traumatic growth are experienced by bereaved parents? A systematic review. *Eur. J. Psychotraumatol.* **2018**, *9*, 1506230. [CrossRef]
77. Kim, M.-G.; Han, S.-W. A Systematic Review and Meta-analysis on the Factors Related to Post-traumatic Growth of Fire Officials. *J. Health Informatics Stat.* **2020**, *45*, 373–384. [CrossRef]
78. Brooks, S.; Amlôt, R.; Rubin, G.J.; Greenberg, N. Psychological resilience and post-traumatic growth in disaster-exposed organisations: Overview of the literature. *BMJ Mil Health* **2020**, *166*, 52–56. [CrossRef]
79. Feng, L.-S.; Dong, Z.-J.; Wu, X.-Q.; Zhang, L.; Yan, R.-Y.; Ma, J.; Zeng, Y. COVID-19-related post-traumatic growth in the general public: A cross-sectional study from Yunnan, China. *Psychol. Health Med.* **2022**, *27*, 925–930. [CrossRef] [PubMed]
80. Duran, B. Posttraumatic growth as experienced by childhood cancer survivors and their families: A narrative synthesis of qualitative and quantitative research. *J. Pediatr. Oncol. Nurs.* **2013**, *30*, 179–197. [CrossRef] [PubMed]
81. Chun, S.; Lee, Y. The Experience of Posttraumatic Growth for People with Spinal Cord Injury. *Qual. Health Res.* **2008**, *18*, 877–890. [CrossRef]
82. Yang, S.-K.; Ha, Y. Exploring the Relationships between Posttraumatic Growth, Wisdom, and Quality of Life in Older Cancer Survivors. *Asian Pac. J. Cancer Prev.* **2019**, *20*, 2667–2672. [CrossRef]
83. Haroosh, E.; Freedman, S. Posttraumatic growth and recovery from addiction. *Eur. J. Psychotraumatol.* **2017**, *8*, 1369832. [CrossRef]
84. Grace, J.J.; Kinsella, E.L.; Muldoon, O.T.; Fortune, D.G. Post-traumatic growth following acquired brain injury: A systematic review and meta-analysis. *Front. Psychol.* **2015**, *6*, 1162. [CrossRef] [PubMed]
85. Askay, S.W.; Magyar-Russell, G. Post-traumatic growth and spirituality in burn recovery. *Int. Rev. Psychiatry* **2009**, *21*, 570–579. [CrossRef] [PubMed]
86. Cui, C.; Wang, K.; An, J.; Jin, C. Current status and influencing factors of post-traumatic growth in maintenance hemodialysis. *Int. J. Nurs. Sci.* **2017**, *4*, 362–366. [CrossRef] [PubMed]
87. Hanetz-Gamliel, K. Associations between the cause of loved one's death, mourner's psychological distress and ongoing relationship with the deceased, and mourner's posttraumatic growth. *Omega J. Death Dying* **2022**, 00302228211068303. [CrossRef]
88. Chan, K.J.; Young, M.Y.; Sharif, N. Well-being after trauma: A review of posttraumatic growth among refugees. *Can. Psychol. Can.* **2016**, *57*, 291–299. [CrossRef]
89. Baillie, S.E.; Sellwood, W.; Wisely, J.A. Post-traumatic growth in adults following a burn. *Burns* **2014**, *40*, 1089–1096. [CrossRef] [PubMed]
90. Blackie, L.E.; Hitchcott, N.; Joseph, S. Looking for Post-Traumatic Growth in Perpetrators of the 1994 Genocide in Rwanda: A Discussion of Theoretical and Ethical Issues. *J. Perpetrator Res.* **2017**, *1*, 64–84. [CrossRef]
91. Rahayu, D.; Hamidah, H.; Hendriani, W. Post-traumatic Growth among Domestic Violence Survivors: A Systematic Review. *J. Educ. Health Community Psychol.* **2019**, *8*, 138–158. [CrossRef]
92. Bryngeirsdottir, H.S.; Halldorsdottir, S. The challenging journey from trauma to post-traumatic growth: Lived experiences of facilitating and hindering factors. *Scand. J. Caring Sci.* **2021**. [CrossRef]
93. Bryngeirsdottir, H.S.; Halldorsdottir, S. "I'm a winner, not a victim": The facilitating factors of post-traumatic growth among women who have suffered intimate partner violence. *Int. J. Environ. Res. Public Health* **2022**, *19*, 1342. [CrossRef]
94. Bryngeirsdottir, H.S.; Halldorsdottir, S. Fourteen Main Obstacles on the Journey to Post-Traumatic Growth as Experienced by Female Survivors of Intimate Partner Violence: *"It Was All So Confusing"*. *Int. J. Environ. Res. Public Health* **2022**, *19*, 5377. [CrossRef]
95. Walker, L.O.; Avant, K.C. *Strategies for Theory Construction in Nursing*, 6th ed.; Pearson: New York, NY, USA, 2019.
96. American Psychiatric Association. Posttraumatic Stress Disorder. In *Diagnostic and Statistical Manual of Mental Disorders: DSM-5*, 5th ed.; American Psychiatric Association: Washington, DC, USA, 2013; pp. 271–280.
97. Marchand, A.; Nadeau, C.; Beaulieu-Prévost, D.; Boyer, R.; Martin, M. Predictors of posttraumatic stress disorder among police officers: A prospective study. *Psychol. Trauma Theory Res. Pract. Policy* **2015**, *7*, 212–221. [CrossRef]
98. Kolassa, I.-T.; Ertl, V.; Eckart, C.; Kolassa, S.; Onyut, L.P.; Elbert, T. Spontaneous remission from PTSD depends on the number of traumatic event types experienced. *Psychol. Trauma Theory Res. Pract. Policy* **2010**, *2*, 169–174. [CrossRef]
99. Kraemer, B.; Schumacher, S.; Winkel, B.; Imboden, C.; Wittmann, L. The "building block" effect of prior trauma for psychological outcome in victims of a natural disaster. *Eur. Psychiatry* **2016**, *33*, S214–S215. [CrossRef]
100. Li, Y.; Herbell, K.; Bloom, T.; Sharps, P.; Bullock, L.F. Adverse Childhood Experiences and Mental Health among Women Experiencing Intimate Partner Violence. *Issues Ment. Health Nurs.* **2020**, *41*, 785–791. [CrossRef] [PubMed]
101. Martin, C.G.; Cromer, L.D.; DePrince, A.P.; Freyd, J.J. The role of cumulative trauma, betrayal, and appraisals in understanding trauma symptomatology. *Psychol. Trauma Theory Res. Pract. Policy* **2013**, *5*, 110–118. [CrossRef] [PubMed]
102. Hing, N.; O'Mullan, C.; Mainey, L.; Nuske, E.; Breen, H.; Taylor, A. Impacts of Male Intimate Partner Violence on Women: A Life Course Perspective. *Int. J. Environ. Res. Public Health* **2021**, *18*, 8303. [CrossRef] [PubMed]

103. Mittal, S.; Singh, T. Gender-Based Violence during COVID-19 Pandemic: A Mini-Review. *Front. Glob. Women's Health* **2020**, *1*. [CrossRef]
104. Alcantud, P.M.; Campdepadrós-Cullell, R.; Fuentes-Pumarola, C.; Mut-Montalvà, E. 'I think I will need help': A systematic review of who facilitates the recovery from gender-based violence and how they do so. *Health Expect.* **2021**, *24*, 1–7. [CrossRef]

MDPI
St. Alban-Anlage 66
4052 Basel
Switzerland
www.mdpi.com

International Journal of Environmental Research and Public Health Editorial Office
E-mail: ijerph@mdpi.com
www.mdpi.com/journal/ijerph

www.ingramcontent.com/pod-product-compliance
Lightning Source LLC
Chambersburg PA
CBHW061558210926
51850CB00009B/2137
* 9 7 8 3 7 2 5 8 0 6 7 6 8 *